Global Migration and the World Economy

Global Migration and the World Economy

Two Centuries of Policy and Performance

Timothy J. Hatton and
Jeffrey G. Williamson

The MIT Press
Cambridge, Massachusetts
London, England

MIT Press books may be purchased at special quantity discounts for business or sales promotional use. For information, please email special_sales@mitpress.mit.edu or write to Special Sales Department, The MIT Press, 55 Hayward Street, Cambridge, MA 02142.

This book was set in Palatino on 3B2 by Asco Typesetters, Hong Kong, and was printed and bound in the United States of America.

Library of Congress Cataloging-in-Publication Data

Hatton, T. J.
Global migration and the world economy : two centuries of policy and performance / Timothy J. Hatton and Jeffrey G. Williamson.
    p.   cm.
Includes bibliographical references and index.
ISBN 0-262-08342-6 (alk. paper)
1. Emigration and immigration—Economic aspects—History. 2. Emigration and immigration—Government policy. I. Williamson, Jeffrey G., 1935– II. Title.
JV6217.H38   2006
304.8—dc22   200505496

10 9 8 7 6 5 4 3 2 1

Once again,
for our wives and best friends
Alison Booth
Nancy Williamson

Contents

Acknowledgments

After mulling it over for eight years, in 1998 we produced *The Age of Mass Migration: Causes and Economic Impact*. A little weary of the eight-year struggle and naively thinking we had set the academy straight on how to think about these problems for the first global century (pre–World War I), we set mass migrations aside and moved on to other, independent projects. Only three years later, we discovered the obvious: that we had only finished half the job, and that it was important to see how the first global century could inform the second global century (post–World War II). So here we are again, offering the reader our take on the economics of world mass migration.

However, *Global Migration and the World Economy: Two Centuries of Policy and Performance* covers a lot more territory than did *The Age of Mass Migration*. Almost two-thirds of this book covers the world mass migration experience since World War I, and much of that attends to the past three decades. Furthermore, the book assesses *world* mass migrations, not just those involving Europe or the New World. In addition, it pays much more attention to the political economy of immigration policy. Finally, we have made an effort to write for a wider audience this time—economists, historians, critical observers of mass migrations, and policymakers. We hope the economics is elegant and correct, but our intent has been to avoid anything formal. We also hope the evidence is compelling and persuasive, but our intent has been to avoid overwhelming the reader with too much.

We have benefited greatly from the help and advice of many who have made insightful comments on our work in progress and who have shared their data, knowledge, and time. The list is long, and we can only single out a few. First, there are our collaborators on related projects: David Bloom, Ximena Clark, Bill Collins, Matt Higgins, Kevin O'Rourke, Max Tani, and Tarik Yousef. Second, there are a pair of superb research assistants who helped make the empirical work possible: Martin Kanz and Rachael Wagner. Third, there are all those scholars—some of whom have been our students—who have shared data and criticism: Roy Bailey, Bob Bates, Barry Chiswick, Davin Chor, Matthew Christenson, Michael Clemens, Paul Collier, Mike Haines, Gregg Huff, Kyle Kauffman, Stephan Klasen, Pedro Lains, Philip Martin, Adam McKeown, Chris Minns, José Antonio Ocampo, Sam Thompson, Alan Taylor, Andy Warner, and participants at the conference "Globalization: Trade, Financial, and Political Economy Aspects" (Delphi, May 24–26, 2000), the conference "Population Dynamics and the Macro Economy" (Harvard, September 11–12, 2000), the PAA annual meetings (Washington, D.C., March 28–31, 2001; Atlanta, May 9–11, 2002), the WIDER conference "Poverty, International Migration, and Asylum" (Helsinki, September 27–28, 2002), the annual meeting of the Economic History Society of Australia and New Zealand (Canberra, September 29, 2003), the Workshop on Demography and Economics (Canberra, November 10, 2003), the conference "Labor Mobility and the World Economy" (Kiel, June 21–22, 2004), the IZA Annual Migration Meeting (Bonn, June 25–26, 2004), and seminars at the Australian National University (ANU), Berkeley, Georgetown, Harvard, Melbourne, Stanford, the American Enterprise Institute, the Center for Global Development, the Inter-American Development Bank, and the International Monetary Fund.

This book would not have been possible without generous funding from several sources. Hatton acknowledges support through a British Academy Research Readership and the hospitality of the Economics Department (headed by Bob Gregory) at the Research School of Social Science (RSSS), which made it possible for the two of us to write the first draft of this book together on the ANU campus in the fall of 2003. Williamson acknowledges the National Science Foundation under grant SES-0001362, the RSSS, and the Department of Economics at the University of Wisconsin, where during the spring of 2004 the second draft was crafted while Williamson was finishing his annual leave from Harvard.

Some of the work in this book appeared earlier. Thanks, therefore, are due to WIDER, which includes our "What Fundamentals Drive World Migration?" in its *Poverty, International Migration, and Asylum* (Hampshire, U.K.: 2005); the American Enterprise Institute, which published Williamson's *The Political Economy of World Mass Migration: Comparing Two Global Centuries* (Washington, D.C.: 2004); and journals that have published various works: our "What Explains Emigration out of Latin America?" in *World Development* (November 2004, with Ximena Clark); Hatton's "Emigration from the UK, 1870–1913 and 1950–1998," in *European Review of Economic History* (August 2004); Williamson's "The Inaugural Noel Butlin Lecture: World Factor Migrations and Demographic Transitions," in *Australian Economic History Review* (July 2004); Hatton's "Seeking Asylum in Europe," in *Economic Policy* (April 2004); our "Demographic and Economic Pressure on Emigration out of Africa," in *Scandinavian Journal of Economics* (September 2003); and our "Out of Africa? Using the Past to Project African Emigration Pressure in the Future," in *Review of International Economics* (August 2002).

We are grateful to the people at MIT Press who expertly steered the book to publication in the final stages. In particular, we would like to thank economics editor Elizabeth Murry and copyeditor Kathleen Caruso.

The best is saved for last. As in our last book together, we again thank our wives, Alison Booth and Nancy Williamson, for their encouragement, patience, and tolerance while we were writing this one. Here's another for them.

T. J. H. and J. G. W.
Canberra, Australia, and Cambridge, Massachusetts
December 2004

1   Goals and Guidelines

There is nothing new about world migration: it has been going on for centuries, and noncoerced *mass* migration has been going on for the last two. Nor are the reasons people move a big mystery: they do it today to improve the quality of their lives, and they did it for the same reason two centuries ago.

The demand for long-distance moves from poor to rich countries, and the ability of potential migrants to finance them, have both soared over the past two centuries. Transport technologies have improved dramatically, so much so that the cost of long-distance moves—as a share of family income at home—are now so low that they are within reach of even very poor Third World citizens, moves that were unthinkable 150 years ago. While only the western European worker was close enough to the labor-scarce New World and far enough above subsistence to be able to invest in a relatively short overseas move in the mid-nineteenth century, workers from poorer and more-distant parts of Europe—Italians, Poles, Slavs, and Russian Jews—were increasingly able to do so as the century progressed. By the mid-twentieth century, poor Mexican and Caribbean workers could finance a move to the United States, and poor Greek and Turkish workers could do the same to western Europe. In the early twenty-first century, there seems to be no distant Asian, African, or Latin American village that is not now within reach of some high-wage Organization for Economic Cooperation and Development (OECD) labor market. Improved transport technologies have lowered the relative cost of long-distance moves, and this has served to increase the number of potential movers. Even though much of the Third World fell behind the rich industrialized First World in the twentieth century, improved educational levels and living standards increased the ability of potential emigrants to make the move. Thus, the passage of time has seen the poverty trap unlocked for poorer and poorer potential migrants, ones increasingly distant from high-wage labor markets. This emigration fact implies an immigration corollary that has important political economy implications: relative to native-born host country populations, world immigrants have fallen in "quality" over time—at least as judged by the way host country markets value their labor. Such an erosion in relative immigrant quality took place during the decades before World War I, and another has taken place during the decades since World War II.

The widening economic gap between rich and poor countries also increased the incentive to move across the twentieth century, although by 1950 it was already big enough to motivate a move for almost any worker in distant Third World villages, towns, and cities—as long as the poverty trap did not lock the potential emigrant in at home. Adding to that demand for emigration, the share of the population at risk increased as poor countries started the long process of economic modernization. Every country passes through a demographic transition as modern development unfolds: improved nutrition and health conditions cause child mortality rates to fall, serving to raise the share of surviving children in the population; after a couple of decades, this swarm of children becomes a swarm of young adults, exactly those who are most responsive to emigration incentives. These demographic events were important in pushing poor Europeans overseas in swelling numbers across the late nineteenth century, and they have been just as important in pushing poor Third World workers to the First World across the late twentieth century. The rich OECD is, of course, at the other end of this demographic transition; there an aging population contributes to a scarcity of working adults and thus to a First World immigration pull that reinforces the Third World emigration push.

Thus, the impressive rise in world mass migration after the 1960s should have come as no surprise to any observer who paid attention to history. Annual immigration to North America rose gradually until the mid-1970s before surging to a million per year in the 1990s. The absolute numbers were by then similar to those reached during the age of mass migration about a century earlier, although they were much smaller relative to the host country populations that absorbed them: the *rate* of immigration in the 1990s was still only a third of what it was in the 1900s. Still, look at what happened to foreign-born shares in host countries. The postwar immigration boom increased the U.S. foreign-born share from less than 5 percent in 1970, to more than 8 percent in 1990, to more than 10 percent in 2000, and to even higher figures as we write. What happened to the United States also happened worldwide. The foreign-born share increased by about a third in Australia and New Zealand between 1965 and 2000 (from 14.4 to 19.1 percent), more than tripled in Europe as a whole (from 2.2 to 7.7 percent), and increased by five times in western Europe (from 2.2 to 10.3 percent). Most of the OECD rise in foreign-born shares took place in the 1990s: two-thirds of the increase in the North American foreign-born share and four-fifths of the increase in the European foreign-born share took place in that decade. In short, OECD immigration has accelerated since 1965 and especially in recent years.

The amazing attribute of this modern boom in world mass migration is that it has taken place in such a hostile policy environment. Prior to World War I, most world mass migration took place without visas, quotas, asylum status, green cards, smuggled illegals, and security barriers. After World War II, *all* of world mass migration took place under those restrictions and limits, and in the face of those hurdles. Imagine how much bigger world mass migration would be today without these modern policy restrictions. Imagine how much bigger those migrations would be today were we still living in the age of unrestricted migration that characterized the first global century before 1914.

While rarely have the poorest been a major part of the mass migrations, it is clear that the nineteenth-century mass emigration from Europe served to diminish poverty there. Indeed, living standards between participating host and sending countries converged during the decades of that century, and the mass migrations were doing most of the convergence work. That is, world mass migration was *much* more important in contributing to convergence than were booming world trade and booming world capital markets in the first global century. If the same cannot be said in regard to the effects of emigration from modern Asia, Africa, the Middle East, and Latin America in the present global century, it is not because the impact of world capital markets and world trade are any more powerful, but rather because the emigrations are so much smaller relative to the huge populations that send these people to the OECD. In the first global century, emigration raised living standards in poor countries a lot. In the second global century, emigration *could* raise living standards in poor countries a lot, but typically it does not. And even when emigration does raise a sending country's living standards, it cannot do so forever. At some point, successful catch-up development diminishes the incentive to leave home, more young adults opt to stay, emigration slows down, and the successful country must rely increasingly on its own productivity devices to continue the catch-up.

If there is even more to be gained by world mass migration today than in the first global century, why are so many potential migrants kept out of the industrial OECD? In large part, the answer has to do with economic adjustment in the host countries and with who pays for the adjustment. Thus, it has to do with the economic damage done to low-skilled native-born workers and their political clout. These factors played a central role when the United States, Australia, Argentina, and other overseas high-wage countries retreated from unrestricted immigration before World War I to tight quotas thereafter. They play the same role today. Modern immigration restriction also has to do with the net fiscal impact of the immigrants, who pays for it, and their political clout. This is a new issue, one that did not arise during the immigration debates in the first global century.

This book covers all of these issues using two centuries of world mass migration experience. It has four parts: Part I deals with the first global century, the age of so-called free world migration; part III deals with the second global century, our current age of restricted world migration; part II deals with the autarchic disaster in between; and the book ends, in part IV, with an assessment of the future of world mass migration.

World mass migration cannot be understood by looking only at the past decade or two. It can be understood only by assessing the present relative to a past that stretches back over two centuries. Let us show you why.

I The Rise of World Mass Migration

2   Evolving World Migrations since Columbus

During the few decades between about 1820 and the mid-nineteenth century, global migrations changed dramatically. Policies changed, restricting global migrations before, while adopting laissez-faire thereafter. Magnitudes changed, with long-distance world migrations soaring to levels never seen before. Migrant composition changed. Most moved under contract or coercion before, while most moved unassisted and free thereafter. Most who moved free and unassisted moved in families and were relatively well-to-do before, while most moved as individuals who were poorer thereafter. And while return migration was very uncommon before, it became increasingly common thereafter. If ever there was a regime switch in world migrations, this was it.

Slavery and Indentured Servitude

The discovery of the Americas stimulated a steady stream of voluntary and involuntary migrants from Europe and Africa. But these streams were a mere trickle compared to what was to follow. High transport costs and big risks (both financial and to life itself) ensured that only the richest and the most intrepid would bear the costs and take those risks. While the flow of free (unassisted) migrants to the Americas almost doubled from 339,000 to 650,000 between the six-decade periods 1580–1640 and 1760–1820 (table 2.1), their numbers were dwarfed by those who came under contract and coercion. Something like 11.3 million had journeyed to the New World by 1820, but most, about 8.7 million, were slaves from Africa. Another large group consisted of indentured servants and convicts from Europe—those whose migration costs were financed by others. Coercion and contracts were the chief means by which the New World recruited its labor force before

Table 2.1
Migration to the Americas, 1492–1880

	1492–1580	1580–1640	1640–1700	1700–1760	1760–1820	1492–1760	1492–1820	1820–1880
Slave and nonslave migrants								
All migrants	265	998	1,358	3,593	5,098	6,214	11,312	15,998
African slaves (thousands)	68	607	829	2,846	4,325	4,350	8,675	2,296
(percentage of all migrants)	(25.7)	(60.8)	(61.0)	(79.2)	(84.8)	(70.0)	(76.7)	(14.4)
Europeans (thousands)	197	391	529	747	773	1,864	2,673	13,702
(percentage of all migrants)	(74.3)	(39.2)	(39.0)	(20.8)	(15.2)	(30.0)	(23.3)	(85.6)
Composition of nonslave migrants								
Servants (thousands)	0	49	236	128	89	413	502	651
(percentage of nonslaves)		(12.4)	(44.4)	(17.3)	(11.5)	(22.1)	(19.0)	(4.7)
Convicts (thousands)	3	8	23	61	34	95	129	20
(percentage of nonslaves)	(1.5)	(2.0)	(4.3)	(8.2)	(4.4)	(5.1)	(4.9)	(0.1)
Free (thousands)	194	339	273	552	650	1,358	2,008	13,051
(percentage of nonslaves)	(98.5)	(85.6)	(51.3)	(74.5)	(84.1)	(72.8)	(76.1)	(95.1)

Source: Eltis 2002b (62, 67).

Note: Some of the individuals recorded in the bottom panel are not Europeans.

the nineteenth century. Over the full period from Columbus to 1820, slaves, servants, and convicts accounted for a little more than 82 percent of the 11.3 million migrants to the Americas, while free migrants accounted for slightly less than 18 percent. These figures switched thereafter: in the 60 years after 1820, free migrants accounted for 81 percent of the 16 million who moved to the Americas.

About 2.6 million Europeans—mostly an equal mix of Spaniards, Portuguese, and British—migrated to the Americas up to 1820, and about one-quarter of these came either under indentured contracts or as convicts (table 2.1; for the allocation by source, see Eltis 2002b, 62). It appears that Spaniards and Portuguese going to South America were much less likely to move under contract, since another source estimates that one-half to two-thirds of all white immigrants to the British colonies in the Americas between the 1630s and 1776 came under indentured servitude contracts (Smith 1947, 336; Galenson 1984). In any case, a passage to America around 1650 would have cost about six pounds, or about five months' wages for an agricultural laborer in southern England (Eltis 1983, 258). Five months' wages was an immense amount for a poor laborer to accumulate, even for workers in the south of England, where living standards were the highest in Europe (Allen 2001). Thus, indentured servitude evolved as the workingman's response to this overwhelming wealth constraint on long-distance migration, a constraint involving a high ratio of costs to income, little or no accumulated working-class wealth, and weak capital markets. Under this system, individuals who signed multiyear contracts were given free passage to the colonies and then, upon arrival, their contracts were sold (at an average price of about eight pounds) to merchants or farmers who needed labor. Of course those with more assets and skills were more likely to make the trip unassisted, and these free migrants dominated the European totals, accounting for more than three-quarters of the nonslave migrants making the long-distance move to the Americas before 1820. Since they were more well to do, these unassisted migrants were *positively selected*; that is, only the best, brightest, luckiest, and most well-connected made the move.

By the end of the eighteenth century, fixed-period contract servitude was in decline, partly because of diminishing European supply, but more importantly, because of the rapid expansion of another form of recruitment: African slavery. European contract or servant labor actually declined from a peak of 236,000 in 1640–1700 to 89,000 in 1760–1820 (table 2.1). As time went on, African slaves became an

increasingly cheaper source of labor compared with European indentured servants. Thus, the sharp rise in slave imports in the early
eighteenth century (table 2.1)—first to the Caribbean and then to the
mainland colonies of the Chesapeake and South Carolina—has been
attributed to the rising price (falling contract length) of indentured
servants (Galenson 1981, 150, 154; Souden 1984, 23). The slave trade
continued to grow in the eighteenth century, partly involving the
North American mainland, but mostly dominated by the sugar colonies of the Caribbean. The documented rise in table 2.1 was really quite
explosive: from 829,000 in 1640–1700, to 2,846,000 in 1700–1760, to
4,325,000 in 1760–1820. Thus, the number of slaves transported to the
Americas came to dwarf that of indentured servants, and black immigration came to exceed greatly white immigration. Of the 11.3 million
migrants to the New World before 1820, about 77 percent were slaves
transported from Africa.

The abolition of the slave trade in the early nineteenth century ended
these forced migrations (although slavery itself lasted longer). It is also
clear that the collapse of the slave trade had everything to do with politics and ideology and nothing to do with economics:

> In 1860, it was possible to buy a prime male slave for thirty dollars in the River
> Congo, and sell the same individual for over nine hundred in Cuba when the
> cost of ferrying a steerage passenger [always assigned more space than a slave
> anyway] across the Atlantic had fallen to less than thirty dollars. Scholars who
> argue that the plantation sector was in decline and therefore slavery died be-
> cause it was no longer profitable have generally not examined the cost struc-
> ture of the slave trade very closely. (Eltis 2002b, 47)

Many have argued that this policy-induced decline in the supply of
slave labor helped contribute to a revival of contract labor—this time
primarily from China and India, and chiefly to sugar-producing and
other tropical plantation areas. We return to this issue farther on in
this chapter.

The Rise of Pioneer Free Settlers

The intercontinental flow of free settlers was very slow at first, but
it gathered speed in the early nineteenth century (Canny 1994). Free
immigrants into the United States outnumbered imported slaves by
the end of the eighteenth century, but elsewhere the transition came
later (table 2.1). Thus, it was not until the 1830s that the decadal flow
of free migrants exceeded that of African slaves for the Americas as a

whole. And it was not until the 1880s that the cumulative sum of European immigration matched that of coerced labor from Africa (Eltis 1983, 255). But the transition from coerced to free migration was spectacular: in the Americas, the share free was only 20 percent in the 1820s, but 80 percent in the 1840s, only two decades later. In Australia, the coerced labor share also declined sharply as the inflow of free settlers began to outnumber that of convicts after the 1830s: the share free was 24 percent in the 1820s and 81 percent in the 1840s (Chiswick and Hatton 2003, 68).

With each new decade of the nineteenth century, free settlers entered the New World in ever larger numbers. Some fled wars and persecution, and some sought political rights and religious freedom, but the vast majority were attracted by the potential economic rewards. In that respect at least, their motives were much the same as those of the indentured servants that preceded them (Galenson 1981, 179). What differed was their improved ability to take advantage of those potential rewards. They traveled in family groups, often with the intention of starting or joining new communities at the New World's frontier. Their numbers were dominated by skilled farmers, craftsmen, and artisans, all with some wealth. The origins of the North American and Caribbean flow were overwhelmingly the more-developed parts of northwestern Europe, while Spain and Portugal supplied South America. Three-quarters of the English and Welsh, two-thirds of the Dutch, and two-thirds of the Germans who migrated to the United States in the 1830s were in family groups, and a third of them were children under fifteen (Erickson 1994, 143).

The onset of free migration to Australia was delayed, since the transport costs were so much greater. The costs of transporting convicts from Europe to Australia fell from forty-five pounds in 1816–1818 to sixteen pounds in 1834–1836; early in the nineteenth century, this was two years' wages for an agricultural laborer (Meredith 1988, 16; Nicholas and Shergold 1988, 58). Given that potential Australian immigrants needed even greater incentives to make the long journey to that region, a policy of assisted emigration was introduced there as early as 1834. The long journey and arduous conditions prolonged the use of coerced and contract labor in South America too, delaying the onset of free migration. Thus, like Australia, Latin America had to use government incentives in the form of free passage and cheap land upon arrival to encourage the flow of free settlers. Assisted-migration policies were less common in North America, where the transport costs (including opportunity costs) facing potential European emigrants were much lower.

This rapid transition to free migration in the first part of the nineteenth century marks a decisive shift in the history of intercontinental migration, but the combination of incentives, constraints, and policy that underlie it have not been given the attention they deserve. Thus, the next chapter explores them at much greater length.

The Age of European Mass Migration

The white populations of the Americas were ... still small ... in the mid-eighteenth century despite two and a half centuries of migration, [and thus] they were overwhelmingly native born.... After 1820, by contrast, free migrants from Europe averaged 50,000 a year to the U.S. alone.

—David Eltis, "Introduction," *Coerced and Free Migration: Global Perspectives*

How did it happen? How and when did the Americas, and North America in particular, evolve from a region with modest to a region with huge numbers of foreign-born, from a region of native-born to a region of immigrants?

The figures for (gross) intercontinental emigration from Europe are plotted as five-year averages in figure 2.1. In the first three decades after 1846, the numbers averaged about 300,000 per annum; in the next two decades, they more than doubled; and after the turn of the

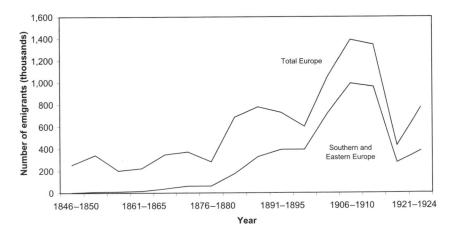

Figure 2.1
Emigration from Europe, 1846–1924 (five-year averages). *Source:* Ferenczi and Willcox 1929 (230–231).

century, they rose to over a million per annum. European emigrant sources also changed dramatically. In the first half of the century, the dominant emigration stream was from the British Isles, followed by Germany. A rising tide of Scandinavian and other northwestern European emigrants joined these streams by midcentury. Southern and eastern Europeans followed suit in the 1880s. This new emigrant stream from the south and east accounted for most of the rising emigrant totals in the late nineteenth century. It came first from Italy and parts of Austria-Hungary, but from the 1890s it swelled to include Poland, Russia, Spain and Portugal.

The overwhelming majority of the European emigrants had the Americas as their destination. Figure 2.2 plots this immigration from 1846 up to the U.S. quotas in the 1920s; the pattern there closely replicates the total intercontinental European emigration plotted in figure 2.1.[1] Migration to the Americas was dominated by the United States, but there were significant flows to South America after the mid-1880s, led by Argentina and Brazil, and to Canada after the turn of the century. A small but persistent stream also linked the United Kingdom to Australia, New Zealand, and South Africa. Still, the United States dominated: during 1846–1850 (years of the great Irish famine), the United States absorbed 81 percent of all emigration to the Americas; during 1906–1910 (years of peak migration before World War I), the United States still absorbed 64 percent of all emigration to the

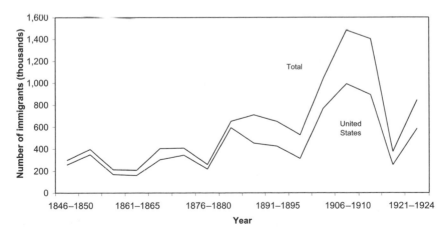

Figure 2.2
Immigration to the Americas, 1846–1924 (five-year averages). *Source:* Ferenczi and Willcox 1929 (236–237).

Americas, its main competitor being Argentina, which took 17 percent (Ferenczi and Willcox 1929, 236–237).

Although they can be measured with far less precision, very important cross-border migrations also took place *within* Europe. The earliest example is offered by Irish migration into Britain between 1781 and 1851, at the end of which the Irish-born had come to account for almost 9 percent of British city population (Williamson 1986, table 3). A second example is offered by the fact that the overwhelming bulk of the migrants leaving Belgium during the nineteenth century went to neighboring France and the Netherlands. To take a third example, in the 1890s, more than half of all Italian emigrants went to European destinations, chiefly France and Germany. A final example is offered by the late-nineteenth-century movement from eastern Europe into Germany, a pattern repeated even today. Significant migrations also took place *within* the New World, especially those from Canada across the border to the United States. Indeed, up to 1900, Canadian gross emigration to the United States typically offset Canadian gross immigration from Europe, yielding only very small net migration flows for Canada (McInnis 1994).

The available statistics almost always refer to gross rather than net migrations. The distinction is unimportant for most of the nineteenth century, and certainly for every century before, simply because the cost of return migration was much too high. However, the distinction between gross and net becomes increasingly important over time as the upward trend in gross emigration was partially offset by an even steeper rise in return migration. Thus, U.S. authorities estimated that between 1890 and 1914, return migration had risen to 30 percent of the country's gross inflow. It varied greatly by nationality; the ratio was nearly half among Italians and Spaniards, but only about 5 percent among Russians, Irish, and Scandinavians. Similarly, the return migration rate was much higher for some New World countries than others. Between 1857 and 1924, return migration from Argentina (Italians and Spaniards) was 47 percent of the gross inflow. The high return migration rate among Italians represented a growing trend toward temporary, often seasonal migration, so much so that eventually such migrants would be called "birds of passage." And what was true of European intercontinental emigration was also true of cross-border migration within Europe.

Since large countries can send out and receive more migrants than small countries, we need some device to standardize the migration experience. What interests us most is the impact of mass migrations, and thus we want to measure the number who emigrate relative to all those in the sending country and the number who immigrate relative to all those in the host country, with whom the migrants live and work. The simplest approach is to divide the migrant flow by the sending or receiving country population or labor force. Table 4.1 reports European emigration rates per decade per thousand of population. These rates include intra-European migrations wherever the data are available. These gross rates exaggerate the net rates, since they understate return migration, but they establish the orders of magnitude well enough. Rates exceeding fifty per thousand per decade were common for Britain, Ireland, and Norway throughout the late nineteenth century, and Italy, Portugal, and Spain reached those levels by the end of the century. Sweden and Finland recorded fifty per thousand rates only in one decade (the former in the 1880s and the latter in the 1900s), but none of the other European countries ever reached such high emigration rates. It must be stressed, however, that even the ten- to fifty-per-thousand rates achieved by the rest are very high by modern standards.

Table 4.1 also reports some New World immigration rates. These are even larger than the Old World emigration rates, an inevitable arithmetic consequence of the fact that the sending populations were bigger than the receiving populations. Every New World country but Brazil had immigration rates far in excess of fifty per thousand in the decade of the 1900s, while only half of the European countries had emigration rates above fifty per thousand, and most of those only barely above. The immigration rates were enormous for Argentina, and they were high everywhere shortly before World War I.

Migration rates of this size imply significant economic effects on sending and receiving labor markets. This is especially so when we recognize that migrations tended to self-select those who had most to gain from the move, namely, young adult males. Thus, the migrants had far higher labor participation rates than either the populations they left or the ones they joined. It follows that the *labor* migration rates were even higher than the already-high population migration rates.

Undocumented return migration rates are not a problem when we look at the share of the population foreign-born reported in census documents. Table 2.2 offers foreign-born share data for late-nineteenth-century Europe and the New World. Just prior to World War I, the highest foreign-born shares (of around 30 percent) were those for Argentina and New Zealand, while that share was 14.7 percent for the

Table 2.2
Percentages of foreign-born in European and New World populations, 1870–1910 and 2000

	1870–1871	1890–1891	1910–1911	2000–2001
Europe				
Germany	0.5	0.9	1.9	8.9[b]
France	2.0	3.0	3.0	10.0
United Kingdom	0.5	0.7	0.9	4.3
Denmark	3.0	3.3	3.1	5.8
Norway	1.6	2.4	2.3	6.3
Sweden	0.3	0.5	0.9	11.3
New World				
Australia	46.5	31.8	17.1	23.6
New Zealand	63.5	41.5	30.3	19.5
Canada	16.5	13.3	22.0	17.4
United States	14.4	14.7	14.7	11.1
Argentina	12.1	25.5	29.9	5.0
Brazil	3.9	2.5	7.3[a]	

Sources: For 1870–1910 figures, Germany: Ferenczi and Willcox 1929 (223); United Kingdom: Carrier and Jeffrey 1953 (15); France, Denmark, Norway, and Sweden: Foreign-born from Ferenczi and Willcox 1929 (308, 381), population from Mitchell 1983 (3–7); Australia (excludes aborigines): Price 1987 (9); New Zealand (excludes Maoris): New Zealand Bureau of Statistics 1883 (107), 1897 (62), and 1918 (76), and Dominion Bureau of Statistics 1942 (1:44); United States: U.S. Bureau of the Census 1926 (4); Argentina (1869, 1895, and 1914): Solberg 1978 (150); Brazil: Conselo Nacional do Estatistica 1958 (28). Figures for 2000–2001 are from OECD 2003 (table 2.1).
[a] 1900.
[b] Foreign nationals.

biggest immigrant economy, the United States. These proportions are considerably higher than those today. As the final column in table 2.2 shows, migrant stocks are now much more evenly spread around the greater Atlantic economy. But the main feature of the table is the rise of western Europe as an immigrant destination and the decline of Latin America. The combination of market evolution and policy change that generated this transition is further examined in part II.

Who Were the European Emigrants?

Understanding the composition of the emigrant streams should help in any quest to explain late-nineteenth-century world mass migrations, and we explore the issue further in the next two chapters. But we need to introduce the topic here. After all, if labor market forces in sending and receiving countries were central to the move, those who moved were likely to have been those most responsive to economic incentives. Furthermore, economic explanations for the mass migrations are likely to look more promising if the composition of the emigrant streams was similar across countries, cultures, and episodes. If instead the composition of the emigrant streams varied widely across countries, then culture, war, ethnic cleansing, and other nonmarket shocks are likely to have dominated economics. So who were the emigrants?

While the emigrants in 1900 were similar to those in 2000, they were *very* different from those in 1800. Early-nineteenth-century global migrant streams were often led by farmers and artisans from rural areas, traveling in family groups, intending to acquire land and settle permanently at the New World's frontier. While many still had rural roots in the late nineteenth century, the emigrants *from any given country* were increasingly drawn from urban areas and nonagricultural occupations. For example, emigrants in the 1830s from Britain, a country that had at that time already undergone a half century of industrialization, were mainly from nonfarm occupations (Erickson 1990, 25; Cohn 1992, 385). This industrialization-induced trend *within* emigrant countries was overwhelmed by the shift *among* emigrant countries, from old emigrant areas (the industrial leaders) to new emigrant areas (the industrial followers). Although emigrants were rarely the poorest in their sending countries, they were typically unskilled, no doubt partly because they were young, but mainly because they had limited formal schooling and training in skilled trades. Thus, the increasing importance of less-industrial eastern and southern Europe as an emigrant source served to raise the rural immigrant proportions and to lower their average skills and literacy.

We return frequently to the issue of positive selection in later chapters, but for the present note that late-nineteenth-century migrants were typically young adults.[2] Only 8 percent of the immigrants entering the United States between 1868 and 1910 were over forty years old; another 16 percent were under fifteen, so that young adults between the ages of fifteen and forty accounted for 76 percent, an enormous share compared with that of the total U.S. population (about 42 percent). The mover-stayer differences were even more dramatic for the Old World: those aged fifteen to thirty-four were only 35 percent of the Irish population, but they were over 80 percent of the Irish emigrants. Thus, European emigrants carried very high labor participation rates with them to the New World. The migrants were also dominated by males, who accounted for 64 percent of all U.S. immigrants between

1851 and 1910 and for more than three-quarters of the emigrants from Spain and Italy.[3] Emigrants tended to be single and moved as individuals rather than in family groups, although a significant minority were young couples with small children. In short, European emigrants also carried very low dependency burdens with them to the New World.

This evidence also suggests that those who emigrated had more to gain from the move and were likely, therefore, to be more responsive to labor market conditions. By emigrating as young adults, they were able to reap the gains over most of their working lives. By moving as single individuals, they were able to minimize the costs of the move, including earnings foregone during passage and job search, as well as to avoid the cost of moving a family (at least until they could afford to do so as an overseas resident).[4] Furthermore, as young adults they had the highest probability of surviving the not-insignificant mortality and morbidity odds during passage.[5] And since the emigrants were often unskilled, they also had little country-specific human capital invested and hence stood to lose few of the rents from acquired skills (except for language). Finally, these young adults had the smallest commitment to family and assets at home.

This characterization of late-nineteenth-century migrants reinforces the premise that labor market conditions at home and abroad were paramount to the migration decision and that most emigrants moved in the expectation of a more-prosperous and more-secure life for themselves and any children and grandchildren they might have. Many moved to escape religious or political persecution, of that there is no doubt, and others did so in convict chains (such as the early "migrants" to Australia). But most moved to escape European poverty, or at least to improve their economic status in the New World. As the technology of transport and communication improved, the costs and uncertainty of migration fell, and overseas migration came within reach of an increasing portion of the European population for whom the move offered the most gain. These forces, accompanied by European famine and revolution, gave rise to the first great surge of mass emigration in the 1840s, the topic of chapter 3.

Macro Instability in the First Global Economy

Recurrent waves and sharp year-to-year fluctuations in nineteenth-century migration were well known even to contemporary observers.

And no wonder: the instability of the migrations was very pronounced. International migration was a vulnerable margin that responded to labor market conditions with a powerful multiplier.

Did foreign conditions matter more in determining the ebb and flow of emigration than conditions at home? This question has long been at the heart of a debate on the determinants of emigration flows. But perhaps that debate can also be informed by the experience of the last fifty years, or even of the last decade. It seems pretty clear that the timing of global migrations today is primarily dictated by the state of the high-wage macroeconomy that is absorbing the immigrants. To the extent that the absorbing economy is subjected to periodic industrial crisis, financial meltdown, productivity slowdown, and rising unemployment, immigration will reflect it, and with very high multipliers. This is true now, and it was true then.

The impact of macro instability on mass migration is illustrated by figure 2.3, which displays emigration rates as deviations from (linear) trend for the six European countries that are central to part I of this book. Two features of figure 2.3 are worth noting. First, since some country emigration rates in the first global economy were much more volatile than others, it seems plausible to infer that local conditions in the sending country must have mattered in accounting for the differences in volatility, for example, high in Ireland and Scandinavia and low in Britain and Germany. Second, since the timing of these fluctuations in country emigration rates exhibit close correspondence, one is encouraged to infer that it was the "shared shock" of conditions abroad that accounted for the common rhythm. Those movements in figure 2.3 have come to be called long swings or Kuznets cycles (Kuznets 1958; Abramovitz 1961). Emigration rates record values well above trend in the late 1860s and early 1870s, again in the 1880s, and again in the 1900s, while those rates fall well below trend during the depressions of the late 1870s and the 1890s. The timing of the migration fluctuations conforms perfectly to macroeconomic boom and bust in the immigrant-absorbing New World. Furthermore, the volatility is big: sharp year-to-year fluctuations often halved or doubled the emigration rate over a single year or just a few years.

This instability was a central focus of the pioneering emigration studies of Harry Jerome (1926), Dorothy Thomas (1941), Simon Kuznets (1952), Brinley Thomas (1954, 1972), and Richard Easterlin (1968). Jerome concluded that the timing of U.S. immigration was determined chiefly by the American business cycle and that conditions in the

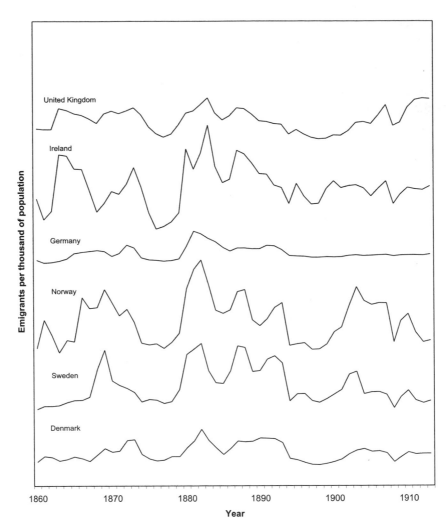

Figure 2.3
Annual emigration rates, 1860–1913 (absolute deviations from trend). *Source:* Ferenczi
and Willcox 1929 (various tables).

countries of origin had only a minor influence. Easterlin argued that long swings reflected the uneven rate of development of the American economy and that immigration was an essential part of the process. In contrast, Dorothy Thomas argued that fluctuations in Swedish emigration were significantly and sometimes decisively influenced by domestic harvest conditions, industrial growth, and demographic factors. Also drawing on Swedish evidence, Brinley Thomas emphasized the importance of lagged natural increase in the sending countries.

Whether assessed with low-tech description or high-tech econometrics, this literature has always been preoccupied with the relative strength of "pull" from abroad and "push" at home. Oddly enough, there has been little discussion of how these terms should be defined. Our strong preference, revealed in chapter 4, is to reserve these terms for describing underlying labor market fundamentals: the forces which served to shift labor demand and supply in the origin and destination countries. When defined in terms of the underlying fundamentals, push and pull take on new meaning. Malthusian pressure at home? Capital formation abroad? Collapse in farm prices at home? Export price boom abroad? Industrialization at home? These are the fundamentals that really should matter in any push-pull debate. The older literature instead typically dwelled on whether the variables representing conditions abroad had larger and more-significant coefficients than those representing conditions at home. Using these criteria, the older literature reached no consensus: pull from abroad was found to have mattered most in some studies, while push at home was found to have mattered most in others. It should be clear that we believe the previous push-pull debate posed the wrong question.

In the wake of John Gould's (1979) critical survey of this literature, interest (by economists, at least) in mass migration during the first global century waned, and many issues were left unresolved. Some historians simply rejected the time series studies involved as too simplistic and inconsistent with more-micro evidence. Grounds for skepticism were that the proxies for labor market variables used in these studies were too crude, that the variables rarely dealt with future expected gains to migration, and that persistence induced by the "friends and relatives effect" (also called chain migration) was too often ignored. Perhaps the key lacuna has been the absence of a coherent theoretical framework within which the roles of different variables could be assessed and in which emigration is a forward-looking decision. Such a model is offered in chapter 4.

The Other Half of the World: Mass Migration in the Periphery

Migration Magnitudes in the Periphery

Twenty-five years ago, Nobel laureate W. Arthur Lewis (1978a, 1978b) reminded us that the flows from labor surplus to labor-scarce parts of the periphery were often comparable to those recorded by the European mass migrations. What we now call the Third World was characterized by the migration of fifty million or more from labor-abundant India and South China to labor-scarce Burma, Ceylon, Southeast Asia, the Indian Ocean islands, East Africa, South Africa, the Pacific islands, Queensland, Manchuria, the Caribbean, and South America. These migrants satisfied the booming labor force requirements in the tropical plantations and estates producing sugar, coffee, tea, guano, rubber, and other primary products. They also worked on the docks and in warehouses and rice mills engaged in overseas trade. The mass migrations involving the periphery imply three questions that are pursued at length in chapter 7: Were the causes underlying the mass migration in the periphery the same as those underlying European emigration before 1914? Did those migrations contribute to real wage, per capita income, or relative factor price convergence within the periphery as they did in the greater Atlantic economy? Was there powerful segmentation between labor markets in the periphery and labor markets in the greater Atlantic economy?

In the wake of empirical work on the Third World after the 1950s, few economists continued to support the labor surplus and (perfectly) elastic labor supply hypothesis which was central to the Lewis (1954) model. However, an economy having *more*-elastic labor supplies implies movement along a different growth path compared with one having *less*-elastic labor supplies. What was the experience of the preindustrial periphery? How much of the labor supply response was due to immigration (e.g., Indian and Chinese immigrants into Assam, the Punjab, Ceylon, Southeast Asia, the Caribbean) and how much to a local response to labor scarcity through earlier marriage, more births within marriage, and higher child survival rates? Chapter 6 shows how mass migrations had an impact on the immigrant-receiving New World and the emigrant-sending Old World prior to World War I, but did they also have an important impact anywhere in the periphery during the preindustrial years before 1940?

Perhaps it is unlikely to expect that these long-distance migrations had the same impact on wage and relative factor price convergence in the periphery. After all, while the immigration rates for booming resource-abundant regions in Southeast Asia, East and South Africa, and the tropical parts of Latin America seem large enough to have left a mark on labor scarcity, this seems far less likely for China and India, the huge labor surplus regions where the emigration rates were so small. True, over the century between 1834 and 1937, India supplied more than 30 million emigrants to the rest of the periphery (Davis 1951, 99). But about 24 million returned, leaving a net emigration of "only" 6.3 million. Six million is a big number, but it was only a tenth of the European emigrations, and furthermore, it was a very small share of India's total population, or even of its major sending regions, like Madras and Bengal. Indeed, while chapter 7 reviews at length a useful comparative assessment taken from Kingsley Davis (1951, 98), it might prove useful to summarize it briefly here. The ratio of British emigrants in 1846–1932 to the British 1900 population was 0.43, while the same ratio for India was only about 0.09, or one-fifth of the British ratio. Indeed, among the eight European emigrating countries listed by Davis, only Russia had a ratio lower than that of India. While the data are inadequate to make the same calculations for China, the consensus seems to be that the ratio was even lower there: "By the time [Chinese] overseas migration became significant, the size of the domestic population was so large that no amount of [external] migration made an impact" (Eltis 2002a, 24).

Migration Timing in the Periphery

Having made these descriptive assertions, securing the evidence to confirm the annual migrations that produced them is quite a bit harder. It is relatively easy to document emigrations out of India; it is far harder to do the same for China. And while it is relatively easy to document the long-distance movements of indentured workers between labor-abundant and labor-scarce parts of the periphery, it is far harder to do the same for those moving unassisted and for those moving under informal and short-term work contracts. Yet the gross migration of indentured workers plotted in figure 2.4 gives a good sense of timing and magnitudes. Indians dominated the indentured migrant trade, but African and Chinese movements were similar. The very low

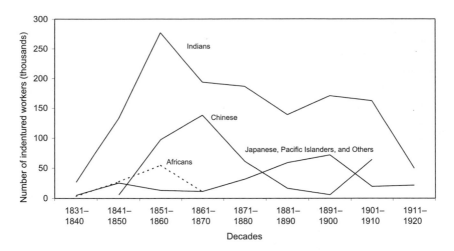

Figure 2.4
Gross migration of indentured workers by origin, 1830–1920. *Source:* Northrup 1995
(table A.1).

levels in the 1820s soared, like those of the European mass emigrations,
in the decades that followed. The gross migration of Indian workers
reached a peak in the 1850s at about one-quarter of a million. It fell
from that peak during the remainder of the nineteenth century, long
before the abolition of contract and indentured migrant labor in the
first third of the twentieth century. While it recorded much smaller
numbers, African indentured migration also reached a peak in the
1850s. Gross migration of Chinese indentured workers reached a peak
in the 1860s, before undergoing a sharp fall thereafter. Figure 2.5 offers
the same gross migration evidence for indentured workers, this time
by tropical estate and plantation destination. The flows to the Indian
Ocean (Mauritius and Reunion) reached a peak in the 1850s, while
those to Peru and the Caribbean (the British and French Caribbean,
British and Dutch Guiana, and Cuba) reached a peak in the following
decade, the 1860s. Gross migration to the Pacific (Fiji, Hawaii, other
Pacific islands, and Queensland) and to Africa (Kenya, Natal, and
other regions) reached peaks somewhat later, the former in the 1880s
and 1890s and the latter in the 1900s.

As a share of total mass migration in the periphery, indentured or
contract labor declined in importance as time went on.[6] Thus, *total* net
migrations, those indentured and those not, reach peaks later than do
net migrations for indentured labor only. Figure 2.6 documents trends

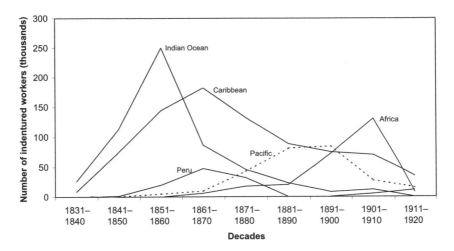

Figure 2.5
Gross migration of indentured workers by destination, 1830–1920. *Source:* Northrup 1995
(table A.2).

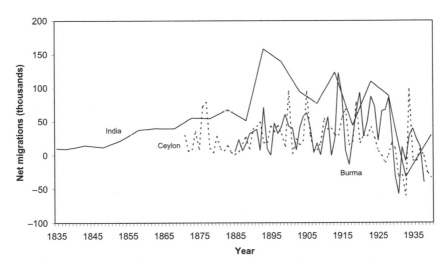

Figure 2.6
Some net migrations involving India. Net migration for India is in half-decade averages;
the series for Ceylon and Burma are annual. *Sources:* India: Davis 1951 (table 6, p. 25;
table 7, p. 27; table 35, p. 99); Burma: Siok-Hwa 1968 (262–263, 265); Ceylon: Snodgrass
1966 (table 2-2, p. 26; table A-14, pp. 305–306; table A-15, p. 308).

Table 2.3
Percentage of foreign-born in populations around the poor periphery

	Burma	Ceylon	Malaya	Dutch East Indies Java	Outer Islands
1870				1.06	2.00
1871		8.14			
1872	4.9				
1880				1.05	2.18
1881	6.5				
1890				1.02	3.24
1891	5.1	8.91			
1900				1.00	3.95
1901	5.4	12.38			
1905				1.00	3.67
1911	6.1	11.61	40		
1921	6.7	10.44	44		
1931	6.9		49		
1941		5.66	49		

Sources: Burma: Siok-Hwa 1968 (265); Ceylon: Sarkar 1957 (table 1); Malaya: Latham 1981 (table 4.8); Dutch East Indies: Latham 1978 (tables 28 and 29).

for net immigration into labor-scarce Ceylon and Burma and net emigration from labor-abundant India. The latter reaches a clear peak in the 1890s, after which it records a gradual secular fall until the 1920s, before collapsing in the 1930s. Census data make it possible to document (in table 2.3) the movements of foreign-born shares in five receiving periphery regions. Foreign-born shares (mostly Chinese) were lowest in the Dutch East Indies, never much more than 1 percent on Java but almost 4 percent in the outer islands in 1900. The share in Burma rose to 6.5 percent in 1881 and stayed around that level between 1911 and 1931. The share in Ceylon was even higher, reaching a peak of 12.4 percent in 1901. Only Malaya reached higher shares, with Indian and Chinese foreign-born making up from 40 to 50 percent of the region's population in 1911–1941. Foreign-born shares were also very high for Trinidad, the Guianas, Mauritius, and Reunion. Indeed, table 2.4 documents foreign-born shares throughout the British Empire in 1901. The shares for Hong Kong, the Orange River Colony (South Africa), and Trinidad and Tobago were the highest, the last almost 37 percent. Excluding India, a major emigrant region, the foreign-born shares around the empire (table 2.4) were pretty much equal to those in the New World (table 2.2).

Table 2.4
Percentage of foreign-born in British Empire populations, 1901

Far East		Americas	
India	0.2	Bermuda	26.5
Ceylon	12.5	Bahamas	2.3
Hong Kong	98.3	Grenada	8.7
Africa		St. Lucia	16.2
Cape of Good Hope	8.5	Trinidad and Tobago	36.7
Natal	12.2	British Honduras	23.9
Orange River Colony	34.8		
Mauritius	17.6		
Seychelles	14.1		

Source: General Register Office 1906 (56–60).

Where Did the Asian Emigrants Come From?

Most of the Chinese emigrants came from the South China provinces of Fukien (Fujian) and Kwangtung (Guangdong), and there was a long tradition of emigration to Southeast Asia from the coastal ports of these provinces, such as Amoy, Canton, Chuanchow, Macao, and Swatow, centuries before the first global boom in the nineteenth century (Lai 2002, 239; McKeown 2004). Early destinations were Java, the outer Indonesian Islands, Indochina, Penang (Malaya), and the Philippines. Most of the Indian emigrants came from Rajputana and Bombay in the west, from Hyderabad and Madras in the southeast, and from Bihar and the United Provinces in the north. Between 1842 and 1870, the Caribbean and the Indian Ocean sugar plantations received about 530,000 Indian contract workers, 64 percent emigrating through Calcutta, 30 percent through Madras, and 6 percent through Bombay. By 1910, Britain's Committee on Indian Emigration estimated that 80 percent of emigrating Indians were from Bengal and the United Provinces (Lai 2002, 240–241). No doubt there are two explanations for this concentration by origin. India shares the first explanation with China, namely, closer location to the source of demand. The second explanation may be related to the impact of nineteenth-century international trade forces, since they seem to have caused deindustrialization (a decline of textiles) in the regions of India that had historically been centers for manufacturing (Roy 2000; Clingingsmith and Williamson 2004). Not only did these deindustrializing regions send labor abroad, but they also sent labor to Indian regions where estate and plantation production was booming, namely Assam and Mysore, as well as to the irrigation-expanded frontiers of the Punjab and the Sind.

Did the Decline in Slave Trade Crowd In Contract Labor Migration?

The timing of events offers seductive support for the popular hypothesis that the demise of the African slave trade and of slavery crowded in Asian contract labor. British abolitionists had been campaigning against the slave trade since the late eighteenth century, and Parliament voted to suppress the trade as early as 1792 (Northrup 1995, 17). While conflict with France made it impossible to implement the 1792 legislation, by 1807 Parliament passed a bill that outlawed British participation in the African slave trade. In the same year, the United States outlawed all slave imports.[7] While other European nations took up some of the slack, slave imports into the Caribbean and the Indian Ocean fell steeply from the 1830s. As figures 2.4 and 2.5 confirm, the migration of indentured Indian and Chinese labor rose steeply in the wake of the antislavery legislation. It is also true that the indentured labor was sent to tropical regions where African slaves had previously been used so extensively, sugar plantations being the dominant source of demand.

Just as the rising cost of indentured servants from Europe helped crowd in African slaves to the North American mainland and the Caribbean in the seventeenth and eighteenth centuries, the successful search for replacements for slave labor was also an important explanation for the rise of the indentured labor migrations in the nineteenth century. A good example is offered by Cuba, where "the contract trade began prior to the end of slavery, but its inception coincided exactly with the first effective Cuban attempts to restrict the slave trade that sent Cuban slave prices soaring in the mid-1840s" (Eltis 2002a, 18). Still, product demand mattered too, and chapter 7 shows exactly how the nineteenth-century global boom created the derived demand for cheap tropical labor. Lewis has been a strong advocate of this demand-led view: "Several writers refer to this [Indian and Chinese labor migration] as a substitute for or successor to the slave trade, but this is a misconception. It is true that after the abolition of slavery the sugar colonies recruited Asian labour, but this was a very small part of the flow of Indian and Chinese labour, most of which ... went to other countries in Asia, working either on European plantations or in mining and construction work" (Lewis 1978a, 186; see also Lewis 1978b, chap. 3). Obviously, both labor demand and labor supply forces were contributing to mass migrations in the periphery, but we argue later that demand forces were doing most of the work.

Chapter 7 seeks explanations for the cessation of the mass migrations in the periphery. The most debated question is whether policy or markets did it. Contract labor in the periphery had a 108-year life (1809–1917), and while it was subject to increasing regulation as time went on, it was not abolished until the First World War. But emigration from China and India had slowed down long before contract labor was abolished. Led by an early decline in the price of sugar, all tropical primary product (relative) prices started a secular decline in the 1890s (Clingingsmith and Williamson 2004), and this cut the pace of recruitment on the tropical estates and plantations. The political tide was certainly moving to choke off indentured labor before 1914, but the demand for *all* labor in tropical export sectors was ebbing. Market forces and political backlash combined to reduce the mass migrations in the poor periphery.

Two More Missing World Migration Parts: Europeans Move East and Chinese Move North

While many western Europeans were moving to the New World, many eastern Europeans were moving in the other direction. Free migration in late-nineteenth-century Russia was big enough to "make the numbers of inhabitants of the Russian Empire crossing the Urals the third largest long-distance migration in history after the transatlantic movement from Europe and the slave trade" (Eltis 2002a, 9). And it is clear that the underlying driving force behind the Siberian settlement was, like the forces pushing Europeans west to the Americas, land abundance and labor scarcity. In 1795, the labor-land ratios were from 140 to 180 times higher (sic!) in the Moscovy, the Ukraine, and the Baltics than in Siberia (Hellie 2002, 294). Migration from west to east tried to redress that endowment imbalance over the subsequent century. By 1911, 87 percent of the Siberian population was of Russian origin (Eltis 2002a, 28).

The migrations eastward within the prerevolutionary Russian Empire were certainly sizable (Burds 1998; Moon 2002), and so were the prewar and interwar migrations from China to Siberia and Manchuria (Gottschang 2000). However, for several reasons, they are not part of this book. First, they are much delayed behind the experience of the rest of the global economy. The late-nineteenth century Russian mass migrations to Siberia are largely a story about the two decades after the 1890s, seventy to eighty years after the big mass migrations took off in the rest of the world in the 1820s. After the 1890s, something like thirteen million Russians moved into Siberia and central Asia (McKeown 2004, 159). The Chinese emigrations to Manchuria and Siberia were also delayed, again until after the 1890s. Second, until very late in the process, Russian migrations eastward were constrained by the absence of the trans-Siberian railroad until Tsar Alexander III initiated the project in 1891. The migrations east were also constrained by tsarist policy: after all, at the time of the serf emancipation in 1861, the Siberian migrations had barely started. While the disappearance of the last vestiges of feudalism helped trigger the mass emigrations from western Europe after 1820, workers in Russia and other parts of eastern Europe had to wait until the early twentieth century to get the same options to move that English and Dutch workers had in the seventeenth century (Eltis 2002a, 21–22). Similarly, for China, it took the Qing government's relaxation of migration restrictions after 1860, homesteading policies in the 1880s, and railroads in the 1890s to trigger the subsequent migration of thirty million Chinese into Manchuria and Siberia (McKeown 2004, 158–159).

The preconditions for European mass migration eastward and Chinese mass migration northward had not been set until the very end of the nineteenth century. As such, this book does not deal with them.

Agenda and Goals

This chapter had modest goals. We have sought only to show that the first global century had distinctly different experience with world migrations than the centuries before. The magnitudes of migration were much greater after the 1820s, and government attitudes toward migration were much more accommodating. Migrants moved mostly under coercion or contract before, while they moved mostly voluntarily and unassisted after. Migrant flows carried higher dependency rates and lower labor participation rates before, but just the opposite thereafter. Return migration was rare before and frequent thereafter. All of these changes require a different way of thinking about these world migrations, and we offer one in chapter 4 that is useful throughout this book. Before we do, however, the next chapter looks in more detail at the characteristics of the transition that changed the world in which world migrations came to operate.

The Transition to Mass Migration: How It All Began

European intercontinental emigration averaged about 300,000 per annum between 1846 and 1876; the vast majority of these emigrants went to the Americas, with their main destination being the United States. Earlier emigration from Europe had been a mere trickle. Spanish migration of colonists, soldiers, merchants, and priests to the Americas over the three centuries after Columbus was only 2,500 per year, and even during its peak in the first half of the seventeenth century, it averaged only 3,900 per year (Sánchez-Albornoz 1994, 27–28, 36). Even English migration across the Atlantic was only 3,500 per year between 1600 and 1776 (Canny 1994, 64). Total Irish emigration to *all* locations (including England) averaged less than 1,650 per year over the same period (Cullen 1994, 139–140). Dutch and German migrations across the Atlantic were no bigger.

To get some sense of how spectacular was the transition from trickle to flood, consider what happened to decade averages of alien passengers entering the United States between the 1820s and the 1850s (Ferenczi and Willcox 1929). The annual average was 12,847 in the 1820s, 53,100 in the 1830s, 152,760 in the 1840s, and 275,458 in the 1850s. Thus, immigration into the United States increased more than *twenty-one times* over those four transition decades! Of those reporting their origin, almost 96 percent of these entering passengers were European by the end of the transition, with the remainder consisting of cross-border emigrants from British North America from above and Mexico, the West Indies, and South America from below. Nor was the United States alone in this surge from trickle to flood. Immigrants through the Canadian ports of Quebec and Montreal rose by an even higher multiple: from barely 1,000 per year between 1816 and 1826, the flow rose to an annual average of 33,550 in the 1840s (the Great Famine year of 1847 alone recorded 74,408) and 29,982 in the 1850s. Immigration into Brazil increased *eleven times* between 1825–1829 and 1855–1859. True, North America and Brazil were relatively short and cheap sea voyages from Britain compared with long-distance moves like those to Australia and New Zealand, but the mass migration boom was apparent there too: arrivals by sea in New South Wales totaled only 4,673 over the three years 1825–1827, while thirty years later, they were more than *ten times* that (49,262 in 1855–1857). The main source of the Australian and North American immigrants was the United Kingdom, and there the recorded number of passengers leaving for non-European destinations rose from 12,510 in 1816 (the year after the Battle of Waterloo, shortly followed by European peace) to 176,554 in 1856, more than *fourteen times* what it had been just four decades before.

While European emigration surged during those four transition decades, the composition of the migration also changed dramatically. The first change was from coerced to free. As we have seen in the previous chapter, it was the rise in free migration over these transition decades that was so dramatic (table 2.1). In the 1820s, only a fifth of the immigrants into the Americas were free, the rest being slaves and indentured servants. Only a decade later, the figure was more than half, and by the 1840s it was four-fifths! This is an amazingly quick transition. The figures for Australia were similar: in the 1810s, convicts accounted for about 95 percent of the immigrants to those distant shores, and free immigrants were the remaining 5 percent; in the 1830s, the free immigration share was 53 percent, and in the 1840s, it was 80 percent.

The other dramatic change that took place during the transition was in the composition of the free immigrants themselves. Prior to the 1820s, the voyage took so long and the steerage costs were so great that only fairly well-to-do artisans, farmers, and merchants could afford to invest in the move. It was simply out of reach of the impecunious laboring class early in the century. It was not out of reach, however, by midcentury, two generations later. The dramatic switch in mix that resulted from this change in migration costs is documented in table 3.1. In the 1820s, only 16 percent of U.S. immigrants reporting an occupation were unskilled servants or laborers. By the late 1840s and early 1850s, the figure had almost tripled to 43 percent, and by the late 1860s and early 1870s, the figure was higher still at 51 percent. We also know something about occupation mix by source country, and it is consistent with these aggregates (Grubb 2003, table 3). The share of laborers and servants in total U.S. country-specific im-

Table 3.1
Occupations of U.S. immigrants, 1820–1898

Occupation	1820–1831	1832–1846	1847–1854	1855–1864	1865–1873	1873–1880	1881–1893	1894–1898
Professional	3%	1%	0%	1%	1%	2%	1%	1%
Commercial	28	12	6	12	6	4	3	4
Skilled	30	27	18	23	24	24	20	25
Farmers	23	33	33	23	18	18	14	12
Servants	2	2	2	4	7	8	9	18
Laborers	14	24	41	37	44	40	51	37
Miscellaneous	0	0	0	0	1	5	3	3
Occupation not listed	61	56	54	53	54	47	49	38
Male	70	62	59	58	62	63	61	57

Source: http://www.eh.net/encyclopedia/cohn.immigration.us.php.

migration rose: for Ireland between 1820 and 1851, by fifty-eight percentage points; for England between 1831 and 1846–1853, by thirty percentage points; and for Germany between 1815–1820 and 1846–1853, by four percentage points. The average rise in the unskilled share of emigrants from these three European countries was thirty-three percentage points.

And once again, what was true of emigration to the United States was also true for European mass emigration streams to every destination. This is not to say that by 1860, the boats were crammed with Europe's poorest, since this would never be true, but it was no longer only the rich and middle class that could afford the move. Later in this chapter, we have more to say about the role of migration costs on emigrant selection. Here we only wish to make two points: first, the cream of the working class and the small farm holder both had a chance to make the move by the end of these transition decades, while they could not afford it at the beginning; and second, even by the end of the transition, the poorest never had that chance to move, illustrated best by the fact that even when the Irish fled their famine in the late 1840s, the poorest stayed home to die (ÓGráda and O'Rourke 1997).

What accounts for the great surge in world migration centered on these four critical decades? A European peace released some pent-up demand to emigrate, and without the peace perhaps the emigration surge would have been suppressed. The fact that international conflict increased the cost of international trade and migration is illustrated clearly during the forty years from the start of the American

Revolution (1776) to the defeat of Napoleon at Waterloo (1815). During the Napoleonic Wars, transportation costs skyrocketed, and even the eighteenth-century emigration trickles dried up. Prior to 1776, Benjamin Franklin estimated that more than 150,000 German speakers lived in and around Pennsylvania, and "only after ... the end of the Napoleonic Wars, with its disruptions on the European continent and in Atlantic shipping, did German and other migration resume at appreciable levels" (Nugent 1995, 103). And what was true of German emigration to North America was even more true of British emigration, since the Revolutionary War was, after all, an Anglo-American conflict. Thus, part of the impressive decline in transport costs and rise in transatlantic migration over the two or three decades up to 1830 was simply a return to peacetime normalcy (Grubb 2003, 5). Anglo-American transportation costs fell from ten to twelve pounds immediately after the war to three to five pounds in the early 1830s (Gould 1979, 621; McDonald and Shlomowitz 1993, table 2, 79). Over the same period, the price for the passage to America from France fell from 300–400 to 120–150 francs (Grubb 2003, 6).

Relative peace reigned in the Atlantic economy for a century after the Napoleonic Wars, the next major interruption to mass migrations being World War I. So apart from the switch from almost sixty years of European conflict to peace, what accounts for the great surge in world migration, and for the change in its composition from richer to poorer migrants, during these four critical decades? This chapter explores three forces that contributed to the transition, forces that were overwhelmed by more-conventional economics during the age of mass migration that followed after midcentury but were important in starting the process: sharply declining transportation costs (and disappearing emigration restrictions), rising government subsidies, and the last great European famine. All three of these were especially important during these four transition decades, and all three began to disappear from the European scene after the mid-nineteenth century. That is, between midcentury and World War I, famines disappeared from the Atlantic economy, the revolutionary fall in transport costs (including steerage) slowed down, there were no more government emigration restrictions to remove, and political violence within Atlantic economy member countries ebbed, and as did conflict between those member countries under Pax Britannica. Of course, western Europe completed the transition into mass migration earlier than did the more-backward eastern and southern Europe, and the same was true of the easing of government emigration restrictions, the ebbing of political violence, and the moderation of transport costs. Thus, our summation of the forces at work in those four decades characterizes emigration from France, Germany, the Low Countries, Switzerland, and the United Kingdom far more than that from the rest of Europe. Indeed, by 1860 those five sources accounted for 90 percent of U.S. immigration.

Transportation costs, government subsidy, and famine can be seen as almost exogenous to labor markets.[1] We argue in the remainder of part I that when the transition to mass migration was complete, labor market forces took over as the instruments driving mass migration. But changing labor market conditions were not the dominant forces accounting for most of the transition to mass migration across those four critical decades. The rest of this chapter elaborates on the three forces that produced the transition.

Transition to Mass Migration and the Cost of the Move

Until well into the nineteenth century, the cost of an overseas move from Europe was simply too great for most potential migrants,[2] and except under conditions of slavery and indentured servitude, it was impossible to secure financing for the move. Declining (time and financial) costs of passage, augmented family resources generated by economic development at home, and financial help from previous pioneer emigrants' remittances would together serve to change this situation as the century progressed. But during the great transition from trickle to flood, it was the decline in steerage rates and in the time in passage that mattered most, the first lowering the direct costs of the move, and the second lowering the indirect costs (mainly the opportunity costs from giving up employment during the move).

Having said as much, it is surprising how little we know about the cost of moving people, when we know so much about the cost of moving goods. Let's start with the goods.

Prior to the railway era, transportation was either by road or by water, with water being the cheaper option by far. Investment in river and harbor improvements increased briskly, and the construction of canals overwhelmed the construction of turnpikes after the mid-eighteenth century. British navigable waterways quadrupled between 1750 and 1820 (Cameron 1989, 172), and canals offered a transport option 50–75 percent cheaper than roads (Girard 1966, 223). On the European continent, French canal construction boomed, while the Congress of Vienna recognized freedom of navigation on the Rhine (Girard 1966, 224). In the United States, construction of the Erie Canal between 1817 and 1825 reduced the cost of transport between Buffalo and New York by 85 percent and cut the journey time from twenty-one to eight days. The rates between Baltimore and Cincinnati fell by 58 percent between 1821 and 1860 and those between Louisville and New Orleans by 92 percent from 1816 and 1860. While it took fifty-two days to ship a load of freight from Cincinnati to New York by wagon and riverboat in 1817, it took only six days in 1852 (Slaughter 1995, 6). Productivity in the U.S. internal transport sector probably rose at about 4.7 percent per annum in the four decades or so before the Civil War (Williamson and Lindert 1980), and as a result, regional price differentials underwent a spectacular fall, from as high as 100 percent to as low as 10 percent (Slaughter 1995, 13). In the four or five decades prior to 1860, transportation began to destroy regional barriers to internal trade, and a national goods market began to emerge within the United States, within Britain, and within countries on the continent. Labor migration into the interior overseas and from the interior at home was made cheaper at the same time.

Steamships were the most important nineteenth-century contribution to shipping technology. The *Claremont* made its debut on the Hudson in 1807; a steamer had made the journey up the Mississippi as far as Louisville by 1815; and British steamers had traveled up the Seine to Paris by 1816. In the first half of the century, steamships were mainly used on important rivers, the Great Lakes, and inland seas such as the Baltic and the Mediterranean. A regular transatlantic steam service was inaugurated in 1838, but until 1860 steamers mainly carried high-value goods similar to those carried by airplanes today, like passengers, mail, and gourmet food (Cameron 1989, 206), especially passengers.

The other major nineteenth-century transportation development was the railroad. The Liverpool-Manchester line in England opened in 1830; early continental emulators included Belgium, France, and Germany. Table 3.2 indicates the phenomenal growth in railway milage during the second half of the nineteenth century, particularly in the United States, where railroads would play a major role in creating a truly national commodity market. Indeed, the railroad was in many ways to the United States what the 1992 Single Market program was to the European Union. But the important point in table 3.2 is what is missing: there are no railroad milage statistics to report for 1830 and only a trivial amount in 1840, but by 1850, where the table begins,

Table 3.2
Railway mileage, 1850–1910

Country	1850	1870	1890	1910
Argentina	—	637	5,434	17,381
Austria-Hungary	954	5,949	16,489	26,834
Australia	—	953	9,524	17,429
Canada	66	2,617	13,368	26,462
China	—	—	80	5,092
France	1,714	1,142	22,911	30,643
Germany	3,637	11,729	25,411	36,152
India	—	4,771	16,401	32,099
Italy	265	3,825	8,163	10,573
Japan	—	—	1,139	5,130
Mexico	—	215	6,037	15,350
Russia (in Europe)	310	7,098	18,059	34,990
United Kingdom	6,621	15,537	20,073	23,387
United States	9,021	52,922	116,703	249,902

Source: Hurd 1975 (appendix 2, 278).

there are more than 1,700 miles of rail in France, more than 3,600 in Germany, more than 6,600 in the United Kingdom, and more than 9,000 in the United States. Note also the tiny railroad milage entries for Austria-Hungary, Italy, and Russia, which made any significant long-distance move impossible for poor workers in the east and south of Europe, at least until later in the second half of the century. The development of railroads in the east made the move from central Europe to Trieste, the rural south of Italy to Naples, and the Jewish Pale to Bremerhaven and Odessa much easier and far less expensive, but that would have to wait until later in the century.

Figure 3.1 provides a sense of the timing and magnitude of the transport revolution in the Atlantic economy. What is labeled the North (1958) index accelerates its fall after the 1830s—its most dramatic decline by far being 1840 to 1860—and what is labeled the British index (Harley 1988) exhibits no trend at all up to 1810, after which the index underwent the same, big fall. The North freight rate index among American export routes dropped by almost 55 percent in real terms between the 1830s and 1850s. The British index fell by about 70 percent, again in real terms, in the half century after 1840. These two indices imply a steady decline in Atlantic economy transport costs of about 1.5 percent per annum after 1840, a big number indeed.

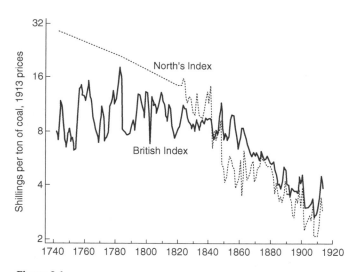

Figure 3.1
Freight rate indexes, 1741–1913. *Source:* Harley 1988 (figure 1), nominal rates deflated by
UK GNP deflator.

To the extent that the direct cost of migrating paralleled this fall in
commodity transport costs, it suggests immense changes. But the indirect costs—the opportunity costs associated with lost work during the
trip—must have fallen as well, especially given that the time in transit
fell. The voyage overseas for the European emigrant started with the
difficult and lengthy trek to Amsterdam, Belfast, Bremerhaven, Cork,
Hamburg, Liverpool, Le Havre, Naples, Trieste, or some other port of
departure, a trip that was expensive and time consuming before the
advent of canals, steamships, and railroads. By the 1850s, every major
port in the northwest of Europe was within relatively inexpensive
reach of the small town and rural interior.[3]

While the extant evidence makes quantification difficult, we do
know something about what happened to costs associated with the
ocean leg of the trip facing the European emigrant. Between the early
1840s and the late 1850s, passenger fares from Britain to New York fell
by 71 percent (Dole 2003), and since this was a period of price inflation,
the real fall was even bigger, 77 percent over these fifteen years. No
doubt the fall would have been quite a bit bigger still if the figures
were quality-adjusted to account for better health services, sanitation
improvements, increased space per passenger, and reduced voyage
time. Indeed, the average time in steerage from Britain to the United

States fell by about 25 percent across the 1840s and 1850s (Dole 2003, figure 6). The cost of long-distance moves fell as well. Over the twenty years between 1839–1840 and 1859–1860, the nominal contract price on government-assisted voyages from the United Kingdom to Australia fell by 16 percent (by sail, McDonald and Shlomowitz 1993, 80), which implies a real cost decline (during these inflationary decades) of 24 percent. Evidence documenting falling steerage costs between 1815 and 1840 is more spotty and anecdotal, but it seems to confirm this maritime revolution. Consider the example of Australia, to which the cheapest fare from Britain fell from thirty pounds in 1828 to eighteen pounds in 1836 (Richards 1993, 256), in real terms a cut of 55 percent over just eight years. The cost of transporting a convict from England to Australia fell from 51.3 pounds in 1816–1827 to 15.6 pounds in 1834–1836, a 70 percent decline over less than fifteen years (Meredith 1988, 18). In the case of the North Atlantic, by the time of the Irish famine in the late 1840s, long-distance travel by sea had become relatively cheap: "A steerage passage from Ireland to Britain could be had for a few shillings and to one of the Canadian maritime ports—the least expensive transatlantic route—for a few pounds" (ÓGráda and O'Rourke 1997, 5).

The ocean leg was, of course, only one dimension of the total cost of an intercontinental move. As we have seen, the ocean leg also took many fewer days in 1860 than in 1820, lowering the wages lost from time away from work, and these lost wages may have undergone an even bigger fall than that for time in steerage to the extent that the real wage, and thus the cost of each day at sea, was rising (Lindert and Williamson 1983). The mortality rate on ships also fell: by 80 percent between the late 1840s and the early 1880s on the government-assisted passage to Australia (McDonald and Shlomowitz 1990). And as we have seen, the cost associated with getting from the European interior to port, and from American port to interior, also underwent a spectacular fall over the four transition decades, perhaps even bigger than that for the ocean leg. Furthermore, the uncertainty surrounding port departure was eliminated with the appearance of Atlantic liners with published schedules (Keeling 1999), thereby reducing the time and cost of waiting for one's ship to leave after making the trip from the interior.

While the real cost of the move dropped sharply over these transition decades, a more-relevant index might be how those costs behaved relative to sending-country incomes. Such an index is shown in the last column of table 3.3, covering Scandinavia, Germany, and the United Kingdom (Galenson 1984, table 1). The numerator for the index is the passenger fare, while the denominator is source country per capita income, the latter a good measure for the early years, when European emigrants were artisans and farmers from the middle of the income distribution, but perhaps a less-perfect measure for later years, as more and more European emigrants were workers from the bottom half of the distribution. Still, since the wage rose relative to per capita income in western Europe across the nineteenth century (table 6.1), table 3.3 understates the size of the fall in the ratio of passage fares to emigrant incomes across the nineteenth century. Of course, as noted previously, the actual fall is also understated to the extent that the quality of steerage improved, with less crowding, better food, lower mortality, and so on.

What does table 3.3 tell us? First, there was very little change in the index for Britain between 1688 and 1816–1821. Second, with the exception of Sweden (a 34 percent fall), there was very little change for any of the countries covered in the table after the 1860s: the index fell by only 7 percent for Denmark between 1870 and 1900; it fell by only 9 percent for Norway between 1865 and 1899; and it actually *rose* by 17 percent for Germany between 1880 and 1900. An average of these four source countries implies a fall of only 8 percent. Most of this slowdown in the rate of fall in the index is due to a slowdown in the rate of productivity advance in shipping after the middle third of the century (Shah Mohammed and Williamson 2004). Third, there was a spectacular fall in the index during the transition decades themselves: between 1816–1821 and 1859–1861, the British-U.S. route index fell by an amazing 80 percent, a fall that appears to have been shared along the Irish-U.S. route. In short, table 3.3 confirms that these four transition decades between 1820 and 1860 were ones of unique and huge declines in the costs of overseas emigration facing Europeans relative to their capacity to pay.

Finally, it should be added that changes in government attitudes toward emigration reinforced the revolutionary decline in transport costs during the transition. Government restrictions on emigration fell in the period before 1830 (Grubb 2003, 5–6). British laws prohibiting the emigration of artisans were repealed in 1825, and remaining restrictions on the emigration of others were eliminated in 1827. The Passenger Act of 1803, which had previously curtailed emigration from Ireland and Scotland, was repealed in 1827. While many German states

Table 3.3
Cost of passage to the United States, 1688–1900

Origin	Date	Fare	Per capita income at origin	Passage fare/ per capita income
Great Britain	1688	£5[a]	£9.8	0.51
Great Britain	1816–1821	£10–12	£20.5	0.40–0.59
Great Britain	1831–1832	£4–6	£20.8	0.19–0.29
Great Britain	1841	£3–7	£24.4	0.12–0.29
Great Britain	1848–1851	£3.5–5	£25.1	0.14–0.20
Great Britain	1859–1861	£3.25	£28.8	0.11
Great Britain	1867–1871	£4.5[b]	£35.0	0.13
Great Britain	1881	£6–6.3	£35.3	0.17–0.18
Great Britain	1890–1891	£3.5	£38.9	0.09
Ireland	1841	£3–7	£15	0.20–0.47
Denmark	1870	$24.33	$91.4	0.27
Denmark	1880	$24.33	$105.3	0.23
Denmark	1890	$24.33–36.50	$117.7	0.21–0.31
Denmark	1900	$36.50	$146.9	0.25
Norway	1865	$24.33	$75.6	0.32
Norway	1887	$24.33–36.50	$88.2	0.28–0.41
Norway	1899	$36.50	$127.3	0.29
Sweden	1860	$24.33	$55.2	0.44
Sweden	1870	$24.33	$57.6	0.42
Sweden	1880	$24.33	$77.5	0.31
Sweden	1890	$24.33–36.50	$86.3	0.28–0.42
Sweden	1900	$36.50	$124.4	0.29
Germany	1880	$24.33	$104.5	0.23
Germany	1890	$24.33–36.50	$133.8	0.18–0.27
Germany	1900	$36.50	$137.1	0.27

Source: Galenson 1984 (table 1, 18).
[a] Fare mainly for indentured servants traveling to the American colonies.
[b] Fare to Canada.

had tried to prohibit emigration before the 1820s, none of them tried to do so thereafter. Sweden repealed restrictions on emigration in 1840. In short, by the middle of the transition period, western European governments had adopted a laissez-faire attitude toward emigration.[4]

Transition to Mass Migration and Government Subsidies

The United Kingdom was by far the most important source of European emigrants in midcentury,[5] and among destinations for British and Irish emigrants, Australia and New Zealand entailed the longest and most costly move. The high cost of the journey required government subsidies to populate these faraway places. How large were the subsidies, how many moved using them, and how were they financed? Since the subsidies arose during the transition, what share of the surge from trickle to flood can they explain? We use Australia to illustrate assisted migration, but we want to stress that by the end of the century, one-tenth of all European emigrants traveled under government subsidy (Northrup 1995, 9).

Australia's colonial government sanctioned free immigration to Australia at the end of the 1820s, having relied on British convict labor until labor supply constraints made it difficult to exploit the European boom for wool exports, created in part by declining transport costs between pastoral source and industrial market. About half of the nineteenth-century mass migration to Australia and New Zealand—almost three-quarters of a million people—was achieved by subsidy and what might be called migrant "quality control." The share subsidized was even bigger during the transition decades, when sending-region wages were lower: between 1832 and 1851, 75 percent of the immigrants to New South Wales were assisted (Madgwick 1937, table 4). The share assisted was about the same for South Australia, but a little lower for Victoria (Haines 1997, 23). For the assisted migrants, not only were the subsidies essential to cover their steerage cost, but also "money was needed to get to the port of embarkation and to the ultimate destination after arrival in Australia; money was required for clothes for the journey;... and [there was] the loss of earnings in transit" (Richards 1993, 253). Australia was simply an impossible destination for the unassisted poor. Earlier we noted that the cheapest fare had fallen dramatically, from thirty to eighteen pounds, in the eight years up to 1836, but what we did not point out is that eighteen pounds in 1836 *still* amounted to about 60 percent of the average male farm laborer's annual earnings in England (Lindert and Williamson 1983, table 2), well beyond his means. If that worker wanted to leave England, the options were to take the cheaper route to North America (at one-sixth the fare to Australia), successfully apply for a government subsidy for the Australian move, or stay. Nor was the fare subsidy large enough to make the move possible for many potential emigrants: "even those falling comfortably within the most eligible categories ... faced substantial costs of entry into the assisted emigration scheme. For instance, all emigrants in 1849 ... were each required to deposit £2 towards the cost of the passage; they were also bound to provide their 'outfit' (and this alone would amount to nearly £5 ...) on top of which was the cost of getting to the port of embarkation" (Richards 1993, 263). For a young childless couple, the unassisted share of the total cost of the move comes close to twenty pounds, or two-thirds of the English male farm laborer's annual earnings. The percentage would have been much higher for an Irish male laborer, since his wages were half those of his English counterpart (Boyer, Hatton, and O'Rourke 1994), and the Irish accounted for about half of the assisted Australian immigrants in 1839–1851 (Madgwick 1937, 234).

We note two features of this account thus far. First, if the total direct cost of the move to Australia was almost forty pounds in the late 1830s or early 1840s, the fare subsidy must have cut that cost in half. Given what we know about migrant elasticities,[6] the introduction of a subsidy scheme like this would have gone a long way toward explaining the surge from trickle to flood of free immigration to Australia over the transition. Presumably, the same was true of other countries that used subsidies extensively later in the century, like Brazil (chapter 9). Second, positive selection—an issue we have promised to revisit in chapter 5—was clearly at work for Australian immigrants, more powerfully than for any other move being considered by potential British emigrants. The poor simply could not afford the move, and it was almost impossible for them to get loans, since they had no collateral. The inference, of course, is that only those of higher "quality" from the middle or upper part of the earnings distribution would have been able to make the move to Australia. This would have been true even of those selected for the government subsidy, since they still had to rely on family resources to cover nonsteerage costs, an amount equal to the subsidy. Presumably, therefore, the 25 percent that left for South Australia and New South Wales in the 1840s without a subsidy were selected from far up the earnings distribution, and even those selected for subsidy could not have been very poor. British and Irish emigrants financing their own move had to have been of "high quality." Did government authorities also make an effort to select "high-quality" candidates among those applying for subsidy?

One of the most contentious debates between British emigrant authorities and spokesmen for colonists' immigrant interests was over "quality,"[7] an issue similar to that involved in the many debates today over the so-called Third World brain drain to the OECD (chapter 15). Australian colonists wanted high-quality immigrants, while British authorities wanted to "shovel" their low-quality poor to Australia (Johnston 1972, chap. 1), keeping the high-quality labor at home. The debate was resolved after 1831, and it was all about who paid the subsidy.

While the British were debating what to do about their poor and their poor laws in the 1820s and 1830s, emigration entered the conversation as a partial solution to poverty—namely, export it. However, just as parish revenues funded the operation of the poor law, the same revenues were seen as the source of funding for emigration subsidies. Britain wanted to export wards of the state, but taxes on parish property holders were thought to be the proper source of the funding. If British taxpayers were being asked to pay the freight, it was thought that they should be able to use their taxes to get rid of the poor—that is, they wanted *negative* selection. Previous experimental efforts to export paupers to Canada and the Cape of Good Hope had proved too costly and failed. The scheme didn't work for Australia either, but perhaps for different, political economy reasons.

The policy debate started with Wilmot Horton, who was undersecretary in Britain's Colonial Office in the 1820s. Horton was "the greatest proponent of the view that public money should be employed to assist large-scale emigration from Britain, to be financed mainly from parish rates" (Richards 1993, 258). He failed in his efforts, but the policy was resurrected by Edward Gibbon Wakefield in 1830. Wakefied retained all of Horton's most important ideas dealing with pauper emigration as a British and Irish safety value *except* the funding source: revenues from the sale of colonial (state) land in Australia would be used to finance the subsidies, not taxes on parish land in England. Since land values were booming in Australia and slumping in England (chapter 6), the idea had a lot going for it. Indeed, booming export prices in Australia implied booming land prices and revenues from land sales, and thus a growing tax fund for assisting immigrants (who might then augment the capacity of the export sector). Slumping export prices would have the opposite effect, thus helping account for the striking instability in the immigration time series. But since the Australian colonies were now paying the subsidy, they wanted full authority over who got the subsidy, and that meant *positive* selection, not the negative selection favored by Britain.[8] The colonists won this brain drain policy battle, and positive selection was the order of the day.

Even though the composition of European emigrants shifted dramatically during the transition between 1820 and 1860, away from middle class merchants, comfortable farmers and skilled artisans and more toward laborers, the Australian example illustrates that positive selection was still at work. Even with the large subsidy, the cost of that long-distance move was out of reach of the really poor, and the immigration authorities made sure that their subsidies financed only the "best and brightest" among farm laborers and domestic servants who wished to leave the United Kingdom. This was true of the Irish immigrants to Australia (Fitzpatrick 1980), Scottish immigrants to New Zealand (McClean 1990), and English immigrants to both (Madgwick 1937, chap. 11; Richards 1993; Haines 1997, chap. 2).

This section cannot end without emphasizing that although Australia has served as an excellent example, other "empty" regions were also trying to lure European immigrants with subsidies. For example, Brazil established a system in 1850 and 1854 whereby immigrants were given public land free of charge. The Brazilian "enactors of the 1850 land law saw [it] as absolutely necessary . . . to compete with the United States, Canada, Australia, Argentina, and other countries in the market for immigrants" (Nugent and Saddi 2003, 12). By the 1860s, both the United States and Canada had generous homestead acts whereby any adult (including an adult immigrant) could get public land at small cost, and by the 1880s about half of Argentina's immigrants were subsidized by the state (Nugent and Saddi 2003, 14).

Transition to Mass Migration and the Irish Famine

The third exogenous and once-and-for-all event that contributed to the transition to the age of free migration was the Irish famine. That sentence implies an agenda for this section: Was the famine really exogenous? How big was the contribution of famine-induced overseas emigration to the surge in mass migration during the transition decades? Was it the poorest and most vulnerable to famine conditions that moved? And did the famine-induced emigration have a permanent impact on subsequent Irish emigration?

Let's start with the first question. There have been two traditions in the literature. One tradition is Malthusian, and it argues that Irish emigration was just another way to deal with overpopulation (ÓGráda 1984). High fertility and early marriage initiated increasing pressure on the land, declining living standards, and increasing vulnerability to harvest shortfalls. The harvest that mattered in the Irish case was the potato, the key wage good for the Irish working poor in the prefamine years. When a harvest shortfall hit, according to the Malthusian theorists, the "excess" population either succumbed at home or escaped death by emigration. In either case, the population fell to some new equilibrium. According to the Malthusian view, the Great Famine in Ireland in the 1840s was inevitable and unavoidable, and since this was the dominant view held by British authorities at that time, it helps explain why Irish famine relief was so modest. For example, one of the most influential economists in the United Kingdom, Nassau Senior, wrote in an 1849 issue of the *Edinburgh Review* that poor relief was the problem, not the famine (ÓGráda 1988, 112). Senior and the other economists who had the ears of politicians at that time certainly were not without their critics: "To leave all the misery consequent upon improvidence and ignorance, to say nothing of imprudence and vice, to their own reward...and to refuse any relief by charity to those who are perishing...would require a heart of iron—a nature from which the natural instinct of sympathy or pity have been expelled or destroyed" (comment attributed to novelist Maria Edgeworth in ÓGráda 1988, 113).

At first glance, the evidence appears to be consistent with this Malthusian view. After all, Irish population increased by more than 70 percent over the fifty years before the Great Famine, from 4.8 million in 1791 to 8.2 million in 1841 (O'Rourke 1991, table 1). And it fell by almost a third between 1841 and 1861, from 8.2 million prior to the famine to 5.8 million a decade or so after the famine. Whether Ireland's working poor were driven to "subsistence" over that half century before 1841 can be debated, but two assertions *cannot* be debated. First, whether they were driven down to subsistence or not, wages were at or very close to subsistence prior to the famine: "the typical farm worker in prefamine Ireland was paid a potato wage not much above subsistence" (ÓGráda 1988, 18). Second, whether at subsistence levels or not, in the middle of the century, Irish farm wages were only a little more than half of those in Britain, and Irish building wages were only a third of those in the United States (Boyer, Hatton, and O'Rourke 1994, figures 11.1 and 11.2). Obviously, the Irish working poor were much more vulnerable to harvest disaster than were farm laborers in England and elsewhere in western Europe. In short, the demographic events we just summarized can be seen as consistent with the Malthusian interpretation.

An opposing view has risen in favor of late, its advocates led by Joel Mokyr (1980, 1985) and Cormac ÓGráda (1988, 1994), and it argues that the potato blight was an exogenous event, unrelated to the half century that preceded it. Even a brief summary of this exogenous-shock view would take us too far afield, but perhaps a quote from one of the proponents will offer a flavor: "The [Malthusians tend] to view the Great Famine as both unavoidable and inevitable. I see it instead as a tragic outcome of three factors: an ecological accident that could not have been predicted, an ideology ill geared to saving lives and, of course, mass poverty. The role of sheer bad luck is important: Ireland's ability to cope with a potato failure would have been far greater a few decades later, and the political will—and political pressure—to spend more money to save lives greater too" (ÓGráda 1988, 122). This opposing view has more to it than simply that the potato failure was truly an exogenous event. It starts with Amartya Sen's (1981) insight that starvation is the result not only of a harvest shortfall but also of a market solution under conditions of unjust property rights (e.g., lack of entitlements). While this is perhaps true of Asian and African famines over the last century, ÓGráda (1988, 79) has argued persuasively that the Irish famine is an exception to Sen's rule: food availability *was* the problem.

How big was the famine-induced Irish exodus? That the Irish made an important contribution to the mass migration surge from trickle to flood is not in doubt. The contribution of the Irish to overseas migration during the critical years 1846–1850 was immense, since they accounted for 71 percent of all European overseas migration over those five years, and they were 50 percent of the U.S. immigration (Ferenczi and Willcox 1929, 230, 380). True, many of those Irish migrants would have moved even in the absence of famine, but it appears that the "famine emigrants...numbered more than half of the one and a half million...who left Ireland for good between the mid-1840s and the early 1850s" (ÓGráda and O'Rourke 1997, 4). They were also important over the longer transition that includes the Great Famine: the rise in Irish immigration to the United States between the 1820s and the 1850s was a third of the rise in all U.S. immigration. The Great Famine accounts for much of the transition to mass migration between 1820 and 1860.

Did the poorest and most vulnerable emigrate from Ireland? So far, we have characterized the transition between 1820 and 1860 as a change from *very* positive selection among free European emigrants to just positive selection. That is, more and more of the working class were able to move, but the poorest of them still could not and did not. What about the Irish during the famine? Did a poverty trap prevent emigration from being an efficient form of Irish famine relief (ÓGráda and O'Rourke 1997, 5)? It appears so. The poorest Irish provinces report the largest human cost of the famine; the biggest population loss was recorded for Connacht (the poorest of Ireland's four provinces) and the smallest for Ulster (the richest). Nor were the emigrants the poorest: "the migrants were not the very poorest or the worst affected by the potato famine. Most of them relied on their own resources in funding their emigration; perhaps fifty thousand of nearly a million were assisted by landlords or the state.... This implies that the very poorest, those with no savings or [compensation for eviction to fall back] on, could not travel. The implication is that the receiving countries were not getting the paupers" (ÓGráda and O'Rourke 1997, 12). Recent estimates imply that excess mortality from the Irish famine was about one million, and those who died were likely to have been the poorest.

The less poor emigrated: one and a half million of them managed to escape the famine by emigration. That the figure is so high might seem somewhat surprising given the poverty of Ireland even among its richer provinces and among its more-favored classes. Surely one of the reasons that the famine emigration was so high is that Ireland had been sending its sons and daughters abroad to North America and Britain for some time, although not in the numbers that the famine generated. The Irish started crossing the Irish Sea in significant numbers in the 1820s, so that by 1841 there were 416,000 Irish-born in Britain (Williamson 1986, 707). The Irish were entering the United States at the rate of 30,000–50,000 per year by the late 1830s and early 1840s (Ferenczi and Willcox 1929, 380). Thus, there were Irish pioneers abroad ready to help many of the Irish escaping the famine in the late 1840s. This friends-and-relatives effect became a very powerful force during the age of mass migration after 1860, but though weaker, it was already at work for the Irish when the disaster hit.

Did the famine-induced migration from Ireland have a permanent impact on that country's emigration experience for the rest of the century? As we show in the next chapter, these famine-pushed emigrants were able to finance the moves of subsequent emigrants. In addition, improvements in the real wage at home—which was permanently raised by the famine depopulation (Boyer, Hatton, and O'Rourke 1994)—would have made it easier for the Irish working poor to finance their move. Evidence in support of this position can be found by comparing the elasticity of emigration to wage differentials between Ireland and abroad, before and after the famine. Low elasticities would be consistent with poverty constraints on the move. High elasticities would suggest that the poverty constraint had been at least partially released by remittances from abroad, or by rising wages at home induced by greater labor scarcity, or both. It turns out that the elasticities were indeed *much* higher in the 1850–1880 postfamine decades than in the 1829–1836 prefamine decades, almost *sixteen times* higher, in fact (ÓGráda and O'Rourke 1997, table 8).

Looking Ahead from the Transition

By 1860, the transition to the age of mass migration was complete, at least for western Europe. Transportation costs had fallen enough to put the cost of an overseas move within reach of a good share of the working class in countries where living standards were highest. Industrial revolutions had begun to raise real wages enough in western Europe to make it easier for families to finance such a move using their own resources. Pioneer emigrants had during the transition established a large beachhead abroad, so they could be used as an additional source of financing for subsequent moves. Demographic transitions in Britain and on the Continent began to generate increasing numbers of young adults eager to move. And not only had emigration policy become laissez-faire, and not only was immigration policy open, but some governments were actually subsidizing moves, especially to overseas locations that were distant and expensive to reach. The Atlantic economy was now ready for the age of mass migration.

4   What Drove European Mass Emigration?

About sixty million Europeans set sail for the resource-abundant and labor-scarce New World in the century following 1820. The overwhelming majority of these arrived as immigrants in the Americas. While the United States was the dominant destination, there were significant flows to South America later in the century, led by Argentina and Brazil, and to Canada after the turn of the century. A small but persistent stream also linked the United Kingdom to Australia, New Zealand, and South Africa. As we pointed out in chapter 2, European intercontinental emigration averaged about 300,000 per annum in the middle three decades of the nineteenth century (after the Irish famine); the figures more than doubled in the last two decades of the century; and they rose to over a million per annum after the turn of the century. The European sources also underwent dramatic change. The dominant emigration stream in the first half of the century was the United Kingdom, followed by Germany. A rising tide of Scandinavian and other northwestern European emigrants joined these streams by midcentury. All of these came to be called the "old" emigrants, but they were joined by the "new" southern and eastern Europeans in the 1880s. These new emigrants accounted for most of the rising emigrant tide in the late nineteenth century. At first they came from Italy, Spain, and Portugal, but after the 1890s, the tide included Austria-Hungary, Russia, and Poland.

Many moved to escape religious or political persecution, and others did so in convict chains. But most moved to escape European poverty, and they did it using family resources, without government assistance, restriction, or, in more-modern terminology, "guestworker" permission.[1] As the technology of transport and communication improved, the costs and uncertainty of migration fell, and overseas migration came within reach of an increasing share of the European population for whom the move offered the largest gain. European famine and revolution may have helped push the first great mass migration in the 1840s, but it was the underlying economic and demographic labor market fundamentals that made each subsequent surge bigger than the last up to World War I.

If the only purpose of this chapter were to explain why so many Europeans left for the New World in an era when state policy was but a modest barrier, it would be very short indeed. To quote a somewhat simplistic overgeneralization by Nobel laureate Robert Lucas (1988):

The eighteenth and nineteenth century histories of the Americas [and] Australia [show] the ability of even simple neo-classical models to account for important economic events. If we . . . treat labor as the mobile factor and land as immobile, we obtain a model that predicts exactly the immigration flows that occurred and for exactly the reason—factor price differentials—that motivated these historical flows. Though this simple deterministic model abstracts from considerations of risk and many other elements that surely played a role in actual migration decisions, this abstraction is evidently not a fatal one. (6)

But this chapter deals with many more questions than the critical one raised by Lucas. Why the variety in intensity? Emigration rates in the latter half of the nineteenth century ranged from a massive fifty or more per thousand per decade from countries like Ireland and Norway to a mere two per thousand from France (table 4.1). Why the variety in trends? The Austro-Hungarian, Italian, Portuguese, Polish, and Russian rates (the latter two not reproduced in table 4.1) trend upward after 1871, while the Danish, German, Irish, and Swedish rates trend downward. This chapter suggests that the variety in European emigration experience can be explained by a common economic framework, rather than by idiosyncratic noneconomic factors embedded in country-specific history and culture.

The biggest challenge, however, is to explain why emigration rates were often lowest from the poorest countries, which had populations with the most to gain from the move. Similarly, why were emigration rates often lowest for the poorest regions and the poorest households within a given country? Why did emigration rates so often *rise* from low levels as successful economic development took place at home? After all, conventional economic theory would suggest that successful development at home would make a move overseas less attractive, not more attractive. It turns out that these apparently counterintuitive historical trends can be easily explained by a framework that dis-

Table 4.1
Migration rates by decade (per thousand mean population)

Country	1851–1860	1861–1870	1871–1880	1881–1890	1891–1900	1901–1910
European emigration rates						
Austria-Hungary			2.9	10.6	16.1	47.6
Belgium				8.6	3.5	6.1
British Isles	58.0	51.8	50.4	70.2	43.8	65.3
Denmark			20.6	39.4	22.3	28.2
Finland				13.2	23.2	54.5
France	1.1	1.2	1.5	3.1	1.3	1.4
Germany			14.7	28.7	10.1	4.5
Ireland			66.1	141.7	88.5	69.8
Italy			10.5	33.6	50.2	107.7
Netherlands	5.0	5.9	4.6	12.3	5.0	5.1
Norway	24.2	57.6	47.3	95.2	44.9	83.3
Portugal		19.0	28.9	38.0	50.8	56.9
Spain				36.2	43.8	56.6
Sweden	4.6	30.5	23.5	70.1	41.2	42.0
Switzerland			13.0	32.0	14.1	13.9
New World immigration rates						
Argentina	38.5	99.1	117.0	221.7	163.9	291.8
Brazil			20.4	41.1	72.3	33.8
Canada	99.2	83.2	54.8	78.4	48.8	167.6
Cuba						118.4
United States	92.8	64.9	54.6	85.8	53.0	102.0

Source: Hatton and Williamson 1998, table 2.1.

tinguishes between what we call supply-constrained and demand-constrained emigration behavior. Poverty traps generated the supply constraints, and they mattered. But the trick is to understand how poor Europeans found ways to release themselves from those supply-constrained poverty traps.

Determinants of Emigration

In a pioneering paper published more than four decades ago, Richard Easterlin (1961) examined the relationship between European emigration and population growth. If emigration was a true vent for surplus population, he argued, then countries that had higher rates of natural population increase should have exhibited higher emigration rates, ceteris paribus. Easterlin viewed the rate of natural increase twenty years prior to any point in time as a proxy for the rate of additions to the labor force current at that point in time: thus, "relatively high additions to the labor market would be expected...to result in labor market slack...and...to relatively higher emigration" (Easterlin 1961, 332). Easterlin argued that past demographic events had an indirect influence on present emigration through the home labor supply. However, if previous baby booms really boosted current emigration through their delayed impact on labor supply, then they would be better captured by an index of current labor market conditions, such as the real wage, reflecting the net impact of both labor supply and demand.

There is another way to interpret Easterlin's correlation. If differences in natural increase were driven chiefly by variations in births and infant mortality, then the rate of natural increase at any given time could act as a proxy for the share of the population who would have been in the prime emigration age group twenty years later. Since this age cohort would have had a much higher propensity to emigrate than those older or younger (see chapter 5), one might observe higher emigration rates associated with faster lagged natural increase, even if real wage gaps between home and abroad remained unchanged. This would offer a *direct* demographic impact of population growth on emigration, quite distinct from the *indirect* effect felt through labor markets that Easterlin stressed. And since rising fertility rates and falling infant mortality rates are associated with early industrialization, rising emigration rates might possibly be correlated with rising real wages at home if the *direct* influence of these demographic variables was sufficiently powerful.

No adequate measure of internationally comparable real wage rates was available to Easterlin when he was writing, and he had to make do with crude pre–Angus Maddison estimates of per capita income. Crippled by lack of adequate data, this important debate lay dormant for about two decades after Easterlin wrote. The appearance of a real wage database for internationally comparable urban unskilled male occupations, however, made it possible to breathe new life into the debate (Williamson 1995). These data have three principal advantages over what was available to Easterlin or, for that matter, even to analysts of modern mass migrations. First, they offer an income measure far more relevant to the decision facing potential migrants. The wage rates were taken from unskilled urban occupations (such as those in the building trades) which were (and are) ubiquitous in all countries, and they were deflated by purchasing-power-parity-adjusted cost-of-living estimates. Second, since these real wage indices are comparable across time and among countries, the country time series could be pooled to form a panel, something that could not be done with the data available to earlier emigration studies. Third, since comparable real wage estimates for major destination countries also became available, indicators of wage gaps between sending and receiving countries could be constructed to measure the gains from migration.

The rows labeled A in table 4.2 report the absolute real wage in various European countries in the second half of the nineteenth and early

Table 4.2
Internationally comparable wage rates and wage ratios

Country		1850–1859	1860–1869	1870–1879	1880–1889	1890–1899	1900–1913
Belgium	A	45.5	52.8	64.2	73.9	85.6	86.9
	B	—	118.2	110.7	109.0	115.9	109.9
Denmark	A	—	—	41.0	52.6	70.6	94.2
	B	—	—	34.6	40.1	47.9	56.8
France	A	—	46.2	52.0	60.4	65.1	71.2
	B	—	—	45.6	45.4	38.3	42.9
Germany	A	52.5	55.4	62.3	68.5	78.1	85.9
	B	—	—	54.1	53.4	53.9	52.7
Great Britain	A	59.4	59.0	70.3	83.5	99.4	98.2
	B	—	—	59.6	63.0	66.0	59.4
Ireland	A	44.4	43.6	51.7	64.5	87.3	90.9
	B	—	—	45.4	50.0	60.2	56.2
Italy	A	—	—	26.2	34.2	37.4	46.4
	B	—	—	37.8	42.6	40.7	45.5
Netherlands	A	45.7	48.9	62.8	79.9	88.1	77.8
	B	—	52.5	53.0	60.9	59.8	46.9
Norway	A	27.2	30.7	40.1	45.8	67.5	83.8
	B	26.0	32.9	25.0	34.9	45.8	50.5
Portugal	A	18.8	19.6	20.1	27.4	23.3	24.6
	B	—	36.2	33.7	36.1	25.1	23.9
Spain	A	30.4	28.0	27.6	25.5	26.8	30.4
	B	—	56.3	52.1	36.6	30.9	31.7
Sweden	A	24.2	34.6	39.0	51.1	70.7	92.2
	B	—	—	36.7	43.2	52.3	59.9

Source: Based on data in Williamson 1995, revised in O'Rourke and Williamson 1997.
Note: A—real wage, Great Britain, 1905 = 100; B—real wage ratio, home to receiving countries. Where there are dashes, there is no information.

twentieth centuries indexed on 1905 Britain. The rows labeled B report
the home real wage in those countries as a percentage of that in the
relevant destination countries. In most cases the destination real wage
is a weighted average of that in the most important receiving countries,
including, where relevant, other European countries. The weights are
based on the distribution of emigrant flows in the 1890s. The main
exception is the destination wage for Spain, which is represented by
the wage prevailing in Argentina alone.

Row A indicates that real wages were rising strongly everywhere in
Europe and the European overseas settlements in the latter half of the
nineteenth and early twentieth centuries. Some countries, like Denmark, Ireland, Norway, and Sweden, were doing especially well, while
others, like Belgium, France, and Spain, were not. If we compared real
wages with emigration rates, the negative relationship would be weak,
since with the exception of Ireland, there is no comprehensive evidence
of a downward trend in emigration rates. There is at best only a very
weak negative correlation between home wages and emigration. Rising real wages at home did not appear to diminish emigration in the
late nineteenth century.

A far better measure of the emigration incentive, however, is the
real wage gap between home and potential destination. Except for Belgium, home wages for emigrants from European countries were substantially below destination wages (row B, table 4.2). Chapter 6 shows
that real wages among the current OECD countries converged in the
late nineteenth century and that most of the convergence was driven
by the gradual erosion in the real wage gap favoring the resource-
abundant New World. For some European countries, the convergence
was dramatic, a finding confirmed in row B of table 4.2. Between the
1870s and the early twentieth century, Danish real wages rose from
about 35 percent to about 57 percent of those in the United States (the
principal destination of Danish emigrants), a very impressive catch-up
over only about three decades. Sweden's real wage catch-up in regard
to the United States was even more dramatic, from about 33 to about
56 percent.[2] But the catch-up was most spectacular in Norway, from
25 to about 51 percent over the same three decades. Ireland sent
her emigrants to North America, Australia, and Britain, and Irish real
wages also enjoyed rapid convergence on real wages in those destinations, from 45 to 56 percent. Dutch convergence on the Netherlands'
major destination, the United States, was a little less impressive—and
there was some backsliding from 1900 to 1913—but the country's rela-

tive real wages rose from 53 percent of destination wages in the 1870s to 60 percent in the 1890s. Similarly, Italian real wages relative to those in France, Germany, the United States, and Argentina rose from 38 to 46 percent. There were exceptions to the convergence rule. The European industrial leaders—Britain, France, and Germany—did not join the convergence; Spain underwent a dramatic collapse in home relative to destination wage, from 56 percent in the 1860s to 32 percent in 1900–1913; Portuguese relative wages also collapsed, from 36 percent of destination wages in the 1860s to 24 percent in 1900–1913. Despite these (important) exceptions, real wage convergence between emigrant and immigrant countries characterized the period, a trend that was driven chiefly by the convergence of European on New World wages.

An inverse correlation between emigration and the wage ratio (home to foreign) is clearly revealed in the raw data for cases like Ireland and Norway. However, over the full intertemporal cross section, the inverse correlation between the wage ratio and the emigration rate is weak, implying that a more-comprehensive explanation is needed.

As the introduction to this chapter pointed out, one central stylized fact makes it clear that real wage gaps do not suffice by themselves to explain emigration: during the course of modern economic growth in Europe, country emigration rates rose steeply at first from very low levels; the rise then began to slow down, emigration rates reached a peak, and subsequently they fell off. This stylized fact—an emigration life cycle, if you will—has emerged from studies both of the time series of aggregate emigration for a number of countries and of regional emigration rates within countries (Gould 1979). It was also used to make predictions about the future of Mexican immigration into America (Massey 1988). Several explanations have been offered for this stylized fact, but we have previously found figure 4.1 useful to capture it; in the figure, movements along some downward-sloping home country emigration function (EM) are isolated from shifts in that function (Hatton and Williamson 1994b; 1998, chap. 2). In preindustrial episodes, we observe low emigration rates (e_0) and low wages (w_0). Industrialization and other events then serve to raise the emigration function to EM' and real wages to w_1. The shift in EM dominates in this example, since emigration rates have *risen* to e_1; in the absence of the shift in EM, emigration rates would have *fallen* to e_1'. In later stages of development, EM is taken to be stable, so that further improvements in real wages at home, to w_2, cut back emigration rates to e_2. Thus, figure 4.1 reproduces the emigration life cycle.

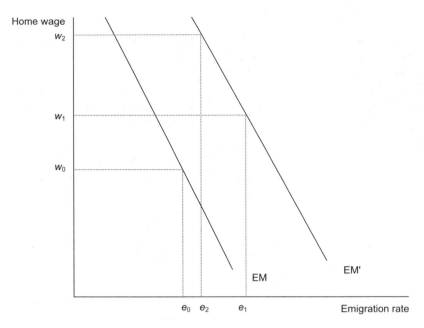

Figure 4.1
Stylized emigration responses

Supply Constraints on Potential Emigrants

What, then, might account for the rightward shifts in *EM* during early industrialization and its stability thereafter? The first explanation appeals to the costs of migration. Although there is a strong incentive to flee preindustrial poverty and rural subsistence, the costs of flight may be prohibitive for most poor laborers. After all, the potential migrant cannot get loans for such a move (a classic case of capital market failure), and his current income is too close to subsistence to make it possible to accumulate the necessary savings to invest in some future move. Thus, enormous wage gaps between an industrializing, resource-rich, high-wage country and an agrarian, resource-poor, low-wage country can be quite consistent with low emigration rates. As industrialization takes place in the home country, real wages rise, and the supply constraint on emigration is gradually released: more and more potential emigrants can now finance the move, and in contrast with conventional theory, the home wage and emigration are positively correlated. As industrialization continues, the backlog of potential migrants is slowly exhausted as more and more workers find it

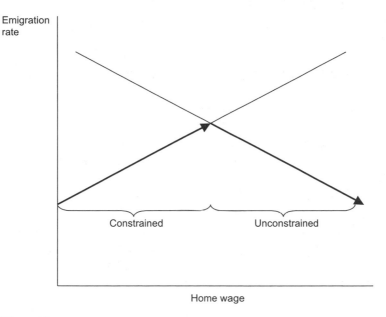

Figure 4.2
Evolution from supply- to demand-constrained emigration

possible to finance the move. When the migration cost constraint is no longer binding, further increases in the real wage cause the emigration rate to decline from the peak. This argument has been used to explain the surge in Italian emigration in the late nineteenth century (Faini and Venturini 1994a).

According to this view, emigration histories should pass through two regimes, the first emigrant supply constrained, and the second emigrant demand constrained, as in figure 4.2. The emigrant-supply-constrained regime is consistent with the rising emigration and rising home wages, and it can also be made consistent with the downward-sloping *EM* function in figure 4.1 by appealing to rightward shifts in that function induced by wage increases. At some point, home wages rise high enough so that financial constraints are no longer binding: further increases in the home wage now reduce the emigration rate as the home economy moves up a more-stable *EM* function, and emigration experience enters the demand-constrained regime. While this tale of regime switch is plausible, we should remember that it takes no account of changing conditions overseas. If the emigration rate is ever to decline from its peak after the regime switch, the sending region has to begin catching up with the receiving region at some stage on the emigration upswing.

Releasing Supply Constraints on Potential Emigrants

The issue is not whether potential emigrants from subsistence economies in the nineteenth century were too poor to move and thus were income constrained: surely that has always been true. The issue instead is whether the constraint was released by rising income at home or by other forces like rising remittances from abroad.

Some scholars have argued that poverty traps prevented the poorest in Ireland from emigrating during the famine of the late 1840s (ÓGráda and O'Rourke 1997). Those poverty traps would be overcome after the famine, even though Ireland did not industrialize: "chain migration" provided the key that unlocked the supply constraint in Ireland, and it was important in other emigrant countries as well. The idea is that rightward shifts in the *EM* function in figure 4.1, or movements up the supply-constrained function in figure 4.2, can also be driven by the remittances of previous (now prosperous) emigrants who finance the moves of impecunious siblings, kin, and friends left behind. As the stock of emigrants abroad increases (and as their earnings catch up with those of the native born: see chapter 5), so too do their remittances, and thus the current emigration rate rises even though the home wage is increasing and the wage gap is falling. The same previous migrants can also, of course, supply room and board for new immigrants as they start their job search. This influence continues as long as potential emigrants find their move financially constrained. In short, the more important are remittances from emigrants abroad, the less important are income improvements at home. Similarly, the less important are remittances from emigrants abroad, the more important are income improvements at home. If some previous exogenous event, like famine in Ireland, has sent pioneers abroad, it can serve to release the supply constraint. Income improvements in the home country (Ireland, in this case) would then not matter as much. If not, as in Italy, then the supply constraint is binding, and income improvements at home help release it.

There is certainly a great deal of evidence relating to chain migration and to the impact of friends and relatives abroad. The influence of letters containing information about prospects in destination countries is well documented, and such information is likely to have reinforced the decision to emigrate. Furthermore, there is abundant evidence that current emigrants' costs of passage were often financed by previous emigrants. This evidence takes the form of large emigrant remittances and frequent use of prepaid tickets: those traveling on prepaid tickets accounted for 30 percent of Finnish emigrants 1891–1914, for 50 percent of Swedish emigrants in the 1880s, for 40 percent of Norwegian emigrants in the 1870s, and for about 25 percent of Danish emigrants in 1881–1895 (Kero 1991, 191; Hvidt 1975, 129). Such evidence clearly argues that past emigration encourages present emigration—what economists call persistence or path dependence, and what historians and sociologists call the friends-and-relatives effect.

The important historical point is that persistence is likely to matter in accounting for the variety in late-nineteenth-century European emigration experience from country to country. Events in the past—like famines, pogroms, and revolutions—are likely to have a potent influence on emigration in the present, even after those events have disappeared from the memory of current generations. Low French emigration in the 1890s may have had its source in the revolution-induced economic reforms a century before, just as high Irish emigration in the 1890s may have had its source in the potato famine a half century before. Persistence and path dependence also imply that nineteenth-century labor markets in the Atlantic economy were getting better integrated through time, an evolution toward true global labor markets that must have been reinforced by the decline in transport costs during that period.

Finally, what about the influence of industrialization and structural transformation? In many qualitative accounts of European emigration, the whole set of changes that accompany industrialization are said to influence attitudes toward emigration. The importance of industrialization in raising labor mobility has been stressed by Massey (1988) to account for late-twentieth-century South-North migrations in which industrialization reduces attachment to the land and raises the frequency of wage labor. The combination of more commercialized agriculture, more consolidated land holdings, diminished small holdings, the erosion of common rights, and relatively high and rising wages in the booming cities all served to produce a nineteenth-century rural exodus (Williamson 1990). The rise of overseas emigration was correlated with the growth of internal migration and can be seen as part of the same phenomenon (Thomas 1954; Baines 1985). To the extent that migrants from rural areas in Europe became urban workers overseas (or in other

European countries), it was simply a rural-urban movement across international boundaries (Thomas 1972).

These, then, are the contending economic and demographic explanations for the European mass emigration.

The Facts

Theory is one thing; fact is another. In previous work, we have explored the theory by incorporating the contending hypotheses in an econometric model that we applied to the nineteenth-century European emigration experience (Hatton and Williamson 1994b; 1998, chap. 3). We explored seven key explanatory variables: the real wage gap between the home country and foreign destinations; the home real wage itself; natural increase lagged two decades (to proxy demographic effects); the level of industrialization (measured by the labor force share in agriculture); the stock of previous migrants (from the same country) living abroad; time (a proxy for declining migration costs); and the dependent variable lagged one decade.

To repeat, the wage gap is the real urban unskilled wage rate in the home country relative to a weighted average of those same real wage rates at the destinations for emigrants from that country (table 4.2). The destination wage varied across emigrant countries to the extent that destinations differed, and different destinations reflected linguistic and cultural preferences as well as overt discrimination. In any case, there was segmentation between different migration streams.[3] The real wage gap measures the expected income gain from emigration. As we argued previously, it is possible that the home wage by itself might also matter if potential migrants were constrained by low incomes. It is an empirical issue as to whether any such constraint was released most by real income improvements at home, by a decline in migration costs, or by remittances and in-kind support (room and board during job search abroad) from those who had already made the move.

The rate of natural increase lagged two decades captures the demographic effect. However, since we have already controlled for the *indirect* influence of demographic gluts on home labor markets by including the home wage and the wage gap, the lagged natural increase should now be interpreted as reflecting a glut in the size of the prime emigration age group two decades later, a *direct* demographic influence. Since emigration was more worthwhile in present value terms to young adults, this age-composition effect should have served to raise the emigration rate for any given wage gap.

The migrant stock variable is intended to capture the friends-and-relatives effect associated with the assistance given by previous emigrants in the form of better information, prepaid tickets, and lower costs of job search. But it may also reflect the broader impact of the attractiveness of migrating to an immigrant community with the same language, culture, and ethnic background. The lagged dependent variable is also included to test whether chain migration was driven mainly by *recent* emigrants to the host country rather than by all previous emigrants.

Finally, a time trend and a set of country-specific dummy variables are also included in the model.[4] The time trend is introduced to capture the influence of declining migration costs, whether due to faster passage, or falling passenger fares, or both. To capture the possibility that noneconomic and nondemographic forces were also significant, country dummies are added.

The only country dummies that emerged as significant are those for Italy and Spain—combined into one Latin dummy—and Belgium. Migration *within* Europe made Latin and Belgian emigration rates higher than international wage gaps suggest should have been the case. None of the other country dummies were found to be significant. Thus, the observed low emigration rates from France and the high emigration rates from Ireland were not due to some deviant cultural behavior, but rather to differences in the economic and demographic fundamentals dictating their emigration experience.

Although the time trend took a positive coefficient as expected, it was not significant. Thus, while the greater part of the variation in emigration experience across countries and through time can be explained by underlying market and demographic fundamentals, declining immigrant transport costs does not appear to be one of them, at least in the late nineteenth century.[5] While we do not have the data to test the hypothesis that the (big) decline in transport costs *before* the 1850s made much of the subsequent mass migration possible, chapter 3 argued that what evidence we do have certainly supports that view.

The real wage gap between source and destination countries had a powerful influence on emigration rates, according to our results, and in the direction that conventional theory predicts: the higher the real wage at home, the lower the emigration rate. This result confirms the downward-sloping emigration function in figure 4.2.

The paradox of rising emigration's coinciding with the convergence between Old World and New World wage rates is largely explained by those demographic and industrialization forces which induced rightward shifts in the emigration function. Demographic forces were a very important part of the shift, but the lagged rate of natural increase had a *direct* impact on emigration, not simply an *indirect* impact through an induced glut in home labor supply and thus on home wage rates. The indirect effect that Easterlin stressed is already captured by the wage variable, but direct demographic effects were powerful by themselves. It appears that these demographic forces accounted for much of the intercountry variation in emigration rates, as well as for the movements in emigration rates through time.

What about the hypothesis that the emigration life cycle might play out according to the following scenario: the home wage first rises, the financial constraint on potential emigrants is released, and the emigration rate rises, but later, as the home wage continues to rise, and the wage gap closes, emigration begins to fall. Stated this boldly, the hypothesis can be rejected: it was relative, not absolute, home wages that drove emigration from Europe in the late nineteenth century. But this result does not imply that poverty traps were unimportant in constraining emigration. They were, but for the typical old emigrant country, rising wages at home did not play an important role in relaxing the constraints those poverty traps imposed; rather, remittances from increasing numbers of pioneer emigrants abroad played the key role in relaxing those constraints. However, rising incomes at home *did* play an important role for the new emigrant countries, for which there were far fewer pioneer emigrants abroad. The stripped-down version of the emigration model reported in table 4.3 shows this more clearly. We have already discussed all of the results here except one, the interaction of the migrant stock with the home wage. As predicted, the coefficient on this term is negative and significant. For countries with large emigrant stocks abroad, income growth at home made a weaker contribution to releasing the emigration supply constraint. For countries with small emigrant stocks abroad, income growth at home mattered far more.

What about persistence? The lagged dependent variable is purged from table 4.3, but it had an estimated coefficient of 0.4, suggesting that the effects of a once-and-for-all shock such as a famine should have died out almost completely after three decades. The influence of past migrations, manifested by the size of the current emigrant stock,

What Drove European Mass Emigration? 65

Table 4.3
Regression estimate for European emigration, 1860–1913

$MigRate = -20.74 - 8.19\ LnWRatio + 0.37\ LagBirth + 0.96\ MigStock$
       (2.2)   (4.2)   (3.6)   (3.0)

$ + 3.19\ LnRWage - 0.18\ MigStock * LnRWage + 5.64\ Dum$
       (1.6)   (2.3)   (4.6)

$ R^2 = 0.72$

Source: Variant of Hatton and Williamson 1998 (table 3.3, column 4, p. 39).

Note: t statistics in parentheses.

Definitions of variables: MigRate = gross emigration rate per thousand of population per decade to all foreign destinations; *LnWRatio* = log of ratio of source country purchasing-power-parity-adjusted wage rates to a weighted average of purchasing-power-parity-adjusted wage rates in destination countries; *LnRWage* = log of source country purchasing-power-parity-adjusted real wage; *LagBirth* = source country birth rate lagged twenty years; *MigStock* = stock of previous immigrants in destination countries at beginning of decade per thousand of source country population; *Dum* = dummy for Belgium, Italy, Portugal, and Spain.

Method: Pooled ordinary least squares regression on forty-eight country/decade average observations.

had a much longer-lasting effect, as table 4.3 shows. Furthermore, the emigrant stock effect was very powerful; for every thousand previous emigrants still living, twenty more were pulled abroad each year. Irish postfamine experience offers a good illustration of how important this stock effect was in practice: the coefficient on the emigrant stock was twice as big for Ireland as it was for Europe as a whole (Hatton and Williamson 1993). A coefficient of this size implies that the famine-induced emigration of one million could have boosted the Irish post-famine emigration rate by as much as six per thousand per annum, and this is in fact exactly the amount by which average postfamine emigration rates exceeded prefamine rates (thirteen versus seven: see O'Rourke 1995). The famine made a crucial contribution to high Irish emigration rates long after the late 1840s and early 1850s. In the words of Roy Geary,

the great exodus of 1847–1854, in placing vast Irish population across the Atlantic and the Irish Sea which created a powerful magnetic field in which millions of Irish were irresistibly drawn from their native country in subsequent decades, was the fount and origin of Irish emigration and depopulation.... [The Famine made] migration part of the ordinary life of nearly every family in Ireland...thus making Irish labour the most mobile in the world and the most free to pursue its best market. (1935–1936, 25, 31)

History matters.

We need to add a final word to this summary of the econometric facts dealing with the determinants of the mass migrations from Europe before World War I. So far, we have said nothing about migration policy. There are, of course, unexplained residuals in the regressions we have summarized above, and policy may well help account for some of them. The problem, however, is getting good measures of the subsidies and restrictions that played a role, sometimes a powerful role, even in this age of "free" migration. We save this issue for chapter 8, in which we explore migration policy in detail.

The Stylized Facts of European Emigration

What role did each variable play in contributing to the observed European mass migration life cycle patterns? Elsewhere we have offered an answer by exploring the product of the estimated coefficients and the changes in the variables themselves. The changing contribution of each variable to mass migration patterns is shown in figure 4.3, in which each variable is normalized to zero in the first decade of the emigration cycle.

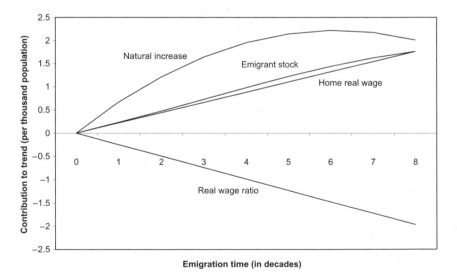

Figure 4.3
Factors in trend emigration. *Source:* Authors' calculations based on regression estimate in table 4.3; for further details of the method used, see Hatton and Williamson 1998 (chap. 4).

The long-run contribution of direct demographic events to emigration rises up to decade 6, when it contributes about two emigrants per thousand of population compared to decade 1. This was clearly an important source of the upswing in European emigration in the nineteenth century, but it gradually weakened as European countries passed through their demographic transitions. It was assisted by the weaker effects of rising incomes at home, which helped release the supply constraint on emigration. This gradually raised emigration rates throughout the emigration cycle, to an extent amounting to 1.5 per thousand by decade 6. These two forces were enhanced by the cumulative effect of the stock of migrants abroad: the emigrant-stock-abroad effect rose strongly through the first six decades of emigration time, contributing over 1.5 per thousand to the annual emigration rate by decade 6. Of course, this emigrant-stock-abroad effect was itself the product of economic and demographic fundamentals acting on emigration and reaching far back in time.

These three variables together jointly implied a trend rising strongly at first, but then flattening out and reaching a peak in the eighth decade of emigration time. At the peak, the total contribution of these variables to emigration compared with the starting decade was 4.2 per thousand. Had there been no other forces at work, the predicted emigration profile would have been very different than the actual emigration trends, such as those demonstrated by figure 4.1. The difference lies in the strong negative influence of the real wage gap between labor markets. As figure 4.3 shows, the impact of changes in the home-to-destination wage ratio was to reduce emigration by over two per thousand by decade 8 of emigration time.

It might be helpful to summarize our argument thus far. First, the increasing ratio of home to destination wages reduced emigration rates, confirming conventional theory. Second, rising incomes at home *increased* the emigration rate by releasing the supply constraint. Third, the rate of natural increase lagged twenty years had a powerful effect on emigration rates. This demographic effect stimulated emigration *directly* by raising the share of the population in the prime emigration age group, rather than only *indirectly* by lowering the domestic wage, raising unemployment, or both. Fourth, there is strong evidence of persistence in these mass migrations. The emigration rate in the previous decade and the stock of previous emigrants living abroad both served to pull many more migrants abroad, and the impact was powerful. Finally, emigration did increase as the proportion of the labor force in agriculture fell (not shown in figure 4.3), but this effect was never very strong. Thus, it offers only weak support for the argument that industrialization induces increased labor mobility.

The emigration life cycle identified for so many European countries can be explained by demographic trends, industrialization, real wage convergence, income improvements at home, and chain migration. High rates of natural increase, wage improvements at home, and a growing stock of previous emigrants abroad dominated the upswing of the emigration cycle. Thus, early industrialization bred European emigration in the late nineteenth century, much like that which has been observed for Mexico, Central America, the Middle East, and Asia since the 1950s. But European real wages were catching up with New World real wages from midcentury to World War I, and this convergence served to lower emigration rates. When the forces of demographic transition eased off, the forces of convergence began to dominate, aided by the weakening pull of the stock of previous emigrants as their numbers abroad leveled out. When the forces of the demographic transition reversed, they joined the forces of wage convergence, causing emigration rates to fall sharply, even before World War I and the quotas of the 1920s.

Were the Latins Different?

The Latin countries—Italy, Portugal, and Spain—were industrial latecomers on the European periphery. They were also late to experience mass emigration.[6] The fact that they joined the mass migrations late, that they were poor by western European standards, and that so many went to Latin America has generated a number of debates on both sides of the Atlantic. The debates imply that the Latins were different. Were they?

Certainly Sir Arthur Lewis thought so. Indeed, he argued that his model of development with immigrant-augmented elastic labor supplies applied well to late-nineteenth-century Latin America (Lewis 1954, 1978b), and many Latin American scholars agreed. Carlos Diaz-Alejandro (1970) wrote that the labor supply in Argentina before 1930 was "perfectly elastic at the going wage (plus some differential) in the industrial centers of Italy and Spain" (21–22). Nathaniel Leff (1972; 1992, 6) believed the same was true of Brazil and that elastic labor supplies could account for stable wages in São Paulo and Santos from the 1880s onward. If this version of the elastic labor supply hypothesis

were correct, then Latin emigrants should have been far more responsive to wage gaps between home and abroad compared with the early
emigrants from northwestern Europe.

If Latin emigrants were more responsive to wage gaps between
home and abroad, why were the wage gaps between southern and
northern Europe so big? Urban real wages for the unskilled in Italy
and Spain were far below those in the United States, Argentina, and
Germany in 1870. Between 1890 and 1913, however, these two countries underwent quite different real wage experiences: the wage gap between Italy and destination countries fell (Italian economic success),
while it rose for Spain (Spanish economic failure). In the 1870s, Italian
wages were only 22 percent of those in the United States, 49 percent of
those in Argentina, and 42 percent of those in Germany (table 4.2). In
the decade prior to World War I, the comparable figures were 28, 48,
and 54 percent, respectively, evidence of strong catching up. Spanish
wages in the 1870s were only 23 percent of those in the United States
and 52 percent of those in Argentina. In the decade prior to World
War I, the Spanish figures were 18 and 32 percent, revealing a serious
fallback. The Portuguese experience was much like that of Spain. These
expanding Iberian wage gaps seem to be inconsistent with elastic emigration responses and contrast with catching up elsewhere.

Why the Latin emigration delay? Since the poorest had the most to
gain by a move to a place with higher living standards, one would
have expected the Latins to have sought higher wages abroad earlier
and faster than the Germans or the British. When they finally did
leave, why were the Iberian rates so low? These questions implicitly
suggest either that Latin migrants behaved differently than those in
the remainder of Europe or that the Latin economic and demographic
environment was different than that in other European countries,
including the possibility that supply constraints were more binding.

Recall the argument that potential emigrants in the poorest European countries were so income-constrained by their poverty that they
could not afford to move. Poverty was greater in Iberia and Italy,
and thus this constraint was even more binding there than elsewhere.
Blanca Sanchez-Alonso (1995, 257, 265) has shown that, when other
influences are controlled for, Spanish provinces with low agricultural
wages did in fact have lower emigration rates in 1888–1990 and 1911–
1913. However, this fact cannot help account for the significant accel-
eration in Spanish emigration, since economic failure in Iberia (Molinas
and Prados 1989) did not produce any significant wage increase. In

Italy, however, both wage increases at home (Faini and Venturini 1994a, 1994b) *and* remittances from abroad helped release the constraint on emigration, especially the latter. It was environment, not behavior, which made the Latins different. Furthermore, Sanchez-Alonso (1998) has stressed the role that policy played in creating an even poorer emigration environment in Spain. While the rest of the world stuck with the gold standard, Spain depreciated the peseta (and raised tariffs on cereals) so that Spanish agriculture could compete with foreign imports in the domestic market. This policy served to raise the demand for unskilled labor at home and reduced emigration push. In short, trade and emigration were complements. Chapter 8 explores whether this proposition can be generalized to the Atlantic economy as a whole or whether it was a Spanish eccentricity.

Is it true that Latin labor supply to the New World was more elastic than that from the rest of Europe? The hypothesis has been soundly rejected (Hatton and Williamson 1994a; 1998, chap. 3; Taylor 1994): Latin emigrants were no more responsive to wage gaps between home and abroad than other European emigrants. It is simply not true that the Latin economies in the late nineteenth century had more-elastic emigrant labor supplies than the rest of Europe. The history of European mass emigration before World War I seems to seriously damage the argument that Latin American development took place under uniquely elastic labor supplies.

Since the Latin emigrants responded to their economic and demographic environment pretty much like the rest of Europe, it must have been the environment that they left behind which was different. The typical northern European patterns are illustrated by Sweden, which was on the downside of its emigration cycle after the 1890s, having reached peak emigration rates earlier. The decline in the predicted gross emigration rate for Sweden is explained entirely by two forces: the decline in the rate of natural increase two decades previously and the spectacular catching up of real wages (Hatton and Williamson 1998, table 3.5). Very different economic and demographic forces were at work in the latecomer Latin countries. True, a boom in the natural rate of population increase two decades earlier was a very powerful force serving to push up emigration rates in Italy and Portugal, an upswing of the demographic transition that replicated a similar upswing in the rest of Europe earlier in the century. These are by far the most powerful forces accounting for the surge in Italian and Portuguese emigration rates after the 1890s. Spain, however, is an exception: two decades earlier, in the 1870s, rates of natural increase were *falling*, not rising, in Spain, a fact well appreciated by demographic historians (Moreda 1987). If emigrant-inducing demographic forces were absent in Spain after the 1890s, why the rise in Spanish emigration rates? The answer seems to lie largely in economic failure at home. The wage gap between Spain and destination countries widened at the end of the nineteenth century (table 4.2), and this event explains almost the entire surge in Spanish emigration. The same was true of Portugal, although the economic failure at home was not nearly as great. In contrast, Italian wages at the end of the century were catching up with those in destination countries—Argentina, Germany, and the United States—and that wage success muted the surge in Italian emigration by partially offsetting the powerful emigrant-inducing demographic forces at work there.

All three Latin countries, shared additional fundamentals that served to contribute to the surge in emigration, especially rising migrant populations abroad. Nonetheless, what really made the Latin countries different from the other countries of Europe after the 1890s was delayed demographic transition and economic failure at home. Oddly enough, economic failure at home also helps explain British experience. British emigration rose to a peak in the 1880s, falling thereafter, thus manifesting an emigration life cycle that was repeated by many countries in nineteenth-century Europe. However, British emigration departed from this standard life cycle pattern after the 1890s: the emigration rate *rose* rather than continuing its fall. What made Britain different after the 1890s? Exactly the same forces that made Spain and Portugal different: economic failure at home.

A European Model of Mass Emigration Emerges

The forces underlying the European mass migrations in the nineteenth century are now much clearer. In the early phases of emigration and modern development, the positive impact of the demographic transition, industrialization, and the increasing number of previous emigrants abroad outweighed the negative impact of real wage catch-up. Thus, even though European real wages were slowly catching up with real wages in more-labor-scarce destinations, emigration rates surged. But as demographic transition forces petered out, as the rate of industrialization slowed down, and as the emigrant stock abroad began to level out, real wage convergence between labor markets at home and

abroad increasingly dominated events. The continued fall in the wage
gap between home and destination areas finally caused emigration
rates to drop off. The fall in emigration rates accelerated on the down-
swing, as direct demographic forces now joined these long-run labor
market effects, that is, as the young-adult cohort—the cohort most responsive to labor market forces—declined in relative importance. Our
guess is that these forces would have stemmed the European mass
migration tide soon after World War I in any case, making American
immigration quotas and the disappearance of immigrant subsidies in
Argentina, Australia, Brazil, Canada, and elsewhere overseas at least
partially redundant.

   This story about the evolution of a true global labor market in the
nineteenth-century Atlantic economy is, however, only one quarter
told. Chapter 5 adds the second quarter: how did the immigrants do
in the destination countries? Chapter 6 adds the third quarter: what
impact did the mass migration have on convergence between countries
and inequality within countries? Chapter 8 adds the final quarter: was
there a policy backlash?

When to Move? Emigration Cycles

So far we have explored European emigration over the long run,
abstracting from business cycles, long swings, and episodic shocks. In
fact, annual emigration rates in European countries in the nineteenth
century were highly volatile, often rising or falling by a half or even
three quarters in a year or two, only to recover again a few years later.
Figure 4.4 displays the annual time series of gross emigration between
1870 and 1913 for the United Kingdom and the three Scandinavian
countries, sending regions that had high absolute emigration rates and
correspondingly large annual fluctuations. How do we explain this
instability?

   Following the pioneering studies of Jerome (1926) and Thomas
(1941), a large literature has debated whether push or pull forces were
the most important determinants of nineteenth-century European emigration. The debate reached no consensus when it blossomed in the
1970s: pull from abroad was found to have mattered in some studies,
while push at home was found to have mattered in others (Gould
1979). Furthermore, the debate explored whether variations in real
wage rates or job opportunities mattered more: when both variables
were included, job opportunities often dominated, especially job op-

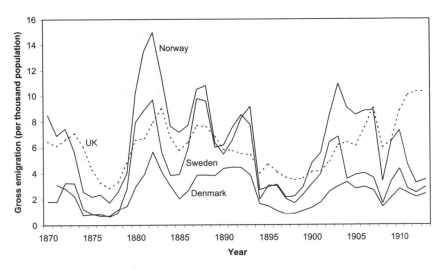

Figure 4.4
Gross emigration rates, 1870–1913. *Source:* Ferenczi and Willcox 1929 (various tables).

portunities in the destination country. Yet it is hard to believe that migrants made decisions based only on conditions at home or only on conditions abroad. Emigration decisions must have been based on some comparison, however approximate, between the two. Similarly, while cyclical conditions clearly mattered in the timing of migration, it is hard to believe that wage rates did not matter as well.

The earlier emigration studies often lacked a coherent economic model of the migration decision, thus making their results difficult to interpret. More-recent approaches have been based on a model in which potential migrants base their migration decision on the comparison of future expected income streams at home and abroad (Hatton 1995), where expected income is simply the wage multiplied by the probability of employment (Todaro 1969). Because migrants are risk-averse, and because greater uncertainty attaches to the probability of employment than to the wage rate, the former takes a larger weight in the migration function.

Estimates on annual time series for gross emigration for the United Kingdom between 1870 and 1813 strongly support these theoretical priors (Hatton 1995; Hatton and Williamson 1998, chap. 4). Wage rates *and* unemployment rates, both at home *and* abroad, all mattered in the way theory predicts. Thus, a permanent 10 percent rise in the foreign-to-home wage ratio raised the emigration rate by 1.9 to 2.4 per thousand of population, a result reassuringly similar to that obtained in the long-run analysis presented earlier in the chapter. The effect of a 10 percent rise in the foreign employment rate (e.g., a fall in the unemployment rate from 10 percent to 1 percent) raised the emigration rate in the long run by between 3.7 to 4.4 per thousand, larger than the effect of an equivalent wage increase and reflecting migrant risk aversion. Changes in the home employment rate had an effect similar to that of changes in the home wage: a 10 percent rise reduced emigration by about 2 per thousand. Finally, the migrant stock, which is also included in the model, had an even more powerful effect than in the cross-country analysis.[7]

Thus, most of the volatility in nineteenth-century European migration is explained by the volatility in employment rates and labor supply dynamics. When these effects are excluded, predicted emigration patterns over time are much smoother. For example, migration volatility in the Scandinavian countries is reduced by up to half when we abstract from these short-run influences. Why do cyclical factors matter so much? Given that long-distance migrations are based on the comparison of future expected lifetime earnings, one might have thought that short-run changes, quickly reversed, would have little effect on migration rates. One reason they instead had such a profound effect in nineteenth-century Europe may be that the time horizon for emigrants intending to return was short, and hence cyclical conditions mattered far more. A second reason relates to the option value of waiting. While it might have been worth emigrating at a given time even though unemployment was high at the destination, it would have been better still to wait a year or two until destination labor market conditions improved. Hence emigrants timed their moves in order to maximize the life cycle benefits overall.

Pogroms and Ethnic Cleansing: Were the East European Jews Different?

Throughout this chapter we have asserted that labor market fundamentals dominated the European mass emigrations. What about non-market forces? The traditional literature points to what it thinks is the best historical example of such forces: the flight of Jewish migrants from eastern Europe in the wake of late-nineteenth-century pogroms. We do not disagree with the position that the *intensity* of Jewish emigration can be explained in large part by persecution. And intense it was. As Leah Platt Boustan (2003, 3) has recently pointed out, net emigration rates of Jews from Russia reached 18.3 per thousand in 1900 when Italian net emigration rates were 13 per thousand. Furthermore, the Jewish net emigration rate was greater in 1900–1913 (19.7 per thousand) than it was even for the Irish in 1850–1859 after the Great Famine (19 per thousand). However, by rejecting economics and the role of markets, the traditional literature creates two unnecessary puzzles for itself (Boustan 2003, 4–5). First, why did the Jews wait until 1881 to emigrate in large numbers even though discrimination had been prevalent throughout the nineteenth century, and even though the 1871 pogroms in Odessa had been even more violent than those closer to the time of the Jewish mass migration? Second, if ethnic cleansing was the dominant force driving Jewish migration, why does the pattern of Jewish emigration correlate so well with that from the rest of the European periphery (labeled "other" in figure 4.5)? There is a less-developed tradition in the economics literature that starts with Simon Kuznets (1975), and it helps erase the puzzles. This tradition was revisited with Andrew Godley's recent study (2001), which argued that the Jewish emigration to New York and London in the late nineteenth and early twentieth centuries was economically motivated. The economic

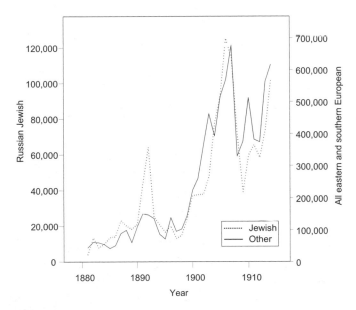

Figure 4.5
Migration to the United States, 1881–1914. *Source:* Boustan 2003 (figure 3).

explanation was strengthened with new data by Boustan (2003), who shows that the timing of Jewish emigration from 1886 to 1913 can be explained by a market-oriented model (like the one discussed earlier in this chapter) just as effectively as can be the Irish emigration in the wake of the Great Famine and the Italian emigration a few decades later. Labor market fundamentals drove the mass migration that occurred during the first global century even for times and places in which persecution, violence, and ethnic cleansing were so pernicious.

Emigrant Origins and Immigrant Outcomes

How do immigrants perform in the host country? Do they do better or worse than the native-born? Are immigrants positively selected from the source country population? Do they utilize their skills, or are they confined to unskilled jobs that are shunned by the native-born? These questions are at the heart of the current immigration debate, but they are not new. In fact they are as old as the mass migrations themselves.

Much of the discussion in this chapter turns on exactly who the immigrants were. The burdens and benefits that immigrants bring to the society that hosts them depend on the whether they are young or old, skilled or unskilled, schooled or unschooled, enterprising or lazy. Much depends on their origins. If the source country is rich in skills and human capital, then it is likely that immigrants from that country will share those characteristics. Equally important is whether immigrants tend to be the best and brightest among the population from which they are drawn. Such characteristics are not accidental. One important lesson that history teaches us is that migration is a selective process. Migrant outcomes are not independent of the factors that drive those who migrate to do so in the first place.

Immigrant Characteristics

As we have seen, European emigration responded to wages and employment opportunities in sending and receiving areas: for those who emigrated, labor market forces were central to the move. The explanations that we have offered for the migrant streams would be more convincing still if they could also be linked to the composition of those streams. In short, those same economic forces should help explain who emigrated as well as how many emigrated. So who were the migrants?

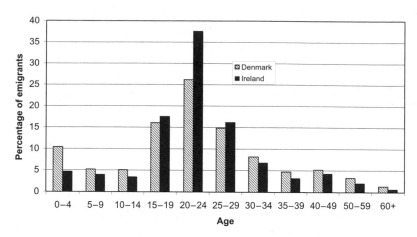

Figure 5.1
Age distribution of emigrants: Denmark, 1868–1900, and Ireland, 1871–1910. *Sources:* Ireland: Carrier and Jeffrey 1953 (108); Denmark: Hvidt 1975 (73).

By the late nineteenth century, European emigrants were typically young adults. This fact supports the view that migration is an economic decision that depends on the comparison of expected future gains with present costs (including loss of income during the move). The younger the migrant, the longer the payback period, and the more worthwhile the investment in a long-distance move. Figure 5.1 shows the distribution of Danish emigrants by age between 1868 and 1900 and of Irish emigrants between 1871 and 1910. Over half the Danish emigrants and nearly two-thirds of the Irish emigrants were aged fifteen to twenty-nine, figures that were typical of emigrants from other European countries as well. Among the Irish, 37 percent of all emigrants and 43 percent of adult emigrants were aged twenty to twenty-four. These individuals had a long working life ahead of them. In addition, while they might have accumulated some general education and occupational skills, they would not have invested heavily yet in country-specific human capital that might have had lower value in the New World.

The selection of young adults for migration is equally striking when compared with the share of young adults in the populations from which they came and to which they went. Among Irish emigrants, 71 percent were aged fifteen to twenty-nine, as compared with 26 percent of the 1881 Irish population. Of all immigrants entering the United States between 1868 and 1910, 76 percent were between the ages fifteen and forty, while the total U.S. population share was only about 42 percent. Immigrants carried both very high labor participation rates and very low dependency burdens with them to the New World, and if anything, this young-adult bias grew even larger as the century progressed.

Furthermore, in almost every decade between the 1820s and the 1890s, more than three-fifths of immigrants to the United States were male (table 3.1). It appears that those who were less involved in the formal labor market, such as children and females, were less likely to be international migrants, since they were less responsive to labor market conditions. Thus, there was a gender bias in the nineteenth-century mass migrations, favoring males, at least when labor market forces were doing most of the work. Furthermore, this bias was more pronounced where the costs of the move were especially high, an assertion that is illustrated by the high male share of Irish going to Australia relative to the share of Irish going to the United States. Males should also have been more dominant in the emigration flows from poorer countries, as indeed they were: in the century before 1928, the male share was 85.5 percent for Indian and Chinese immigrants into the United States, 74.6 percent for southern and southeastern Europeans, and 59.8 percent for northwest Europeans (Gabaccia 1996, 92). Finally, the male gender bias in European emigration declined over time (Gabaccia 1996).

Emigrants in 1900 were certainly different from those in 1800. Early-nineteenth-century migrations often took place as family groups, with those who emigrated intent on acquiring land and settling at some overseas frontier (chapter 2). While many still had rural roots in the late nineteenth century, the emigrants from any given country were increasingly drawn from cities, towns, and urban occupations. Thus, emigrants in the 1830s from Britain, a country that by then had already undergone a half century of industrialization, were mainly from nonfarm occupations. This industrialization-induced trend was overwhelmed by the shift from old emigrant sources (the industrial leaders) to new emigrant sources (the industrial followers). This shift in source left its mark on trends in the occupational composition of U.S. immigration across the century (table 3.1): for example, the proportion of immigrants that were unskilled laborers and servants rose from 16 percent in the 1820s to 55 percent in the 1890s.

While most of these migrants became permanent residents of the countries to which they migrated, return migration became increasingly

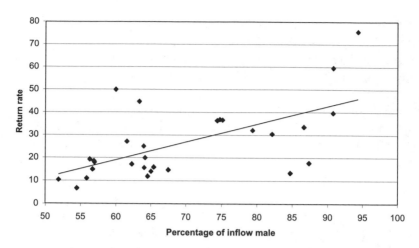

Figure 5.2
Return migration and sex composition, United States, 1910–1914. *Source:* Calculated from
U.S. Bureau of the Census 1926 (88, 90).

common over the course of the nineteenth century. This reflected
both the declining costs of travel (especially the time involved) relative
to migrant incomes and the change in immigrant source. In the decade
before 1914, emigrants returning home from the United States
amounted to about a third of the inward flow. Return migration rates
differed more by source country than by destination. Thus, among Italian emigrants, the return flow from both Argentina and the United
States averaged about half the outward flow. But these were much
higher than the return migration rates among the northwestern Europeans. Figure 5.2 shows that the higher the percentage of males in the
inflow for a given source country, the greater the return migration rate
to that country. Thus, for a large and increasing minority across the
century, emigration to the New World was temporary. These were the
male migrants who intended (and could now afford) to return home to
marry and start families after accumulating a nest egg working abroad.
Return migration was not the result of failure and disillusion: it was
part of a lifetime strategy for improving living standards and escaping
poverty.[1]

How Did Immigrants Do in the Host Country?

Immigrant assimilation experience has been a source of debate for
some time. The key questions have been: How large was the earnings

disadvantage that nineteenth-century immigrants faced upon entry into the destination labor market? How rapidly did that initial disadvantage erode as they gained labor market experience in the host country? Did the earnings of immigrants catch up with, or even overtake, the earnings of native-born workers? Were differences in assimilation related to country of origin, schooling, and occupational background as well as religion, ethnicity, and culture?

This debate started a century ago when the U.S. Immigration Commission (known as the Dillingham Commission) devoted four years (1907–1911) to examining every aspect of the economic and social life of immigrants in the United States. The background to the inquiry was the "changed character of the immigration movement to the United States during the past twenty-five years" (1:13). The commission drew a sharp distinction between immigrants from old northwestern European immigrant sources, such as Britain, Ireland, Germany, and Scandinavia, and those from new southern and eastern European immigrant sources, such as Italy, the Balkans, Russia, and what is now Poland. The commission viewed the new immigrants as "largely a movement of unskilled laboring men, who have come, in large part temporarily, from the less progressive and advanced countries of Europe," characterizing them as "far less intelligent" and "actuated by different ideals" than the old immigrants. Thus, the commission took a dim view of the new immigrants—a view that was not fully justified by the voluminous evidence that was provided in its own report. The commission's view was restated and popularized by Jeremiah Jenks (a leading member of the commission) and Jett Lauck in their book *The Immigration Problem*, which went through six editions between 1911 and 1926.

The commission's findings (and those of Jenks and Lauck) have been widely criticized, both by contemporaries and by historians (Hourwich 1922; Handlin 1957; Jones 1992, 152–156). The critics have raised two particularly telling points. First, the commission failed to allow for the fact that the most recent immigrants at the time the report was published were still in the process of assimilating—climbing the occupational ladder or catching up with the native-born and earlier immigrant cohorts. Part of their apparent disadvantage was therefore due to their recent arrival rather than to their origin. Second, the commission's old-new classification was arbitrary, according to the critics, who have argued that there was as much variety in the upward mobility of nationalities *within* the old and new immigrant categories as

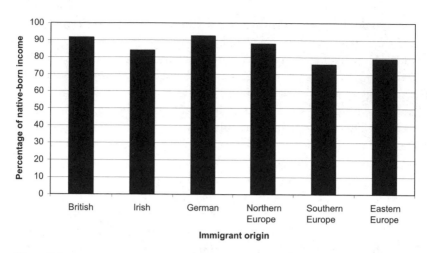

Figure 5.3
Occupational earnings of foreign-born men by immigrant origin as a percentage of native-born men, United States, 1910. *Source:* We are grateful to Chris Minns for kindly providing these data.

there was between them: "What was thought to be the old-immigrant pattern applied to the British but not to the Irish: what was taken to be the new immigrant pattern applied to the Italians but not to the East Europeans" (Thernstrom 1973, 135). Still, many historians present a pessimistic picture of immigrant progress. According to one of the most influential accounts, although "most immigrants had no direction to go but upward if they remained in the United States, the overall impression is that such movement was an unrealistic expectation in their lifetimes" (Bodnar 1985, 170).

So how did immigrants perform in the U.S. labor market? The most comprehensive measure comes from the occupations recorded in the census. These can be converted to an income measure by attributing to each individual the average earnings for that individual's occupation. Figure 5.3 shows, for 1910, the average occupational earnings of foreign-born U.S. males as a percentage of the incomes of native-born males whose parents were also native-born. The figure shows occupational earnings for the employed only and excludes those employed in agriculture. The height of the bar indicates that the occupational earnings of U.S. immigrant males born in Great Britain amounted to a little over 90 percent of native-born U.S. male incomes. Irish-born males in the United States earned somewhat less than their British-born counterparts, while the German-born earned a shade more, and immigrants

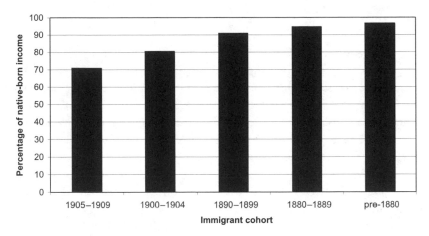

Figure 5.4
Occupational earnings of foreign-born men by date of immigration as a percentage of native-born men, United States, 1910. *Source:* We are grateful to Chris Minns for kindly providing these data.

from elsewhere in northwestern Europe were somewhere in between. By contrast, those from eastern and southern Europe earned less than 80 percent of native-born incomes.

But southern and eastern European immigrants were on average more-recent arrivals in the United States than those from other parts of Europe, so some of these differences might be attributed to the assimilation process itself. As immigrants gained labor market experience and improved their language skills, their earning power increased. In figure 5.4, the occupational earnings of different cohorts by year of arrival are compared with the average for native-born workers in 1910. Those who had arrived most recently, in 1905–1909, received about 70 percent of average native-born earnings, with the figure rising to 80 percent for those arriving in 1900–1904 and reaching 97 percent for those with more than thirty years of U.S. experience. It is tempting to interpret this progression as reflecting the assimilation process, but there are at least two reasons why the steep upward slope in figure 5.4 may be exaggerated. First, the most recent arrivals were much younger, and thus less skilled, than the average native-born person, while those who arrived before 1880 were much older and thus more skilled. Second, perhaps the Immigration Commission was right in suggesting that those who arrived most recently were in some respects "inferior" to previous immigrants, and hence the upward earnings progression simply reflects the declining labor market "quality" of successive immigrant cohorts.

Several econometric studies have examined the assimilation of U.S. immigrants around 1890 using earnings data from workers surveyed by a number of state labor bureaus. The immigrants in these surveys were chiefly from northwestern Europe—the old immigrants that the Immigration Commission believed had assimilated relatively well. The most recent research confirms the commission's belief.[2] Immigrants were largely assimilated by the time they were mature workers. That is, those who arrived as adults certainly suffered an initial wage penalty of about 20 percent relative to comparable native-born workers. But in the first twenty years after arrival, their earnings grew about 1 percent per year faster than those of the native-born. In short, they were in the process of catching up. For immigrants who arrived as children (under the age of sixteen), earnings profiles were very similar to those of the native-born.

So much for the old immigrants. What about the new immigrants from southern and eastern Europe? Does their experience also support this optimistic assimilation view? Based on the occupational earnings from the 1910 census, new U.S. immigrants suffered upon arrival a wage disadvantage of about 15 percent compared with old immigrants, but their subsequent income growth was somewhat faster (Minns 2000). The Immigration Commission's own inquiry into the earnings of male immigrants and native-born males in sixteen manufacturing and extractive industries yields evidence that suggests that old immigrants earned 17 percent less than the native-born soon after arrival, while new immigrants earned about 25 percent less, a difference of eight percentage points (Hatton 2000, 517). Both groups experienced wage growth about 1 percent per annum faster than the native-born in the subsequent twenty years.

Immigrant occupational mobility in the antebellum decades also supports the more-optimistic assimilation view. It is now possible to trace the progress of those early immigrants who arrived in the 1840s, through the 1850s and up to the 1860 census, and the effort reveals that the number of adult males who were unskilled fell from 57 percent upon arrival to 20 percent a decade later, although it is true that the Irish rose up the occupational ladder less quickly than did the British or the Germans. Of those who brought skills with them, 70 percent were able to put those skills to use within four years of arrival (Ferrie 1999, 87).

High occupational mobility was true of post–Civil War immigrants as well, at least based on a comparison of the occupational composition of different arrival cohorts observed in the 1900 census with that of the same cohorts observed ten years later in the 1910 census (Minns 2000). It appears that immigrants moved up into white-collar jobs considerably faster than did native-born males in similar age groups. Perhaps most surprising is the substantial movement of those from new immigrant origins into white-collar jobs. But it fits well with detailed local studies such as that of Kessner (1977), who found considerable upward occupational mobility among Jews and Italians in New York around the turn of the century. For younger immigrant arrivals, this reflects the postarrival acquisition of skills and English language proficiency but for those who arrived with greater labor market experience, it probably reflects better use of pre-existing skills acquired at home before the move.

But pre-existing skills of what quality? There was considerable heterogeneity by origin within the groups that the Immigration Commission labeled old and new. Table 5.1 shows the earnings for groups of different origin relative to those of the native-born after twenty years

Table 5.1
Immigrant earnings in U.S. industry, 1909 (percent higher or lower than the native-born, after twenty years)

Immigrant origins	Wage difference	Immigrant origins	Wage difference
Old immigrant		Croatian/Slovenian	−0.6
Scandinavian	5.5	Greek/Macedonian	−7.5
Dutch/Flemish	4.9	Hebrew	4.9
English	10.8	North Italian	−1.3
Finnish	4.8	South Italian	−7.6
French/Belgian	6.4	Lithuanian	−4.3
German/Swiss	0.1	Magyar	−5.3
Irish	−3.6	Polish	−3.9
Scottish/Welsh	7.9	Portuguese/Spanish	1.3
New immigrant		Romanian	−3.3
Armenian	−7.9	Russian	−3.1
Bohemian/Moravian	1.4	Ruthenian	−6.3
Bosnian/Herzegovinian	6.4	Slovak	−3.2
Bulgarian/Serbian	−3.0	Syrian/Turkish	−9.6

Source: Calculated from Hatton 2000 (table 2, column (1), 516–517).

in the United States. Among those with old immigrant origins, those from Britain, France, and the Low Countries earned more than the Irish or the Germans, while Jews (labeled "Hebrews" in the table) and Iberians earned more than almost all other new immigrants. Still, after twenty years' experience in the United States, immigrants from northwestern Europe typically earned more than the native-born, while most of the ethnic groups from southern and eastern Europe earned less.

The quality of the skills that immigrants brought with them is likely to explain these differences. Immigrants from those parts of Europe that were the least industrialized and urbanized and had the lowest levels of education and literacy typically earned less than those from the more-advanced parts of Europe. These country-of-origin differences should have been reflected in the characteristics of immigrants on arrival in the United States, and they were (Hatton 2000, 519). Every increase of ten percentage points in the share of immigrant arrivals who were literate raised average earnings by 1.2 percent. And an increase of ten percentage points in the share of skilled and professional among male immigrants raised average earnings by 1 percent. Thus, the earnings of immigrants from any given country reflected the education and skills they brought with them to the United States, and that in turn depended on the level of development of the society from which they came.

Did Immigrant Quality Decline?

The Immigration Commission concluded that the new immigrants were inferior to the old. True, the commission failed to allow for the assimilation process when it compared new and old immigrants. But even when such allowances are made, it appears that significant differences between origin groups remain and that these can be traced largely to the characteristics upon arrival of immigrants belonging to those origin groups. Drawing on the commission's evidence, Jenks and Lauck (1926, 36) demonstrated that among those admitted to the United States in 1899–1909, 22 percent of old immigrants but only 9.2 percent of new immigrants were classified as either professional or skilled. They also found that among adults, only 2.7 percent of old immigrant arrivals were illiterate, compared with 35.8 percent of new immigrants. Jenks and Lauck interpreted this as powerful evidence that immigrant quality had fallen as a result of the shift in immigrant source. Yet as table 3.1 shows, there is little evidence of any decline in the share of immigrants that were classified as having skilled, professional, or commercial occupations after the 1870s, when new immigrants began arriving in large numbers.[3]

These opposing views can be reconciled by noting two trends that were pushing in opposite directions. On the one hand, immigrants from each country were becoming more skilled and educated as industrialization proceeded and schooling in their home countries expanded. On the other hand, the immigrant composition was shifting toward the less-developed sending regions. The right question to ask is: what effect did the shift in source country composition have *by itself* on average immigrant quality? If we focus only on European males and only on those who reported an occupation, the share of skilled workers and professionals fell by 4.3 percentage points between 1873 and 1913 (Hatton 2000, tables 1, 4). But had the source country composition stayed constant, the share of skilled workers and professionals would have *increased* by 2.7 percentage points. More dramatic still, between 1893 and 1913, the share of adult immigrants who were literate (in any language) fell by 4 percentage points, whereas with a constant source country composition, it would have *increased* by more than 6 percentage points.

Jenks and Lauck seem to have been vindicated: source country composition effects reduced immigrant quality by quite a bit, at least according to literacy and occupational status. But how much difference did those attributes make to immigrants' labor market performance? That is, did the destination labor market place high value on those home-acquired attributes? The decline in immigrant earnings relative to the native-born that can be attributed to the changing country of origin is less than five percentage points, a decline that was associated mostly with the effects of the shifting source country composition of immigrants on the proportions who were literate and skilled (Hatton 2000, 520).

Is a 5 percent decline in the relative earnings capacity of the immigrant inflow over forty years big or small? As we show in part III, whether immigrant quality declined in the post–World War II United States has been one of the most hotly debated immigration topics. To anticipate that discussion, the estimates provided by Borjas (1992) indicate that source country composition effects account for a fall of twenty-six percentage points between 1940 and 1980 in the relative earnings of newly of arrived immigrants. This is five times as large as the composition effects on immigrant earnings between 1873 and 1913. Part of the reason for the big difference is that the gaps in living standard between the new and old immigrants of the 1960s and 1970s (Latin Americans and Asians versus Europeans) were *much* larger than those between the new and old immigrants of the 1890s and 1900s. Had the Immigration Commission been able to look forward seventy years, it might have had a higher opinion of the new immigrants of its own day.

Were Immigrants Positively Selected?

Even if the labor market quality of U.S. immigrants declined as a result of their changing origin, it might still have been true that immigrants were positively selected. Indeed, it is widely believed that international migrants were and are the best and brightest—that on average they are more skilled, more ambitious, and more enterprising than those who stay home. Although this may be widely believed, the late-nineteenth-century evidence is far from clear-cut. Selection could occur along a number of observable characteristics like education, skill, wealth, and family background, but what about unobservable characteristics like ambition, energy, and motivation? The issue of selection is further complicated by the fact that we cannot observe how migrants would have done had they stayed in the home country. Given these complications, much of what follows should be viewed as informed speculation.

Inferences about selection can be drawn from immigrant performance in destination labor markets. Given sufficient time to assimilate, nineteenth-century immigrants from northwestern Europe often, as we have seen, achieved higher earnings than the native-born. This fact implies that the advantage of positive selection eventually outweighed the initial disadvantage of being an immigrant. Those from southern and eastern Europe may also have been positively selected, but even if they were, the positive selection effect failed to outweigh the immigrant disadvantage, since their skills—valuable in the home country— were of lower value in the destination country. A further piece of evidence comes from second-generation immigrants, who inherit some of their parents' characteristics but do not suffer the initial immigrant disadvantage that their parents did. Native-born workers with one or two foreign-born parents had earnings that were 6.5 percent *higher* than those with native-born parents (Hatton 1997, 2000; Minns 2000). Second-generation immigrants appear to have had an advantage over those with native-born parents, implying an element of inherited positive selection.

What about evidence from immigrant origins? As we have seen, emigrants in the early nineteenth century—the pioneers of mass transatlantic migration—were frequently farmers and artisans. While they were not upper class—like merchants and landed rich—these pioneer migrants *were* from the middle class of their day. For example, emigrants from the German region of Hesse-Cassel in 1832–1857 were "positively selected because the highest skilled were over-represented. In terms of financial wealth, the emigrant population was negatively selected because the richest were under-represented" (Wegge 2002, 390). Similar patterns emerge among emigrants who moved later in the nineteenth century. Thus, among emigrants from Denmark between 1868 and 1900, craftsmen and artisans were overrepresented: their share among emigrants was about twice that among the source population. Laborers were underrepresented even though they accounted for the majority of the emigrants (Hvidt 1975, 113). It was not always true that unskilled laborers were underrepresented among emigrants, however, as the Irish illustrate. Irish laborers still accounted for 80 percent of male emigrants in 1881, long after the famine, but only 22 percent of the Irish labor force, and 84 percent of female emigrants from Ireland were servants, compared with 33 percent of the population. Still, for most countries, the poorest were underrepresented in emigrant flows.

This finding is consistent with the analysis in chapter 4, in which we argued that poverty constrained the volume of emigration from the poorer parts of Europe. It is also consistent with the view that transatlantic migrants were more positively selected than they would have been in the absence of poverty constraints. Selection also suggests a reason why the Irish seem to have done less well in the U.S. labor market than did the British, the Germans, and other northern Europeans. No doubt it was partly because Ireland was poor and rural, and thus a random selection of the Irish might have done less well than a random selection of the more-urban and more-industrial British. But it may also have been partly because the poverty trap was less binding in Ireland, because of the very large emigrant stock abroad that served to unlock the constraint. In short, the Irish may have been an exception among the nineteenth-century new emigrants: they were of "low quality" because they came from an exceptionally poor country, but they also may have been *negatively*, not positively, selected.

Table 5.2
Skill premia in the United States and Europe, 1890

	United States	Great Britain	France/ Belgium	Germany/ Switzerland
Premium for semiskilled over unskilled	28.4	16.1	25.2	17.9
Premium for skilled over unskilled	53.0	32.6	63.1	35.2

Source: Based on an econometric analysis of microdata from the U.S. Commissioner of Labor Survey. For a discussion of this survey, the industries included, and the occupational classification used, see Hatton, Boyer, and Bailey 1994. We are grateful to Roy Bailey for help with the data.

Note: Figures in table are coefficients from a regression of log earnings for male household heads on age, age-squared industry dummies (that differ between Europe and the United States), and skill-by-country dummies. All the coefficients reported here are significant at the 5 percent level.

So much for constraints; what about incentives? The modern literature on migration discussed in part III suggests that one factor determining immigrant selection is the relative return on skills at home and abroad. If the return to skills is higher in the (rich) destination country than in the (poor) origin country, then the skilled have a greater incentive to emigrate than the unskilled. Was that the case in the nineteenth century? Truly comparable cross-country evidence is sparse for most of the nineteenth century, but table 5.2 presents skill premia for blue-collar occupations for four Atlantic regions in 1890. The premium for semiskilled and skilled workers over the unskilled was considerably larger in the United States than in Britain or Germany. Other things equal, this would imply a greater incentive for the emigration of skilled workers from these countries. The same was not true of France and Belgium, and it may not have been true of less-developed European countries, for which we do not have comparable data. Thus the incentives for positive selection were greater late in the century for some source countries than for others.

Hard evidence from early in the century is almost nonexistent, but there is a tradition that points out expensive unskilled labor and cheap skills in the early industrial United States compared with Britain (Habbakuk 1962; Rosenberg 1967). For example, while in the 1820s U.S. skilled machine makers received a wage only 2 percent higher than that of their British counterparts, unskilled U.S. labor manning those machines earned 22 percent more. Thus, compared with the United States, the British skill premium was 20 percent higher in the 1820s

(Brito and Williamson 1973, 237–238). Such evidence suggests that, in the absence of poverty constraints, Anglo-American migration should have *negatively* selected British unskilled labor early in the century. But Anglo-American migration should have *positively* selected British skilled labor in the 1890s, after fifty to sixty years of hothouse American industrialization, when the skill premium was pushed up dramatically by an explosion of skilled labor demands. The qualification "in the absence of poverty constraints" is important, since such constraints were probably the dominant force even in the antebellum period. Income incentives (negative selection) and poverty constraints (positive selection) were working against each other early in the century, whereas they were working together late in the century.

We should also observe systematic differences across destinations that offered different incentives or costs to the migrant. The skill composition of the immigrant flows to Canada and the United States were very similar at the turn of the century. New evidence suggests a good reason for this: skill premia were also very similar in the two countries (Green, MacKinnon, and Minns 2002, 681).[4] It seems likely that skill premia were similar in Australia. Yet British emigrants to Australia were much more often skilled, compared with those heading for North America (Pope and Withers 1994). Since the costs of migration to Australia were so much larger (even when subsidized), any difference in positive selection favoring Australia was likely to have been driven by poverty constraints (only the best could afford the move) rather than by wage relativities.

What about other streams of mass migration? One puzzle is why Italians from the *mezzogiorno* (the southern regions of Italy) who crossed the Atlantic typically went to the United States, while those from the more-industrial northern part of the country typically went to South America.[5] On the face of it, this fact seems anomalous, since the more-literate, more-skilled, and more-urban northern Italians would seem to be better matched with U.S. labor markets, while the less-literate, less-skilled, and more-rural southern Italians would have been better matched with South American labor markets.[6] Historians have argued that those at the bottom of the occupational ladder in the poor and backward *mezzogiorno* gained most by working as unskilled laborers in cities like New York, while those from the north had better opportunities to become middle-class entrepreneurs or skilled workers in places like Buenos Aires (Klein 1983; Baily 1983, 296). The costs of migration mattered too, of course: government subsidies for migration to the São Paulo coffee plantations were offered exclusively to northern Italians.[7] But as the coffee boom faded and as living standards in North America outstripped those in South America, emigration among *all* Italians, both those from the north and those from the south, shifted increasingly to the United States.

Clearly, cultural affinities, location preferences, and the friends-and-relatives effect all influenced who emigrated and where they went. But we can also detect the influence of strong economic forces on immigrant selection. It seems plausible to conclude that while positive selection was driven by wage incentives for British and German emigrants, it was driven more by poverty constraints for those from the poorer parts of Europe. In Ireland, where poverty constraints were relaxed by an enormous stock of previous (famine-driven) emigrants, current emigrants were less positively selected, as were those from the Italian south. It also seems likely that the degree of positive selection differed across destinations: the more distant the destination from the home country, the greater the costs of emigration and the more likely immigrants would be positively selected; the closer the destination to the home country, the lower the cost and the more negative the selection.

Was There Brain Drain?

The idea that emigration seriously reduces human capital in the source country is a recurring theme today, and we return to it in part III. Because of the fear of brain drain, there were legal restrictions in the eighteenth century on the emigration of artisans and engineers from Britain to the European continent. But public concerns about losing vital skills through emigration seem to have vanished by the late nineteenth century. There may have been good reasons for this. First, where positive selection was weak, emigration would not have made a major dent in the per capita skill base at home. Second, much of the human capital embodied in the emigrants who disappeared across the Atlantic had not been financed by the public purse. Third, immigrant remittances from abroad may have offset the foregone income at home.

So was there a big brain drain from Europe to the New World during the age of mass migration? While there seems to have been positive selection, it probably did not translate into big brain drain losses. Table 5.3 shows rates of literacy (in any language) for adult immigrants to the United States between 1899 and 1909 for five European countries,

Table 5.3
Literacy in Europe and the brain drain

	France	Britain	Italy	Spain	Portugal
Literacy rate of adult immigrants to the United States, 1899–1909	94.6	99.0	47.0	85.4	31.8
Literacy rate of adult population, 1901	83	97	52	44	22
Literacy loss (outflow of literates as a percentage of literate adults)	0.4	1.6	8.6	0.6	2.0
School enrollment as a percentage of literate adults in 1901	25.9	23.4	24.2	31.3	29.5

Source: Calculated from Jenks and Lauck 1926 (33) and Tortella 1994 (13).

as well as the literacy rates of the adult home populations of those countries in 1901. As the table shows, literacy rates among immigrants were generally somewhat higher than they were among the source populations, implying positive selection. Perhaps this was inevitable. After all, immigrants were younger than the source populations, and late-nineteenth-century Europe was undergoing an educational revolution that raised literacy among the young movers compared with the old stayers (Easterlin 1981). Italy may appear to be an exception to the rule of higher literacy rates among immigrants than among source populations, but the observed lower literacy among immigrants relative to the Italian population simply reflects the dominance of southern Italians in the immigrant inflow.[8] The third row of table 5.3 reports the outflow of literate emigrants (over the decade) as a proportion of literate adults in the 1901 source population. For Britain and France, the loss to the United States across the decade was small in relation to the stock, less than 2 percent. It was larger for Italy because of that country's higher emigration rates. It would have been larger for Spain and Portugal if the flows to South America were taken into account, but those flows are still small.

Even if the human capital losses were small for Europe when measured in terms of education and literacy, they may have been larger in terms of unobservable "best and brightest" characteristics. One piece of evidence supporting such a view comes from evaluations of Swedish clergymen of the intellectual abilities of their parishioners. Comparison of those who subsequently emigrated with those who did not reveals that the former had a higher intellectual level, did better at school, and had a wider view of the world (Hvidt 1975, 109). On these grounds, one might have expected that immigrants to the New World were more likely to become entrepreneurs and business leaders than the native-born. Consistent with that prediction, it turns out that among those born between 1816 and 1850, immigrants were overrepresented among the top businessmen in the United States. This evidence of positive selection and brain drain was much less apparent among those born between 1850 and 1890, however, reflecting the declining quality of U.S. immigrants by origin (Ferrie and Mokyr 1994).

How Much Did Immigrants Gain by Moving?

The discussion of immigrant performance in the destination country often obscures the enormous gains that accrued to immigrants simply by having moved from low-wage to high-wage labor markets. As we showed in chapter 4, wage rates in the New World were significantly higher than in Europe. While immigrants initially earned less than similar native-born workers, they later caught up with and sometimes overtook their native-born peers. So how large were the gains to European emigrants over their lifetimes?

One way to evaluate emigrant gains is to calculate the increase in net present value attributable to the move. Table 5.4 reports discounted lifetime earnings at home and abroad for a twenty-year-old male, based on the wage ratios in the last column of table 4.2. Over a forty-

Table 5.4
Net present value of emigration

	Germany	Britain	Ireland	Italy	Spain	Sweden
Present value of lifetime income at home (1905 pounds)	359	410	380	194	127	385
Net present value of lifetime income abroad (1905 pounds)	585	648	574	356	339	576
Percentage gain in lifetime income	63	58	51	83	167	50

Note: Calculations based on wage ratios for 1900–1913 in table 4.2 for a forty-year working lifetime starting at age twenty-one and using a discount rate of 10 percent. Mean earnings at home and abroad are adjusted by age using age-earning profiles from the estimates underlying table 5.2. Earnings in the destination are adjusted to allow for assimilation effects and for differentials relative to the native-born displayed in table 5.1. Migration costs are assumed to be direct costs of twenty pounds plus three months' foregone income.

year working life, the expected net present value of earnings to an un-skilled urban laborer in Germany would have been about 360 pounds. If he had emigrated at age twenty, his expected discounted lifetime earnings would have amounted to 585 pounds. This gain nets out his cost of migration, allows his earnings upon arrival to be lower than those of the native-born, and assumes the postassimilation earnings differential observed in table 5.1. At the wage differentials observed in the decade before 1914, the typical German emigrant would have increased his lifetime earnings by 63 percent over the alternative of staying at home. The gains to the British emigrant were similar, 58 per-cent, while those to the Irish emigrant were a little lower, 51 percent. Whereas the gains for Swedes (50 percent) were similar to those for other northern Europeans, those for southern Europeans were *much* larger: Italians stood to increase their discounted lifetime earnings by 83 percent and Spaniards by a massive 167 percent.[9]

Where Did Immigrants Find Employment?

To some observers the concentration of U.S. immigrants in the urban Northeast and Midwest, as well as in certain unskilled occupations, is evidence of labor market segmentation and immobility. This immi-grant concentration was even more marked for individual national-ities than for immigrants as a whole. Thus, it might be concluded that while the existence of ethnic neighborhoods made for easy entry into immigrant-dominated niches, it also limited the immigrant's integra-tion into the wider community and retarded progress up the occupa-tional ladder. While historians now take a more-optimistic view of these issues than was once accepted, it is still argued that escape from the ghetto was a long process, one measured in generations rather than years. We are persuaded by the accumulating evidence that there was a well-integrated national labor market in the United States by the late nineteenth century and that immigrants exploited it. That assertion is not inconsistent with the fact that they clustered and concentrated.

Where did nineteenth-century immigrants find employment? We can discriminate between two views on this question. The first view is optimistic: it argues that the immigrants entered rapidly growing, high-wage employment, thereby easing short-run labor supply bottle-necks in leading industries. The second view is pessimistic: it argues that immigrants crowded into slow-growing, low-wage employment in industries undergoing relative decline, thereby crowding out unskilled natives. These competing views can be examined by comparing the share of immigrants in a given occupation with employment growth in that occupation. If the share of immigrants in rapidly expanding industries and occupations was high and rising, then immigrants could be regarded as the "shock troops" of structural change.[10] Elsewhere, we have explored this issue for male immigrants between 1890 and 1900 (Hatton and Williamson 1998, chap. 7). The evidence from that exploration confirms that immigrants found employment more frequently in unskilled jobs, compared with natives. More to the point, immigrants located in slow-growth sectors, not fast-growth sectors. In short, there is no evidence to support the view that the foreign-born flowed disproportionately into or dominated fast-growing occupations and sectors prior to World War I. In fact, the evidence suggests the contrary: immigrants flowed disproportionately into the slowest-growing parts of the economy.

We have a ready explanation for these facts: given that occupational growth reflects shifting comparative advantage, and given that the United States was exploiting its comparative advantage in resource- and capital-intensive industries, it follows that fast-growing sectors should have generated buoyant demand growth for skilled labor (a complement with capital) and sluggish demand growth for unskilled labor (a substitute for capital). Thus, unskilled immigrants *should* have flooded into unskilled-labor-intensive industries and occupations in which growth was slower. Indeed, these findings are consistent with those concerning immigrants in the 1980s and 1990s, a time period for which the flood of new, less-skilled immigrants into services and import-competing manufacturing has raised the same concern (Baumol, Blackman, and Wolff 1989; Borjas 1994) that New York immigrant sweatshops did in the 1890s. The evidence from the 1890s also seems to confirm a mismatch between labor demand, which was shifting away from unskilled occupations (i.e., becoming more skilled), and booming immigrant labor supplies that were declining in quality (i.e., becoming less skilled). The mismatch had, of course, inequality implications then just as it does now (Goldin and Margo 1992; Borjas, Freeman, and Katz 1992). It crowded out native unskilled workers (including southern blacks; Thomas 1972, 130–134, chap. 18; Collins 1997) and thus widened the gap between the working poor and the rest.

Did Immigrants Displace the Native-Born?

The question of whether immigrants "rob jobs" from the native-born or reduce their wages was just as contentious in the nineteenth century as it is today. If, as we have argued, European immigrants integrated well into New World labor markets, it follows that they must have been competing directly with native-born workers over a wide range of occupations, industries, and locations. That raises a perennial question (to which we return in the next chapter) about whether unemployment at that time was higher and wages lower for the native-born than they would have been in the absence of the immigrants. The answer must distinguish between the short run and the long run.

Some observers have argued that in the short run, immigration was one of the mechanisms through which New World economies were able to adjust to temporary excess labor supply created by recession and industrial crisis. Thus, in the years before 1914, the United States has been viewed as being, "like some West European countries in the 1970s, able to export its unemployment problem by massive repatriation of Mediterranean labor" (Tyrrell 1991, 1047). There are good reasons why immigration should have been particularly sensitive to cyclical conditions in destination countries before World War I. Does it follow from this that the cyclical ebb and flow of migration eased the burden of unemployment among nonimmigrants? Yes, but only to a small extent. Between 1890 and 1913, the average year-to-year change in employment in the United States was nine times as great as the average year-to-year change in net worker immigration. Thus, even if the correlation between changes in employment and immigration had been perfect, the so-called guestworker effect would have provided only a very modest safety valve.

But what about the medium term? In a protracted depression like that of the 1890s, gross immigration remained low (and net immigration was probably negative, as the unemployed immigrants returned home), and this reduced the size of the labor force competing for scarcer jobs. One calculation suggests that the U.S. labor force would have been about 3 percent smaller in 1900 as a result of the slowdown in the immigration rate during the depressed years of the 1890s (Hatton and Williamson 1998, 174–177). Similarly, in Australia, the recession of the 1890s cut the immigration rate sharply, and the unemployment rate rose by less than it would have otherwise. Thus, in protracted recessions the responsiveness of immigration provides some relief to an overstocked labor market.

Theory tells us that in the long run shocks to employment and labor supply should be absorbed by real wage adjustments, rather than by changes in the unemployment rate. So did late-nineteenth-century immigrants crowd out the native-born and lower their wages? This was certainly the view of the U.S. Immigration Commission (1911), which argued that immigration "has undoubtedly had the effect of preventing the increase of wages to the extent which would have been necessary had the expansion of local industries occurred without the availability of the southern and eastern Europeans" (8:440; see also Jenks and Lauck 1926, 206–207). Such counterfactuals are easier to state than to prove, since they depend on holding other things constant. Some have argued that since wages in the United States grew more slowly between 1890 and 1914 than they did in the 1920s, when the immigration rate was much lower as a result of the quotas imposed on immigration, unrestricted mass immigration must have slowed the rate of growth of real wages in the earlier period (Douglas [1930] 1966, 564; Lebergott 1964, 163).[11]

Real wage effects are difficult to infer with confidence because it is so hard to control for all the other influences on the wage and because the wage itself is one of the determinants of immigration. An alternative approach, followed in the literature on the more-recent era, is to look

Table 5.5
Net immigration and internal migration in the United States, 1880s to 1900s

Region	Foreign-born net immigration			Native-born net immigration		
	1880s	1890s	1900s	1880s	1890s	1900s
New England	14.2	13.0	14.1	−1.3	−1.5	−1.6
Mid-Atlantic	12.0	10.0	16.1	−1.9	1.4	−0.1
South Atlantic	0.9	0.6	1.2	−3.0	−3.0	−2.4
East North Central	9.4	5.3	7.2	−5.2	0.4	−3.4
West North Central	11.5	3.6	4.5	8.1	−5.5	−6.0
East South Central	0.4	0.2	0.3	−6.3	−4.3	−7.1
West South Central	1.9	1.7	1.9	6.6	7.3	7.6
Mountain	18.0	7.6	11.7	32.0	14.1	24.8
Pacific	20.8	7.7	19.8	32.8	14.0	38.8

Source: Calculated from Eldridge and Thomas 1964 (tables A1.11, A1.12, and A1.14). Migration rates are per thousand of the native-born population per decade.

at the effects of immigration across states or cities in the same country. Historical studies that use the same methodology are rare. But Claudia Goldin (1994) estimated the relationship between immigration and wage changes across American cities between 1890 and 1915. She found that a one-percentage-point increase in the foreign-born population share reduced unskilled wage rates by about 1 to 1.5 percent. Similar results were found for artisans and for different industry groups. Thus there is evidence that where immigration was greater, real wage growth was slower.

While such evidence sheds light on the local wage effects of immigration, it does not necessarily measure the economy-wide effects. When immigrants move into a state or locality, natives and previous immigrants may elect to move out or not to move in. If the native-born (and previous immigrant) population migrates across states and regions in response to economic incentives, then the effects of immigration in a local labor market would be only partially reflected in the local wage. To the extent that native-born workers (and earlier immigrants) are displaced to other regions, wage effects will be spread across the entire economy. Is there evidence of such displacement effects? Table 5.5 documents that while immigrants moved into New England, the Mid-Atlantic, and the North Central states in the 1880s through the 1900s, these regions also experienced net outflows of native-born. This was no coincidence. It has been estimated that after controlling for other relevant influences, 40 native born residents moved out of a northeastern state for every 100 immigrants that flowed in during a decade, mainly to the west (Hatton and Williamson 1998, 168). Two implications follow from this. While much has been written about the attractions of moving west, less attention has been given to the immigrant-induced "push from the east." More important to the issues at hand, the magnitude of these displacement effects is large enough to suggest that, although immigrants were largely concentrated in the urban Northeast and Midwest, the labor market effects of immigration percolated through the whole U.S. economy.

With that notion in mind, the next chapter turns to the economy-wide effects of international migration in both sending and receiving countries.

The Impact of Mass Migration on Convergence and Inequality

Two important features characterized the late-nineteenth-century Atlantic economy. First, it was one of rapid globalization: capital and labor flowed across national frontiers in unprecedented quantities, and commodity trade boomed in response to sharply declining transport costs. Second, it underwent an impressive convergence in living standards. Poor economies around the European periphery tended to grow faster than the rich industrial leaders at the European center, and often even faster than the labor-scarce economies overseas. However, catching up was not universal. Those catching up on the European leaders were not in Asia, Africa, the Middle East, or eastern Europe, and even around the fast-growing European periphery, there were some that failed. Still, there *was* catching up in the Atlantic economy. At the same time, dramatic income distribution changes were also taking place *within* these economies—inequality rose in the labor-scarce New World, and inequality fell in the labor-abundant Old World.

The first half of this chapter asks whether mass migration and economic convergence were connected. The second half of the chapter asks whether mass migration had an impact on income distribution trends in sending and receiving countries.

Is Convergence a Recent Phenomenon?

Since the academic literature on the topic has become so plentiful, and since the issue even gets abundant media exposure, it is hard to imagine any intelligent citizen, and certainly any economist, who is unaware of the dramatic (unconditional) convergence that the OECD has undergone since 1950. The OECD's members include western Europe, southern Europe, North America, and Australasia. By convergence, we refer to the process by which the world's poorer countries have grown faster since the middle of the twentieth century than richer countries, to such a degree that the economic distance between them might almost disappear a half century later. By *unconditional* convergence, we refer to the process by which those poor countries have tended to catch up on the rich, period. Later in the chapter, we use the term *conditional* convergence, by which we mean that while some poor countries may not have experienced much catching up with rich ones, they *would* have exhibited some catching up had it not been for some offsetting disadvantage.

Most economists take an ahistorical position when writing about convergence in the late twentieth century. So it is that Robert Barro, Gregory Mankiw, and their collaborators (Barro and Sala-i-Martin 1992, 1995; Mankiw, Romer, and Weil 1992) ignore pre–World War II or even pre-1970 experience, focusing instead on the last two or three decades. The implicit assumption seems to be that the data for this kind of analysis are absent prior to the 1960s, or that the experience then was irrelevant, or, even worse, that there could not possibly have been any convergence in pre–World War II history.[1] They are mistaken on all three counts. In short, history has a great deal to say about convergence.

What history? Our interest is in what Simon Kuznets called modern economic growth, and that translates here into almost 200 years, from the early nineteenth century, when the British industrial revolution really took off, to the early twenty-first century, when even the poorest parts of Asia have become part of it.

Convergence among whom? Our net will capture only members of the present OECD club with European origins (plus Argentina and Brazil). True, much of the unconditional convergence before World War I would disappear if the net were widened to include eastern Europe. If it were widened still further to include the Third World, unconditional convergence would totally evaporate. Why the small net? First, because we think the sources of convergence in the OECD club are themselves misunderstood, and it matters to get the facts about these sources straight before venturing outside the club. Second, because we want to assess the impact of the mass migrations involving the club.

Convergence of what? The yardstick that matters to us is the gap between workers' living standards in rich and poor countries. Convergence implies an erosion in this gap, at least in percentage terms. There appear to be two ways to explore the issue over long time periods. Estimates of gross domestic product (GDP) per worker hour offer one (Maddison 1994, 1995). Real wage rates offer another (Williamson 1995; O'Rourke and Williamson 1997). Abramovitz, Baumol, and other economists writing about the late twentieth century all use GDP per capita or per worker hour to measure convergence. This chapter favors instead purchasing-power-parity-adjusted real wage rates (typically those of the urban unskilled). Real wages are certainly the right measure if our interest is the impact of globalization on labor markets. But we can think of three other reasons why it pays to look at both factor prices and GDP aggregates.

First, real people earn unskilled wages, or skill premia, or profits or land rents, not that statistical artifact known as GDP per capita. While GDP per worker hour may be the right measure of labor productivity, workers' living standards are better indicators of economic well-being.

Second, economic change nearly always involves winners and losers, and this fact is crucial to the evolution of policy. Changes that might increase GDP per capita are often successfully resisted, and examining the behavior of factor prices is a necessary first step toward understanding these political responses.

Third, understanding the sources of wage and other factor price changes helps us understand the sources of convergence. The open economy mechanisms which we argue were central in driving late-nineteenth-century convergence—trade, migration, and capital flows—operated directly on factor prices, and thus only indirectly on GDP per capita. By focusing only on GDP per capita, macroeconomists are likely to miss a large part of the story. Suppose that we want to know whether convergence is due to technological catch-up, gains from trade, or the impact of mass migration. If the dominant force is technological catch-up, then it seems likely that wage rates, skill premia, land rents, and profit rates will all rise with GDP per capita and GDP per worker, albeit at different rates depending on some technological bias. If the dominant force is trade, then standard theory predicts that wage-rent ratios will move in opposite directions in the two trading partners and that relative factor prices and real wages will converge much faster than either GDP per capita or GDP per worker. If the dominant force is mass migration, then given that migrants tend to be young adults, GDP per capita in immigrant countries should rise faster than GDP per worker, and wage rates should fall relative to land rents and profit rates. The opposite would be true of emigrant countries. By relying solely on GDP data, macroeconomists are missing a chance to discriminate between these and other competing explanations for convergence.

Divergence Shocks and Convergence Responses in the Nineteenth Century

The Atlantic economy was perturbed by two profound shocks during the first half of the nineteenth century: early industrialization in Britain, which then spread to a few countries on the European continent, and resource "discovery" in the New World, triggered by sharply declining international transport costs. Tariff barriers were high prior to midcentury even in Britain (the Corn Laws were repealed only in 1846, with liberal trade reform following on the European continent a decade or two thereafter); commodity trade was still modest; migration across national borders was not yet "mass" (the famine-induced Irish flood of migrants was not released until the late 1840s); and global capital markets were as yet underdeveloped. Divergence in the Atlantic economy can be documented only starting in 1830, and even then the sample for which data are available is relatively small (eight countries in 1830, rising to thirteen by 1869). Nonetheless, the limited evidence available points to steep divergence in the Atlantic economy during the first half of the nineteenth century.

Figure 6.1 documents real wage dispersion between 1830 and 1869. The summary statistic $C(N)$ plotted there (where N is the sample size) has been used extensively in the convergence debate, and it is our measure of convergence.[2] Based on the eight Atlantic countries for which data are available (Brazil, France, Great Britain, Ireland, the Netherlands, Spain, Sweden, and the United States), $C(8)$ rises from 0.143 in 1830 to 0.402 in 1846, a near tripling in the index of real wage dispersion. Industrial revolutionary events in Europe certainly contributed to this divergence, but most of it was due to New World success: the United States increased its real wage advantage over England from 45 percent in 1830 to 89 percent in 1846.

Figure 6.1 suggests a secular turning point somewhere between 1846 and 1854. Since convergence persists for the next six decades or so, the mid-nineteenth century appears to date the start of modern convergence in the Atlantic economy.

Economists are taught that really important shocks to any market are followed, with a lag, by transitions to a new equilibrium or a new steady state. The Argentinians call the transition from 1870 to 1913 the

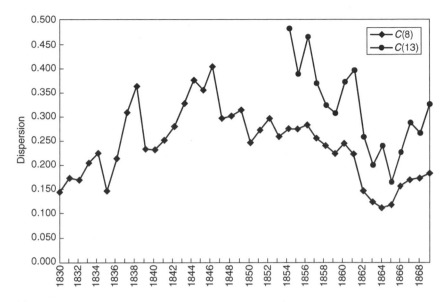

Figure 6.1
International real wage dispersion, 1830–1869. *Source:* Williamson 1995 (table A2.1); revised in O'Rourke and Williamson 1997.

belle époque, North Americans refer to it as their gilded age, and revealingly, the English dub it their Victorian and Edwardian failure. Figure 6.2 plots the transition from the midcentury to World War I: it was the most extensive living standard convergence the Atlantic economy has ever seen, *including* the better-known convergence of the post–World War II era. True, most of the convergence was completed by the turn of the century, and the speed per decade wasn't as fast as that recorded during the post–World War II epoch (Crafts and Toniolo 1996). But it *was* an impressive convergence nonetheless. In fact, real wage dispersion in the Atlantic economy dropped by more than a third over the three decades 1870–1900,[3] and it dropped perhaps by two-thirds over the half century following 1854.

Our summary measure of real wage dispersion can be decomposed into three parts: dispersion within the New World, dispersion within Europe, and dispersion between Europe and the New World, the last measured by the average wage gap between the two. When these three components are computed, we get the following results (Williamson 1996). First, the average wage gap between Europe and the New World accounts for about 60 percent of the real wage variance across these seventeen countries. The remainder is explained by the variance

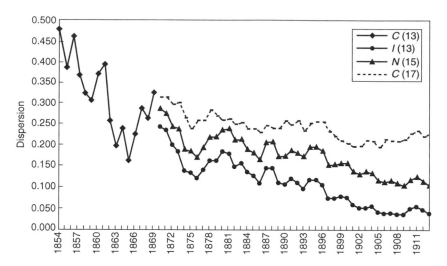

Figure 6.2
International real wage dispersion, 1854–1913. *Source:* Williamson 1995 (table A2.1); revised in O'Rourke and Williamson 1997.

within Europe and within the New World. Furthermore, real wage variance within the New World accounts for more of the total variance than does real wage variance within Europe. All of this implies that real wage variance among the late-nineteenth-century European countries in our sample was a very modest part of real wage variance in the Atlantic economy as a whole (although we have already confessed that the absence of poor eastern European nations from the sample probably accounts for much of this result). Second, about 60 percent of the convergence between 1870 and 1900 can be explained by the collapse in the gap between Europe and the New World.

Convergence was ubiquitous in the late-nineteenth-century Atlantic economy, but it is less a story about Germany and the United States catching up with Britain, and more about European industrial late-comers catching up with European industrial leaders. Convergence *did* take place within Europe, but it was more-modest affair in the aggregate since spectacular catching-up successes on the continent were offset by some equally spectacular failures. And in spite of the enormous outpouring of literature on Britain's loss of economic leadership to America and Germany, it is definitely the wrong place to look if the purpose is to understand convergence in the Atlantic economy. The switch in roles between these big three involved an exchange of eco-

Table 6.1
Relative economic performance of the European periphery in the late nineteenth century:
Percentage growth per annum

Country	Real wage per urban worker 1870–1913	Wage-rent ratio 1870–1910	Real GDP per capita 1870–1913	Real GDP per worker hour 1870–1913
Denmark	2.63	2.85	1.57	1.90
Finland	n.a.	n.a.	1.44	1.80
Norway	2.43	n.a.	1.31	1.65
Sweden	2.73	2.45	1.46	1.74
Italy	1.74	n.a.	1.28	1.33
Portugal	0.37	n.a.	0.69	1.10
Spain	0.44	−0.43	1.11	1.52
Austria	n.a.	n.a.	1.46	1.76
Ireland	1.79	4.39	n.a.	n.a.
The European periphery	1.73	2.32	1.29	1.60
Belgium	0.92	n.a.	1.05	1.24
France	0.91	1.80	1.30	1.58
Germany	1.02	0.87	1.63	1.88
Great Britain	1.03	2.54	1.01	1.23
The Netherlands	0.64	n.a.	1.01	1.34
Switzerland	n.a.	n.a.	1.20	1.46
The European industrial core	0.90	1.74	1.20	1.46
Europe	1.39	2.10	1.25	1.54
Argentina	1.74	−4.06	n.a.	n.a.
Australia	0.14	−3.30	0.87	1.08
Canada	1.65	n.a.	2.29	2.31
United States	1.04	−1.72	1.81	1.93
New world	1.14	−3.03	1.66	1.77

Source: O'Rourke and Williamson 1999 (table 2.2).
Note: n.a. = not available.

nomic leadership among the rich leaders, an interesting event, but marginal to the issue at hand. What mattered far more was the behavior of the poor countries relative to the rich ones, and the rich ones included Belgium, France, Germany, and the New World, not just Britain.

Table 6.1 reports the growth in real wages, GDP per head, and GDP per worker hour for twenty countries in the late nineteenth century. Let's start our narrative with the spectacular catching up with the leaders by Scandinavia, where real wages grew at rates almost three times those prevailing in the European industrial core: Swedish workers enjoyed real wage growth about 2.7 times that of British workers; Danish workers enjoyed real wage growth about 2.6 times that of German workers; and Norwegian workers enjoyed real wage growth about 3.8 times that of Dutch workers. In fact, no other country in our European sample underwent real wage growth even close to that of Sweden, Denmark, or Norway. Consistent with the predictions of conventional trade and migration theory, product per worker hour documents a less-spectacular Scandinavian catch-up than real wages, but even these data confirm an impressive growth performance compared with the European industrial core (1.77 versus 1.46 percent per annum). Consistent with the fact that Scandinavian emigrants were economically active, the superiority of Scandinavian GDP per capita growth over that of the industrial core (1.45 versus 1.2 percent per annum) is smaller than that of real wages or GDP per worker hour, but Scandinavian GDP per capita growth is still superior to that of the industrial core.

Scandinavia outperformed the rest of Europe (and probably the rest of the world) in the late nineteenth century. The Scandinavian countries were overachievers even by catching-up standards. What about the rest of the periphery? Austria seems to have done about as well as Scandinavia. In contrast, while Ireland certainly obeyed the laws of convergence, it was no overachiever. Real wages grew twice as fast in Ireland as they did in the industrial core, but they grew about as fast as the periphery average, and they recorded only three-quarters of the Scandinavian growth rate. The western Mediterranean Basin did very badly. Real wages crawled upward at about 0.4 percent a year in Iberia, while they surged *five and a half times* as quickly elsewhere around the periphery. Like most of Africa during the second great globalization boom (that since 1970), Spain and Portugal seem to have missed out on the first great globalization boom—as did Egypt, Turkey, and Serbia at the other end of the Mediterranean Basin (Williamson 2000a). Maddison's real GDP per worker hour data also confirm a poor Iberian performance, but the gap is not quite so great as open economy arguments would predict. Italy does somewhat better, but even it—except for real wages—falls below the average for the periphery. The importance of the Iberian failure to overall Atlantic economy convergence can be seen in figure 6.2: the convergence from 1854 to 1913 is steeper when Iberia is removed ($I(13)$ versus $N(15)$).

Let us now return to the average wage gap between Europe and the
New World, the variable which accounted for so much of the convergence over the second half of the nineteenth century. Four countries illustrate the process best: Ireland and Sweden (with heavy emigrations
from the late 1840s onward), the United States (with heavy immigrations from the late 1840s onward), and Britain (the industrial leader,
losing its dominant grip). In 1856, unskilled real wages in urban Sweden were only 49 percent of those in Britain, while in 1913 they were
at parity with Britain's, an impressive doubling in the Swedish wage
relative over the fifty-seven years. Real wages in Sweden rose from 24
to 58 percent of those in the United States over the same period. In
1852, shortly after the famine, unskilled real wages in urban Ireland
were only 61 percent of those in Britain, a figure that had changed
hardly at all over the previous three decades. Real wages in Ireland
started a dramatic convergence on those in Britain during the 1850s
(and notably, in the absence of any Irish industrialization), so that they
were 73 percent of those in Britain by 1870 and 92 percent of those in
Britain by 1913.

When Convergence Stopped

Between 1914 and 1934, the secular real wage convergence which had
been at work in the Atlantic economy since the middle of the nineteenth century stopped. Following 1934, real wage gaps in the Atlantic economy widened so much that measures of global labor market
(dis)integration retreated all the way back to the levels of the late
1870s.

How much of the cessation in convergence can be explained by the
First World War and by the interwar breakdown of global commodity,
capital, and labor markets? A positive correlation is certainly apparent.
After the passage of the Quota Acts in the 1920s, the United States
would never again have an open immigration policy, and Argentina,
Australia, Brazil, and Canada followed suit. Migrations between members of the Atlantic economy dropped from a massive flood to a modest trickle, not to become a public issue again until the 1980s, when
nonmembers from Asia, Africa, and Latin America began to send emigrants (legal and illegal) in large numbers to the Atlantic economy.
Governments intervened in capital markets, restricting the movements
of financial capital across their borders. The enormous flow of private
capital from western Europe (led by Britain) to the Americas, to eastern

Europe and to Europe's colonies dried up, not to recover until the 1970s. Commodity trade was choked off by tariffs, quotas, preferential agreements, and exchange rate intervention, a protectionist shift that was to take decades of the General Agreement on Tariffs and Trade (GATT), the European Community (EC), the North American Free Trade Agreement (NAFTA), and other agreements to erase.

Is the correlation spurious? No. If the convergence in the late-nineteenth-century Atlantic economy was driven largely by open economy forces, then it would invite the inference that the disintegration of the Atlantic economy between 1914 and 1950 had a great deal to do with the cessation of secular convergence that started in the middle of the previous century. Chapter 10 explores this inference more deeply.

Searching for Convergence Causes: The Role of Mass Migration

How much of the convergence in the pre–World War I Atlantic economy was due to mass migration? How much was due to other forces like trade, capital accumulation, and productivity advance?

Table 6.2 assesses the labor force impact of late-nineteenth- and early-twentieth-century mass migrations on each Atlantic economy country in 1910. The impact varied greatly: Argentina's labor force was augmented most by immigration (86 percent), Brazil's the least (4 percent), and the United States' somewhere in between (24 percent) but below the New World average of 40 percent; Ireland's labor force was diminished most by emigration (45 percent), those of France and the Netherlands the least (1 and 3 percent, respectively), and Britain's somewhere in between (11 percent) but just a little below the Old World average of 13 percent. These, then, are the Atlantic economy mass migrations whose labor market impact we wish to assess.

The standard way of dealing with this question on a classroom blackboard is illustrated by figure 6.3, and we simplify the answer by looking only at the wage gap between New World and Old World labor markets. The figure shows New World wages and labor's marginal product on the left-hand side and Old World wages and labor's marginal product on the right-hand side. The world labor supply is measured along the horizontal axis. An equilibrium distribution of labor, of course, occurs at the intersection of the two derived labor demand schedules (O and N). Instead, we start at I_1, where labor is scarce in the New World, and thus where the wage gap between the two

Table 6.2
The cumulative impact of mass migration, 1870–1910

	Persons		Labor force		Impact on real wage 1910	Impact on GDP per capita 1910	Impact on GDP per worker 1910
	Net migration rate 1870–1910	Cumulative impact 1910	Net migration rate 1870–1910	Cumulative impact 1910			
Argentina	11.74	60%	15.50	86%	-21.5%	-8.2%	-21.0%
Australia	6.61	30	8.73	42	-14.6	-6.8	-14.4
Brazil	0.74	3	0.98	4	-2.3	-0.5	-1.5
Canada	6.92	32	9.14	44	-15.6	-7.6	-15.5
United States	4.03	17	5.31	24	-8.1	-3.3	-8.1
New World	6.01	29	7.93	40	-12.4	-5.3	-12.1
Belgium	1.67	7	2.20	9	-4.4	-3.1	-5.1
Denmark	-2.78	-11	-3.67	-14	7.6	3.7	7.4
France	-0.10	0	-0.13	-1	1.4	0.2	0.3
Germany	-0.73	-3	-0.96	-4	2.4	1.3	2.2
Great Britain	-2.25	-9	-2.97	-11	5.6	2.8	5.8
Ireland	-11.24	-36	-14.84	-45	31.9	n.a.	n.a.
Italy	-9.25	-31	-12.21	-39	28.2	14.2	28.6
Netherlands	-0.59	-2	-0.78	-3	2.7	1.1	1.9
Norway	-5.25	-19	-6.93	-24	9.7	3.1	10.4
Portugal	-1.06	-4	-1.40	-5	4.3	0.0	0.0
Spain	-1.16	-5	-1.53	-6	5.9	0.0	0.0
Sweden	-4.20	-15	-5.55	-20	7.5	2.5	8.2
Old World	-3.08	-11	-4.06	-13	8.6	2.3	5.4

Source: Taylor and Williamson 1997 (tables 1, 3, 4).
Notes: Migration rates are per thousand per annum. Minus denotes emigration. The New World and Old World averages are unweighted. See Taylor and Williamson for the calculation of the real wage, GDP per capita, and GDP per worker impact. n.a. = not available.

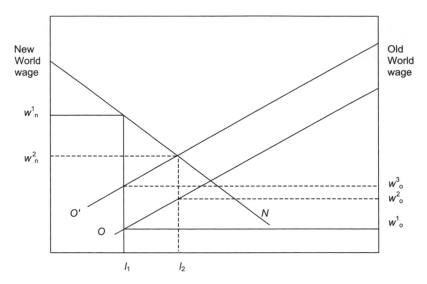

Figure 6.3
Allocating labor supplies between New and Old Worlds

regions is very large, $w_n^1 - w_o^1$. If mass migrations redistribute labor toward the New World, say to I_2, the wage gap collapses to $w_n^2 - w_o^2$, and all the observed convergence is attributable to migration. However, the same kind of convergence could have been achieved by a relative demand shift: a shift from O to O', an event driven perhaps by a trade boom favoring labor in the Old World or by faster accumulation and technological change there. The no-migration counterfactual invokes the ceteris paribus assumption: we adjust population and labor force according to the average net migration (and labor participation) rate observed during the period and assume that technology, capital stocks, prices, and all else remain constant. Such assumptions impart an upward bias on the measured impact of mass migration, but let's determine whether the magnitudes for the Atlantic economy as a whole are large enough to warrant further debate over such bias.

Migration affects long-run equilibrium output and wages to the extent that it influences aggregate labor supply. The labor demand elasticities have been estimated econometrically, and the results have been used to assess the impact on real wages, GDP per capita, and GDP per worker in 1910, had there been zero net migration after 1870 in all countries (Taylor and Williamson 1997, table 4). The last three columns of table 6.2 present the results.

The experiment suggests that the mass migrations lowered wages and labor productivity a lot in the New World and raised them a lot in the Old World; they typically (but not always) lowered income per capita marginally in the New World and typically (but not always) increased income per capita marginally in the Old World. Not surprisingly, the biggest impact is reported for those countries which experienced the biggest migrations: emigration raised Irish wages by 32 percent, Italian by 28 percent, and Norwegian by 10 percent, and immigration lowered Argentine wages by 21 percent, Australian by 15 percent, Canadian by 16 percent, and American by 8 percent.

This partial equilibrium assessment is higher than it would be in general equilibrium: after all, it ignores trade responses and changes in output mix, both of which would have muted the impact of the counterfactual no-migration impact, and it also ignores global capital market responses, although this latter shortcoming is repaired in a moment. Whether it is an overstatement or not, Table 6.2 certainly lends strong support to the premise that mass migration made an important contribution to late-nineteenth-century convergence. In the absence of the mass migrations, real wage dispersion would have *increased* by 7 percent, rather than having decreased by 28 percent as it did in fact. GDP per worker dispersion would have decreased by only 9 percent, rather than by 29 percent as it did in fact. GDP per capita dispersion would also have decreased by only 9 percent, rather than by 18 percent as it did in fact. Wage gaps between New and Old World in fact declined from 108 to 85 percent, but in the absence of the mass migrations, they would have *risen* to 128 percent in 1910.

Pairwise comparisons are also easily constructed using table 6.2. Wage gaps between many Old World countries and the United States fell dramatically as a result of mass migration: without Irish emigration (some of whom went to America) and U.S. immigration (some of whom were Irish), the American-Irish wage gap would have risen by 33 percentage points (from 135 to 168 percent), while in fact it fell by 48 (from 135 to 87 percent); without Italian emigration (a large share of whom went to America) and U.S. immigration (many of whom came from Italy), the American-Italian wage gap would have risen by 32 percentage points, while in fact it fell by 102; without British emigration and Australian immigration, the Australian-British wage gap would have fallen only by 14 percentage points, while in fact it fell by 48; and without Italian emigration and Argentine immigration, the Argentine-Italian wage gap would have risen by 75 percentage points, while in fact it fell by 45. Furthermore, the mass migrations to the New World also had an impact on economic convergence *within* the Old World: without the Norwegian emigration flood and the German emigration trickle, the German-Norwegian wage gap would have fallen by 63 percentage points, while in fact it fell by 71; and had Irish emigration not exceeded British emigration by far (as it in fact did), the British-Irish wage gap would have fallen by only 7 percentage points, while in fact it fell by 33.

The counterfactual results in table 6.2 suggest that more than all (125 percent) of the real wage convergence in 1870–1910 (log measure of dispersion) and about two-thirds (69 percent) of the GDP per worker convergence was attributable to migration. In contrast, perhaps one-half (50 percent) of the GDP per capita convergence might have been due to migration.

The contribution of mass migration to convergence in the full sample and in the New and Old World differ. Indeed, in two out of three New World cases, convergence would have been *greater* in the absence of mass migration. While those two cases may at first appear counterintuitive, the fact that the Atlantic labor market was segmented should account for it. Immigrant flows were not everywhere efficiently distributed, since migrants did not always obey some simple market wage calculus; kept out of the best high-wage destinations, or having alternative cultural preferences, many went to the "wrong" countries. The south-south flows from Italy, Spain, and Portugal to Brazil and Argentina were a strong force for local (Latin), not global (Atlantic economy), convergence. Furthermore, policy (such as assisted passage) still played a part in violating any simple market wage calculus. However, the small contribution of migration to convergence within the Old World and within the New illustrates our opening point: the major contribution of mass migration to late-nineteenth-century convergence was the enormous movement of about sixty million Europeans to the New World.

The relative insensitivity of GDP per capita convergence to migration is a result of countervailing effects inherent in the algebra. For real wages or GDP per worker, high migrant-to-population ratios of labor participation rates amplify the impact of migration, but with GDP per capita the impact is muted. Why? In the former two cases, migration has a bigger impact on the labor force, GDP and wages, the bigger is the labor content of the migrations. In the case of GDP per capita, things are less clear. For example, with emigration, population outflow generally offsets diminishing returns in production for a net positive impact on output per capita, but selectivity assures that emigration will take away a disproportionate share of the labor force, lowering output via labor supply losses, with a negative impact on output per capita. The latter effect dominated in the late-nineteenth-century Atlantic economy (Taylor and Williamson 1997), so muted GDP per capita effects are no surprise.

Qualifying the Convergence Bottom Line

The previous section argues that mass migration accounted for 125 percent of the real wage convergence observed in the Atlantic economy between 1870 and 1910. In short, we have overexplained late-nineteenth-century convergence. But remember that there were *other* powerful forces at work too. Consider capital accumulation. We know that capital accumulation was more rapid in the New World than in the Old, so much so that the rate of capital deepening was faster in the United States than in any of its competitors (Wright 1990; Wolff 1991), and the same was probably true of other rich New World countries. Thus, the mass migrations may have been at least partially offset by capital accumulation, and a large part of it was being carried by international capital flows, which reached magnitudes unsurpassed before or since (Obstfeld and Taylor 2003; Clemens and Williamson 2004). The evidence on the role of global capital market responses to migration is very tentative, but Taylor and Williamson (1997) make exactly this kind of adjustment to the results reported in table 6.2. They implement the no-net-migration counterfactual in a model in which labor supply shocks generate capital inflows or outflows in order to maintain a constant rate of return on capital in each country. The capital-chasing-labor offsets are very large. Whereas mass migration overexplained 125 percent of the observed real wage convergence using the model without capital chasing labor, it explains about 70 percent of the convergence using the model with capital chasing labor, leaving approximately 30 percent to other forces. The findings for labor productivity are similar.

In theory, the forces of late-nineteenth-century convergence could have included trade expansion, technological catch-up, and human capital catch-up, but in fact mass migration was the central force. These results offer a new perspective on the convergence debate, one relevant for macroeconomists and policymakers. The convergence power of free migration, when such migration is tolerated, can be substantial. Convergence explanations based on technological or accumulation catch-up in closed economy models miss this point. The millions on the move in the late nineteenth century didn't.

Who Gained and Who Lost? A Relative Factor Price Assessment

Shortly after the First World War, two Swedish economists looked back on the pre-1913 episode and thought they could discern the distributional consequences of globalization. Both Eli Heckscher, an economic historian, and Bertil Ohlin, a trade theorist, argued that the trade boom and labor migration had important income distribution consequences within both Europe and the New World: they argued that trade, commodity price convergence, and labor migration combined implied factor price convergence (Flam and Flanders 1991, 90–92).

The insights of Heckscher and Ohlin still inform public debate today, as the ongoing controversy about the causes of rising inequality in the OECD testifies. Is commodity market integration between the industrialized North and the developing South leading to an increase in wage inequality in rich, skill-abundant countries by forcing down the prices of goods intensive in unskilled labor, which can be more efficiently produced in the Third World? Does immigration into the OECD displace native unskilled workers, leading to wage inequality? And what about sending countries in the Third World: does emigration raise wages and reduce inequality there? Given the intensity of the current debate, it is of obvious relevance to ask whether declining transport costs and mass migration had an impact on income distribution in the late nineteenth century, the period that motivated Heckscher and Ohlin in the first place.

Note, however, that Heckscher and Ohlin asked us to view trade as a substitute for factor migration. If labor, capital, and skills had been perfectly mobile, then relative factor prices would have been the same everywhere in the Atlantic economy. They were not, but trade was a partial substitute, by helping those factor prices converge, if not making them equal. Thus, trade and mass migration were working together to make factor prices converge. And what did factor price convergence imply for changes in the income distribution? Who gained and who lost? Labor's wage should have fallen relative to land rents in the New World. Since landlords were at the top of the distribution pyramid and laborers at the bottom, globalization should have contributed to rising inequality in the resource-abundant New World. Similarly, globalization should have contributed to rising wages relative to land rents in Europe, and thus to falling inequality there. So were Heckscher and Ohlin right?

The evolution of relative factor prices has now been documented for the late-nineteenth-century Atlantic economy, so we can explore whether the big globalization winners were New World land and European labor and whether the big losers were European land and New World labor. Were globalization forces strong enough to leave their mark on the first global century? After all, the Heckscher-Ohlin predictions are based on a static trade theory which assumes that commodity market integration and mass migration were the only shocks affecting the world economy. Nothing could be farther from the truth. This was a period of dramatic industrialization, technical change, and demographic revolution, forces which also must have had their impact on real wages, farm rents, and income distribution more generally. In particular, economic growth meant that wages across the present-day OECD were rising rapidly: American (and Australian) labor certainly did not lose in absolute terms. In an expanding world like this, the Heckscher-Ohlin prediction becomes a counterfactual one: world commodity market integration and mass migration meant that European real wages grew more rapidly than they otherwise would, and it meant that New World real wages grew less rapidly than they otherwise would. Clearly, factor price trends cannot by themselves tell us whether or not these counterfactual predictions were fulfilled, but recent economic analysis has shown the predictions to be accurate.

There are four questions that we can sensibly ask of the data. First, did real wages converge in the late-nineteenth-century Atlantic economy? Second, did land rents converge? That is, did European rents fall, and did overseas rents rise? Third, was there relative factor price convergence? That is, did the ratio of wages to rents rise in Europe and fall in the New World? Finally, if there was relative factor price convergence, did it translate into rising inequality in the New World and falling inequality in Europe?

Early in this chapter we examined the first question using purchasing-power-parity adjusted real wages, and the answer we got was an unambiguous yes. There *was* real wage convergence within the OECD club during the late nineteenth century, and the bulk of this convergence was accounted for by convergence in real wages between the Old and New Worlds.

To answer the second and third questions, we need rent data for land of comparable quality across countries and over time. Alas, such data are unavailable, a point which Heckscher himself appreciated (Flam and Flanders 1991, 48). Nevertheless, if we make the plausible assumptions that European quality-adjusted land was initially more expensive than New World quality-adjusted land and that land rents moved as land prices did, then land rent convergence during this period is a certainty. Between 1870 and 1910, real land price increases in Australia (over 400 percent) and the United States (over 250 percent) were enormous, far greater than the biggest real land price increases we can document for Europe (Denmark, where land prices increased by only 45 percent between 1870–1873 and 1910–1913: O'Rourke and Williamson 1999, figures 4.1–4.3). Moreover, in three important European countries—Britain, France, and Sweden—land prices actually *fell*, in Britain by over 50 percent. Land rents and prices rose in the American Midwest, the Australian outback, and the Argentine pampas relative to those in Europe, as predicted.

It is the third question that is really central to any test of any globalization theory, especially in the context of a growing economy, and especially since the theory relies so heavily on *relative* factor endowments and *relative* factor prices. The answers are supplied by the second column of table 6.1, in which the evolution of the ratio of wages to land prices is documented for three New World countries (Argentina, Australia, and the United States), for four European free traders (Denmark, Britain, Ireland, and Sweden), and for three European protectionists (France, Germany, and Spain). Relative factor price convergence certainly characterized the period from 1870 to 1913. In the New World, the wage-rent ratio plunged. By 1913, the Australian ratio had fallen to one quarter of its 1870 level, the Argentine ratio had fallen to one-fifth of its mid-1880s level, and the U.S. ratio had fallen to less than half of its 1870 level. In Europe, the ratio boomed: the British ratio in 1910 had increased by a factor of 2.7 over its 1870 level, while the Irish ratio had increased even more, by a factor of 5.5. The Swedish and Danish ratios had both increased by a factor of 2.3. This increase was less pronounced in protectionist economies: the ratio increased by a factor of 1.8 in France and 1.4 in Germany and actually decreased a bit in Spain.

What factor price evidence we have seems to offer support for the predicted impact of the mass migration and trade boom on income distribution in the late nineteenth century. While real wages grew everywhere before 1913, they grew faster in labor-abundant Europe compared with the labor-scarce frontier overseas. Rents surged in the land-abundant New World and plunged in land-scarce, free-trading Britain, while remaining relatively stable on the European Continent, which either protected its agriculture or made profound structural changes in farming practice. And the wage-rent ratio increased dramatically in Europe, especially in free-trading countries, while declining equally dramatically in the frontier economies overseas.

Of course correlation is not causation. Just as rising inequality in the OECD today may plausibly be attributed to technical change, rather than globalization, so there may have been other forces at work affecting nineteenth-century income distribution independent of any globalization-induced shocks. Mass migration should have—and did—contribute to international real wage convergence during this period. Trade did the same, although its impact was more modest. Technical change should have—and did—save on labor and use land at the frontier, while it should have—and did—save on land and use labor in Europe.

All in all, globalization had exactly its predicted impact on relative factor prices around the Atlantic economy between the mid-nineteenth century and World War I (O'Rourke, Taylor, and Williamson 1996), but did it translate into the predicted income distribution trends? For the modern economist reading this, it may seem odd to discuss changing distribution without reference to skill premia while stressing land rents. Yet land and labor were the dominant factors of production a century ago, not skills and capital as is true today. Complete income distributions are, of course, unavailable between the mid-nineteenth century and World War I, except for those for a few countries and a few benchmark dates. But even if they were available, it is not obvious that we would want to use them to test the impact of mass migration. Like economists involved in the late-twentieth-century debate, our interest is in the structure of factor prices and factor rewards—the size of the average income gap between the upper and lower classes. Indeed, if rising inequality was explained by an increase in unskilled workers who were all new immigrants, then the rising inequality would be far less interesting and certainly less dangerous politically. But suppose the new immigrants also lowered the relative incomes of the poor native-born with whom they competed? Inequality trends of this sort are far more interesting *and* have more-dangerous political implications.

How, then, did the typical unskilled worker near the bottom of the distribution do relative to the average income recipient; that is, how did the ratio of the unskilled wage (w) to GDP per worker hour (y) trend over time? Changes in the ratio w/y measure changes in the economic distance between the working poor near the bottom of the distribution and the average-income recipient in the middle of the distribution. When the index is normalized by setting w/y equal to 100 in 1870, we get the following: powerful Danish and Swedish equality trends establish the upper bound (the index rises from 100 to about 153 or 154), and powerful Australian and U.S. inequality trends establish the lower bound (the index falls from 100 to about 53 or 58). An alternative way to standardize these distributional trends is to compute the annual percentage change in the index relative to its 1870 base: the per annum rates of change range from 0.97 and 0.98 for Denmark and Sweden to -1.22 and -1.45 for Australia and the United States. This measure of the annual rate of change in inequality is plotted against the 1870 real wage in figure 6.4, which offers a stunning confirmation of the hypothesized globalization-inequality connection: between 1870 and 1913, inequality rose dramatically in rich, land-abundant, labor-scarce New World countries like Australia and the United States; in-

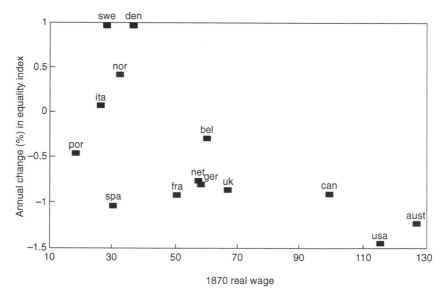

Figure 6.4
Initial real wage versus equality trends, 1870–1913. *Source:* Williamson 1997 (figure 6).

equality fell dramatically in poor, land-scarce, labor-abundant, newly industrializing countries like Norway, Sweden, Denmark, and Italy; inequality was more stable in European industrial economies like Belgium, France, Germany, the Netherlands, and the United Kingdom; and inequality was also more stable in the poor European economies which failed to play the globalization game, like Portugal and Spain.

When Kuznets gave his presidential address to the American Economic Association in 1955, he hypothesized that inequality should rise in early stages of modern development, reach a peak during what we have come to call the newly industrialized country stage, and then fall thereafter. Since then, the thesis has taken a beating, most recently from a newly constructed late-twentieth-century database (Deininger and Squire 1996). What is surprising about this literature, however, is that it treats a very complex problem so simply. There are a number of forces that can drive inequality in the long run, and we listed some of them above: mass migration, trade, demography, schooling, and technology. The technological forces which Kuznets thought were pushing his Curve cannot by themselves explain the trends in figure 6.4, since while inequality should have been on the rise in newly industrializing but poor European countries, it was not, and while it should have been on the decline in richer, more-mature industrial economies, it was not.

It appears likely that globalization must have been producing the late-nineteenth-century Atlantic economy distribution trends. Furthermore, we think that mass migration was the most important part of that globalization-distribution connection. As we already noted, the mass migration significantly influenced labor supplies in sending and receiving countries. We also noted that migration's impact on the labor force was highly correlated with initial labor scarcity, causing the biggest reductions in low-wage emigrating countries and the biggest increases in high-wage immigration countries. Figure 6.5 plots the migration-inequality connection: where immigration had a large positive impact on the labor force, inequality underwent a steep rise; where emigration had a large negative impact on the labor force, inequality underwent a steep fall.

Mass migration appears, therefore, to be the leading candidate in accounting for the distribution trends we observe in the Atlantic economy. We stress that this *appears* to be the case, since it is impossible to decompose globalization effects into trade and migration given that the correlation between migration's impact, trade's impact, and initial

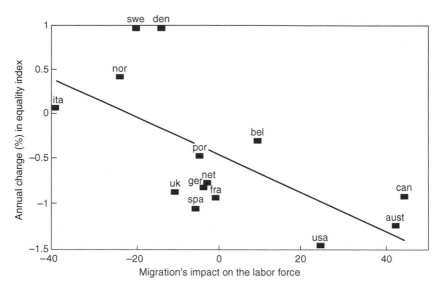

Figure 6.5
Equality trends versus migration's impact on the labor force, 1870–1913. *Source:* Williamson 1997 (figure 7).

labor scarcity is so high. Yet an effort has been made to finesse this problem by constructing a trade-globalization-impact variable as the interaction of initial labor scarcity and openness (Williamson 1997). The former is proxied by dummies for the labor-scarce New World, the labor-abundant European periphery, and the core European industrial leaders making up the remainder. Openness is proxied by trade shares (*trade*). The per annum rate of change in the equality index, here called *e*, is explained by ($R^2 = 0.72$, *t*-statistics in parentheses; O'Rourke and Williamson 1999, 179):

$$e = -52.07 - 0.31mig + 0.25trade + 0.55(d_1 * trade) + 2.42(d_2 * trade)$$
$$(2.56) \quad (1.00) \quad\quad (0.36) \quad\quad\quad (3.38)$$

where *mig* stands for the impact of net migration on labor supplies, $d_1 = 1$ when Australia, Canada or the United States, and $d_2 = 1$ when Denmark, Italy, Norway, Sweden, Spain, or Portugal. The impact of mass migration is powerful, significant, and of the right sign: when immigration rates were big, *e* was small, and inegalitarian trends were strong; when immigration rates were small, *e* was bigger, and thus inegalitarian trends were weaker; and when emigration rates were big, *e* was even bigger, and thus egalitarian trends were strong.

Around the European periphery, the more-open economies had more-egalitarian trends (bigger *trade* implying bigger *e*, [0.25 + 2.42] * *trade*). It appears that the open, industrializing "tigers" of that time enjoyed benign egalitarian trends, while those among them opting for autarky did not. Furthermore, the coefficient 2.42 on (d_2 * *trade*) passes conventional significance tests. In the European industrial core, the effect was far less powerful, since the smaller coefficient 0.25 on *trade* does not pass any significance test. It appears that open economy effects on income distribution were ambiguous among the European industrial leaders with moderate initial income levels. In the labor-scarce New World, however, the more-open economies also had more-egalitarian trends ([0.25 + 0.55] * *trade*), which is certainly *not* what Heckscher and Ohlin would have predicted. The result is not statistically significant, however.

Overall, we read this evidence as strong support for the impact of mass migration on distribution trends: the effects were great everywhere in the Atlantic economy where the migrations were large. The evidence offers weak support, however, for the impact of trade on distribution trends, except around the European periphery, where trade lowered inequality. This econometric exercise was able to explain about two-thirds of the variance in distributional trends across the late nineteenth century.

Did citizens living through these events prior to World War I feel that migration accounted for most of these distributional trends? Did they modify their open and liberal policies in response? Chapter 8 establishes the migration backlash connection for New World immigration policy, but it might be useful to determine whether distributional trends changed during the interwar period when quotas were imposed in immigrant countries, capital markets collapsed in the face of government intervention, and trade barriers soared to autarkic heights—that is, under conditions of deglobalization.

Earlier in this chapter, we established that convergence ceased after 1913. It now turns out that the globalization-inequality connection was also broken. Figure 6.6 shows the correlation between distributional trends as measured by changes in w/y and a 1921 real wage measure of labor scarcity. The late-nineteenth-century inverse correlation completely disappeared, replaced after 1921 by a positive correlation. In the interwar period of deglobalization, the poorer countries underwent sharply increasing inequality, while the richer countries underwent more-moderate increases or, in four cases, egalitarian trends. This

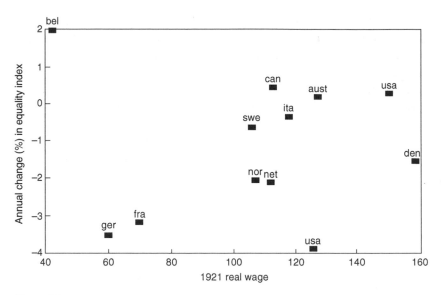

Figure 6.6
Initial real wage versus equality trends, 1921–1938. *Source:* Williamson 1997 (figure 9).

finding is consistent both with the cessation of the mass migrations *and* with the Stolper-Samuelson theorem: protection should raise demand for the scarce factor, thus improving the position of the unskilled in rich countries and contributing to egalitarian trends there, while eroding the position of the unskilled in poor countries and contributing to inegalitarian trends there. Whether it really *was* deglobalization which precipitated this dramatic switch in distribution trends has yet to be established with firmer evidence, but there seems to be no doubt about the switch itself: the pre-1914 egalitarian trends in Scandinavia and Italy disappeared and were replaced by post-1921 inequality trends; the pre-1914 inequality trends in the New World disappeared and were replaced by post-1921 egalitarian trends which Arthur Burns (1954) called a revolutionary leveling; and the relatively stable pre-1914 distribution trends in industrial France and Germany were replaced by dramatic post-1921 inequality trends, consistent with the rise of fascism (Rogowski 1989, chap. 3).

Who Gained and Who Lost? Looking in Labor Markets

The impact of the immigrants on late-nineteenth- and early-twentieth-century U.S. labor markets obsessed contemporary American observers. Here we confront two questions that are just as relevant today as they were when posed almost a century ago when the Immigration Commission published its 1911 report: Did immigrants crowd out natives? Did they reduce their wages? It appears that they did.

Recall that Claudia Goldin (1994) estimated the correlation between immigration and wage changes across cities between 1890 and 1915, finding that a one-percentage-point increase in the foreign-born share reduced unskilled wage rates by 1 to 1.5 percent. Another study estimated the impact of immigration on the real (unskilled) wage by looking at the wage adjustment mechanism from time series data. By altering labor supply and unemployment in the short run, immigration should drive down the wage along some long-run Phillips curve. The long-run solution to one such model estimated for 1890–1913 suggests that, holding output constant, an increase in the labor force by 1 percent lowered the real wage in the long run by 0.4 or 0.5 percent (Hatton and Williamson 1998, table 8.6). Based on the stock of foreign-born and their children enumerated in the 1910 census, immigration after 1890 accounted for about 12 percent of the 1910 labor force and immigration after 1870 accounted for about 27 percent of the 1910 labor force. These magnitudes suggest that the real (unskilled) wage would have been 5 to 6 percent higher in the absence of immigration after 1890 and 11 to 14 percent higher in the absence of immigration after 1870.

Both the city cross section and the time series results are consistent with those based on computable general equilibrium models. For example, the first effort to apply computable general equilibrium techniques to the late-nineteenth-century United States estimated that immigration after 1870 lowered real wages in 1910 by 11 percent (Williamson 1974, 387), almost identical to the time series estimate. A more-recent computable general equilibrium experiment got pretty much the same result: immigration reduced urban real wages in 1910 by 9.2 percent (O'Rourke, Williamson, and Hatton 1994, 209). In short, it does indeed appear that there were powerful crowding-out forces at work in immigrant countries before World War I, and these must have contributed to the rising inequality observed there.

Mass Migrations in the
Poor Periphery

The global boom between 1820 and World War I involved more than simply the greater Atlantic economy (which includes the distant colonies of Australia and New Zealand). The periphery was pulled into the boom as well, and the central global shock that triggered the periphery's participation was, first and foremost, a massive favorable terms-of-trade shock that stretched out over more than a half century. Only then, second, did mass migrations respond thus to help the periphery generate the impressive export supply response that followed. The relative price of exportables had to rise dramatically if this process was to be set in motion in the resource-abundant parts of the periphery: Southeast Asia (Burma, Java, Malaya, the Philippines, Siam, and the Straits Settlements), South Asia (Assam, the Punjab, and Ceylon), tropical and semitropical Latin America (the Caribbean, the Brazilian northeast, British and French Guiana, and coastal Peru), North Africa, East Africa, and the Indian Ocean (Egypt, Kenya, Mauritius, Natal, and Reunion).[1] And rise they did.

This chapter starts by describing the forces that account for the terms-of-trade boom, then goes on to document that boom. With those foundations in place, the chapter then explores the mass migrations that followed: one estimate has it that between forty-eight million and fifty-two million emigrants left India and China for labor-scarce and resource-abundant locations elsewhere in the periphery (McKeown 2004, 156), although confirmation of the high return migration rates are hard to come by (Lai 2002, 230). To what extent was there segmentation between labor markets in core and periphery? How important were distance and transport costs in creating big wage gaps between labor-scarce and labor-abundant regions around the periphery? Was poverty a binding constraint on free migration within the periphery? What were the various institutional solutions to this poverty constraint? Did the mass migrations produce the same real wage and relative factor price convergence in the periphery that took place in the core (chapter 6)?

Export Booms in the Resource-Abundant and Labor-Scarce Periphery

Setting the Stage: Thinking about Prices

As chapter 3 documented, transport costs dropped very fast between 1820 and 1860. Here, we document their continued fall during the rest of the century. These powerful globalization forces were partially offset by a rising tide of protection in the greater Atlantic economy after midcentury—but only partially. Declining transport costs accounted for two-thirds of the integration of world commodity markets over the century following 1820 and for *all* of world commodity market integration in the four decades after 1870, when globalization backlash offset some of it (Lindert and Williamson 2003, table 1). Note, however, that the late-nineteenth-century tariff backlash that occurred elsewhere did not take place in Asia, the Middle East, and Africa, partly because they were colonies of free traders, partly because of the power of gunboat diplomacy, and partly because of the political influence wielded by natives who controlled the natural resources that were the base of their exports (Lewis 1978a, 1978b; Rogowski 1989; Williamson 2004, 2005). Without the greater Atlantic tariff backlash to mute them, trade-creating, positive external price shocks turn out to have been even bigger and more ubiquitous in the periphery than those which occurred in the greater Atlantic economy during the first global century.

There are at least two reasons why commodity prices had bigger effects on wages and returns to natural resources in Asia, Africa, and the rest of the tropical periphery. First, the commodity price shocks were bigger, for the reasons already given. Second, land and other natural resources were much more important factor endowments in primary product exporters. The impact of price shocks on relative factor prices are much bigger in economies in which (immobile) land and other natural resources are important: changes in the returns to land, natural resources, and plantation labor relative to both "free" labor and industrial capital are far bigger in the specific-factors model[2] than those between capital and "free" labor in the more-standard two-factor Heckscher-Ohlin model; that is, while specific factors could not escape bad price shocks when they hit their products, they *did* enjoy big gains in wages and rents when the price shocks favored them. Why do we care? Because it is the derived demand for those factors of production that will spill over into excess demands for unskilled labor in the export sector and thus create a potential role for mass migrations.

Transport Revolutions, Colonial Administrations, and Gunboats in the Periphery

Every historian knows the components of the nineteenth-century worldwide transport revolution, and we have reviewed some of them already in chapter 3. But it is important to stress that the transport revolution was not limited to the Atlantic economy.

Except in regard to exotic high-value and low-bulk products, distance seems to have almost isolated Asian producers and consumers from Europe until the early nineteenth century. Transport innovations subsequently changed all that. The Suez Canal (opened in 1869), cost-reducing innovations on seagoing transport, and railroads penetrating the interior began to liberate Asia from the tyranny of distance by 1914.[3] The decline in freight rates between 1870 and 1914 was just as dramatic on routes involving Black Sea and Egyptian ports, and perhaps even more so (Harlaftis and Kardasis 2000). The tramp charter rate for shipping rice from Rangoon to Europe fell from 74 to 18 percent of the Rangoon price between 1882 and 1914, and the freight rate on sugar between Java and Amsterdam fell by 50–60 percent (Williamson 2000b, 2004; O'Rourke and Williamson 1999, chap. 3). Furthermore, there was an equally dramatic decline in transport costs *within* the periphery. The freight rate on coal between Nagasaki and Shanghai fell by 76 percent between 1880 and 1910, and total factor productivity on Japan's tramp freighter routes serving Asia advanced at 2.5 percent per annum between 1879 and 1909 (Yasuba 1978, tables 1, 5).

While the fall in transport costs was dramatic, it was not the most important event opening up nineteenth-century Asia to global forces. Under the persuasion of Commodore Matthew Perry's American battleships, Japan signed the Shimoda and Harris treaties and in so doing switched from autarky to free trade in 1858. It is hard to imagine a more-dramatic switch in commercial policy, since Japan's foreign trade quickly rose from nil to 7 percent of national income.[4] Other Asian nations followed the same liberal path, most forced to do so by colonial dominance or gunboat diplomacy. Thus, China signed a treaty with

Britain in 1842 that opened its ports to trade and set a 5 percent ad valorem tariff limit. Siam avoided China's humiliation by going open on its own and adopting a 3 percent tariff limit in 1855. Korea emerged from its autarchic Hermit Kingdom about the same time, undergoing market integration with Japan long before colonial status became formalized in 1910. India went the way of British free trade in 1846, and Indonesia followed Dutch liberalism. Thus, in contrast with the Atlantic economy, sharply declining transport costs contributed to commodity price convergence in Asia without any offsetting rise in tariffs.

What was the impact of these transport innovations on the cost of moving goods between markets? Liverpool wheat prices exceeded Chicago prices by 58 percent in 1870, but by only 18 percent in 1895, and by only 16 percent in 1912. Overall price convergence was even greater when account is taken of the collapse in price gaps between midwestern farm gates and Chicago markets, as well as between Liverpool and British consumers. A price convergence similar to that in Anglo-American wheat markets occurred as well for other foodstuffs, like meat, butter, and cheese, although convergence for these three had to wait for the advances in refrigeration made toward the end of the century. Trends parallel to these Anglo-American ones can also be documented for price gaps between London and Buenos Aires, as well as Montevideo and Rio de Janeiro. The Ukraine and the rest of the eastern European periphery was also part of this worldwide price convergence: wheat price gaps between Odessa and Liverpool of about 40 percent in 1870 had just about evaporated by 1906. Commodity price convergence involving the eastern Mediterranean was just as powerful. The price spread on Egyptian cotton between Liverpool and Alexandria plunged off a high plateau after the 1860s. Liverpool price quotes exceeded those in Alexandria by 63 percent in 1837–1846, but only by 41 percent in 1863–1867, and only by 5 percent in 1890–1899 (Issawi 1966, 447–448).

Transport cost declines from interior to port and from port to Europe ensured that Asian and African export-oriented enclaves became more integrated into world markets. The raw cotton price spread between Liverpool and Bombay fell from 57 percent in 1873 to 20 percent in 1913, and the jute price spread between London and Calcutta fell from 35 to 4 percent. The same events were taking place even farther east, involving Burma and the rest of Southeast Asia: the rice price spread between London and Rangoon fell from 93 to 26 percent in the four decades prior to 1913. These events had a profound impact on the creation of an Asian market for wheat and rice, as well as a truly global market for grains (Latham and Neal 1983; Brandt 1985; Kang and Cha 1996).

This narrative is summarized in table 7.1, in which we add an attempt to quantify the magnitudes of the transport revolution over the century or so between 1870 and 1990. The evidence presented in the table confirms the assertion that the spectacular pre–World War I decline in transport costs was biggest in Asia. It also confirms that the decline slowed down a bit during the interwar decades and that transport costs have declined only modestly since 1950, thus pointing to the nineteenth century as a special globalization episode.[5]

Terms of Trade Facing Export Enclaves in the Periphery

What happened to the relative price of the primary products exported by the periphery to the booming industrial markets of Europe and North America during the first half of the nineteenth century? The way to answer this question is to look at what happened to the terms of trade facing the world's industrial leader (and colonist), Britain. Figure 7.1 plots Britain's net barter terms of trade, the ratio of its export (manufactures) to import (primary products) prices, which underwent a spectacular fall: it decreased by half over the four decades between 1820 and 1860. Therefore, the terms of trade facing Britain's Asian, African, and Latin American trading partners, the primary product exporters, must, on average, have at least doubled. They probably increased even more, since as we argued earlier, the world transport revolution ensured that the relative price of primary product exports increased by even more at the source. Of course, it isn't just a transport revolution that explains this terms-of-trade behavior, since very rapid productivity advances in the core's export sector (manufactures, especially textiles) probably made an even greater contribution. Whatever the case, this huge improvement in the terms of trade facing primary product exporters in the periphery is illustrated by Latin America in figure 7.2, in which it is apparent that the boom continued until the early to mid-1890s. Furthermore, it appears that the terms of trade in this part of the periphery doubled over the seven decades following 1820. Things were pretty much the same elsewhere, except that the secular terms-of-trade bubble burst somewhat earlier. Thus, the Egyptian terms of trade rose 2.5 times between the early 1820s and their secular peak in the early 1860s, while the Ottoman terms of trade rose the

Table 7.1
Global transport cost changes and commodity price convergence

Indicator	Period	Change
The Big-Bang era before World War I		
The Greater Atlantic economy		
Transport cost declines		
American export routes, deflated freight cost index (1869/71 = 100)	1869/71–1908/10	100 to 55
American east coast routes, deflated freight cost index (1869/71 = 100)	1869/71–1911/13	100 to 55
British tramp, deflated freight cost index (1869/71 = 100)	1869/71–1911/13	100 to 78
Freight costs as percentage of wheat price	1870–1910	41 to 22.6
Commodity price convergence		
Liverpool–Chicago wheat price gap (percentage)	1870–1912	58 to 16
London–Cincinnati bacon price gap (percentage)	1870–1913	93 to 18
Philadelphia–London pig iron price gap (percentage)	1870–1913	85 to 19
London–Boston wool price gap (percentage)	1870–1913	59 to 28
London–Buenos Aires hides price gap (percentage)	1870–1913	28 to 9
The Third World		
Transport cost declines		
Rangoon–Europe freight costs as percentage of rice price	1882–1914	74 to 18
Java–Amsterdam sugar freight cost index (1870 = 100)	1870–1914	100 to 45
Nagasaki–Shanghai coal freight cost index (1880 = 100)	1880–1910	100 to 24
Commodity price convergence		
Liverpool–Odessa wheat price gap (percentage)	1870–1906	40 to 2
Liverpool–Bombay cotton price gap (percentage)	1873–1913	57 to 20
London–Calcutta jute price gap (percentage)	1873–1913	35 to 4
London–Rangoon rice price gap (percentage)	1873–1913	93 to 26
Liverpool–Alexandria cotton price gap (percentage)	1837/46–1890/99	63 to 5
The era of slowdown to steady state, 1920–1990		
Transport cost declines		
World Bank deflated ocean freight cost index (1920 = 100)	1920–1940	100 to 68
Freight costs as percentage of wheat price	1920–1940	27.5 to 18.7
World Bank deflated ocean freight cost index (1950 = 100)	1950–1990	100 to 76
Freight costs as percentage of wheat price	1950–1990	18.7 to 14.2

Source: Williamson 2002 (table 1).
Note: A commodity price gap is calculated as the percentage by which the price at the high-price importing location exceeds that at the low-price exporting location.

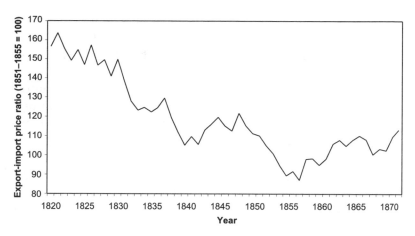

Figure 7.1
Britain's terms of trade, 1820–1872. *Source:* Bértola and Williamson 2003 (figure 1).

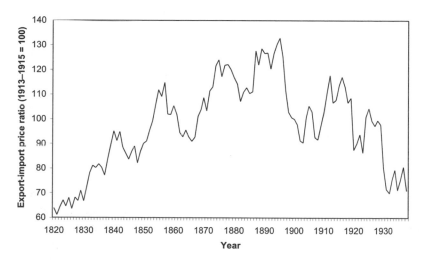

Figure 7.2
Latin America's terms of trade, 1820–1938. *Source:* Bértola and Williamson 2003 (figure 2).

same amount between the late 1810s and their peak in the early 1860s
(Williamson 2004, figures 2.7 and 2.8). Meanwhile, the Indonesian
terms of trade rose by 2.7 times between the late 1820s and the late
1860s (Korthals Altes 1994, 159–160).

The terms of trade boomed everywhere in the tropical and semitropical periphery up to the 1860s and 1870s; they sputtered around high
levels over the next two decades, and then they fell everywhere thereafter. The terms of trade collapse across the twentieth century is, of
course, well known and has been central to debate over policy in what
we now call the Third World. Indeed, it provoked Raoul Prebisch
(1950), Hans Singer (1950), and W. Arthur Lewis (1978a, 1978b) to infer
that the primary product boom was over and that an epoch of deterioration had set in, a turn of events that they thought warranted
proindustry intervention. Our interest at present, however, is the nineteenth century.

Impact in the Periphery: Theory

What were the effects of the soaring terms of trade facing the tropical
periphery over the half century after 1820 and the steep descent over
the half century after 1890? Lewis (1954, 1978a, 1978b) pioneered
exploration of this question, looking at factor market responses in the
primary-product-exporting economies. Lewis composed a long list of
effects that included what is central to this chapter: international labor
migration, real wages, and income distribution. Since the factor inputs
that mattered most in the tropical economies were land and labor, the
best way to explore the income distribution impact there is to focus
on the wage-rent ratio: the returns to labor relative to land. Since Eli
Heckscher and Bertil Ohlin wrote about the problem almost a century
ago, we have learned that primary product export price booms raise
the relative demand for land and other natural resources. Note that we
have been talking about *relative* factor prices, not *absolute* factor prices.
We have said nothing so far about real wages and living standards
for common labor. Positive terms-of-trade shocks of the magnitude
observed for the tropical periphery across most of the nineteenth century must have raised real wages and living standards there, at least in
the short run and medium term. But in the long run, living standards
are also driven up when technological advance, capital deepening,
and human capital improvement surpass population growth. In the
tropical periphery before 1914, the effects of these forces were pretty

modest. After all, this is the period during which growth in the center far outstripped that in the periphery, one during which the gap between the West and the rest became very large (Maddison 1995; Pritchett 1997; Landes 1998).

We document below the wage-rent (w/r) evidence, but first we need to elaborate a bit on the theory. If the price of primary products (here called "agriculture," and thus Pa for its price) rises, the isoprice curve for primary products shifts outward, land rents rise, and the rent-wage ratio rises still more. In this example of a favorable price shock to the country specializing in agriculture, there is a magnification effect, since the rise in rents exceeds the rise in Pa. By symmetry, when Pa/Pm (where Pm is the price of manufactures) falls, the wage-rent ratio rises, again by a magnification effect.

How big is the magnification effect? In his classic paper on the specific-factor model, Ronald Jones (1971) showed exactly what determines the size of the magnification effect. Suppose the agricultural sector uses mobile labor, earning the wage w as before, and immobile land, earning the rent r as before. Suppose further that the manufacturing sector uses mobile labor and immobile capital, the latter earning an interest rate i. Now, introduce a shock into this economy by an improvement in its terms of trade, Pa/Pm. It must follow that

$$\Delta r > \Delta Pa > \Delta w > \Delta Pm > \Delta i,$$

where the delta refers to rates of change, and where it is clear that changes in the returns to the specific factors, land and capital, are more pronounced than the return to the mobile factor, labor: after all, while labor can flee the sector absorbing an unfavorable price shock and race to the sector absorbing a favorable price shock, an immobile factor cannot. If instead plantation labor and "free" labor do not move among sectors smoothly, then the wage on plantation labor should rise even more. What happens to the real wage is determined by what the workers consume. If they do not consume much of the export good (tea, sugar, rubber, guano, coffee, cotton, spices, jute, hemp, tin) but consume a lot of the import good (textiles, grains), then real wages will rise $(\Delta w > \Delta Pm)$, and there will be a spillover demand for immigrants. Furthermore, the rent-wage ratio responds as

$$(\Delta r - \Delta w) = \lambda(\Delta Pa - \Delta Pm),$$

where $\lambda(> 1)$ denotes the magnification effect. Thus, globalization-induced terms-of-trade shocks can have different effects on wage-rent ratios depending on the size of the shock and the structure of the tropical economy in question, but the expectation is that $\lambda > 1$ everywhere. Typically, then, a positive terms-of-trade shock favoring the tropical periphery's export sector should have raised real wages but created more inequality.

These are likely to have been the essentials driving factor demand, inequality, real wages, and mass migration in the tropical periphery across the first global century.

Wage Gaps and Costs of Moving in the Nineteenth-Century Periphery

The relative price boom for the exports of tropical products certainly increased the demand for unskilled labor in the tropical parts of the periphery after about 1820, but there was already plenty of incentive to move from labor-abundant to labor-scarce areas.

Recall from the previous three chapters the size of the wage gaps between emigration and immigration regions in the greater Atlantic economy. In the 1850s, the western European emigrant who faced the biggest gap between his home wage option and what he could get abroad was one from Norway, where home wages were only 27 percent of those in the New World (table 4.2); that is, the average Norwegian unskilled male could increase his real earnings by 3.7 times by emigrating across the Atlantic. The figures for the richer western European countries ranged from 44 percent (Ireland) to 59 percent (Britain). In short, at the end of the transition to mass migration in the Atlantic economy, the ratio of wages in labor-scarce regions abroad to those at home ranged from 3.7 for Norway to 1.7 for Britain. The potential gains from a move were immense, although as we have seen, the poorest could not scrape up the funds to make the costly investment.

Things were no different in the periphery. The average Indian indentured immigrant in British Guiana, the famous sugar-growing area in the northeast shoulder of Latin America, earned a monthly wage of $4.45 in 1869 (Northrup 1995, 129). If he had stayed home in the Madras Presidency to work as a rural laborer, he would have made about $1.50 per month, for a ratio of three to one. But the wage received by the indentured worker in Guiana was over and above the lodging, board, medical care, and (some) clothing furnished by his employer. For a poor unskilled coolie in those times, expenses for food, clothing, and lodging would have almost exhausted his income back home in

Madras. Thus, it seems fair to say that when income in kind is added to his wage income in Guiana, his monthly wage would have been more like $8 or more, and the ratio to monthly wages back home in India would have been five or more to one. According to this Guiana-Madras example from 1869, these wage gaps—measures of relative labor scarcity between the export enclaves and one of the two main labor surplus sources of the estate and plantation workers—were far higher around the periphery than they were around the greater Atlantic economy.[6]

Perhaps this huge 1869 Guiana-Madras wage gap exaggerates the incentive for mass migration within the periphery in the nineteenth century. After all, it could have been that Guiana had the highest wages (partly to compensate for high malaria-induced mortality risk there), or 1869 might have been a year of peak disequilibrium in this South-South labor market. However, applying the same rules to other regions yields similar, or even more spectacular, results: wages in the West Indies in 1870 implied a destination-to-home ratio of 4.8; Trinidad in 1870, 7.8; Hawaii in 1870, 9.0 (Northrup 1995, 130; Tinker 1974, 186). There is additional evidence supporting the large wage gap characterization: indentured Indian migrants returning from Mauritius in the late 1870s brought back cash equal to, on average, about four years of income at home, a figure that must understate the accumulated gains from the move, since so many used postal savings to remit earnings while in Mauritius and brought home (unreported) gold, silver, and jewelry (Northrup 1995, 137).

The distances from south India to the Caribbean or Hawaii were, of course, very large, while those for the Chinese coolie trade connecting the South China provinces of Fukien and Kwangtung to Southeast Asia were much shorter. So what were wage gaps like for these great Chinese emigrations? In the 1870s, the unskilled labor wage ratios between Siam and China were almost three (Williamson 2000b, table 1.1, assuming no change in Chinese real wages in 1873–1909).

This benign description of the gains from migration as an indentured or contract worker should not imply that we ignore the abundant evidence documenting poverty and hard times for these migrants, as well as abuse of their contracts (Lewis 1978a, 187; Tinker 1974, chap. 6; Northrup 1995, chap. 5). First, mortality rates on ships transporting indentured Chinese and Indian migrants were much higher than those for ships carrying nonindentured passengers on the same routes and at the same time (McDonald and Shlomowitz 1990, 1993; Northrup 1995, chap. 4). On the other hand, nonindentured passengers were financially much better off and thus had much lower mortality rates back home, too. Furthermore, ship mortality rates declined sharply between midcentury and the 1870s (Northrup 2002, 219), and while health and working conditions were certainly very bad on the estates and plantations abroad, they may well have been even worse at home. While the authorities and reformers pointed to examples of physical cruelty, restricted freedom, arbitrary wage deductions, and penal sanctions, they scrutinized the coolie trade far more critically than they did the abject conditions in the regions from which the migrants came.

Given wage differentials like those just cited, "the miracle," in Kingsley Davis's (1951) words, "is that there was not an even greater exodus" (102). True, 30.2 million left India, but 23.9 million returned, so that "only" 6.3 million left India for good between 1834 and 1937. Most of these headed south, east, or southeast: about 42.2 percent went to Burma, another 24.9 percent to Ceylon, and another 19.3 percent to British Malaya (Davis 1951, 99, 101). The Caribbean, the Pacific and Africa got the rest, 13.6 percent. But all of these net migrations over the century between the 1830s and the 1930s added up to only 9.4 percent of India's 1900 population (Davis 1951, table 34, 98), while the comparable percentages for European emigration were 43.3 for the British Isles, 33.3 for Portugal, 31.1 for Italy, 19.8 for Austria-Hungary, and 9.7 for Germany. Of course, there were very significant migrations taking place *within* India that were driven by much the same forces as those that drove migrations *from* India: migration to the tea, coffee, and rubber estates in Mysore and Assam and migration to the Punjab and Sind, where government irrigation investment created an enormous addition to hectarage. The movements to Assam were the biggest and the most similar to the international migrations (Davis 1951, chap. 14),[7] and they were also driven by large wage gaps. In summary, India was and is a huge country, so small percentages imply big numbers, but 6.3 million making permanent moves abroad is surprisingly small *especially* given the enormous incentive to move.

The mass migration data for the other main labor surplus area, China, are not as good—perhaps because so much more of it was not contract labor—but we are told that nineteen million Chinese moved to Southeast Asia, the Indian Ocean, and the Pacific in the first global century (McKeown 2004, 157), although "only" 8.2 million were residing abroad in 1922 (Ferenczi and Willcox 1929, 149). As with India, most of China's emigrants were in Asia: 32.4 percent in Formosa,

Hong Kong, and Macao; 28.3 percent in Java, the Straits Settlements, and the Philippines; 18.3 percent in Siam; 16.6 percent in Annam, Burma, and Ceylon; and 4.4 percent in the rest of Asia. While 8.2 million is a big number, it was less than 2 percent of China's 1910 population, implying a very small emigration rate compared with European experience. Yet it was a bigger share of the *male* population, since few women moved: in 1900–1903, almost 89 percent of the Chinese immigrants entering Singapore were men (Huff 1994, 154, 402–403), and the share of Chinese immigrants to the United States that were male in the century before 1928 was 96 percent (Gabaccia 1996, 92). Furthermore, the emigration rates were much higher in the *coastal regions* from which most of the Chinese emigrants originated.[8] Still, these emigrations were small compared to the sending-country populations.

Why was South-South migration over the century after 1820 so low compared with North-North migration? We must at the start dispatch any notion that South-South migration was shut off by policy at the origin. In this case, stated policy and implemented policy are two quite different things. Long before the height of the coolie trade involving China, "imperial edicts ... forbade [e]migration over two dynasties," but they were ignored (Hui 1995, 52). Thus, new emigration was prohibited in 1718, and all Chinese residents abroad were recalled. A decade later, a sentence of banishment was pronounced on those who failed to return, and those who did return were viewed as having committed a capital offense (Ferenczi and Willcox 1929, 149–150). Port authorities and other officials could not and did not implement any of these decrees, but on the contrary, became implicit facilitators for the coolie trade. By 1860, what had been a reality was codified by legalizing the coolie trade in China (Ching-Hwang 1985, chap. 3). It is fair to say, therefore, that Chinese migrations went largely unrestricted during the period of great South-South migrations.

The same is true of India, although in this case there was some active intervention to subsidize the migrations. For example, Trinidad tried, through economic incentives, to stem return migration and encourage immigrants to stay. In 1851, the government of Trinidad started to pay Indian immigrants at the end of their contract $50 to stay, a financial incentive replaced by even more lucrative free land in 1869, and then both in 1873 (Northrup 1995, 134). No doubt partially as a result, Trinidad became the most popular destination for West African immigrants, and the Indian return migration rates from Trinidad were the lowest for any emigrant destination. Thus, 40 percent of the population of Trinidad and Tobago was Indian or of Indian descent in 1938 (Davis 1951, 102).

Government policy was even more immigrant-friendly in Burma. In the early 1870s, Lower Burma was sparsely populated (31 persons per square mile, while Bengal had 269 per square mile), and the British government moved to reclaim swamp and jungle, thus increasing acreage for rice production. The movement of Burmese from Upper Burma into the new acreage was too slow, so in 1874 the government turned to direct recruitment of Indian workers for settlement in Lower Burma (Siok-Hwa 1968, 117–120). The scheme died two years later as the recruits from Calcutta were found to be unfamiliar with farm tasks or simply preferred urban employment. Subsidization and recruiting was tried again in 1877, this time with Madras workers, another scheme of direct recruiting which was soon abandoned. Finally, in 1882 the British government switched from direct recruitment to transport subsidy, and it worked; the subsidy served to reduce by a third the fares for "deck passengers" (immigrant workers taking the cheapest passage) on routes from Calcutta, Ganjam, and Madras. The subsidy was removed in 1884 since "the government decided that enough labourers could be obtained without a subsidy" (Siok-Hwa 1968, 121–122).

If policy was benign and wage gaps huge in the nineteenth century, what, then, explains the low South-South migration rates? The answer is clear, and it is certainly consistent with the European mass emigrations: the cost of the move was very big, and the living standards in India and China were very low, so that no unskilled worker could, on his own, possibly secure sufficient funds to invest in the move and thus to reap the high returns available abroad. Recall table 3.3, which gave the ratio of passenger fare to income per capita at home for European emigrants heading for the United States. The biggest ratio reported there was for the British emigrant in 1821 and before, ranging from about 0.4 to about 0.6. With the subsequent transport revolution, the British ratio fell to 0.1 by the end of the century. The ratios of passage fare to home country per capita income were *much* higher for workers pondering emigration from India and China (Galenson 1984, table 1): for indentured Chinese to the West Indies in 1859–1880, the ratio was 5.3 to 9.9; for indentured Chinese to Hawaii in 1877–1880, it was 6.8; for contract Chinese labor to California in 1877–1880, it was 5.5 to 6.8; and for indentured Indian labor to the West Indies in 1859–1901, it was 3.6 to 11.8. These figures are at minimum *ten times* those for the Atlantic economy.

No poor Indian or Chinese laborer would have made the move under those cost conditions given the inability of such laborers to get loans to finance the move. However, estates and plantations in the export enclaves—or their recruiters—were happy to make the investment, especially as transport costs fell after 1820 and the soaring terms of trade raised the demand for labor on these estates and plantations. Indeed, an index of the ratio of moving costs for an indentured migrant (recruitment, board en route and passenger fare) to the wage at the export enclave fell from four to one between 1852–1874 and 1881–1909.[9]

Government and Private Assisted Passage in the Periphery

As we noted in chapter 2, the problem of high moving costs, poverty constraints, and capital market failure had in the centuries prior to the nineteenth been solved in the most obscene way: by African slavery. That option began to disappear in 1807 when Parliament banned all British subjects from engaging in the slave trade. Other, less-squeamish European colonialists took up some of the slack left by the British, but in 1834 slavery was abolished in the British colonies, and the rest of the world followed suit over subsequent decades. The alternative to slavery was to seek something between it and free labor, contracts whereby the investor would fund the cost of passage, but the migrant would agree to work for the investor (or whomever he or she represented) for a specified number of years and at some below-market wage. In theory, the agreement allowed the investor to recoup and get a market return on his investment, while the migrant was allowed to collect the remaining (big) wage gains from the move.

The most famous form of this type of contract was indentured servitude, but there were a variety of other arrangements in which the most important condition was contract length (Northrup 1995, 115–116). Given these countries' distance from source, Chinese recruits were expensive in Cuba and Peru, thus generating arrangements early in the century in which passage and recruiting costs covered by the recruiter could be recouped over a contract length of eight years. Since they were a little closer to China than were Cuba and Peru and the passage to them from China was cheaper, contracts in the Windward Caribbean colonies and South America were for five years. Hawaii was closer still to China, and contracts there were typically for three years. Clearly, the higher the cost of passage and recruitment, the longer the time necessary to recoup the investment with an adequate market return. By the

1850s, "five-year contracts became the norm in... British colonies... with migrants... closer to their homelands having the right to a free return passage after five years" (Northrup 1995, 116). Since political rhetoric in the mid-nineteenth century viewed long contracts as too close to slavery and a source of abuse, progressive legislation constantly pushed for shorter contracts. The progressives met with less and less resistance as steerage costs fell across the century.

As Ferenczi and Willcox (1929) noted seventy-five years ago, "Chinese emigration was often assisted, [but] compared with free emigration, this type of emigration was of minor importance" (153). The assistance offered to Chinese emigrants took the form of what became known as the credit ticket system, a system that was in operation at least as early as 1823, and by 1887 it accounted for 27 percent of the Chinese arriving in Singapore (Northrup 1995, 59). Under the credit ticket system, "the cost of the passage was advanced to the coolie by brokers acting as agents for large European trading houses, or for coolie ships recruiting on contract to planters and others.... Repayment through earnings gave the coolie more control over the period during which he provided his labour" (Hui 1995, 52).

The vast majority of Indian emigrants were assisted under contracts that varied by length, but the really short-term arrangements were those typical of moves within South and Southeast Asia. These were called *kangani*, and they were common for emigration from southern Asia to nearby areas like Burma and Ceylon (two-thirds of the Indian emigration). The *kangani*, or head man, was the professional recruiter, and often he recruited whole gangs from a given village (Davis 1951, 104). This system started in Ceylon, but it had become common in British Malaya by 1890. In the case of the Burmese migrations, the professional recruiter was called a *maistry*, but the system was similar to the *kangani* (Siok-Hwa 1968, 123).

Plantation employment requirements were driven by demand. As the terms of trade of tropical economies improved, the quest for contract labor gained in intensity; when export prices declined, so did recruitment of contract labor for the estates and plantations. These migrations offer a classic example of elastic labor supplies that goes back to the writings of W. Arthur Lewis. While the employer-recruitment-driven approach to migration (Piore 1979) has gone out of fashion, it still seems an appropriate characterization of these nineteenth-century migrations. Since the numbers migrating were small in relation to the stock of potential emigrants, labor supply at

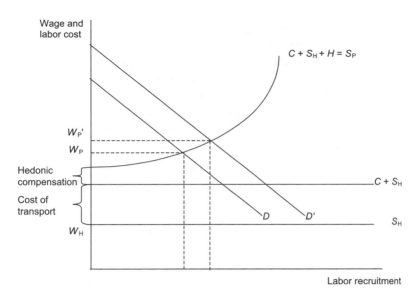

Figure 7.3
Market for contract labor

home was highly elastic, as in figure 7.3. However, the labor supply facing the plantation abroad included the fixed transport cost (C, returned to the investor) and some "hedonic" compensation to the worker (H), who would have preferred to be home, had to forego family formation, and got exposed to high mortality risk. While it seems plausible to expect this hedonic compensation to rise as the search for willing recruits gets harder, the underlying supply curve at the origin (S_H) is horizontal. Thus, a booming terms of trade shifts demand outward (from D to D'), increasing migrant recruitment without appreciably raising labor costs.

Figure 7.3 highlights several other things too. One is that the decline in recruitment costs, especially transportation, must have reduced labor costs facing plantation owners and increased the demand for contract labor. Another is that even though supply was elastic at home, plantation employers' labor costs must have increased when favorable demand shocks raised the compensation premium at the destination. A third is that the wage paid to contract labor was a recruitment-cost-plus-hedonic-premium markup over the real wage at the origin. The hedonic premium must have risen as contract labor requirements increased (at least in the short and medium term), since the marginal indentured migrant needed to be compensated for leaving home, for tolerating oppressive work regimes, and for exposing himself to cholera and other mortality risks. Clearly, the low disamenities-adjusted estate wage (w_P), much lamented by the critics, largely reflected conditions at the origin (w_H). Finally, this simple framework says nothing about who paid for the transport costs, C. But cheap Asian contract labor meant recruiting poor people; the poverty constraint was binding, and hence employers or their representatives had to pay the upfront costs in return for a labor contract.

Compared with Indian migrations, Chinese migrations appear to pose a paradox. While the vast majority of Indian migrants were indentured and otherwise assisted, the vast majority of the Chinese migration was free (Northrup 1995, 52). True, free migration for the Chinese migrant "was often another form of the credit-ticket system, the difference being that the sponsors might be kinfolk or clan associates" (Hui 1995, 52). Still, Chinese emigrations appear to have taken the same form as European emigrations: late in the first global century, a very large share of Chinese migrations were voluntary and unassisted, involving family, clan, and village networks (Lai 2002, 235). This was not true of the indentured Indian migrants. Why the difference? Perhaps the explanation lies in the fact that Chinese workers had been migrating to Southeast Asia for centuries, and thus new emigrants could get funding from previous pioneer emigrants established abroad. Or perhaps the Chinese coolie market was sufficiently old to have gotten much more professional and efficient compared with the newer Indian market, illustrated by the ubiquitous "lodging house" system. Or perhaps the explanation lies in the fact that the move from the South China provinces of Fukien and Kwangtung to Southeast Asia was much shorter in time and distance and thus less costly than that from major Indian sending regions.

The Impact of Immigration and Emigration around the Periphery

The flows from labor surplus to labor-scarce parts of the periphery seemed to obey many of the same laws of motion as those recorded in the European mass migrations. Is it plausible to expect, therefore, that they had the same impact on wage and relative factor price convergence? Perhaps not. While the immigration rates for booming resource-abundant regions in Southeast Asia, eastern and southern Africa, and tropical parts of Latin America seem large enough to have left a mark on relative labor scarcity, it seems far less likely to have been true of China and India, the huge labor surplus regions where the emigration *rates* were so small. In addition, it is difficult to sort out the role of the terms of trade, labor migration, and other factors, as we show in a moment.

Early in this chapter, we predicted that globalization should have fostered *relative* factor price convergence within the periphery, manifested mainly by falling wage-rent ratios in labor-scarce areas and rising wage-rent ratios in labor-abundant areas. That is, labor migration and favorable terms-of-trade shocks should have worked together toward relative factor price convergence. The terms-of-trade boom for each region's exportable should have served, ceteris paribus, to raise the relative price of the region's abundant and cheap factor: thus, it should have raised the relative price of cheap arable hectares in Burma and Siam (relative to labor), while it should have lowered the relative price of expensive arable hectares in South China and Madras (relative to labor). Initial relative scarcities should have been at least partially dissipated by the terms-of-trade boom. At the same time, migration should also have served to raise the price of the abundant and cheap factor: emigration from China and India should have served to raise the relative price of labor and lower the relative price of land at home, while immigration into Burma and Siam should have had the opposite effect. From 1820 to the terms-of-trade peak in the late nineteenth century, mass migration and the terms-of-trade boom should have worked together to create relative factor price convergence within the periphery.

So much for theory. What about fact? Table 7.2 documents the predicted behavior, although it can be documented only starting in 1870 and only for four land-abundant regions in Asia (Burma, Siam, Egypt, and the Punjab) and three land-scarce regions (Japan, Korea, and Taiwan). Wage-rent ratios fell dramatically in land-abundant immigrant regions (Siam being the most spectacular case) and rose dramatically in land-scarce regions (Japan being the best-documented case).

But how much of this predicted wage-rent convergence can be attributed to trade and how much to migration? Here we are on shakier ground, since we simply do not know whether migration or the terms of trade mattered most in the convergence, but our best guess would be the terms of trade. We are pushed to that conclusion by two facts: first, the migrations were, as we have seen, very small shares of total population and labor force in the sending, and perhaps even some receiving, regions;[10] and second, it was changing land rents, not

Table 7.2
Wage-rent ratio trends in the periphery, 1870–1939 (1911 = 100)

	Land abundant				Land scarce		
Period	Burma	Siam	Egypt	Punjab	Japan	Korea	Taiwan
1870–1874		4,699.1		196.7			
1875–1879		3,908.7	174.3	198.5			
1880–1884		3,108.1	276.6	147.2			
1885–1889		2,331.6	541.9	150.8	79.9		
1890–1894	190.9	1,350.8	407.5	108.7	68.6		
1895–1899	189.9	301.3	160.1	92.0	91.3		
1900–1904	186.8	173.0	166.7	99.8	96.1		68.1
1905–1909	139.4	57.2	64.4	92.4	110.4	102.8	85.2
1910–1914	106.9	109.8	79.8	80.1	107.5	121.9	96.6
1915–1919	164.7	202.1	83.5	82.5	104.9	109.4	111.2
1920–1924	113.6	157.9	124.3	81.1	166.1	217.4	140.0
1925–1929		114.9	120.8	72.6	202.4	209.2	134.8
1930–1934		113.1	116.2	50.4	229.5	194.0	130.7
1935–1939		121.6	91.0	33.2	149.9	215.4	123.6

Source: Williamson 2002 (table 1).

wages, that were driving those wage-rent ratios. Indeed, while migration should have served to raise real wages in emigration areas and lower them in the immigration areas, it did not do so, or at least the influence was not sufficiently big to offset other forces. The other force that mattered most was the terms-of-trade boom, producing the $\Delta w > \Delta Pm$ result in labor-scarce estate and plantation locations. The best way to illustrate this is to compare real wage trends reported in table 7.3 for India and Japan with those for Siam and Indonesia. The data are limited, but they certainly do not confirm real wage convergence in the periphery during the first global century. On the contrary, there appears to be real wage *divergence*. Either the terms-of-trade shocks were simply too big and favored the land- and resource-abundant regions, or the net migrations were too small, or both.[11]

The proponents of the migration-was-too-small view are many (Davis 1951, 98), but they all appeal to the small ratio of *net* emigration or even *net* immigration to the population and labor force of the participating regions. We do not disagree, but this view needs far greater support before the case can be considered clinched. And when future research makes the sharper assessment required to give this view the additional support it needs, it should pay more attention to the impact

Table 7.3
Real wage performance in four parts of Asia, 1820–1914 (1913 = 100)

Period	Japan	India	Indonesia	Siam
1820–1824			48	91
1825–1829			49	100
1830–1834	72		49	84
1835–1839	52		49	90
1840–1844	68		50	81
1845–1849	78		50	82
1850–1854	78		51	100
1855–1859	83		63	103
1860–1864	88		75	116
1865–1869	75		78	150
1870–1874	79	184	94	165
1875–1879	74	154	93	156
1880–1884	73	180	113	171
1885–1889	76	186	135	163
1890–1894	64	156	121	130
1895–1899	81	149	130	79
1900–1904	85	142	111	87
1905–1909	90	117	100	68
1910–1914	99	106	99	91

Source: Williamson 2000b (table 1.2).

of remittances on living standards in the sending regions of China and India, the average length of time that the migrant stayed overseas, and the age and sex selection (young adult males), which had a far bigger impact on the labor force in sending and receiving regions (which is rarely measured) than on population. It should also pay more attention to the issue of regional labor market segmentation *within* sending regions. If labor markets in Madras were poorly integrated with other regional labor markets across India, then the relevant denominator for the emigration rate is population or labor force in Madras, not India. The same applies to Fukien and Kwangtung provinces in China.

Race, Prejudice, and Labor Market Segmentation Involving the Periphery

Immigrants from the less-developed parts of the world were effectively shut out of the greater Atlantic economy. Several countries of European settlement began in midcentury to introduce Indian and Chinese labor: New South Wales in the 1840s, Victoria in the early 1850s, and Queensland and Natal a few years later. But as the forces of resistance gathered strength, restrictive legislation escalated in response to the perceived threat of "colored" immigrants (Huttenback 1976, 75), culminating in the total exclusion of Chinese and Indian migrant workers. Victoria led the way in 1857 with a residence tax, and in the 1880s all the Australian colonies moved to increase the ratio of shipping tonnage to colored immigrants that was allowed to land, backing up the measures they enacted with heavy fines. Similarly, small flows of Chinese immigration into California produced the Chinese Exclusion Act of 1882. The response in British Columbia was similar, although the Ottawa government first used a tonnage ratio rule similar to that used in the Australian colonies, with heavy fines imposed for violations, until complete Chinese exclusion was enacted in 1903.

These pre-emptive policies in the immigration regions of the greater Atlantic economy ensured that contract labor was cut off and Chinese and Indian immigration suppressed to no more than a trickle. But it produced tensions in the British Empire, where British subjects were all equal under the crown—at least in principle, if not in fact. Nowhere were these tensions higher than in Natal, where Indian contract labor had been introduced in 1859 and where by 1891 there were nearly as many Indians as Europeans. The key issue there was not contract labor per se (although that attracted criticism too) but the fact that post-indentured Indians and their descendants were denied the right to live and work on equal terms with whites. The solution was Natal Act 14 of 1897, which introduced a dictation test in a European language that was designed to stop further Indian immigration. This same formula became the basis of the White Australia Policy (Act 17 of 1901) introduced by the newly federated Australia, with comparable policies implemented by New Zealand in 1899 and by British Columbia in 1907.[12]

Even though the costs of migration were high and few free Asian migrants would or could move to the distant American West Coast or to Australasia, they were never allowed to gain more than a toehold in the greater Atlantic economy. Thus, the currents of European and non-European international migration were strictly segmented. Where contract labor could be restricted to plantation economies distant from white settlement—particularly in island economies like the West Indies, Mauritius, Reunion, and Fiji—it flourished. Where there was potential for Asian contract laborers to seep into settler economies and to compete head on with workers of European origin, it was fiercely, and for the most part successfully, resisted.

But even in the plantation enclaves, indentured laborers worked under harsh restrictions. Policy toward Indian immigrants in Natal was hardly friendly. In an effort to make the previously indentured immigrants recontract, they were taxed three pounds annually until they did (but 69 percent did not: Northrup 1995, 133). Further discriminatory restrictions on Indian immigrants provoked protests, including those led by the young Mohandas K. Ghandi, and some violence, so much so that many left for home after 1908. Things might have been even worse in Mauritius where, in addition to a tax of two pounds, eighteen shillings imposed on them, "free" Indian immigrants were harassed by vagrancy laws and licenses which were intended to reduce economic alternatives facing them upon the termination of their indentured contracts (Thiara 1995, 66).

Race and prejudice are even easier to document, as is conflict. Immigrant labor's resistance to poor treatment was given frequent illustration by demonstrations: "Mass worker protests...took place in Mauritius in 1872..., but the most significant occurred in Natal.... In Fiji, the most serious strike took place in 1886 [when workers] marched to the agent general of immigration in Suva" (Thiara 1995, 67). Kingsley Davis (1951) reports all of this as "the Indian problem abroad":

In every country to which they went, [the Indians] found themselves a minority differing both culturally and racially from the native population, and under European masters. In these four elements—racial difference, cultural difference, European domination, and government ambivalence—are to be found the main ingredients giving rise to the Indian problem abroad.... There was unmistakeable evidence of a rising prejudice against Indians in such areas as South and East Africa, Burma, and Fiji. (103–104)

In the Caribbean, Indians were often looked upon by whites as heathen and by Africans as scab labor, and "in Trinidad, British Guiana ... and Surinam, ethnic tensions eventually manifested in political confrontations" (Vertovec 1995, 61). Indeed, violent race riots broke out in Burma in 1930 and 1938, resulting in a dramatic fall in Indian immigration to that country and a surge in emigration (Siok-Hwa 1968, 136).

Why Did Assisted Migration Come to an End in the Periphery?

In the 1870s, China moved first to regulate, then to abolish the indentured migrant trade. Portuguese officials in Macao agreed to join the movement and stopped the trade from that port in 1874. Cuba, Peru, and the United States supported the move. British officials continually intervened to shut down the indentured migrant trade from India wherever abuses were reported. All of this culminated in the British government's decision to end the Indian trade as of March 1916 (Northrup 1995, 144–145).

Why did "assisted" migration come to an end? Was it ideals or economics? We think it was economics, and we think the economics had two parts. First, net emigration of all Indian workers—assisted and unassisted—fell off very sharply from the early 1890s to War World I, from 790,000 in 1891–1895 to 383,000 in 1906–1910, and by 1936–1937 it was down to 59,000 (Davis 1951, 99). It appears to us that this sharp drop was induced by poor economic conditions in the estates and plantations on which the Indian emigrants worked, manifested by the secular decline in their terms of trade after a peak somewhere between the 1860s and the 1890s (the exact year varying depending on the export staple involved), after which they fell sharply. Second, the migration of indentured labor fell off much earlier and even more steeply than did total migration. Indian indentured migration reached its peak in the 1850s, Chinese in the 1860s. The decade totals of indentured immigration from all sources—African, Chinese, Indian, Japanese, and others—rose from about 34,000 in the 1830s to almost 420,000 in the 1850s. It never came close to regaining that level thereafter, dropping to 212,000 in the 1880s. It peaked in the 1850s in Mauritius and Reunion and in the 1860s in Cuba, Peru, and the Caribbean. Only in Africa and the Pacific did the peaks come late enough to have been cut off by policy. In short, the share of the Indians and Chinese migrating under indentured contracts fell sharply after the 1850s and 1860s, *long* before restrictive legislation was passed and implemented.

Although some vestiges of contract labor survived into the interwar period, it was largely abolished during or immediately after the First World War. Sharp declines in the price of sugar in the 1880s cut the pace of recruitment to the sugar plantations. Other primary-product-producing plantations elsewhere in the tropics followed suit. In addition, from the turn of the century, the level of protest regarding contract labor increased in India and throughout the British Empire.[13] If the political tide was moving against indentured labor and the demand for it was ebbing, the war-induced shipping shortage was the event that ultimately brought it to a halt by 1917. High wartime transport costs coincided with demonstrations in India, both stopping recruitment on the supply side. The Indian government invoked the formal abolition of recruitment for British Guiana in 1919, for Fiji in 1920, and for Mauritius in 1921.

Economics and idealism combined, through interest group politics, to bring an end to the indentured labor system in the poor periphery. Economics and backlash combined to reduce the mass migrations there. The underlying fundamental forces often accumulated over long periods before sudden shocks caused a radical change in policy, just as was true of New World immigration policy regarding European mass migrations. Declining derived labor demand was the underlying fundamental at work, but it was helped by a rising backlash manifested in a discriminatory reaction to postindentured laborers in the poor periphery and in their outright exclusion from most of the greater Atlantic economy. As the next chapter confirms, it appears that late-nineteenth-century immigrant backlash was on the rise in both center and periphery.

II

The Fall of World Mass Migration

Political Debate and Policy
Backlash

There was a gradual closing of New World doors to immigrants after the 1880s. The doors did not suddenly and without warning slam shut on American immigrants when the U.S. Congress overrode President Wilson's veto of the Literacy Act (aimed at immigrants) in February 1917, or when it passed the Emergency Quota Act of May 1921. Over the half century prior to the Literacy Act, the United States had been imposing restrictions on what had previously been free immigration (e.g., contract labor laws, Chinese exclusion acts, exclusion of classes of immigrants, and head taxes). And the United States was hardly alone. Argentina, Australia, Brazil, and Canada enacted similar measures, although the timing was sometimes different, and the policies often took the form of an enormous drop in, or even disappearance of, large immigrant subsidies rather than of outright exclusion. Contrary to the conventional wisdom, therefore, there was not simply one big regime switch around World War I from free (and often subsidized) immigration to quotas, but rather an evolution toward more-restrictive immigration policy in the high-wage New World. Attitudes changed slowly and over a number of decades; they didn't change all at once.

What explains this evolution in immigration policy? A number of candidates have been nominated: increasing racism and xenophobia, a rising immigrant threat to the dominant Anglo-Saxon culture, widening ethnicity gaps between previous and current immigrants, increasing numbers of immigrants, decreasing quality of immigrants, the threat of even lower-quality immigrants, crowding out native unskilled workers, deteriorating labor market conditions and rising inequality, greater awareness of that inequality by the powerful (informed by activist reformers), and greater voting power in the hands of those hurt most: the working poor. The goal of this chapter is to identify the fundamentals that might underlie changes in immigration policy, to distinguish between the impact of these long-run fundamentals and the determinants of short-run timing, and to clarify the differences between market and nonmarket influences on the evolution of and changes in immigration policy. In addition, the chapter will have something to say about the extent to which policy waited for immigrants to have their impacts on labor markets and the extent to which it tried instead to anticipate those impacts by responding to the immigrations themselves. Finally, we ask which countries were most sensitive to immigration policies elsewhere and to what extent the biggest among them, the United States, set the pace for the rest.

A Word about Emigration Policy

No doubt sending-country policy toward emigrants has never played the role that receiving-country immigration policy has. Still, it has varied across time and space in predictable ways that deserve some of our attention.

Except for a modest lapse in the 1870s, Britain maintained a fairly stable and strong policy of emigrant support from midcentury onward (O'Rourke and Williamson 1999, figure 10.1), although that policy certainly had a powerful proempire bias. Not only was there no restriction on emigration, but Britain even took an active role in disseminating information to potential migrants about job prospects overseas and actually offered some significant subsidies for the cost of overseas passage.

British emigration policy was not always as benign as it was between 1850 and 1930, nor was emigration policy that benign in poorer parts of Europe. Recall that in chapter 3, we noted that many early European industrializers, fearing skilled artisan (brain) drain, tried to restrict emigration. Prior to the 1820s, Britain actually prohibited the emigration of artisans, and the Passenger Act curtailed eighteenth-century emigration from Ireland and Scotland. Many German states had tried to prohibit emigration before the 1820s, and Sweden had emigration restrictions before 1840. Since so much of the European emigration at that time involved skilled artisans, such restrictions certainly were predictable: these governments wanted to keep scarce factors at home. They were not always successful, however, since most countries on the Continent had porous land borders. And in spite of its stated policy, England had been a net emigration country since the sixteenth century (Wrigley and Schofield 1981, 528–529). In any case, as the cost of emigration dropped during the transition decades after the 1820s (chapter 3) and as European emigration became less a move of the rich and more of the poor, relative factor endowments offered less reason for emigration restriction. After all, unskilled labor was the abundant factor in Europe and a poor-law burden. Military manpower needs offered another reason for eighteenth- and early-nineteenth-century government restrictions on emigration. But after the Napoleonic Wars and under Pax Britannica, European conflicts diminished, and military manpower needs fell off sharply.

Since the political motivations for keeping emigration restrictions evaporated in the early nineteenth century, it is hardly surprising that emigration prohibitions on British artisans were repealed in 1825 and remaining restrictions on others were eliminated in 1827. Britain's restrictive Passenger Act was repealed in 1827. Germany never tried to police emigration restrictions after 1820, and Sweden repealed its emigration restrictions in 1840. In short, by the middle of the transition period between 1820 and 1860, western European governments had adopted a laissez-faire attitude toward emigration.

The backward parts of Europe were slower to adopt liberal policies toward emigration. Portugal still restricted the emigration of young men of military age. In response, young Portuguese men and boys avoided the restriction by misreporting their ages and illegally emigrating to Brazil (Baganha 1990). Italian emigrants from rural areas lost their official claim to the community safety net if they stayed away too long, thus encouraging return migration. And as chapter 2 pointed out, Russia retained serfdom until 1861, tying potential emigrants to their villages before and even for some time after (Domar and Machina 1984; Burds 1998; Eltis 2002a).

Measuring Immigration Policy

The standard view of globalization history seems to be that there was an exogenous—and this is the key word—collapse of the world economy after 1914, a deglobalization implosion driven by two world wars, a period of fragile peace, the Great Depression, and a cold war. The late twentieth century, according to this view, marked a successful struggle to reconstruct the pre–World War I global economy. This view ignores the fact that tariffs protecting economies in the European periphery, in Latin America, and in the non-Latin New World were very high and on the rise prior to 1914 (Coatsworth and Williamson

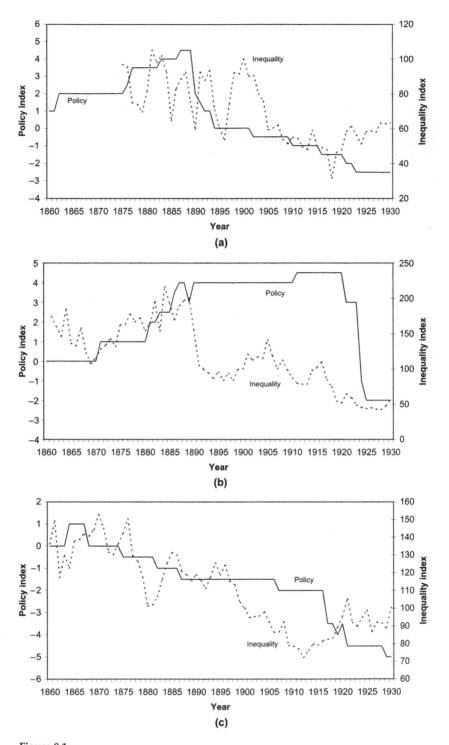

Figure 8.1
Policy and inequality: (a) Argentina, (b) Brazil, (c) United States, (d) Australia, (e) Canada. *Source:* Timmer and Williamson 1996.

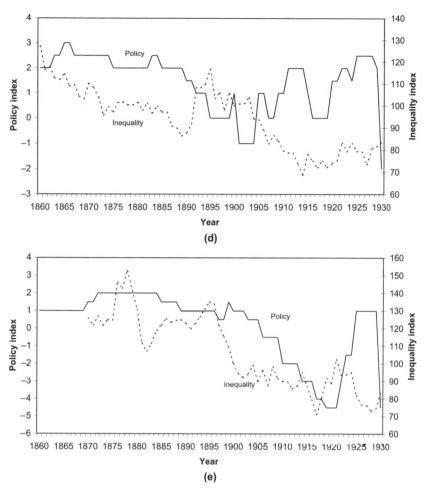

Figure 8.1
(continued)

2004; Williamson 2004, 2005) and that immigration policy was becoming more restrictive (O'Rourke and Williamson 1999, chap. 10). To ignore this fact is to miss important evidence of globalization backlash.

How do we construct an index that can quantify immigration policy? We want one that reflects policy stance toward immigration, not one that attempts to measure the impact of immigration policies. Such an index could then be used to assess the extent to which globalization backlash was at work and, if so, to identify the form that it took. Following the lead of political scientists, recent work has designed a policy index that ranges from +5 to −5, covering the seventy years from 1860 to 1930 (Timmer and Williamson 1996, 1998). A positive score denotes a proimmigration policy, typically including comprehensive subsidies for immigrants' overseas passage, temporary housing for them upon arrival, free transportation for them to the interior, and nondiscriminatory treatment of immigrants relative to natives, including the availability of cheap public land. A negative score denotes anti-immigration policy, typically an outright ban on some groups of immigrants, quotas on other groups, head taxes, literacy tests, and discriminatory treatment of immigrants after arrival. A score of zero denotes policy neutrality (politically unrestricted and unassisted migration) or a wash between conflicting pro- and anti-immigration policies. It takes some doing to summarize a country's immigration policies with a score for each year, but international economists struggle with the same problem in gauging just how open a country's trade policy is at any point in time (Anderson and Neary 1994; Anderson 1995; Sachs and Warner 1995; Rodríguez and Rodrik 2001).

The solid lines in figure 8.1 are quite clear about the very long run. Despite universal openness to immigration in the 1860s, the doors to the New World were effectively closed by 1930. Argentina's index (figure 8.1a) dropped from +4.5 in the late 1880s to −2.5 in the mid-1920s, a 7-point fall (out of a possible 10). Brazil's index (figure 8.1b) underwent a similar decline, although it all came in a rush at the end of the period. The U.S. index (figure 8.1c) fell from 0 in the early 1860s to −5 by 1930, a 5-point fall. Australia's index (figure 8.1d) fell from +3 in the mid-1860s to −1 shortly after the turn of the century and to −2 in 1930, for a total 5-point fall. Canada's index (figure 8.1e) fell from +2 in the mid-1870s to −4.5 by 1930, a 6.5-point fall. The evolution of immigration policy varied widely among these five countries over the seven decades covered by the index: Argentina and the United States exhibited a steady drift away from free immigration; Brazil remained open much longer, suddenly slamming the door shut in the 1920s; and the trend in Canada reversed itself in the 1920s, while that in Australia did so more than once over the period.

Although there are a few cases of remarkable short-term variance, strong policy persistence is the more-notable aspect of figure 8.1. Immigration policy was very slow to change, sometimes constant over a decade or more, even though there was often intensive political debate underlying that apparent quiescence. The best examples of this stability are Brazil over the three decades from 1890 to 1920, a period that ended in 1921 when immigration restrictions were imposed, and the United States from 1888 to 1916, a period that ended with the override of President Wilson's veto of the anti-immigrant Literacy Act in 1917.

Given that immigration policy was so slow to change, it is important to look for long-run fundamentals that were responsible for its evolution and distinguish them from short-run influences on the timing of changes in it.

Immigration Policy before the 1930s: Searching for Hypotheses

As we have seen, immigration flows have always been sensitive to differentials in wages and unemployment rates among countries. But the literature suggests that immigration *policy* has also been sensitive to labor market conditions.[1] For example, there was a strong push for immigration restrictions in the United States in the late 1890s, a time of economic recession and high unemployment (Goldin 1994). At that time, however, the rate of immigration slowed dramatically, reaching a nadir in 1897, the same year that the first vote on immigration restriction was taken in the House of Representatives. Similarly, Australian inflows dropped sharply in the recession of the 1890s, when attitudes toward immigrant subsidies hardened (Pope and Withers 1994). These events would seem to suggest that the impetus to restrict immigration was far more sensitive to deteriorating labor market conditions than to immigration magnitudes, regardless of what observers at the time may have believed was the source of high unemployment and/or poor real wage gains.

On the other hand, the ethnic composition of immigrants has always been a factor in the politics of restriction. Australia maintained a strict policy aimed at keeping the country one of British and Irish descent and certainly not "yellow" (Pope and Withers 1994). The United States banned immigrants from China in 1882 and immigrants from all of Asia in 1917 (Green 1995). Increasing demands for restriction of immigration in the 1880s and 1900s paralleled an increase in the relative numbers of immigrants from southern, central, and eastern Europe, the so-called new immigrants. Partly as a result of these policies, by 1890 the world labor market was almost completely segmented into what economists today would call North and South (Lewis 1978b; Hatton and Williamson 1994b). What is difficult to sort out is whether these policies were a result of racism and xenophobia or whether ethnic origin merely served to signal, however imperfectly, the human capital content or quality of the immigrants (Foreman-Peck 1992).

Nor is this all, since any understanding of immigration policy in a particular country requires us to pay close attention to the influence of immigration policies implemented by other countries. Did Latin America, by implementing its own restrictions, anticipate a wave of deflected European emigrants when the United States imposed (or even debated imposing) quotas? Or did it wait instead until the deflected wave flooded its own labor markets, only then dealing with the problem? Did Australia and Canada take their cues from U.S. immigration and British emigration policy? What about even smaller immigrant countries: did they anticipate how policy and labor market conditions in the bigger immigrant countries would affect their own?

Who Had the Vote?

The two central questions for any political economy model of immigration policy are first, who gains and who loses? and second, who decides the policy? Let us focus briefly on the second, specifically, who had the vote in the second half of the nineteenth century?

A lively literature has emerged recently which explores the relationship between growth, inequality, and suffrage in the Americas (Engerman, Haber, and Sokoloff 2000; Sokoloff and Engerman 2000),[2] and it should be helpful in identifying when and where anti-immigration policies emerge in the New World. In 1850, 12.9 percent of the U.S. population could vote. If this figure seems small, consider that it almost doubles when restricted to males (25.3 percent), doubles again when restricted to male adults (52.3 percent), increases still further when restricted to white adult males (60.9 percent), and increases still more when it is restricted to citizens. In any case, there was no wealth or literacy requirement for voting in the United States in 1850, and there was no other country that had a higher political participation (i.e., the share in total population eligible to vote): the comparable figure for Argentina was 1.8 percent in 1896, that for Brazil was 2.2 percent in 1894, that for Canada was 7.7 percent in 1867, that for Chile 1.6 was percent in 1869, that for Ecuador was 2.8 percent in 1888, and that for Britain was 3.5 percent in 1832 (Sokoloff and Engerman 2000, 225–226; Engerman and Sokoloff 2003, 43). Only after the 1867 Reform Act did the vote reach down far enough in Britain so that "working-class voters became the majority in all urban constituencies," and only after 1870 did "all adult males over the age of 25" have the vote in Germany (Acemoglu and Robinson 2000, 1184).

In short, by the end of the transition to mass migration and at the end of two decades of American immigration rates that were the highest the country would ever record, the free, white workingman— native-born or naturalized—had the vote in the United States, long before most of the world's male adults. Thus, the workingman had an important voice in the choice of immigration policy in the United States, and the rest of the non-Latin overseas immigrant regions were not far behind. But even in Latin America, where suffrage lagged behind that in the rest of the New World, U.S. working-class voters had an impact on immigration policy to the extent that Latin American policy followed the U.S. lead.

Three Models of Immigration Policy

Let us now return to the first question raised above: Who gains and who loses as a result of immigration? There is a clear consensus on this question: a country's resident wage earners lose in the face of more immigrants, as the labor pool swells and wages sag. If the immigrants are mostly unskilled, then the unskilled native-born lose the most. Owners of other factors of production—land, capital, and perhaps even skills—gain to the extent that the more-abundant unskilled labor supply makes these other factors more productive. Land rents go up as more labor is applied to a fixed acreage. Profits go up as more labor is applied to a fixed stock of capital. Skill premia rise as more unskilled labor works with the same supply of skilled labor. In addition, the middle class and rich (i.e., those who hold or control the other factors of production) also gain to the extent that they consume heavily the services of unskilled labor. Having said that much, two caveats deserve to be stressed. As we showed in chapters 5 and 6, most attempts to measure the impact of mass migration on wages prior to 1914 have found that wages were pushed down by immigration. But one historical study found that wages in Australia actually increased with immigration, if only marginally (Pope and Withers 1994). This perverse Australian result could be explained if immigrants augmented labor demand enough to offset their impact on increased labor supply: for example, by working previously unsettled land, or by inducing an accumulation response as capital from the home country chased after labor.[3] If labor demand keeps pace with labor supply, native labor is apparently not hurt by immigration. The problem for politicians and their constituents, however, is to distinguish between labor demand conditions that are dependent on the immigrants and those that are not. Under conditions of sagging wages and high unemployment, policy might still be used to keep out new immigrants—and even to send old immigrants home—even if their presence had nothing to do with the deteriorating labor market conditions.

Alternatively, suppose over the business cycle wages were sticky downward and unrelated to the size of the unemployment pool.[4] Immigration in this case could not have had any effect on wages, but it would have added to the number of unemployed. But suppose, too, that the new immigrants were last hired and first fired (Hatton and Williamson 1995; Collins 1997). Under these conditions, employed natives would not benefit from immigrant departure; capitalists would not gain either, since wages would not fall; and the unemployed native-born would not gain, since no new jobs would be created. But the unemployed may express their discontent by strikes and street violence. While perceptions of immigrants as the root cause of the problems may differ from the economic reality, all sides may nonetheless respond to the discontent by uniting in favor of immigration restriction. It appears this alignment of interests is exactly what happened in the United States during the 1890s (Goldin 1994) in response to discontent over economic conditions, some of which were attributed to the influx of immigrants.

Suppose, as we previously argued, that new immigrants actually *do* crowd natives out of the labor market, rather than being the last hired and first fired. Under these alternative conditions, what we have called guestworker effects should minimize the impact of an economic downturn on native-born unemployment, as recent (but now jobless) immigrants return home. That is, immigrants do voluntarily what a restrictive immigration policy aims to do. Indeed, immigrants do it even better. A policy of immigrant exclusion can do no better than reduce the gross inflow to zero, while voluntary return migration in bad times can drive up the gross outflow to levels high enough to make net immigration negative during recessions, as it did in the 1930s. While these guestworker effects were certainly present in the United States in the 1890s, the return migration flows were never big enough to take a really big bite out of the high unemployment rates typical of that critical decade (chapter 5).

Most discussions of the politics of immigration assume that the interests of capital and labor are divided on this issue. Land ownership might have mattered too, as a determinant of where one's interests lay in regard to immigration, especially in the late nineteenth century, when agriculture was still a very big sector, especially in the overseas destinations for so many European emigrants.[5] Assume that individuals receive their incomes from one of the following three sources: wages, profits, or land rents. Depending on the voting franchise, the government maximizes a weighted objective function that includes rents, profits, and wages of native labor (but not immigrant labor). The critical question is whether immigrant and native labor are complements or substitutes in production: if they are substitutes, then immigration hurts native wages. Most economic historians think they were substitutes in the late-nineteenth-century U.S. economy.[6] Thus, the larger the weight that a country's politicians attached to labor interests, the more restrictive its immigration policy; the larger the weights they attached to capitalist or landlord interests, the more liberal its immigration policy. According to this reasoning, labor scarcity in the New World should have fostered immigration restrictions, since labor scarcity and strong working-class political clout went together.

Now expand the argument to include two types of immigrant labor, skilled and unskilled. Suppose further that skilled immigrant labor is a complement to domestic labor, whereas unskilled immigrant labor is a substitute. We would then expect to see a policy that encourages immigration of skilled workers and discourages unskilled ones. James Foreman-Peck (1992) argues that this concern over skill levels of immigrants, rather than racism or xenophobia, was responsible for late-nineteenth-century policies in the Americas that restricted Asian immigration and for policies in South Africa that restricted African immigration. It might also be responsible for the U.S. immigration policies being debated in the quarter century before World War I, particularly literacy requirements and quotas favoring the higher-quality old immigrants.

Although the work by Foreman-Peck does not implement a formal empirical test, his discussion of Argentina, Britain, South Africa, and the United States indicates that some of the facts are consistent with his theory. For example, landed interests were largely in control of Argentina's immigration policy, and the Argentinian government offered generous immigration subsidies to attract farm laborers from the Mediterranean. In contrast, the United States had a more-universal franchise, rejected subsidies, and gradually closed the door as the frontier itself was closed (by 1890, or so said the census commissioner at the time).

Goldin (1994) takes a different approach. Following a long tradition in American historiography that has focused on sectional interests, Goldin looks at regional splits and rural-urban differences in the United States in a way consistent with a median-voter model. She assumes that individual senators and congressmen pursued policies that favored their constituents, in proportion to the numbers represented by each urban, rural, and regional interest group. The passage of the anti-immigrant Literacy Act, which failed in its first attempt at passage in 1897 and was finally successful in 1917, seems to have been the result of two (often opposing) forces: demographic changes and changes of heart. The changes of heart were many. Goldin suggests that capitalists were for the first time aligned with labor in opposing immigration during the recession years of the 1890s when unemployment was high and wages sticky downward. In later years, faced with full employment and rising wages, capital would shift back to its more-typical proimmigration stance. The South would shift to an anti-immigration stance, a change of heart probably motivated by the urge to protect its relative population share and voting clout in Congress. Finally, the Midwest, fairly pro-immigration in the 1890s, would undergo an anti-immigration switch following World War I. Goldin argues that this was mostly a change of heart on the part of older immigrant groups, pushed to patriotism by the war.

Where does demographic change enter the story? Goldin finds that the probability that a legislator would vote for immigration restrictions was negatively related to the proportion of foreign-born in the district he represented and was also negatively related to its level of urbanization. This relationship suggests that what we might now call family reunification effects were operating in the cities. A large stock of urban foreign-born voters created a political environment favorable to open immigration, since the flows of new immigrants flooding the cities were likely to be from the same region as the stock, and the migration must have involved some family, village, and kin reunification between the immigrants and the resident foreign-born. Since cities were on the rise, proimmigration interests increasingly made themselves heard.

More important than either of these nonmarket forces, however, was the impact of increasing immigration on wages and the subsequent effect on votes. Goldin finds, especially after the turn of the century, a significant negative impact of immigration on wages, a result consistent with other historical studies we reviewed in chapters 5 and 6. This change in real wages is, in turn, a significant explanatory variable in accounting for the 1917 congressional vote to override the presidential veto of the Literacy Act. The higher the growth in wages in his district, the less likely was the congressman to vote for an override (and thus for restriction).

These two findings—that wages influenced U.S. immigration policy and that immigrants influenced wages in American labor markets— are useful in our comparative assessment of immigration policy in the New World. However, for our purposes, it is necessary only that politicians and their constituents *believed* that immigration retarded wage advance, not that it actually did so, for it to have affected their votes on immigration policy issues. It appears that they did.

William Shughart, Robert Tollison, and Mwangi Kimenyi (1986) take a somewhat different approach, examining shifting degrees of enforcement of immigration restrictions. Workers want high wages and (if they have the vote) pressure politicians to enforce immigration restrictions. Capitalists and land owners want lower wages, and they try to reduce enforcement. The model predicts that as the economy goes through business cycles, the ideal policy mix shifts, resulting in changes in the degree of immigration restriction enforcement. The authors test their model using data from the United States from 1900 to 1982, and the results support their theory. Even taking into account official changes in immigration policy, the size of the enforcement budget, and the party in the White House, the degree of enforcement is significantly, and negatively, related to real gross national product (GNP). Unemployment and the real wage are also significant predictors of enforcement, but not so consistently as real GNP. Had these authors also looked at U.S. policy toward indentured labor contracts prior to 1900, they would have seen the same correlation: harsh enforcement during slumps, soft enforcement during booms.

Until quite recently, these were the only studies that offered empirical support for any theory of immigration policy in the century before World War II. All three studies addressed the role of labor markets, but they limited their attention to the *absolute* gains and losses associated with some given immigration policy. What about *relative* gains and losses? What about income distribution and inequality?

Income Distribution and the Politics of Immigration: Some Qualifications

While we may still wish to argue over how much, recent debate has agreed that immigration can create more inequality in receiving countries. Certainly this has been true of recent experience in the United States, but the debate has spilled over to confront European immigration as well. Chapter 6 showed that the distributional impact of migration is confirmed for the late nineteenth century, since inequality increased in receiving countries and decreased in sending countries. How should policy have responded?

Citizens might vote in favor of immigration restrictions for other reasons than simply those derived from special interests. For example, rational and farsighted voters might consider the impact of immigration on future economic growth. If they were to do so, how would they assess it? Immigration induces falling wages and greater inequality, but does that inequality augment or inhibit economic growth? The traditional Smithian view had it that the rising inequality would place relatively more income in the hands of those who save, thus raising the investment rate and growth. Modern political economists take a different view, arguing that if a country lets its poorest voters become too poor, richer voters might join poorer voters to pass distortionary redistributive policies that can slow growth (Alesina and Perotti 1994; Forbes 2000; Lindert 2003). What are the facts? Economists do not yet have a clear answer—especially for the years prior to the 1930s when government redistributive intervention was so modest.

Citizens might vote for immigration restriction for other reasons too. For example, they might dislike, and fear the results of, the increased inequality around them or the deterioration of the living standards of their unskilled neighbors.

Trade, Immigration, and the U.S. Nineteenth-Century Policy Paradox

The literature on the political economy of trade policy is mature and large. Models of endogenous tariffs flourish, and some new historical evidence now helps us choose among them. A review of this trade policy literature should be relevant if one believes, as did Eli Heckscher and Bertil Ohlin (Flam and Flanders 1991), that trade is a partial substitute for labor migration. If these two factors are partial substitutes, then policies toward them should be influenced by similar political economy forces, resulting in similar open or closed attitudes toward them.

Who are the interest groups in trade theory? In the short run, when factors are assumed to be relatively immobile, protection of a given industry (such as textiles or steel) will benefit both capital and labor in that sector. As local industrial prices rise in response to protection, the value-marginal product of all factor inputs there increases, including wages and profits. In the long run, when capital and labor have time to relocate, protection helps the scarce factor (labor in rich countries), since the import-competing industries typically use more of the scarce factor. Most models of trade policy take the short-run approach, focusing on the pressure from specific industries, although some of the empirical tests focus on the long-run importance of factor endowments (the most notable example being Rogowski 1989). Stephen Magee, William Brock, and Leslie Young (1989) presented some evidence for the United States from 1900 to 1988 which exploited the median-voter model; Jonathan Pincus (1977) and Howard Marvel and Edward Ray (1983) also used U.S. history, this time to find support for the pressure group approach. Most recently, however, one of the present authors (Williamson 2005) has used a thirty-five-country world sample covering the period 1870–1938 to show that Stolper-Samuelson forces were very important in explaining different tariff levels across countries and changing tariff levels over time. There were many other powerful forces at work in the century before World War II, one of which was that high tariffs in the New World were compensation for the scarce factor, labor, and for the import-competing sector, industry. Similarly, high tariffs in Europe were compensation for the scarce factor there, land, and the import-competing sector, agriculture.

There is an obvious historical symmetry between trade and immigration policy. While trade policy may seek to protect wages by restricting imports made with cheap labor, immigration policy may seek to protect wages by restricting growth of the labor pool. If trade is a partial substitute for labor migration, tariffs and immigration restrictions should go hand in hand. The important point is that trade policy can easily undo what immigration policy has done and vice versa: thus, we expect consistency between them. How, then, does one account for the fact that between the 1820s and 1870s, the United States had high tariffs,[7] while it also maintained a free immigration policy? What accounts for this policy paradox?

The best historical illustration of this policy paradox is offered by antebellum immigration. Between 1820 and the mid-1840s, the annual
immigration rate in the United States averaged around four or five per
thousand, but it rose dramatically in 1847 following the failure of the
potato crop in Ireland and elsewhere on the Continent, fueled further
by European political instability in 1848 (Ferrie 1999, 35). As a result,
the U.S. immigration rate soared in the 1850s, peaking at fifteen per
thousand in one of those years, a rate even higher than those reached
in the 1900s. We know that the impact of this flood of immigrants
was substantial, although it was muted by an equally spectacular westward migration and settlement as well as an accelerating rate of capital
accumulation. Most importantly, anti-immigration feelings appeared
at the time in the popular press, nativist political organizations got
more powerful and louder, and organized labor rebelled, sometimes
violently:

The pressures immigration placed on labor markets, particularly in the urban
Northeast, produced a remarkable backlash in the 1850s. The first response of
native workers was increased labor militancy: dozens of new labor organizations sprang to life...and a wave of more than 400 strikes swept the
country.... The second response was political: increasing support for those
who preached the nativist creed.... [In particular], the Order of the Star
Spangled Banner (popularly known as the "Know-Nothings") grew from a secret band of 43 adherents in 1852 to a national political organization boasting
one million followers in 1854. (Ferrie 1999, 162)

Recall that by the 1850s, urban workingmen in the United States had
the vote, and it is clear that they were using their voice! Also recall
that this was a period of high tariffs in the United States (although
they were to become much higher after the Civil War). However, the
Know-Nothings never advocated "the restriction of immigration. They
merely suggested extending the period before which immigrants could
become naturalized (and therefore eligible to vote)," a party position
that suggests a fear of immigrant political power but not of economic
impact (Ferrie 1999, 162; see also Anbinder 1992).

    How can we account for this policy paradox? As we noted previ-
ously, in the 1850s, the U.S. political system produced tariffs on
trade—favoring industry and labor in the industrial Northeast—but
free immigration, exposing resident labor to immigrant competition.
Why the paradox in the 1850s, and why did it evaporate by the turn of
the century?

We do not have any firm answers, but we can offer some plausible speculation. Explanations for protection are not hard to find: industrial interests and the labor they hired were being compensated for the damage created when the United States entered the global economy and was invaded with imports of manufactures. These conditions may have also prevailed in the 1890s, but they were far weaker (Wright 1990). Why, then, were tariffs even higher in the 1890s? Probably because the South (the major exporting and thus free trade region) lost the Civil War to the protectionist North, and certainly because population (i.e., voter) growth was much slower in the South than in the North between the 1850s and 1890s. Why do free immigration policies prevail in the 1850s while restrictionist forces win in 1917? Labor absorption rates mattered (Williamson 1982). First, western land settlement was faster in the middle of the century than at any time in U.S. history. By comparison, the commissioner of the U.S. census asserted in 1890 that the frontier was closed. Second, the rate of capital accumulation—aided by British capital inflows—soared to levels that were never exceeded in U.S. history (Williamson 1979). Third, the immigrants were more positively selected (of higher quality) in the 1850s than in the 1890s, and as we subsequently show, it was the interaction of poor immigrant quality with high immigrant numbers that mattered. These forces appear to have suppressed immigrant restriction in the 1850s, since real wages surged in spite of the immigration (Margo 1992). They did not surge in the 1890s, however, and voters thought immigration was the cause. In short, labor absorption rates were much higher in the 1850s than in the 1890s.

What Explains Immigration Restriction? A Menu of Hypotheses

This brief review of the literature offers some promising explanations for the New World retreat from open (and often subsidized) immigration policies to increasingly restrictive policies, which reached a crescendo with the immigration quotas imposed after World War I. First, immigration policy may respond to either the quantity or the quality of immigration, or both. Thus, the size of the immigrant flow as a share of the native labor force is one obvious candidate for explaining immigration policy, although the experience of the 1890s has already suggested that labor market conditions might have mattered far more. The quality of a country's immigrants measured in comparison with the native labor force, is another candidate. The vast majority of nineteenth-century immigrants came from and entered unskilled jobs. Some had good health, high levels of literacy, on-the-job training, and considerable exposure to work discipline. Others did not. Immigrant quality and quantity were highly correlated prior to World War I. The shift in immigrant source from higher-wage to lower-wage areas of Europe coincided with the rise in immigration rates. It seems likely that these two effects reinforced each other in their impact on policy.

Second, immigration policy may respond to labor market conditions. The likelihood of this occurring may be increased by distinguishing more sharply between short-run and long-run influences on such policy. Unemployment, wage growth, and other macroeconomic indicators should serve to isolate the role of business cycles, trade crises, world price shocks, and other short-run events that might influence the timing of immigration policy. Long-run labor market fundamentals should be captured by the behavior of real unskilled wages (a measure of absolute performance) or by the behavior of unskilled wages relative to average incomes (a measure of relative performance). Such a proxy for inequality was used in chapter 6, and it is used again here. The right-hand side of each panel in figure 8.1 (scaled 1900 = 100) is keyed to this index of inequality in the five countries, represented by the broken lines in the figure.[8] The inequality index gauges the unskilled worker's economic performance against that of an average that includes profits, farm rents, house rents, skilled workers' wages, and white-collar incomes. It is a measure that politicians and voters can most easily understand. The use of this measure in the analysis presented here does not assume that immigration had a powerful influence on living standards of the working poor in the New World. It assumes instead that politicians and voters *believed* that immigration had a powerful influence on the living standards of the working poor. Whether it was absolute or relative wage performance that mattered is an empirical issue, but figure 8.1 suggests that inequality is a promising explanation, since the secular fall in the inequality variable is everywhere (other than Brazil) highly correlated with the retreat from open immigration policies.

Results from a opinion surveys of some Kansas and Michigan workers conducted in the middle of the 1890s depression might illustrate the potential of immigrant quantity and labor market conditions in explaining policy. Here is what these workers said in response to questions put to them by interviewers from their state labor bureaus:

62.8 percent of 438 Kansas wage earners surveyed in 1895 thought immigration should be "restricted" and another 24 percent thought it should be outright "suppressed," leaving only 8.5 percent happy with free immigration; 67.5 percent of the 992 Kansas wage earners surveyed in 1897 thought immigration should be restricted and another 24 percent thought it should be suppressed, leaving only 3.7 favoring the status quo; about half of the 5,524 Michigan railway employees surveyed in 1895 thought that immigration injured their occupation; and 61.9 percent of the Michigan owners of public conveyances in 1895 thought immigration hurt their business through greater competition, with 92.1 percent favoring immigrant restriction.[9]

Third, a lagged dependent variable should help identify just how slowly policy responds even to long-run labor market fundamentals, especially in democratic countries in which debate over these issues, and the resolution of bicameral and other differences, takes time. This is illustrated very clearly by the United States in the period between the first vote on the proposed anti-immigration Literacy Act in the 1890s and the override of President Wilson's veto in 1917. When the House of Representatives first voted in 1897, 86 percent of those voting favored the literacy test and thus more restriction of immigration. Yet it took twenty more years to get the Senate to agree, to defeat the presidential veto, and to get the act on the books (Goldin 1994, table 7.1).

Fourth, a country's immigration policy may be influenced by the immigration policies of other countries, either directly or indirectly. If the country anticipates the influence of immigration policies abroad on immigration inflows at home, the impact is direct. Since the labor market in the United States was so enormous relative to that of the rest of the New World, and since so many European emigrants went there,[10] it seems very unlikely that the United States paid much attention to the immigration policies being introduced elsewhere. Australia may have paid little attention to other countries' immigration policies as well, to the extent that it was at least partially shielded from events in the United States by British Empire settlement policy, a policy of labor market segmentation. In contrast, Argentina and Brazil must have paid close attention to the immigration policies of the United States, since they could reasonably expect the marginal European emigrant to be pulled from or pushed toward Latin America in response to less- or more-restrictive policy in the United States. Presumably, authorities might have moderated the impact of those policy changes abroad by mimicking U.S. policy before being confronted with the actual migrant response. It seems likely that the same might have been at least partially true of Canada, which, in spite of British Empire settlement policy, had to accommodate that long porous border with its big neighbor to the south.

Fifth, what nonmarket forces remain after these market forces have been allowed to have their impact? After immigrant quality is controlled for, did racism have an independent influence? Did the resident population have less sympathy for free immigration if new immigrants were not of the same ethnic origin as the previous immigrants? Did the political response to market events change as the working poor found their political power increasing?

Finally, there was the belief that immigrants threatened the mainstream culture of a country, not only by their numbers, but also to the extent that immigrants marry younger and have larger families than the native-born, rhetoric often heard during the eugenics movement. Although Samuel Huntington (2004) may fear today's Mexican immigrants for this very reason, fears of this type were never borne out at the end of the first global century, since immigrant fertility converged rapidly on the U.S. norm (King and Ruggles 1990; Guinnane, Moehling, and ÓGráda 2004).

What Explains Immigrant Restrictions? Some Evidence

The empirical literature on the determinants of immigration policy is very new, but the main outlines are beginning to emerge (Timmer and Williamson 1996, 1998). Table 8.1 gives a representative regression result, based on a panel data set including our five New World countries and covering the years 1860 through 1930.

The most consistent effect reported in table 8.1 is that immigration policy was slow to change (i.e., the coefficient on the lagged dependent variable is positive, big, and significant). This was especially true of Brazil and the United States: in the latter case, the result is driven by the 1888–1916 period, which included twenty years of congressional debate, ending in the 1917 anti-immigrant Literacy Act and the quotas which followed; and in the former case, the result is driven by the 1890–1920 period, when heavily subsidized immigration (financed by fat export earnings generated by high coffee prices) was replaced by restriction (when export earnings contracted as coffee prices plunged). It is worth noting that where historical persistence was strongest, the shift in policy, from open to closed, was greatest. Substantial immigra-

Table 8.1
Determinants of immigration policy, circa 1860–1930

$Policy_t = 0.809\ Policy_{t-1} + 0.015\ WtoY_{t-1} + 0.005\ WageR_{t-1} + 0.009\ Unemp_t$
  (9.74)   (2.65)   (0.64)   (1.24)
  $+ 0.005\ [X+M]/Y_t - 0.028\ ImWage_{t-1} - 0.847\ Threat_{t-1}$
  (0.80)   (1.90)   (2.57)
  $R^2 = 0.87; SE = 0.91$

Source: Timmer and Williamson 1996.

Note: t statistics in parentheses.

Definitions of variables: *Policy* = index of immigration policy ranging from liberal (+5) to restricted (−5); *WtoY* = ratio of unskilled wage to GDP per worker; *WageR* = unskilled real wage; *Unemp* = unemployment rate; $[X+M]/Y$ = trade share measure of "openness"; *ImWage* = unskilled wage in immigrant origin; *Threat* = immigrant supply threat.

Method: Ordinary least squares regression with country fixed effects on fifty-six country/half-decade observations.

tion policy changes typically required long periods of debate. However, this was not always true, as can be seen by the enormous switch in Argentina's policy in only five years, 1889–1894, when the country was hard hit by world depression.

Measures of macroeconomic conditions—like unemployment rates—are, predictably, of little help in accounting for long-run policy changes. Only Australia offers any evidence that these factors contributed to long-run policy formation (not reported in table 8.1). Of course, the *timing* of the introduction of such policies can be and was, during the period covered by the regression, influenced by short-run macroeconomic conditions.

Labor market conditions had a consistent influence on immigration policy over the period, and they did so through both the absolute and the relative income performance of unskilled workers. Real wage growth mattered most in the United States, and nominal wage growth mattered most in Australia, while real wage levels mattered most in Brazil. In all cases, poor labor market performance was associated with more-restrictive immigration policy. However, the most consistently significant variable in the analysis is *WtoY*, the ratio of the unskilled wage to per capita income, or of income near the bottom of the distribution to income in the middle. Rising inequality was associated with increasingly restrictive immigration policy. As we have seen, new immigrants tended to cluster at the bottom of the income distribution, a tendency that held increasingly true as the nineteenth century unfolded. Regardless of what else is included in the regression equation, this measure of labor's relative economic position stands up as an important influence on policy. Rising relative labor scarcity encouraged more-open immigration policies; declining relative labor scarcity encouraged more-restrictive immigration policies.[11]

The evidence just summarized speaks to the *indirect* impact of immigration on policy by looking at absolute and relative wage performance in labor markets. What about the *direct* impact of immigration on policy? Perhaps the size and character of the current and expected future immigrant flow precipitated policy change, the latter serving to anticipate the labor market impact. Two variables might serve to measure these direct immigration effects. First, one might use a proxy for the quality of the immigrants—here the real wage of unskilled urban workers in the source countries. Second, one might measure immigrant quantity by the foreign-born population share in the destination country. Examination of these variables reveals that low and falling immigrant quality tended to precipitate immigration restrictions in Australia, Canada, and the United States, even after other forces are controlled for (Timmer and Williamson 1998). The variable *Threat* in table 8.1 uses information on both immigrant quality and quantity, and the sign on the variable is as predicted: rising *Threat* induced restrictive policy. To some extent, therefore, policy in these countries anticipated the impact of rising numbers of low-quality immigrants on unskilled wages and moved to exclude them. In addition, Argentina seems to have looked to the north across the Rio de la Plata to watch labor market events in Brazil, acting as if it knew that those events would divert immigrants to or from Argentina's borders. Thus, rising relative and absolute wages in Brazil tended to produce more-open policy in Argentina. This result is consistent with the policy spillovers that we discuss subsequently.

The other measure of immigration's attributes—the difference in ethnic composition between the current immigration flow and the foreign population stock (not shown in table 8.1)—seems to have had little bearing on policy over the time period covered in the regression. This is not the result that the popular literature favors: according to that view, a rising gap between the ethnic origins of previous immigrants— who had become residents and probably voting citizens—and that of current immigrants would serve to erode commitments to free immigration. While there is some weak Brazilian support for this view, it does not appear for any of the other countries in our sample after we control for other influences. It should be quickly emphasized to whom this benign antiracism conclusion applies: most New World immigrants were of *European* ethnic origin, since the United States and other high-wage countries had acted to exclude most Asians for most of the period studied, and free Africans rarely applied for admission into the historically slave-based New World.

To what extent was a change in a country's immigration policy during this period in part a reaction to policy changes abroad? As expected, the United States was not responsive to competitors' policies at any point during the time period under consideration, presumably because it was too big and an immigration policy leader. Nor, for that matter, was Canada, a surprising result that seems to confirm Canadian success in shielding its labor market from the eastern and southern European exodus to North America. For the other countries in our sample, policy abroad mattered a great deal. For Argentina, it was the combined impact of Australian, Canadian, and Brazilian policy that mattered, more-restrictive policy abroad inducing more-restrictive policy at home. Brazil tended to mimic the policies followed in Argentina and the United States. Australia, in turn, tended to favor open immigration policies when the United Kingdom offered more-generous subsidies to its emigrants and also, to some extent, when Canada adopted more-open policies.

To summarize, while the *size* of the immigrant flow did not seem to have any consistent impact on New World policy up to 1930, the low and declining quality of the immigrants it comprised certainly did, provoking restriction. Racism and xenophobia do not seem to have been at work in driving the evolution of policy toward potential European immigrants. Rather, it was immigrant quality, labor market conditions, and policies abroad—especially those set by the economic leaders, Britain and the United States—that mattered most for policy. New World countries acted to defend the economic interests of their scarce factor, unskilled labor.

How Big Were the Effects?

How much did each factor contribute to closing the doors to immigrants (Timmer and Williamson 1998, table 5)?

When the Brazilian door slammed shut in the 1920s, almost 62 percent of the 6.5-point drop in the country's policy index was due to deteriorating labor market conditions, a good share of which resulted from rising inequality. Labor market forces account for nearly two-thirds of this major Brazilian policy shift, from an open immigration policy with generous subsidies in 1917 to a restrictive policy with no subsidies in 1927. Canada offers even stronger evidence in support of the view that labor markets mattered. During that country's Prairie Boom, from 1899 to 1919, its policy index dropped 6 points. Two-thirds of this drop can be attributed to rising inequality over those two decades, and another tenth or so to diminished immigrant quality. Between 1888 and 1898, the policy index for Argentina fell by 4.5 points. Indirect labor market effects at home apparently made only a modest contribution to this big policy change. However, it could be argued that Argentina anticipated the likely labor market effects at home of labor market events in Brazil, in which case rising inequality and deteriorating wage growth in Brazil account for three-quarters of Argentina's policy shift. The increasing foreign-born presence in Argentina accounts for an additional quarter of the policy shift. The immigration policy index for the United States dropped by 2 points between 1865 and 1885. Almost all of that drop can be attributed to labor market effects and the deteriorating relative income conditions of the unskilled. Direct immigrant effects captured here by declining immigrant quality (86 percent), mattered almost as much. In contrast with the powerful labor market effects apparent between 1865 and 1885, almost none of the 2.5-point drop in the index for the United States between 1885 and 1917 can be assigned to labor market conditions. Thus, American historians are right when they attribute much of the passage of the Literacy Act to nonmarket factors. Yet deteriorating immigrant quality *does* account for two-fifths of the move toward restriction in the United States during the period.

Summing Up

These results point to long-term influences driving immigration policy that are very different from the short-term influences about which so much has been written. Thus, while unemployment and macro instability certainly influenced the *timing* of policy changes toward restriction of immigration in the late nineteenth and early twentieth centuries, labor market fundamentals were the central forces driving policy in the long run. Furthermore, there is no compelling evidence that xenophobia or racism was driving immigration policy in the New World economies, once underlying economic variables are given their due, and given that we ignore Asian exclusions and absent Africans.

Over the long haul, the New World countries tried to protect the economic position of their scarce factor, the unskilled worker. Labor became relatively more abundant when immigrants poured in, and governments sought to stop any absolute decline in the wages of the native unskilled with whom the immigrants competed, and often even in their wages relative to the average-income recipient. The greater the perceived threat to these wages from an increase in the number of immigrants, from lower-quality immigrants, or from both, the more restrictive policy became.

Late-nineteenth- and early-twentieth-century immigration policy in New World countries seems to have been influenced indirectly by conditions in the labor market and directly by immigration forces which, if left to run their course, would have had their impact on labor market conditions. Yet the shift in these countries to more-restrictive policies was less a result of rising immigrant flows and foreign-born stocks and more the result of falling immigrant quality. Furthermore, very often immigration policy at home was driven by immigration policy abroad, a correlation that suggests that countries tended to anticipate the likely impact of policies abroad on labor markets at home. Finally, the United States was a clear policy leader during this time, showing no evidence of responding to policies adopted elsewhere, but the remaining immigrant-receiving countries were very sensitive to the leader's policies and to the policies of their competitors.

This chapter offers strong support for the hypothesis that rising inequality in countries with high levels of immigration can help account for the globalization backlash that started in the late nineteenth century and became so powerful in the interwar period. New World governments acted to defend the economic position of unskilled labor, and thus gradually moved to insulate themselves from global market forces, by restricting immigration. Still, immigration restrictions came late in the century, partly because labor absorption rates remained high until late in the century, and perhaps also because unskilled workers did not have a full political voice until late in the century (and even later than that in Latin America). Economic forces matter for immigration policy, but so do the political institutions with which those forces interact.

9   The Demise of Mass Migration and Its Impact

World War I brought an end to mass migration and closed the door on the first global century. The combined effects of two world wars, the Great Depression, and the introduction of restrictive immigration policy served to choke off emigration to the New World, and thus migrations never regained their pre-1914 levels in the half century that followed. What was true of absolute levels was even more true, of course, of emigration and immigration rates.

The magnitude of the collapse in the global mass migrations is apparent in figures 9.1 and 9.2, both based on the impressive work of Dudley Kirk (1946) and that which issued from the famous collaboration between Imre Ferenczi and Walter Willcox (1929), scholars who lived through the global implosion between 1914 and 1950. Three central facts leap out at us from these two figures. First, the migrations of the 1920s were never able to recover the migration levels of the 1880s, let alone those of 1895–1914, and they fell to much lower levels after the 1920s. By the 1950s, the United States was no longer a melting pot or a nation of immigrants, but rather a closed economy whose youth were mostly native born, a characteristic that fit awkwardly on the shoulders of this new twentieth-century world leader. Second, most of the collapse in mass migration was due to the sharp decline in emigration from the new source countries located in southern and eastern Europe: the Austro-Hungarian Empire, the Russian Empire, Iberia, Italy, and the Balkans. Emigration from the old sources in northwestern Europe—the British Isles, Scandinavia, the Low Countries, Germany, France, and Switzerland—hardly declined at all. Third, the United States underwent the biggest fall in immigration, far exceeding that of the other top three overseas destinations (Argentina, Brazil, and Canada).

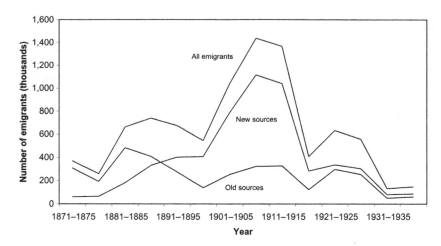

Figure 9.1
Emigration from Europe, 1881–1939 (five-year averages). *Source:* Kirk 1946 (289).

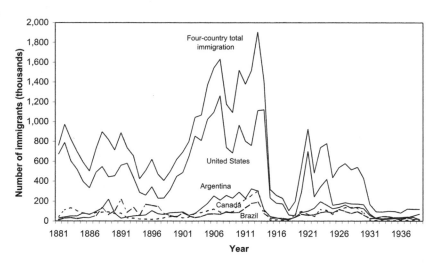

Figure 9.2
Immigration to chief New World destinations, 1881–1939. *Sources:* Kirk 1946 (280); Ferenczi and Willcox 1929 (361, 384–389, 539–540, 550).

The U.S. immigration data plotted in figure 9.2 offer the story line. When the guns of August started thundering in 1914, European immigration to the New World began to dry up: overseas immigration to the United States fell from 1.1 million annually in both 1913 and 1914 to 60,000 in 1918 and 54,000 in 1919. Potential immigrants in the European interior found it difficult or even impossible to make their way to the traditional ports of departure, and even had they arrived at those ports, they would have found steerage space extremely scarce and expensive. To make matters worse, as the war in the trenches dragged on, economic hardship made it increasingly difficult for potential emigrants in source countries to find the resources necessary to finance the move. Postwar recession and unemployment kept the immigration figures low in 1919 and 1920. With economic recovery in 1921, the United States recorded an overseas immigration rate of 702,000, as high as any level it had experienced over the fifteen years between 1885 and 1900, but that brief spurt was the last. The average between 1922 and 1929 was 232,000, a figure about one-third of the 1881–1914 average. During the Great Depression decade, the flood dried up to a trickle, averaging about 50,000 each year.

The great mass migration was over.

What Form Did Immigration Restriction Take?

How much of this collapse in European emigration was due to policy and how much to war and the Great Depression?

It seems quite clear that in the short run, much of the collapse in global migration can be attributed to world wars and the Great Depression. The clearest evidence of this fact is that none of the U.S. country quotas were binding from the early 1930s to the mid-1940s, even for the "excluded" new source countries located in southern and eastern Europe. Although the country quotas were set far below pre-1914 immigration levels, the new regions of emigration were only able to fill small shares of their quotas between 1932 and 1937: southern and eastern Europe were able to fill less than 40 percent of their quotas; Asia, less than 30 percent; and Africa, less than 10 percent (Gemery 1994, figure 9.1). However, chapter 8 taught us two lessons that apply here. First, changes in immigration policy usually come in very big, discrete steps and only after long, acrimonious, and time-intensive debates. The fact that the policy steps are big when implemented serves to maximize their impact at the destination. Second, when the underlying fundamentals favor immigration restrictions, they are usually not imposed until an industrial crisis occurs, and thus when short-run labor market problems are most apparent and affected citizens are most verbal. These are precisely the episodes when labor demand slumps, labor markets go slack, emigrants postpone their move, and immigration totals fall to low levels, even in the absence of policy restriction. Thus, the impact of immigration restrictions must be assessed over the long run, when capacity rather aggregate demand determines output, employment, and productivity and when peacetime normalcy rather than wartime scarcities dominate.

Four pieces of U.S. immigration legislation were enacted over the decade 1917–1927, and all were restrictive in intent and impact.[1] The first of these, the 1917 act, imposed a literacy test that, as noted in the previous chapter, was precisely the mode of restriction which had been debated by Congress from 1895 onward. By the end of the Great War, the literacy test (in English "or some other language...including Hebrew or Yiddish" [Hutchinson 1947, 85]) proved ineffective in stemming the inflow, mainly because a revolution in the provision of free and public elementary education had spread east and south to backward and illiterate Europe from the 1880s onward (Easterlin 1981; Lindert 2003). Italy certainly illustrates this schooling diffusion. Between 1881 and 1931, Italian regional literacy rates soared: from less than 20 percent to more than 60 percent in southern Italy, Sicily, and Sardinia; from less than 35 percent to almost 80 percent in central Italy; from about 40 percent to about 85 percent in Venice and Emilia; and from almost 60 percent to more than 95 percent in the northern industrial triangle (Kirk 1946, 183–185). The literacy rate for Italy as a whole was about 80 percent by 1931. Is Italy really a relevant example of the European literacy revolution? After all, while it was certainly a major supplier of emigrants from the new European region, one could also argue that it was more economically advanced than the other nations in that region. In any case, the literacy rate for young adults is much more relevant evidence for any prediction regarding the effectiveness of the 1917 Literacy Act, since these were the individuals most responsive to labor market signals. Repairing the evidence to respond to these two critiques (that Italy was nonrepresentative and that the overall literacy rate was not especially relevant) fails to damage the point: the literacy rate in poor European source countries (including Italy) for those aged fifteen to twenty-nine ranged from 80 to 83 percent in 1931.[2] No wonder the literacy criteria failed to offer an effective U.S. bar to immigrants from poor European countries. However, the 1917 legislation *did* include an "Asian Barred Zone" provision that was *very* effective in keeping out almost all potential immigrants from that part of the world.

The second piece of restrictive legislation was the Quota Act of 1921 (the Johnson Act) that set limits to immigration from Eastern Hemisphere countries. This second act was implemented in a congressional rush when 700,000 immigrants arrived from Europe that year (passing over the literacy bar) and with the election of President Warren Harding, who was much more comfortable with anti-immigration interests than his predecessor, Woodrow Wilson, had been. The annual number of immigrants of a given nationality was limited to no more than 3 percent of the U.S. population of that nationality as recorded in the 1910 census (Bernard 1982, 94–95). Under the 1921 act, the quotas for immigrants from the various countries of northern and western Europe were set at about 198,000, and those for immigrants from all other source countries, mainly in southern and eastern Europe, were set at about 158,000, or about 356,000 in all. The legislation was clearly targeted to limit new immigrants who, the prewar Dillingham Commission had argued, had a harder time assimilating, were a source of poverty and a potential welfare burden on the state, and became poor citizens (or failed to become citizens at all). The targeting worked: annual quotas for southern and eastern European countries were in all cases less than a quarter of the numbers admitted before the Great War. The Asian Barred Zone remained in place, embodying a racial restriction that applied everywhere in overseas destination countries including Australia, Brazil, Canada, and Natal (Daniels 1995, 39–40; Davis 1947). This Asian restriction embedded in the 1917 and 1921 U.S. acts had its source in the increasingly strong lobbying interests on the West Coast, which managed to get Congress to accept a Chinese exclusion act as early as 1882. Had British Colombia, California, Nevada, Oregon, and Washington formed an independent nation in 1870, the New World would have seen an Asian exclusion act even sooner. Furthermore, U.S. Asian restrictions stayed in place for almost a century, until the reforms of 1965.

The 1921 act also had a pro–Western Hemisphere bias, since such immigration was not subject to quotas. After all, there appeared to be no reason to set quotas for Western Hemisphere countries, since South America would have seemed to be too poor and too distant to generate

Table 9.1
Net U.S. immigration by region of origin, 1910–1939

	1910–1919	1920–1929	1930–1939
Old Europe	910,309 (21.2)	991,128 (32.9)	77,839 (37.0)
New Europe	2,548,453 (59.5)	542,058 (18.0)	113,016 (53.7)
Mexico	135,678 (3.2)	455,502 (15.1)	−75,240 (−35.8)
Canada	417,016 (9.7)	912,651 (30.3)	144,325 (68.6)
Other	274,809 (6.4)	107,441 (3.6)	−49,503 (−23.5)
Total	4,286,265 (100.0)	3,008,780 (100.0)	210,437 (100.0)

Source: Gemery 1994 (table 9.2, 178).
Note: Numbers in parentheses are percentages of total immigrants. Canada includes Newfoundland.

a viable pool of emigrants, at least at that time. Furthermore, Canada was viewed as a member of the British family with old European origins. Finally, farm interests in the Southwest were lobbying for cheap Mexican unskilled labor to work their fields, the products of which were by that time supplying national and international markets. These facts had one important, but perhaps unpredictable, implication: illegal immigrants poured over the border from Canada and Mexico, trying to sidestep the European quotas and the Asian restrictions by passing through contiguous neighbors and over porous borders. One estimate has it that "hundreds of thousands (perhaps millions) of illegal immigrants" entered the United States in the 1920s via Canada and Mexico (Briggs 1984, 48). In any case, the share of U.S. immigrants coming from Canada and Mexico rose from 12.9 percent in 1910–1919 to 45.4 percent in 1920–1929. Mexican immigration by itself rose by about 320,000 over the decade (table 9.1), a harbinger of things to come later in the twentieth century.

Finally, the 1921 act also introduced a nonquota category. This category was based on individual characteristics (rather than nationality) and would come to represent the "family reunification" part of U.S. immigration.

The 1921 act was not restrictive enough for some anti-immigration interests, and their power in Congress was on the rise. Thus, the third piece of restrictive U.S. immigration legislation, the Johnson-Reid Act of 1924, lowered the immigrant quota from 356,000 to 165,000, mostly by reducing the new-source-country quota from 158,000 to 21,000 (Bernard 1982, table 3.1, 96). The more-restrictive quotas of the 1921 act were set at 2 percent of the foreign-born by nationality in the 1890 census. Finally, the fourth piece of restrictive legislation, the national origins act of 1927, completed a decade of U.S. experimentation with immigration restriction which set the overall immigration quota at about 150,000, based now on national origins of the U.S. 1920 population.

As previously noted, there were quota and nonquota categories for immigrants, and the 1924 act made it far easier for relatives of those currently in the country to enter as nonquota immigrants. Since wives and children were exempted from the numerical quota by the 1924 act, the number of persons admitted each year from any given country in the late 1920s was often much higher than that set by the quota. Thus, while actual gross immigration into the United States from southern and eastern Europe was 101.5 percent of the quota in 1924, the figure was 316.1 percent in 1929 (Gemery 1994, table 9.4, 182).

Family reunification had become an important part of U.S. immigration policy by the late 1920s, and it was reinforced in the 1965 reforms. It has stayed that way ever since.

Whom Did the U.S. Quotas Keep Out, and What Did It Do to Positive Selection?

As table 9.1 shows, net immigration to the United States fell dramatically from 4.3 million in 1910–1919 to 210,000 in 1930–1939. But the composition by source also changed dramatically, reflecting the intent of the legislation. The share coming from new sources in Europe fell from almost 60 percent in the 1910s to 18 percent in the 1920s, and the share from "other" (mainly Asia) fell from 6.4 to 3.6 percent over the same period. In short, immigration from "undesirable" sources dropped from 65.9 to 21.6 percent of the total. In contrast, the European and Canadian share rose from 30.9 to 63.2 percent.

The national-origins policies of the U.S. immigration legislation clearly served to increase positive selection to the extent that a larger share of U.S. immigrants were coming from developed regions. Indeed, table 9.2 documents that the share of entering immigrants with skilled, professional, or commercial occupations rose from 17.9 percent in 1911–1916 to 24.1 percent in 1926–1930 and 30.6 percent 1936–1940. Among those in the labor force and thus reporting occupations, the rise is even more dramatic, from 24.6 to 40.4 and to 69.1 percent in those same years, respectively. But note the impact of family reunification. The share of females in the total rose from 35.1 to 54.8 percent

Table 9.2
Distribution of U.S. immigrants by gender and occupation, 1911–1940

	1911–1916	1916–1920	1921–1925	1926–1930	1931–1935	1936–1940
By gender						
Male	64.9%	58.7%	56.6%	53.8%	40.8%	45.2%
Female	35.1	41.3	43.4	46.2	59.2	54.8
By occupation						
Skilled, professional, and commercial	17.9	22.6	23.7	24.1	21.0	30.6
Unskilled, servants, and farmers	54.9	40.0	37.6	35.6	17.6	13.7
No occupation	27.2	39.3	38.7	40.3	61.4	55.7

Source: Gemery 1994 (table 9.3, 178).
Notes: "No occupation" includes mainly women and children.

over the two decades, almost a 20-percentage-point rise, and the share of individuals not in the labor force (mainly women and children) rose from 27.2 to 55.7 percent, a 28.5-percentage-point rise.

The quotas changed the immigrant mix by source, from new back to old origins. On those grounds alone, they raised the quality of the immigrants. At the same time, however, family reunification also sharply lowered the high labor participation rates and low dependency rates U.S. immigrants had been bringing with them since 1820. If the latter dominated the former, a century of positive selection of young adult males might have been completely overturned by the U.S. policies introduced during the quota decade, a result which was certainly not the intent of the policy.

It should be added that as new emigrants from the east, southeast, and south of Europe were deterred from first-best options by restrictive immigration policy overseas, many of them explored second-best options *within Europe*. For example, aliens accounted for only 2.9 percent of the French population in 1911 but were 6.2 percent in 1926; in that year, they came mainly from Italy (31.7 percent), Russia and Poland (15.7 percent), and Spain (13.5 percent) (Cross 1981, chap. 3). Germany was much less friendly to immigrants, but where interwar European countries allowed immigration, potential European emigrants were deflected by restrictive immigration policy from first-best labor markets overseas to second best labor markets in the European west.

Population and Labor Force Impact

Did the collapse in world migration have an impact on sending and receiving countries? The United States was the biggest immigrant labor market, and it also underwent the biggest decline in immigration after 1914, so our focus is there. Whether because of a switch to restrictive immigration policy, war, the Great Depression, or all three in concert, did the rate of labor force and population growth in the United States slow down in the three decades after the Great War? If so, how much of the decline can be attributed to declining immigration? Only if we can show that the switch in immigration policy contributed to a labor force slowdown can we then ask whether it had an impact on economic events within the U.S. economy.

Three studies have explored the impact of immigration on U.S. population and labor supply in the interwar years, but we believe that all three asked the wrong question. Simon Kuznets and Ernest Rubin (1954) adopted a foreign-born measure and counted net migrants of labor force age as well as immigrant children born abroad as they reached employment age. Richard Easterlin's (1968) measure was narrower and excluded the impact of immigrant children. More recently, Henry Gemery (1994) extended the analysis, also using the Easterlin measure, the narrow definition that we use in what follows. However, all three of these scholars measured only the share of the *observed* or *actual* labor force or population increase accounted for by immigrants. While such accounting decompositions are useful, they do not assess the impact of the demise of mass migration on labor force or population growth. What we want instead are estimates of a counterfactual world in which the mass migrations continued. Only then can we identify the role of the demise of mass migration.

First, what was the extent of the labor force slowdown? Table 9.3 documents a dramatic fall in the rate of labor force growth in the United States, from 2.29 percent per annum over the three prewar decades (1880–1910) to 1.14 percent per annum over the three war and interwar decades 1910–1940. This slowdown in the rate of labor supply growth amounted to 1.15 percentage points—a massive regime switch in which the growth rate was cut in half. Would we find similar large numbers for other immigrant countries? The answer depends on two factors. First, which economies were most dependent on immigration prior to the Great War? We have already reported the answer to that question in table 6.2 for both sending and receiving countries:

Table 9.3
U.S. labor force growth, 1910–1940: Some counterfactuals

	Labor force growth rate (percentage per year)	Percentage due to net immigration
Actual: 1880–1910	2.29	40.1
Actual: 1910–1940	1.14	11.6
Counterfactuals for 1910–1940 with immigrant participation rate of 1910–1940		
Net immigration rate of 1910–1940	1.14	11.6
Absolute net immigration of 1880–1910	1.38	30.9
Net immigration rate of 1880–1910	1.66	44.1
Counterfactuals for 1910–1940 with immigrant participation rate of 1880–1910		
Net immigration rate of 1910–1940	1.17	14.5
Absolute net immigration of 1880–1910	1.48	35.6
Net immigration rate of 1880–1910	1.82	50.4

Sources: Statistics on sources of population growth kindly provided by Michael Haines. Labor force participation rates from Maddison 1995 (106–107, 246) and Gemery 1994 (178).

immigration between 1870 and 1910 served to raise the 1910 labor force of Argentina by 86 percent, that of Canada by 44 percent, that of Australia by 42 percent, and that of the United States by 24 percent; and emigration between 1870 and 1910 served to lower the 1910 labor force in Ireland by 45 percent, that of Italy by 39 percent, that of Norway by 24 percent, and that of Sweden by 20 percent. Second, which economies underwent the biggest fall in mass migration? With the evidence provided by the answers to those two questions in hand, we would then predict that the biggest labor force slowdown occurred in those economies in which net migration had the biggest impact on prewar labor force totals and where net migration underwent the biggest decline after 1914. Australia would be one candidate; indeed, the rate of labor force growth in Australia fell by 1.41 percentage points between 1870–1913 and 1913–1938 (Maddison 1991, 266). Statistics for the other immigrant countries are harder to document, but similar magnitudes are likely.

Next, does the demise of mass migration explain the slowdown? Table 9.3 poses the following counterfactual: What would have been the rate of labor force growth between 1910 and 1940 in the United States had the 1880–1910 immigration experience persisted? Our expectations are, of course, that the demise of mass migration accounted for a very large share of the slowdown in U.S. labor force growth. The counter-factuals are calculated to take account of two forces. First, immigration into the United States fell after 1910. So what would have been the impact in 1910–1940 if, on the one hand, the immigration *rate* had remained at the 1880–1910 average thereafter, and if, on the other hand, the *absolute level* of immigration had remained at the 1880–1910 average thereafter? The pre-1910 *rate* sets an upper bound and the pre-1910 *level* a lower bound on the counterfactual impact. Results for these counterfactuals are reported in the second panel of table 9.3. Second, the age and sex distribution of U.S. immigrants changed dramatically after 1910—partly induced by immigration policy—thereby serving to lower the labor participation rate (and to raise the dependency rate) of the interwar immigrants. So what would have been the impact on post-1910 U.S. labor force growth if, in addition, the immigrant labor participation rate had remained at its pre-1910 average thereafter? These counterfactuals are reported in the third panel of table 9.3.

The bottom line in table 9.3 is this. The observed decline in the rate of labor force growth, 1880–1910 to 1910–1940, was 1.15 percentage points, but the decline under the no-mass-migration-demise counter-factual would have been only 0.47 (2.29 − 1.82: bottom panel) or 0.63 (2.29 − 1.66: middle panel) percentage points. The demise in mass migration accounted for 45 to 59 percent (or about half) of the massive slowdown in U.S. labor force growth around World War I. Since the immigrants were less skilled than the native-born, it seems likely that the demise of mass migration contributed even more than half to any slowdown in the growth of the unskilled labor force.

The demise in mass migration wasn't the only force at work, of course, since the crude birth rate in the United States also fell, from about thirty-seven per thousand in the 1880s to about eighteen per thousand in the 1930s. But the demise in immigration accounted for about half of the changing demographic and labor supply growth events during the interwar years when the world went antiglobal.

Did the Absence of Immigrants Contribute to the Great Leveling in America?

Does immigration foster inequality and does its absence foster equal-ity? The Reverend Thomas Malthus thought so. When appearing be-fore a parliamentary committee on the state of Britain's poor in the 1820s and 1830s, he argued that Irish immigration into industrial

England reduced the real wages of the working class (Williamson 1986, 694). When Paul Samuelson published the sixth edition of his famous *Economics* textbook a century and a half later, he joined Malthus with the statement: "After World War I, laws were passed severely limiting immigration. Only a trickle of immigrants has been admitted since then.... By keeping labor supply down, immigration policy tends to keep wages high" (Samuelson 1964, quoted in Borjas 2003, 1335). Also in 1964, while writing his *Manpower in Economic Growth*, Stanley Lebergott joined Malthus and Samuelson with this statement about the impact of the immigration quotas: "It [is] most unlikely that the rate of productivity advance or the nature of productivity advance changed so [much in the 1920s] as to explain [the spurt in real wage growth]. Instead we find that halting the flow of millions of migrants ... offers a much more reasonable explanation" (27). This question has a very old empirical tradition in the United States that goes back to the late nineteenth century and to the appearance of the Dillingham Commission report. But the tradition was alive and well even a half century earlier: "[T]he 1850s witnessed the highest immigration rates in U.S. history.... The pressures immigration placed on labor markets, particularly in the urban Northeast, produced a remarkable backlash in the 1850s.... The popular press took up the anti-immigrant cry with [an editorial stating that] 'the enormous influx of foreigners will in the end prove ruinous to American workingmen'" (Ferrie 1999, 161–163).

The economics underlying all of these statements is straightforward. A glut in the labor supply lowers the wage relative to the returns to capital and rents on land. Since capital and land are held by those at the top of the distribution pyramid, immigration-induced labor supply growth should create more inequality, and the demise of immigration should create less, ceteris paribus. If, in addition, immigrants tend to be less skilled than the native-born, then immigration should also raise the premium on skills as they get scarce relative to unskilled labor, and the demise of immigration should reduce the premium on skills as they get relatively abundant, ceteris paribus.

Not everyone has agreed with this traditional argument, mostly because of the "ceteris paribus": many other dynamic forces were driving the American economy, thus offering potential offsets to any measured immigrant glut or scarcity. Potential offsets invite debate. For example, Vernon Briggs (1984, 50) thought that the premise of the traditional argument was false, since he believed that immigration was still substantial in the 1920s and that productivity advance was very different in rate and bias. Others have argued that immigration generates accumulation responses, forces that, if indeed generated, mute the immigration impact. Chapter 14 grapples with this issue at length in the context of the more-recent late-twentieth-century evidence. Thus, we do not try to resolve this debate here but only pose the arguments and present an impressive and suggestive correlation in the historical time series.

Chapter 6 explored the correlation between migration rates and inequality trends, where countries were the unit of observation. During the mass migrations between 1870 and 1913, rich labor-scarce countries with big immigration rates underwent rising inequality, and poor labor-abundant countries with big emigration rates underwent falling inequality (figure 6.5). During the antiglobal and immigrant-restricted interwar years 1921–1938, the correlation disappeared. Indeed, some previously emigrating countries like Italy now underwent rising inequality, while some previously immigrating countries like Australia, Canada, and the United States underwent falling inequality (figure 6.6). This is only a correlation, of course: immigration policy may have been correlated with some omitted variables, and the omitted variables may have been doing all the work. Still, at least the correlation cannot be used to reject the immigration-breeds-inequality hypothesis out of hand.

Now consider figure 9.3, which plots the correlation for the United States only, but over 150 years. Figure 9.3 is taken from a book by Jeffrey Williamson and Peter Lindert (1980) that was published some time ago, and the underlying data have since been revised. Still, the correlation has not been overturned by those revisions: namely, rapid rates of labor force growth in the United States took place during episodes in which earnings inequality was on the rise and the skill premium was increasing, while slow rates of labor force growth took place during episodes when earnings inequality was decreasing and the skill premium was falling. And note the observations that are the focus of this chapter: 1909–1929 and 1929–1948 in the lower-left quadrant, where the skill premium was falling and the growth rates of the labor force were slow; and 1879–1899 and 1899–1909 in the upper-right quadrant, where the skill premium was rising and the growth rates in the labor force were fast. Correlation is not causation, but figure 9.3 is certainly consistent with the immigration-breeds-inequality hypothesis.

The twentieth-century evidence available on the evolution of U.S. inequality has improved over the past decade or so, and it confirms a

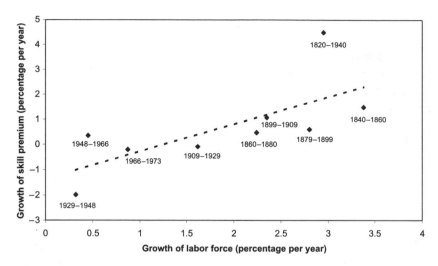

Figure 9.3
Labor supply and the skill premium in the United States, 1820–1973. *Source:* Williamson and Lindert 1980 (205).

great egalitarian leveling in American incomes between the first and second thirds of the century. The ratio of wages among the top 10 percent in manufacturing to those among the bottom 10 percent fell by almost a third between 1890 and 1940, a period of labor force slowdown as we have seen; half of this slowdown we have attributed to the demise of mass migration. Pay ratios of skilled to unskilled workers fell by two-thirds between 1907 and 1952. The ratio of college professors' incomes to that of unskilled workers was cut in half between 1908 and 1960. Weekly wage dispersion measures among white men fell by more than a quarter between 1940 and 1965, as did the share of total income accounted for by the top 10 percent of income earners. And the gap between male and female wages also fell from 1900 to 1935 (Goldin 1990, 60).

Among the authors contributing to the evidence presented in figure 9.4, Claudia Goldin and Lawrence Katz have made the greatest effort to explain the great leveling (Goldin and Margo 1992; Goldin and Katz 1998, 1999a, 1999b, 2001), and the relative demand and supply of skills is central to their story: "[The] long-run change in the distribution of earnings is shaped by a race between the demand for skill, driven largely by industrial shifts and technological advances, and the supply of skill, altered by changes in educational investments, demographics

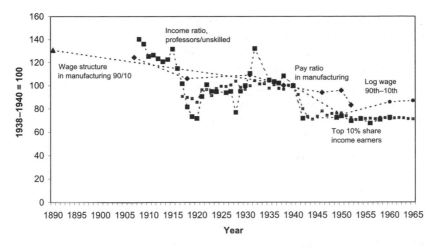

Figure 9.4
American inequality trends, 1890–1965. Wage structure in manufacturing 90/10 = wage ratios, male production workers, top 10 percent relative to bottom 10 percent (*Source:* Goldin and Katz 2001, table 2.1); income ratio, professors/unskilled = ratio of earnings of college full professors to low-skilled workers (*Source:* Goldin and Katz 2001, table 2.3); log wage 90th–10th = wage dispersion of white men, log weekly wages 90th–10th percentiles (*Source:* Goldin and Margo 1992, table 1); pay ratio in manufacturing = pay ratios, skilled to unskilled in urban manufacturing (Goldin and Margo 1992, table 7); top 10 percent share income earners = income share of the top 10 percent of earners (Piketty and Saez 2003, table 2).

and immigration" (Goldin and Katz 2001, 68). While Goldin and Katz are cautious, they appear to favor the view that an exogenous and revolutionary change in the supply of secondary and tertiary schooling must have overwhelmed the skill-using bias that has characterized twentieth-century economic progress. Such schooling forces would, of course, help erase the skill premium, compress the wage structure, and level incomes. But what about exogenous and revolutionary changes in unskilled labor supplies associated in part with the demise of mass migration? These exogenous policy-induced immigration forces would reinforce the exogenous policy-induced schooling forces: as the growth of the unskilled labor force slowed down, unskilled labor would have gotten scarcer relative to skilled labor.

If mass migration before the First World War contributed to high and rising inequality and skill scarcity in New World host countries, while its essential elimination after the quotas contributed to the decline in skill scarcity and falling inequality there, then we should see somewhat different trends in the European sending countries. While both sides of the Atlantic may have shared the same technological events and perhaps even the same schooling events (Europe was undergoing a schooling revolution too, although at the elementary school level: see chapter 8), the boom and bust in mass migration must have left different inequality marks on labor markets on either side of the Atlantic. Much more work remains to be done on this issue, but what evidence we have at hand seems to be consistent with our hypothesis. Two recent papers have documented comparative skilled versus unskilled wage gap trends for Europe and North America between 1870 and 1960, and they show the following: first, the skilled wage premium started falling in the United Kingdom thirty-five years before it did in the United States and Canada (1880 versus 1915: Anderson 2001, 96; Betrán and Pons 2004, 39); second, while the skilled wage premium declined very dramatically after 1915 in the United States and Canada, it declined only very modestly in the United Kingdom (Anderson 2001, 96; Betrán and Pons 2004, 39); and third, these same two comparisons also hold for America relative to Denmark, France, Germany, Italy, Spain, and Sweden (Anderson 2001, 94; Betrán and Pons 2004, 39). The mass migration secular boom and bust appears to be a good candidate to help explain the asymmetric inequality trends in Europe and the New World before and after the imposition of immigration quotas.

So is the schooling-oriented literature on twentieth-century American inequality only half right? A good illustration of how policy-induced immigration forces created greater unskilled labor scarcity and lower inequality in the United States is not hard to find, and it involves disadvantaged black Americans. Did European immigrants crowd out southern blacks from northern jobs that offered much better earnings and living standards than did sharecropping in the South? This is a very old question, and the evidence in regard to it was, until recently, illustrated only by compelling correlations. Thus, more than thirty years ago Brinley Thomas (1972, 130–134, chap. 18) noted the striking inverse correlation between black migration out of the South and European migration into northern cities. The problem left unanswered by these correlations, however, was causation:

The exit rate out of the south was high in the 1870s, high in the 1890s, high during World War I, and high after the quotas, all of which were years of low European immigration. Is this evidence of unskilled European immigrants crowding out unskilled (black, male, southern) Americans? Or is this evidence that during a slump, when unemployment was high in eastern cities and immigration low, things were even worse for southern agriculture, thus pushing farm labor north in spite of the high unemployment incidence there? (Hatton and Williamson 1998, 165)

William Collins (1997) has now unraveled the issues of causation and supplied the answers. While only about a half million southern blacks left for the urban North in the four decades before 1910, *seven times* that—about 3.5 million—left in the four decades after 1910. By 1950, about 20 percent of all the blacks born in the South lived in the North, while the figure was only a little more than 4 percent at the turn of the century (Collins 1997, 607), or only a fifth of the 1950 figure. Not only did those who moved improve their economic lives, but those who stayed behind gained too, since the wage gap between North and South declined sharply as the Great Black Migration served to better integrate what had been regionally segmented labor markets (Wright 1986). Collins concludes that the mass migrations from Europe did indeed crowd out southern blacks from better jobs in the urban North, and symmetrically, the demise of the mass migrations crowded them in. A very large share of the Great Black Migration can be explained by the disappearance of new European immigrants in northern U.S. cities after 1914. Since the Great Black Migration greatly improved the relative income position of blacks between 1910 and 1950, it helps account for the great leveling of incomes in the middle third of the twentieth century and offers one important channel through which exogenous changes in European mass migration contributed to this leveling.

Did the Presence of Immigrants Contribute to the Schooling Revolution in America?

Goldin and Katz (1999a, tables 6, 7) have documented a decline in the returns to schooling in the United States from World War I to the 1960s that is consistent with the evidence of the great leveling of U.S. incomes in the middle third of the twentieth century. For young men, the return to a high school degree fell from 11–12 percent in 1914 to 7 percent in 1959, while the return to a college degree fell from about 15 percent to 9 percent over the same period (Goldin and Katz 2001, table 2.4). How much of this was due to a policy-induced scarcity of unskilled and unschooled immigrants that lowered the rate of return to schooling by raising the opportunity costs of staying in school and out of the labor market? How much of it was due instead to a schooling glut that lowered those rates? If a schooling glut was the more substantial cause, how much of that glut was triggered by exogenous policy changes, and how much of it was instead an endogenous response to the observed skill scarcity created, at least in part, by the open immigration policy before 1914?

It is important to stress that the immigrant scarcity and the schooling glut hypotheses are not in competition with one another: instead, they are mutually supportive. The exogenous and endogenous schooling hypotheses also need not be competing, since both forces might have been operating. Still, we would like to know, if both were operating, which was doing most of the work.

Goldin and Katz clearly favor the exogenous schooling hypothesis. There is no doubt that secondary school enrollment soared in the United States from 1910 to 1940, rising from about 14 percent to 71 percent (Goldin 1998; Goldin and Katz 2001, figure 2.5), and an increasing number of secondary school graduates took white-collar office and factory jobs. That is, more and more high school students were using their diplomas in the marketplace, rather than only as a way to gain entrance to college, and the number of terminal degrees granted by secondary schools increased: "The increase in high school enrollments and graduation served to flood the market with literate and numerate workers whose skills enabled them to move into white-collar office jobs. It also increased the supply of those capable of filling blue-collar positions that required the reading of manuals, deciphering of blueprints, computing of formulae, and use of elementary science" (Goldin and Katz 2001). Moreover, "'mass' secondary school education was unique to the United States at that time. Most European countries did not have mass non-vocational, non-industrial secondary school education that was fully publicly funded until the post–World War II era" (Goldin and Katz 1999a, 15).

But why did the schooling movement in the United States begin around 1900 or 1910? Why not later, as it did in Europe? We may agree that the schooling supply response helped erase schooling scarcity and inequality in America, but surely previous schooling scarcity played a role in triggering that supply response? Goldin and Katz think it did not and believe instead that the relative cultural and wealth homogeneity of the early twentieth century explains the timing and location of the schooling boom. For them the key was social and economic egalitarianism in America, which supported the belief in externalities—especially in New England and the West, where the high school movement led the nation. Perhaps, but some part of the schooling boom could have been an endogenous response to the large skill premium, schooling scarcity, and high return to education in the late nineteenth century, when mass migration reached its crescendo. The issue has not yet been resolved, but Rodney Ramcharan (2001, 2003) has offered some evidence in support of the schooling endogeneity hypothesis, although his evidence also offers some support for the alternative offered by Goldin and Katz. Ramcharan's results are reassuring for those who, like us, believe that schooling endogeneity and exogeneity forces were *both* at work.

The payoff to future research on the schooling endogeneity hypothesis will be great, since the hypothesis speaks to modern brain drain debates and whether and how human capital formation responds to mass migration in host and source country, a topic we discuss at length in chapter 15.

Would European Emigration Have Dried Up without Restrictions?

The demise of mass migration accounts for about half of the great slowdown in labor force growth after World War I, and that slowdown appears to have had an important impact on the performance of the twentieth-century U.S. economy. In the short and medium run, war and the Great Depression explain a good share of the decline, but in the long run it was policy that mattered. Or did it?

In the absence of the two world wars, the Great Depression, and even the quotas, would emigration from Europe have dried up of its own accord over the half century following 1914? The answer is a definite yes, if nineteenth-century experience is any guide. Chapter 4 showed how countries pass through emigration life cycles, rising from low levels to peak emigration rates, then falling from those peaks. Furthermore, we know why they pass through those life cycles: spreading industrial revolutions make it possible for lagging countries to catch up with the leaders; unfolding demographic transitions generate a surge, then a collapse, in the growth rate in the number of young adults; and rising outflows allow each emigrant country to exploit more-efficient networks and to develop stronger friends-and-relatives effects, at least up to some optimal rate. Thus, there is every reason to believe that countries in eastern and southern Europe would have undergone the same life cycle after 1914 that the countries in north-western Europe did before 1914—in the absence of war, depression, and policy.

The only uncertain issue is when Latin America, Africa, and Asia would have joined the mass migrations—in the absence of war, depression, and policy. But that brings us to 1950 and part III of this book.

III

The Rise (Again) of World Mass Migration

10   Resurrection: World Migration since World War II

Although intercontinental migration resumed after World War II, the resumption of its pre–World War I pattern by source did not last long. Nor was the magnitude the same as it had been, since the restrictive immigration policies introduced two or three decades earlier persisted. Yet U.S. policies were to change sharply in the 1960s with a shift away from the quotas that had so strongly favored immigrants from western Europe since they were introduced in the 1920s.

Annual immigration to North America and Oceania rose gradually from the end of World War II to the mid-1970s before surging to a million per year in the 1990s (figure 10.1). The absolute numbers were by then similar to those reached during the age of mass migration about a century earlier, but they were much smaller relative to the host country populations that had to absorb them. Thus, the U.S. annual immigration rate fell from 11.6 immigrants per thousand in the 1900s to 0.4 immigrants per thousand in the 1940s, before rising again to 4 immigrants per thousand in the 1990s. Most Americans are aware of the fact that there has been a surge in U.S. immigration over the past three or four decades, but the *rate* of immigration in the 1990s was still only a third of what it was in the 1900s. Still, even a relatively low immigration rate can generate very fast growth in foreign-born population shares when it starts from a low base and a faster-growing foreign-born population combines with a slower-growing host population. The proportion of the U.S. population foreign-born had fallen from a 1910 peak of 15 percent to an all-century low of 4.7 percent in 1970. The postwar immigration boom increased the foreign-born share to more than 8 percent in 1990 and more than 10 percent in 2000.[1] Thus, the United States has come two-thirds of the way back to reclaiming the title "a nation of immigrants" after a half-century retreat. While the immigration rate is now only a third of what it was at its peak in the

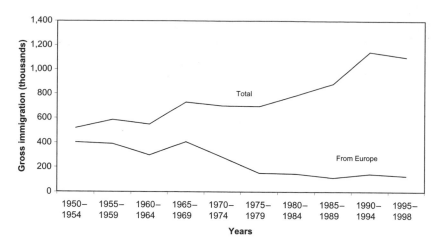

Figure 10.1
Gross immigration to the United States, Canada, Australia, and New Zealand, 1950–1954
to 1995–1998 (annual averages). *Source:* United Nations, *World Population Monitoring,*
various issues.

first decade of the twentieth century, the contribution of immigration
to population and labor force growth is similar to what it was then, because the rate of natural increase has also declined.

What happened to the United States after World War II also happened worldwide. Table 10.1 reports trends in the foreign-born around
the world over the thirty-five years between the mid-1960s and the
turn of the century. The data are based on country censuses, sources
that are likely to be of higher quality than those that report annual
immigrant flows, and they deal with unambiguous net permanent
moves. The most revealing entries appear in the last three rows of the
table. There we see that the foreign-born share in the total population
increased by about third in Oceania between 1965 and 2000 (from 14.4
to 19.1 percent), more than doubled in North America (from 6 to 13
percent), and more than tripled in Europe (from 2.2 to 7.7 percent).
The sources of the data in table 10.1 make it clear that North America
is defined to exclude Mexico, so in this case we are talking exclusively
about a high-wage, immigrant-absorbing region. Alas, the same is
not true of Europe, since the sources also make it clear that the latter
is defined to include eastern Europe and the former Soviet Union,
two net emigrating regions and, increasingly, a significant source of
migrants for the European Union. The foreign-born share in *western*

Table 10.1
Migrant stock around the world, 1965–2000

Year	1965	1975	1985	1990a	1990b	2000
Migrant stock (millions)						
World	75.2	84.5	105.2	119.8	154.0	174.9
Africa	8.0	11.2	12.5	15.6	16.2	16.3
Asia	31.4	29.7	38.7	43.0	50.0	50.0
Latin America and Caribbean	5.9	5.9	6.4	7.5	7.1	5.9
North America	12.7	15.0	20.5	23.9	27.6	40.8
Europe	14.7	19.5	23.0	25.1	48.4	56.1
Oceania	2.5	3.3	4.1	4.6	4.8	5.8
Percentage of world migrant stock						
World	100.0	100.0	100.0	100.0	100.0	100.0
Africa	10.6	13.2	11.9	13.1	10.5	9.3
Asia	41.8	35.1	36.8	35.9	32.4	28.6
Latin America and Caribbean	7.9	6.8	6.1	6.2	4.6	3.4
North America	16.9	17.8	19.5	20.0	17.9	23.3
Europe	19.6	23.1	21.8	20.9	31.4	32.1
Oceania	3.3	3.9	3.9	3.9	3.1	3.3
Migrant stock as a percentage of population						
World	2.3	2.1	2.2	2.3	2.9	2.9
Africa	2.5	2.7	2.3	2.5	2.6	2.1
Asia	1.7	1.3	1.4	1.4	1.6	1.4
Latin America and Caribbean	2.4	1.8	1.6	1.7	1.6	1.1
North America	6.0	6.3	7.8	8.6	9.8	13.0
Europe	2.2	2.7	3.0	3.2	6.7	7.7
Oceania	14.4	15.6	16.9	17.8	18.0	19.1

Sources: 1965–1990a from Zlotnick 1998 (431); 1990b and 2000 from United Nations 2002b.
Note: There are differences of definition in the figures for 1965–1990a and 1990b–2000. The most important is due to the breakup of the Soviet Union, which is included with Europe for the earlier years. Reclassification of the area encompassed by the former Soviet Union into individual republics added about 27 million to the world international migrant stock in 2000.

Europe (not reported in table 10.1) rose much more dramatically in the late twentieth century than it did in Europe as a whole: from 2.2 percent in 1965 to 10.3 percent in 2000, an increase of *five times*, even larger than the comparable rate of increase for North America. In sharp contrast, the foreign-born slaves in Africa, Asia, and Latin America and the Caribbean declined.

Most of the OECD rise in the foreign-born share took place in the 1990s: two-thirds of the increase in the North American foreign-born share and four-fifths of the increase in the European foreign-born share. Thus, immigration into the OECD has accelerated since 1965 and especially recently.

Next, consider where the migrants have gone. The share of the total world foreign-born in Europe and North America increased from 36.5 to 55.4 percent over the thirty-five years covered in table 10.1. Asia accounted for most of the rest, 28.6 percent in 2000, and almost half of that Asian share can be attributed to the Persian Gulf region. Thus, three-quarters of the world's foreign-born are now located in western Europe, North America, Oceania, and the Persian Gulf.

The source regions for these immigrants are, of course, Africa, Asia, eastern Europe, Latin America, and the Caribbean. Foreign-born shares are low and falling in all of these emigrating regions. The foreign-born share of Asia, as the first major Third World source of immigrants, declined between 1965 and 1975—when Asia was sending rather than receiving migrants—and its share has stabilized since. The foreign-born share in Latin America has undergone two big drops, one between 1965 and 1975 and then another across the 1990s. The decline in Africa came later, but again in two steps, 1975–1985 and 1990–2000. Although it is not shown in the table, the share of the foreign-born in eastern Europe has also undergone a steady fall throughout the thirty-five years.

Where Have the World Migrants Come From? Five Seismic Changes

World migration patterns by source and destination have undergone five seismic shifts over the half century since World War II. The first involved Europe's decline as an emigrant source: European emigration to North America and Oceania collapsed from 400,000 per annum in the early 1950s to less than 100,000 per annum in the early 1990s (figure 10.1). Part of this drop can be explained by the resurgence of migration *within* Europe.

Emigration from southern Europe has a long tradition going back to pre-nineteenth-century colonization, but it involved migrations between continents. Toward the 1950s, this more-traditional outflow from southern Europe to the Americas was replaced by migration heading north within Europe, led by Italy, Greece, Portugal, and Spain, later joined by Turkey (Venturini 2004, 13). To take only one example, the share of Portuguese emigrants moving *within* Europe rose from a tiny minority of 1.5 percent in 1950–1954 to a large majority of 57.1 percent in 1970–1974 (United Nations 1979). Migration *within* Europe (including Turkey) grew rapidly in the early postwar years through guestworker arrangements, particularly in Germany, where the share of the foreign-born among workers rose from 0.6 to 11.2 percent between 1957 and 1972. This European south-north migration came to an end in 1973 "due to economic recession and to social problems arising from immigration. . . . The flows from southern [Europe decreased], but [southern European immigrants] were replaced by immigrants from other countries" (Venturini 2004, 13). Foreign nationals increased from 1.3 percent of the western European population in 1950 to 4.5 percent in 1990. The 1990 figure would easily double if it included the foreign-born who had become naturalized (Stalker 1994, 189–190).

More recently, western and southern Europe have become destinations for immigrants from Asia, the Middle East, and Africa, and since the demise of the Soviet Union in the 1990s, western Europe has also absorbed immigrants from the east, including the former Soviet republics. As a result, annual net immigration into the European Union rose from 200,000 in the 1980s to over a million in 1989–1993, before falling again to 640,000 in 1994–1998: over the 1980s and 1990s, EU immigration more than tripled. Indeed, EU immigration now surpasses that of the United States and would exceed it by even more if (estimated) illegal immigrants were included.

The second seismic shift involved the transformation of Latin America from a major migrant destination to a major migrant source. The Latin American evolution is a mirror image of the European transformation from a major source to a major destination, and it appears to be unique. The nineteenth-century mass migration experience reported in part II shows that poor, low-wage, agrarian countries send out few emigrants at first but that the numbers surge during early industrialization, before falling off during late industrialization. The late twentieth century illustrates how at some point these countries start to receive immigrants as they get rich, labor scarce, and high wage. Latin

America is the sole exception to this secular pattern, and the explanation for its being an exception appears to be that the region has an even richer and faster-growing neighbor to the north. Since the 1920s, Latin America has never been able to catch up with North America in terms of living standards, or even to reduce the gap between the two regions. Thus, it is hardly surprising that the stock of immigrants in Latin America and the Caribbean who were born outside the region fell from 3.7 million in 1960 to 3 million in 1980, while the number of Latin Americans and Caribbeans residing outside the region increased from 1.9 million to 4.8 million over the same two decades. The magnitude of this change has been really quite phenomenal: Latin America went from hosting (net) 1.8 million foreign-born to having (net) 1.8 million Latin Americans hosted abroad, a secular regime switch adding up to a net change of 3.6 million over only two decades!

The changing source of U.S. immigrants is particularly instructive in illustrating this Latin American migration revolution (table 10.2). Whereas only about a fifth (22.2 percent) of all U.S. immigrants came from south of the border in the 1950s, almost half (47.2 percent) did so

Table 10.2
Source area composition of U.S. immigration, 1951–2000 (percentage of total)

Region of origin	1951–1960	1961–1970	1971–1980	1981–1990	1991–2000
Europe	52.7	33.8	17.8	10.3	14.9
West	47.1	30.2	14.5	7.2	5.6
East	5.6	3.6	3.3	3.1	9.4
Asia	6.1	12.9	35.3	37.3	30.7
Americas	39.6	51.7	44.1	49.3	49.3
Canada	15.0	12.4	3.8	2.1	2.1
Mexico	11.9	13.7	14.2	22.6	24.7
Caribbean	4.9	14.2	16.5	11.9	10.8
Central America	1.8	3.1	3.0	6.4	5.8
South America	3.6	7.8	6.6	6.3	5.9
Africa	0.6	0.9	1.8	2.4	3.9
Oceania	0.5	0.8	0.9	0.6	0.6
Total (thousands)	2,515	3,322	4,493	7,338	9,095

Source: U.S. Citizenship and Immigration Services 2003 (table 2).
Note: National origin based on country of last residence. Totals include 2.7 million former illegal aliens receiving permanent resident status under the Immigration Reform and Control Act of 1986. Of these, 1.3 million fall in the decade 1981–1990 and 1.4 million in the decade 1991–2000.

in the 1990s, the latter about equally split between Mexico and the rest of Latin America plus the Caribbean. The share of U.S. (legal) immigration accounted for by Mexicans increased from almost 12 percent in the 1950s to almost 25 percent in the 1990s. No doubt the measured share would have increased even more had it included illegals.

The third seismic shift during the postwar decades involved Asian and African immigrants, whose numbers rose from negligible to very large. Postwar Asian migrants to the United States have come mainly from India, Pakistan, China, Korea, the Philippines, and Vietnam. Europe has undergone the same surge in Asian immigration, as well as a surge in immigration from Africa and the Middle East. Annual immigration from the developing world into five major European destination countries—Belgium, Germany, the Netherlands, Sweden, and the United Kingdom—rose from 97,000 in 1975–1979 to 225,000 in 1990–1993 (United Nations 1997, 32–33). For Germany alone, annual immigration from North Africa and western Asia more than tripled from 20,000 in 1975–1979 to 67,000 in 1990–1993, while the numbers from sub-Saharan Africa over the same period rose from 1,200 to 22,000.

The fourth seismic shift involved the Persian Gulf. The development of oil production and exports in the countries bordering the Persian Gulf—particularly, thinly populated Saudi Arabia, Kuwait, Bahrain, and the United Arab Emirates—led to a large labor demand boom which spilled over into an increasing demand for foreign workers. The rapid job creation appeared in construction, trade, and low-skilled service industries, as well as in occupations requiring more highly educated workers, such as teaching, engineering, and medicine. Initially, the rising excess demand for labor was satisfied by importing temporary contract workers from nearby parts of the Arab world, like Egypt, Palestine, and Yemen. With the formation of the Organization of Petroleum Exporting Countries (OPEC) cartel and with the continuing increase in world demand for oil, crude oil prices reached unprecedented heights in the 1970s. OPEC revenues tripled over about five years, from less than $200 billion in 1971–1975 to over $600 billion in 1976–1980 (Abella 1995, 418). The increase was much bigger if calculated over the decades following the late 1960s.

This price boom raised local income and generated an extraordinary increase in the demand for foreign workers. Contract workers from other Arab states continued to move to the Persian Gulf, but they were soon far outnumbered by the millions of temporary workers from nearly all parts of Asia. The annual flow of Asian workers to the Middle East increased from less than 100,000 in 1975 to nearly one million in 1991, with the sources moving eastward as time went on. The share from Pakistan and India decreased from 97 percent in 1975 to 36 percent in 1991. Taking the place of immigrants from Pakistan and India were those from Bangladesh and Sri Lanka, whose share increased to 22 percent, and those from Southeast and East Asia, whose share increased to 42 percent. By 1990 the stock of Asian workers had grown to about 400,000 in Kuwait, to nearly half a million in the United Arab Emirates, to over 1.5 million in Saudi Arabia, and to over 3.5 million in the Gulf region as a whole (Abella 1995; United Nations 2000a). The shift from Arab to Asian foreign labor in the Persian Gulf countries arose in part because of the lower Asian reservation wage, but also because the receiving countries wanted foreign labor that would not settle permanently and would be less of a cultural or political threat to the indigenous population than other Arabs would be. The eastward movement in the recruitment of Asian migrant workers reflected an attempt to diversify origins and prevent any one group from dominating the region.

Asian workers came to the Persian Gulf under short-term contracts (generally only one to two years). To facilitate the transfer, private agencies were established in the sending countries early on, and some governments (e.g., those of South Korea and the Philippines) actively promoted labor contracts for their construction workers. After all, the arrangement provided benefits in the form of higher-paying jobs for many of their nationals, profitable contracts for their construction firms, and substantial foreign exchange earnings from remittances and repatriated wages and profits (Amjad 1989).

The fifth seismic shift involved emigration from eastern Europe. The movement of European labor from the less-industrial and poor east to the more-industrial and rich west has a long history that goes back to the industrial revolution almost two centuries ago. Even during the troubled interwar years, migration from Poland and Czechoslovakia to Belgium and France was extensive.[2] In the five years following the end of World War II, something like 12 million ethnic Germans returned to Austria or Germany from Poland, Czechoslovakia, and the Soviet Union. When the Soviet Union annexed eastern parts of Poland at the end of the war, some 1.5 million Poles emigrated. In addition, there was migration "churning" within eastern Europe associated with postwar political readjustment.

This traditional east-west flow of European migrants was stopped dead by postwar emigration policy in the centrally planned economies: "By 1950, the newly established communist regimes imposed strict emigration controls. Migration to countries with established market economies was practically forbidden. Migration between centrally-planned economies occurred on a very limited scale." (United Nations 2002a, 12). Thus, a historically important world migration flow almost ceased for three or four decades after 1950—almost, but not quite. There were important exceptions: reunification of Jews with their families in Israel was allowed by the Soviet regime after the mid-1960s; in 1963, the Yugoslav constitution recognized explicitly the right of its citizens to emigrate, making it possible for about a half million to flow to Germany as guestworkers; and the political events in Hungary (1956) and Czechoslovakia (1968) drove out two bursts of refugees.

Things changed dramatically in the 1980s when Poland and Romania opened up, and they changed even more dramatically when the Berlin Wall fell in November 1989. Emigration from what came to be called the transition economies increased five times between 1985 and 1989, from about 240,000 to about 1.2 million. The annual outflows stayed at those high levels until 1993, when they eased off a bit, averaging around 700,000 in 1997 and 1998 (United Nations 2002a, tables 3, 5). At the start of the new century, Europe seems to have reestablished its old east-west migration tradition.

World Migration Trends since 1950—Legal and Illegal

Legal Migration

The same fundamentals that drove mass migration in the late nineteenth century also help explain world migration more recently, especially its changing composition by source. During its so-called golden age of growth from 1950 to 1973, the dramatic convergence of income and earnings within Europe and between Europe and the overseas countries contributed tremendously to the sharp decline in the share of Europeans in New World immigrant totals (figure 10.1, table 10.2). The rise in Asian immigration to a peak in the 1980s coincides with *their* growth miracle too, conforming to the life cycle pattern that was so common to nineteenth-century European emigrations. Secular booms and busts in the growth of the emigration-age cohorts also contributed to secular changes in the composition of migration (table 10.3),

Table 10.3
Growth of emigration age group on four continents, 1955–1995

	1955	1965	1975	1985	1995
Percentage growth in previous five years of population aged 20–29					
Europe	3.1	−3.2	14.0	1.9	−3.7
Latin America and Caribbean	11.1	12.3	19.9	15.5	8.5
Asia	10.6	4.8	21.4	13.1	9.0
Africa	11.6	10.4	14.4	17.0	14.3
Population aged 20–29/population aged 20–64					
Europe	28.5	25.6	27.1	26.8	24.1
Latin American and Caribbean	35.0	34.9	37.2	37.8	35.6
Asia	34.4	32.8	35.3	35.5	34.7
Africa	37.0	36.1	37.4	38.7	38.6

Source: Calculated from United Nations 1999 (various tables).

as precocious East Asia, then imitating Southeast Asia, and finally lagging South Asia passed through their own demographic transitions (Bloom and Williamson 1998). In Europe, Asia, and Latin America, the growth of populations aged twenty to twenty-nine slowed after 1975, although much less so in Latin America than in Europe and Asia. By contrast, African populations in this emigration-age group continued to surge, a fact that clearly influenced migration out of Africa, a topic to which we return at length in chapter 12.

Immigration has, of course, been heavily constrained by quotas and other regulations since the Second World War. Thus, the underlying fundamentals driving world migration are harder to identify, since immigration flows and patterns by source reflect immigration policy as well as those fundamentals. The next chapter has far more to say about this, but some introduction to the role of policy in the postwar decades might be useful at this point.

When in the 1960s North America and Oceania eliminated selective policies and quotas based on national origin and ended their virtual ban on Asian immigration, those policy changes broke the preexisting link between allocated quotas and nineteenth-century European immigration and opened the door to immigration from the Third World, Asia in particular. Subsequent legislation further altered the country composition of the quotas and the rules governing employment-based immigration. Where these constraints were absent, economic and demographic fundamentals clearly shaped the pattern of immigration. For example, spouses of U.S. citizens who are not themselves U.S. citizens are not subject to numerical restrictions on immigration, and when their experience is examined for the years between 1972 and 1990, origin country per capita income has the expected negative effect on the number admitted, while origin country education has the expected positive effect (Jasso, Rosenzweig, and Smith 2000, 219). To take another example, when an ex ante measure of immigration—applications for skilled immigration visas—is examined for Australia, real GDP ratios as well as relative unemployment rates between home and destination countries are found to have determined the flow of applicants as predicted (Cobb-Clark and Connolly 1997).

Economic forces also explain ex post (policy-constrained) outcomes. A study of postwar immigration into Germany (1964–1988) has demonstrated that migrant flows were determined by short-term cyclical factors, as measured by unemployment rates, and by long-term forces, as measured by income per capita in Germany and the sending countries (Karras and Chiswick 1999). The lagged net migration rate, representing chain migration effects, was also important. Income, unemployment, and a variety of other economic and demographic variables have been shown to influence U.S. and Canadian immigration rates, across source countries and through time (Karemera, Oguledo, and Davis 2000). Other evidence points to the U.S. immigrant stock as the single most important determinant of the country composition of U.S. immigration (Yang 1995, 119). This finding suggests that the relationship of a potential immigrant to a U.S. citizen or resident alien has been the single most important channel of entry since 1965, a result consistent with nineteenth-century experience.

The famines, revolutions, and pogroms that augmented nineteenth-century emigration magnitudes, influenced its timing, and often changed its source (chapter 4) have also left their mark on postwar mass migrations. As we show in chapter 12, civil wars in Africa displaced annually across international borders sixty-four per thousand of population, while government crises, coups d'etat, and guerilla warfare had similar, although somewhat smaller, effects (Hatton and Williamson 2003). Some really massive political upheavals have generated even larger migrant flows to the developed world. The fall of Saigon in April 1975 produced a large-scale refugee exodus to the United States from Vietnam, Laos, and Cambodia, and twenty years later, the disintegration of Yugoslavia generated a large exodus to the European Union. Yet the numbers seeking asylum in developed countries are also influenced by economic fundamentals, as we show in chapter 13. German asylum applications from the Third World were, between 1984 and 1995, influenced by relative incomes in the home country and Germany and by the existing migrant stock in Germany, as well as by terror and armed conflict (Rotte, Vogler, and Zimmermann 1997). Thus, asylum seekers also respond to economic conditions and asylum policies, suggesting that even they compare the economic advantages and disadvantages of alternative destinations.

While the same variables may have influenced world migration before 1914 and after 1950, the size of their impact may well have been different. There are really two issues here. First, we need to know whether the *unconstrained* effects are the same now as then. Net emigration from African countries, largely across the porous borders within the region, provides one benchmark (Hatton and Williamson 2003). Chapter 12 shows that a 10 percent rise in the foreign-to-home wage ratio increased net African out-migration by 0.9 per thousand, roughly comparable to the 1.3 per thousand recorded for late-nineteenth-century Europe. Demographic effects also appear to be just as powerful in modern Africa as they were in late-nineteenth-century Europe. Thus, it appears that the relevant elasticities characterizing *unconstrained* emigration may not have changed very much over the last two centuries.

Second, we need to know how much difference policy makes. The effects of immigration policy can be illustrated by comparing econometric estimates for U.K. emigrants after 1975, when they faced immigration controls, with those for U.K. emigrants before 1914, when they did not (Hatton and Williamson 1998, 65; Hatton 2004b). The friends-and-relatives or chain migration effect operates even more powerfully now than in the late nineteenth century, since it has been reinforced by family reunification policies. Each thousand added to the migrant stock in the host country generates between 50 and 100 percent more new migrants per year in the postwar period compared with before 1914.[3] By contrast, the effect of source country unemployment is only a fifth to a third as large and relative income only a tenth to a fifth as large in recent times compared with a century ago. Thus, immigration policy acts as a filter that enhances immigrant stock effects but mutes wage and employment effects on international migration.

Such orders of magnitude are only very rough approximations of the effect of policy, and the next chapter tries to make them sharper. Nevertheless, they clearly suggest that liberalizing barriers to migration would dramatically alter the demographic landscape, partly because of the increased responsiveness to migration incentives that would occur in the absence of barriers and partly because the magnitude of those incentives are *much* bigger now than they were in the past. New World real wages were double those in western Europe in the late nineteenth century, while today, real wages in the OECD are five to ten times those in the Third World. Chapter 11 elaborates on research findings that estimate that an EU expansion to include the ten central and eastern European accession candidate countries (with income levels 40 percent of those in the EU) would trigger a westward movement of three million people into the existing EU within just fifteen years (Bauer and Zimmermann 1999). Liberalizing immigration from the Third World would produce *much* larger effects, both relatively and absolutely, effects that would accumulate as rising immigrant stocks in the destination and rising real wages at home both served to relax the poverty constraint on emigration.

Illegal Migration

Restrictive immigration policy has caused the demand for visas among potential immigrants to outstrip the supply made available by host countries. The result has been queues for visas of increasing length in those host countries that ration and a growing population of illegal aliens residing in the host countries who have bypassed the queue entirely. Since there were few restrictions on entry to most countries a century ago, illegal immigration was not a significant issue then. The first illegal aliens to appear in the United States were Chinese in the 1880s, since they were the first group to be excluded by law (1882). The second illegal aliens to appear were those who crossed porous Canadian and Mexican borders in the 1920s, evading the new quotas (chapter 9). Illegal aliens include persons for whom the cost of obtaining a legal visa is very high, or who cannot obtain a visa at all, or who are jumping ahead of others in the queue. While some of the host countries experiencing large illegal immigration are New World countries of overseas settlement—such as Australia, the United States, and Canada, others are traditionally countries of emigration that only recently have experienced rising immigration pressure—like those in southern Europe and Japan (Weiner and Hanami 1998; OECD 2000a; Venturini 2004).

The estimated illegal immigrant magnitudes worldwide are very large. Even conservative estimates set the stock of foreign-born living illegally in host countries at ten million (Skeldon 2000). One source estimates that half of all new OECD immigrants are now illegal and that the vast majority of these gain entrance through the purchase of smuggler services (IOM 2003). Descriptions of human smuggling "contracts" prevailing today (Friebel and Guriev 2004) sound remarkably like the contract labor and indentured-servitude arrangements that were so common in the eighteenth and nineteenth centuries, only such arrangements were made illegal a century ago (chapters 2 and 7). Today's smugglers can serve two functions—to get the immigrant illegally under the wire and also to finance the move: "Smugglers and other intermediaries finance the costs of undocumented entry, and the debt repayment is taken out of migrants' wages in sweatshops and restaurants that are related to these intermediaries" (Friebel and Guriev 2004, 1). Furthermore, theory can be used to show how a crackdown on illegals—deportation, not stricter border controls—can increase, rather than decrease, the inflow of illegals and also make them even more unskilled and negatively selected (Friebel and Guriev 2004). Everything hinges on the debt contract and the ability and incentive of the indebted illegal to escape into the legal sector.

Illegal workers tend to be very low-skilled (Chiswick 2001). This fact is explained only in small part by the fact that immigration policy favors high-skilled applicants. A more-important influence has been the increase in income and labor market information at home, both of which have made it easier even for low-skilled workers in poor sending developing countries (now with higher income as a result of development at home) to purchase professional illegal migration services (now cheaper as a result of increased experience and volume). Another reason that illegal workers tend to be low-skilled is that high-skilled workers find it much harder to mask their illegal status and to secure illegal employment which fully exploits their skills. Low-skilled jobs are less likely to require licenses, certifications, and other documentation that might reveal legal status. Limited transferability of skills acquired in the origin country is far more relevant for skilled workers than for unskilled workers. Illegal aliens are also less likely to bring dependent family members with them, as this would increase the probability of their illegal status being detected. As a result, they are more likely to move back and forth between origin and destination. Repeated migration is costly for skilled workers, since the value of location-specific skills depreciates when they are transferred to another location. Finally, the wage differential between the origin and destination is much larger for low-skilled than for high-skilled potential illegal migrants. Thus, there is no shortage of economic explanations for the common observation that illegal migrants are disproportionately low-skilled.

Policy response to illegal migration has taken three forms (OECD 2000a; Chiswick 2001). One response has been to increase border enforcement. Although this certainly has reduced the flow of illegal alien workers, borders remain porous, and thus the impact of such enforcement has been modest. Our guess is that border enforcement has done more to raise the cost of illegal migrant services than to reduce the flow of illegals, in much the way that attempts to limit the drug trade have raised the prices for illegal drugs while being less successful at reducing their availability. Even island nations, such as the United Kingdom and Japan, have discovered that liberal democracies cannot seal their borders.

A second response has been to improve the effectiveness of interior enforcement of immigration regulations, mainly by imposing penalties on employers of illegal aliens. Although employer sanctions of this type have been adopted in many countries, including the United States in the 1986 Immigration Reform and Control Act, they have been weakly enforced at best, as have other instruments intended to enforce immigration law away from the borders. Obviously, there are good political economy reasons for the weak enforcement.

A third response has been to convert illegal workers into legal workers through amnesty, that is, to "regularize" their immigration status. The United States has implemented the largest amnesty program of this type. Under the provisions in the Immigration Reform and Control Act, nearly three million individuals received legal status in 1986, primarily low-skilled workers from Latin America and their family members (Chiswick 1988). Although the combination of amnesty and employer sanctions was supposed to "wipe the slate clean" (amnesty) and "keep it clean" (sanctions), illegal immigration to the United States has continued unabated: it has been estimated—after almost two decades since the 1986 amnesty—that there are something like five to seven million illegal aliens now living in the United States. In the late 1990s, the very tight labor market, the growing size of the illegal alien population, and the difficulty labor unions were having maintaining their membership base all resulted in a call from many quarters for another amnesty. The political pressure for another large amnesty diminished with the economic slowdown in 2001 and the terrorist attack by aliens in September of that year.

Labor-scarce liberal democracies are in a quandary. They offer wage opportunities that are very high by the standards of the countries that send immigrants to them. The increase in origin country wealth, the fall in transportation costs, the increased ease of staying in contact with families at home through ever-cheaper communication, and the emergence of new immigrant enclaves in host countries have all spurred incentives for and lowered costs associated with low-skilled migration. Immigration barriers are introduced in part to protect low-skilled native workers from the labor market competition posed by low-skilled immigrants, as well as to suppress the public income transfers, low-cost housing demands, and added pressure on the social service delivery system that results from the immigration of low-skilled immigrants. These immigration barriers and sanctions on the employment of illegals have never been fully effective. It appears that liberal democracies have thus far refused to adopt the draconian measures that would be needed to prevent illegal migration or discourage its continuance once it occurs. Because of the negative externalities and social problems associated with an alien population living and working outside the law, amnesties are introduced.

Amnesties do not wipe the slate clean. Since they do not address the causes of illegal immigration, they do not keep the slate clean either. Indeed, amnesties encourage others to become illegal immigrants, since once instituted, amnesties offer the likely prospect of amnesties in the future as well.

The Evolution of Immigration Control

Early in the age of world mass migration, immigration controls were either nonexistent or largely ineffective. But as the numbers of immigrants mounted toward the end of the nineteenth century, host countries became increasingly interested in immigration control. As chapter 8 has made clear, the door to immigrants was closed gradually rather than slammed shut overnight as it is often supposed. The shift away from proimmigration policies began with the removal of various subsidies for immigration. Cheap land at the frontier lost its value to potential immigrants to Brazil and the United States as they turned increasingly to urban jobs. Argentina abandoned its immigration subsidies in 1890, as did Chile in 1891. Australia and New Zealand progressively reduced their levels of assistance to immigrants after the 1880s, with subsidization policies revived only briefly in the subsidies provided by the British government under the Empire Settlement Act of 1922. The subsequent shift away even from neutral immigration policies began with the regulation of shipping companies dealing with the immigrant trade and with emigration agents, bans on contract labor, bans on those who were likely to become public charges, and bans on those considered undesirable as immigrants because of their race or origin.

The interwar story was told in chapter 9, but it might be helpful to review it briefly here. Chinese immigrants were excluded from the United States by an act of 1882 and those from Japan by a "gentlemen's agreement" in 1908. All Asians (other than those from the Middle East) were excluded as part of the Asian Barred Zone in 1917. After several attempts at passing legislation to do so over a quarter century, the United States finally introduced a literacy test for immigrants in 1917, although illiterate relatives (spouses and children) of an admitted literate immigrant were given visas despite their illiteracy. As we have noted, the literacy test proved to be an ineffective barrier to immigration, so it was followed by quotas based on national origins in acts passed in 1921 and 1924, legislation whose intent was to choke off immigrants from southern and eastern Europe. A literacy test was introduced in Natal in 1897 and it was followed by similar tests introduced in Australia in 1901 (the White Australia Policy), New Zealand in 1907, and Canada in 1910. Similar patterns of escalating restrictions were adopted in South Africa and Brazil, culminating in quota systems in the early 1930s. Even the British dominions adopted severe restrictions limiting immigration from Britain in the 1930s.

Post–World War II immigration policies have been even more heterogeneous, but they can be roughly classified under four regimes. The first regime included the famous guestworker systems of the early postwar years. The best known is that of Germany, where wartime forced labor was replaced first by inflows of ethnic Germans displaced from territories lost in the east, and then, through a series of bilateral agreements, by guestworkers from southern Europe and Turkey. Recruitment for guestworker programs was abruptly stopped in 1973, but between 1960 and then, about a million were recruited annually to work in Germany. Guestworker programs in France, Belgium, and the Netherlands were less well known and on a smaller scale, but all of

them were abruptly halted as a result of the oil price shock in 1973 and
the recession that followed. Active recruitment of low-skilled temporary migrants took place in North America too: the *Bracero* program
(1942–1964) was initiated in the United States during the tight labor
markets of World War II, when labor, mainly Mexican, was recruited
to work under short-term contract in agriculture. And as we have
noted, new guestworker streams were established in the Persian Gulf
after the 1970s.

The second regime involved a dramatic policy shift in the major immigrant host countries from systems based on national origins to systems based on worldwide quotas. The 1965 amendments to the U.S.
Immigration and Nationality Act broke the link between allocated
quotas and past immigration, ended the virtual ban on immigration
from Asia, and introduced a quota for immigrants from the Western
Hemisphere. Similarly, Canada abolished preferences for British, Irish,
and other western European immigrants in 1962. The White Australia
Policy was abandoned, gradually in the 1960s, and then decisively in
1973, while New Zealand waited until 1987 to abandon its comparable
policy.

It is not likely to have been mere coincidence that the three major
English-speaking countries of overseas settlement abandoned their
pro-western-European immigration policies at about the same time.
Rapid economic growth and tight labor markets in these countries,
plus the decline in emigration from western Europe resulting from the
tight labor markets there, were both important factors. In addition, racist immigration policies in the United States, Canada, and Australia
did not sit well with the newly independent African and Asian countries that were to become increasingly important trading partners and
neutrals or participants in the cold war between western democracies
and communist countries.[4] As if these forces were not enough, the
growing Civil Rights movement in the United States also made the
openly racist national-origins quota system political anathema.

The third regime gave a more-important role to humanitarian considerations. An increase in refugee admissions was often followed by
policies that made subsequent immigration through family reunification easier. These were underpinned by a growing body of international agreements aimed at protecting human rights.[5] Humanitarian
agreements such as the 1951 Geneva Convention on Refugees, to
which a growing number of countries subscribed, also opened the
door to an increasing number of asylum seekers from the 1980s on-

ward. Amnesties to illegal immigrants became more frequent, with notable ones in Italy (1977–1978), France (1981–1982), Argentina (1984), and the United States (1986), and a further wave among EU countries in the 1990s (Stalker 1994, 152). However, chapter 13 shows how the European Union has begun to tighten up on the conditions for family reunification and to limit its generosity toward asylum seekers and illegal immigrants.

In the fourth regime, OECD countries have increasingly sought to allocate visas on the basis of skill. A skills component was introduced into the Canadian points system in 1965, which was later given more weight. Australia and New Zealand also shifted away from policies targeting immigrants in specific occupations and more toward their selection on the basis of education and experience (Winklemann 2001). The systems in these two countries award points for education, experience, language skills, and being in a prime age group and also include categories for business migrants bringing capital or intending to start a business. The United States sharply increased its employment-related immigrant visas in 1990, more than doubling what had been a small skill-based employment visa program. Although a Canadian-style point system was seriously considered by the U.S. Congress in the late 1980s, the 1990 Immigration Act retained the employer petition and job-targeting method of rationing skill-based visas. Cumbersome administrative procedures have limited the use of the employment-based visas in the United States, and the quotas for such visas have not been filled.

The Political Economy of Postwar Policy Regimes

Dramatic shifts in policy over time and significant differences in policy among countries are explained in the older literature typically on a purely ad hoc basis, but a newer literature has recently emerged which accounts systematically for policy formation. The idea is simple enough: if those who stand to gain by immigration are politically powerful, then immigration policy will be less restrictive. If instead those who stand to lose by immigration wield the strongest political muscle, then immigration policy will be more restrictive.

Chapter 8 explored the late-nineteenth-century evidence regarding this simple but powerful idea and found that the evidence supported it. However, that chapter also reported that economics did not always dominate, since politics also mattered, and in several different ways.

First, shifts in the political balance, either through the adoption of democratic institutions or through the extension of the franchise, often tipped the balance in favor of immigration control. This shifting political balance implied a weakening of landed interests and the strengthening of labor interests, particularly unskilled labor, from the mid-nineteenth century onward, shifting the political balance against immigration. Second, changing attitudes toward immigrants and outright racial prejudice often mattered. Third, ethnic politics were often important, where members of an ethnic group sought to encourage the immigration of those who would add to the group's size and power but limit that of others. Fourth, the political elite were often captured by particular interest groups or were sufficiently powerful to pursue strategic aims independent of their political mandate. The bottom line is that the same economic forces often translated into different policy outcomes across countries and over time.

The late-nineteenth- and early-twentieth-century restrictionist forces identified in chapter 8 also seem relevant for the early postwar period, but working in reverse. Rapid real wage growth, narrowing income distributions, diminishing skill differentials, and falling foreign-born shares all served to ease the pressure for restriction early in the postwar period. This was reflected by a broadening in the market and an extension of political access to previously excluded groups. European recruitment policies of the 1960s, the 1965 U.S. amendments to the Immigration and Nationality Act, and Australia's abandonment of its British-only policy were each preceded by a rising scarcity of the most-desired immigrants. For example, Germany turned to southern European guestworkers only after the Berlin Wall went up and traditional sources of East German and central European immigrants dried up. The United States introduced its immigration reforms in 1965 only after two decades of impressive economic growth, increased labor scarcity, and Soviet anti-emigration policy which stanched the traditionally large outflow of eastern European emigrants. Finally, Australia dismantled its ultra-pro-British policy only as the available immigrants fell far short of national targets for "population or perish" goals.

So much for underlying fundamentals. What about the timing of policy change? During times of high unemployment, immigrants augment the pool of the unemployed or push natives into the pool. All groups who fear social unrest have an interest in tightening immigration restrictions under such poor macroeconomic conditions. Thus, unemployment has been found to have been a key determinant of the timing of restrictive immigration policy in the United States since the turn of the century, as reflected either in deportations or required departures relative to the immigrant flow (Shughart, Tollison, and Kimenyi 1986; Timmer and Williamson 1996, 1998). Similarly, unemployment has been found to be the key variable explaining the timing of moves from less- to more-restrictive policy in OECD countries since the 1960s (Money 1999, chap. 2). The abrupt termination of European guestworker policies in 1974 surely owes much to deteriorating economic conditions.[6] In postwar Australia, the unemployment rate has been found to be the single most important determinant of the annually announced targets for immigrant intake (Wooden et al. 1994, 304).[7]

Macroeconomic conditions have helped dictate the timing of OECD immigration policy change throughout the postwar period, just as they did a century ago in the New World.

An Agenda for What Remains

This survey in this chapter suggests an agenda for the remainder of the book. The next chapter explores exactly how the fundamentals driving immigration have interacted with policy over the past half century. Chapter 12 dwells on the emigration experience of what should become the next major source of mass migration, Africa. Demography turns out to matter in somewhat different ways as the AIDS epidemic races against the demographic transition in influencing emigration out of Africa. Asylum seeking rose dramatically after the 1980s, and chapter 13 explores the reasons why. It will also try to understand the political economy of reactions to the asylum seekers. Chapter 14 returns to a question that organized much of the discussion in chapters 6, 8, and 9: Do immigrants crowd out unskilled residents and thus contribute to inequality in incomes? The modern literature has tended to reach quite a different conclusion than has the historical literature, and chapter 14 explores the reasons why. Chapter 15 shows how interconnected are the issues of immigrant assimilation in the destination countries and emigrant brain drain in the sending countries. Finally, we explore explanations for anti-immigrant feeling in chapters 16 and 17 before concluding with a look to the future in chapter 18.

11 World Migration under Policy Constraints

In two markets at least—goods and capital—globalization forces since 1950 have brought world economic integration back to where it was in 1913. The progressive relaxation of controls on international capital flows, extensive tariff reductions, and the removal of nontariff barriers have led the way. As we have seen in the previous chapter, the same has not been true of the third market, labor. World migration revived in the decades following World War II, but it has never returned to the levels observed in the Atlantic economy prior to World War I. Indeed, the world labor market has not been reintegrated to anywhere near the same degree as world markets for goods and capital. Immigration controls introduced in the 1920s and 1930s remain in place and new ones have been added, clearly inhibiting the flow of labor across national boundaries.

That said, it might seem odd that so little has been done to assess the impact of these restrictive policies on world migration. While tariffs and other trade barriers have been measured and their impact assessed, the same has not been true of restrictive migration policy. Accordingly, this chapter examines the impact of shifting immigration policies over the past half century. It is guided by two questions raised in the previous chapter. First, do the same economic and demographic fundamentals that drove mass migrations before 1914 still matter in explaining the volume and composition of immigration flows today, even in the presence of restrictions? Second, how have shifts in immigration policy affected the volume and composition of these flows?

Explaining Migration

Chapter 4 examined the forces that drove transatlantic migration before World War I. Are the same forces equally important in an era

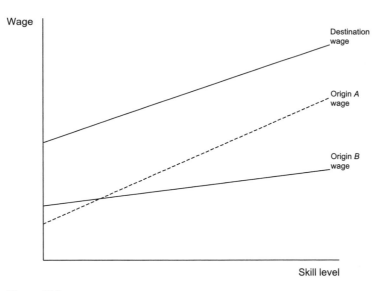

Figure 11.1
Wages by skill in origin and destination

when restrictive immigration policy is so pervasive? One view has it
that restrictive immigration policy acts as a dam holding back potential
migrants, such that while the size of the lake created by the dam may
be influenced by the usual economic and demographic fundamentals,
they play no part in determining the volume of water coming over the
spillway. According to this view, it's the height of the spillway that
matters. We reject this view and offer an alternative in which policy
acts as a filter. While policy may attenuate and modify the effects of
the fundamentals on the numbers and types of migrants who are admitted to a particular country, it does not eliminate those effects. Our
view is that immigration outcomes are very much the joint product of
both migrant self-selection and government policy selection.

The incentive to migrate is depicted in figure 11.1, in which the wage
received at the origin and destination depends on skills. Skill here represents various human capital endowments that are rewarded in the
labor market: education and training, both age-related, as well as talent
and other attributes that are not age related. As the figure shows, the
wage is higher at the destination than at the origin for every skill level,
but along the origin *A* skill-wage function (the broken line in the figure), the wage gap decreases with skill, whereas it increases along the
origin *B* function. In both cases, individuals at all skill levels in the

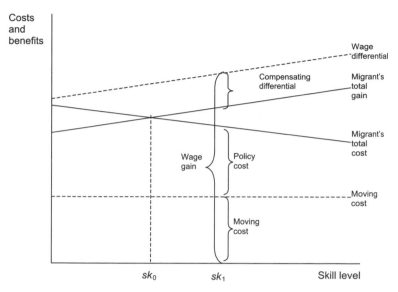

Figure 11.2
Costs and benefits of migration

origin country have an incentive to migrate. Furthermore, the absolute gap depends, among other things, on age: in origin A, the younger the potential migrant, the larger is his absolute wage gain; in origin B, the opposite is true. In addition, the skilled have a greater incentive to move from B than from A. All of these comparisons between A and B still apply when the lifetime of the migrant is considered and the gain is expressed in present value terms.

The migration gains from B are compared with the costs in figure 11.2. The top (broken) line represents the wage differential, the gap between destination and origin wages in figure 11.1. As figure 11.2 shows, the return to skill is greater in the destination than in the source country, so the skilled have most to gain from making the move. If the return to skill were greater at the origin than at the destination (as is true for origin A in figure 11.1), then the unskilled would have the most to gain from making the move, and the total wage gains function would be downward sloping.

Any migration decision must also take into account noneconomic considerations. These are represented in the figure by the vertical distance between the wage differential function and that describing the migrant's gain—in this case, a parallel downward shift. Potential migrants prefer home country, home culture, and family contact. Thus, they must be sufficiently compensated to get them to leave their origin (the compensating differential). For many individuals, the compensating differential required to persuade them to move may be large enough to wipe out any potential wage gain from migration. Even when the costs of moving are close to zero, not everyone will move. Figure 11.2 assumes that there is no correlation between skill level and this compensating differential (hence the parallel shift). If instead the compensating differential is thought to be smaller for the skilled than for the unskilled, then the migrant's gain function will be steeper than that for the wage differential.

The cost of migration has two parts. The first is the cost of the move itself: travel costs, job search costs, income foregone in both travel and job search, and psychic costs associated with the process of migrating. Once again, these moving costs are assumed to be invariant with skill, but they may not be. After all, since income foregone during the move is greater for the more skilled, the moving cost function should slope upward for that reason alone. Alternatively, the skilled may be more efficient in organizing the move and face lower job search costs, in which case the moving cost function will slope downward (Chiswick 2000). Figure 11.2 assumes that these two forces are offsetting.

The second part of the cost of migration is that imposed on the potential mover by immigration policy in the destination country, represented by the vertical distance between the constant moving costs just described and the total migration cost function. Some of this cost is obvious, such as application fees and the frustration generated by bureaucratic procedures. But there are other, more-important costs too, such as the long delays that result from visa rationing, delays that will also reduce (the present value of) the benefits of migration. These costs may be relatively low for some potential migrants, in particular, for those with relatives at the destination, which makes it possible for them to enter through family reunification schemes. For those without relatives at the destination or without other characteristics that meet immigration policy criteria, it may be almost impossible to gain access. For them, migration costs may be higher than any conceivable wage gain. The total migration cost curve slopes downward in figure 11.2 to reflect the lower costs faced by the skilled: immigration policy provides easier access (and therefore lower costs) for skilled compared with unskilled individuals. Indeed, where immigration policy is strongly skill-selective, total migration costs should include the costs of acquiring the necessary skills. A good historical example of this is offered by the rise in European literacy that made it easier for potential migrants to leap over the literacy bar imposed by the United States in 1917. It raised the cost for both individual and state in the European sending regions.

Any potential migrant with skills higher than sk_0 in figure 11.2 will migrate; to the right of sk_0, the gains outweigh the costs. With skill level less than sk_0, the individual will not migrate. A general tightening of immigration policy can be thought of as increasing the policy cost, shifting the total migration cost curve upward, while a shift to a more-skill-selective policy will produce a steeper downward slope. The same tightening will also, of course, encourage unskilled potential migrants to move as illegals.

Figure 11.2 applies the standard investment criterion to migration decisions, as first suggested by Sjastaad (1962). But the Sjastaad approach ignores an important theme of this book, namely, that many potential migrants are too poor to bear the cost of long-distance migration and face borrowing constraints. It is hardly surprising that borrowing for migration is difficult, since distance makes it so much easier to default on such loans. Thus, even if the gains from migration are large for the poorest unskilled workers, a substantial share of them may be unable to reap those gains, something we observed in the centuries before 1914. As a more-restrictive immigration policy raises the costs of the move, it serves to screen out a larger and larger share of the poor from poorer emigrant countries. In contrast, a policy that stresses family reunification reduces migration costs for the poor from poorer countries and thus helps break their poverty constraint.

Immigration Policy in the English-Speaking New World: Skilled Labor Requirements versus Family Reunification

The previous chapter showed how postwar immigration policy in the English-speaking New World shifted away from the country-of-origin quota systems that originated in the early 1920s. It is well worth dwelling on some of the details, since we plan to assess their impact in the next section.

The 1952 U.S. Immigration Act preserved the country-of-origin quota system. Most visas subject to quota were still allocated to European countries, and among these, two-thirds went to just two countries, Germany and the United Kingdom. Children and spouses of native-born and naturalized U.S. citizens were exempt from the quota. Visas were allocated according to a system of preferences that gave up to 50 percent of the issued visas to those with special skills and the remainder to (nonimmediate) relatives of U.S. citizens and alien residents. While Western Hemisphere immigrants were not subject to a quota, those from countries in the Asia-Pacific region were, and those quotas were small.

The 1965 amendments to the Immigration and Nationality Act embodied a radical shift in a policy that had prevailed for four decades. It established a maximum quota of 20,000 immigrants from each Eastern Hemisphere country annually, subject to an overall annual ceiling of 170,000. Within the quota, visas were allocated according to a seven-category preference system, which gave 64 percent to relatives of U.S. citizens and alien residents, 6 percent to refugees, and 30 percent to employment-based categories. As before, children and spouses of U.S. citizens were exempt from the quota. This new system strongly favored family reunification over employment-based immigration. Indeed, family reunification had been the main mechanism for entry even before the new legislation came into force in 1969. Many observers believed that while the revised policy would be seen as nondiscriminatory, the composition of the foreign-born would nevertheless ensure that new immigrants would continue to come from traditional European sources (Briggs 1984, 69; Daniels and Graham 2001, 43–44). In fact, the abolition of the national-origins quota system greatly increased immigration opportunities for non-Europeans, as we show subsequently.

The Western Hemisphere quota of 120,000 introduced in the 1965 act did not initially include country-specific quotas and a system of preferences, but these refinements were included by an act of 1976. This was followed in 1978 by an act that combined the quotas for the two hemispheres into an overall quota of 290,000. The preference category for refugees was removed in 1980, and the worldwide ceiling was reduced to 270,000. The 1986 Immigration Reform and Control Act provided for the legalization of illegal immigrants who had resided in the United States since before 1982. It also expanded the H-2 program for temporary foreign workers and introduced temporary visas for agricultural workers with three years' residence.

The most important amendment to the post-1965 regulations came in the 1990 Immigration Act. This legislation introduced an overall quota of 675,000 divided into three classes: 480,000 visas were allocated to family immigrants, with immediate relatives of U.S. citizens being subject to the quota for the first time; employment-based visas were increased to 140,000 (from 54,000 previously), under a five-part preference system; finally, visas were used to diversify immigrants by allocating 55,000 of them to those from countries with relatively low immigrant presence since 1965.

In contrast with the United States, Australia, Canada and New Zealand all elected to follow a postwar immigration policy that focused on national labor market needs. The preference given in Canada to immigrants from the United Kingdom, France, and the United States was abolished in 1962 and replaced with a scheme that allocated visas chiefly to sponsored dependants, nominated relatives, and independent migrants. The second and third of these categories became subject to a points test in 1967, which served to make Canadian and U.S. policy very different. In addition to those given for having relatives in Canada, points were awarded for youth (older adults got fewer points than younger ones), education, certain strategic occupations, employment arranged prior to immigration, and fluency in English or French. The Canadian system was modified by the Immigration Acts of 1976, 1988, and 1993. As a result, the share of Canadian immigrants admitted under the points system was reduced in the 1980s but increased again in the 1990s (Green and Green 1995, 1999). Modifications to the points system further increased the skill selectivity of immigration policy, and by 1994 nearly half of all Canadian immigrants were admitted principally according to characteristics relating to the labor market.

After its World War II experience, the postwar Australian government took the view that its population was too small to ensure economic and strategic security and that it needed to "populate or perish."[1] With a firmly established preference for British immigrants, Australia introduced the U.K. Assisted Passage scheme in 1947, which offered passages for ten pounds per adult and five pounds for those aged fourteen to eighteen. This was followed in 1957 by the "Bring out a Briton" campaign, with the result that 90 percent of U.K. immigrants to Australia were assisted in the 1960s (Appleyard 1988, 43). These assistance schemes were all reined back in the next decade, and the discriminatory White Australia Policy was abolished by the Whitlam government in 1975 (Hawkins 1989; Jupp 1991). New methods of immigrant positive selection were sought to replace these schemes, and thus Australia's first points system was launched in 1979. Over the following two decades, the proportion of Australia's immigrants that were subject to the points test was raised, and a business skills stream was introduced (DIMA 2000).

New Zealand was the last country to record this switch in immigration policy, and it followed the Canadian and Australian lead. A 1947 assisted passage scheme offered ten-pound passages for key workers, and it continued until 1975. The preference for British and European immigrants was weakened in 1974 and abolished in 1987. The points system adopted in 1991 resembled those of Canada and Australia but gave more weight to general skills rather than to specific occupations (Winklemann 2001). By the mid-1990s, 65 percent of New Zealand's immigrants were points-tested. As in Australia, the minimum threshold points score is adjusted depending on conditions in the domestic labor market.

Deglobalizing British Labor

These four English-speaking countries—the United States, Canada, Australia, and New Zealand—kept the immigration doors open to the British longer than to immigrants from the rest of Europe. Even so, British emigration fell over the postwar period, suggesting that British labor became less globally involved as time went on. Why? Late-twentieth-century British emigration experience provides an opportunity to assess the quantitative impact of immigration policy abroad on potential British emigrants before trying to do the same for potential emigrants from other parts of the world.

Between 1871 and 1913, U.K. passenger statistics recorded a gross emigration outflow of about ten million and a net emigration outflow of about six million, equivalent to about 13 percent of the 1913 population. The United States, Canada, Australia, and New Zealand jointly accounted for 88 percent of the gross and 93 percent of the net emigration of these British citizens. Gross emigration rates reached highs of around 8 per thousand in the early 1880s and again in 1910–1912. A significant share of these emigrants came from Ireland, but for Great Britain alone, the average net emigration rate was about 3 per thousand, as compared with 3.6 per thousand for the United Kingdom as a whole.

After an interwar lull and a wartime cessation, British emigration revived in the 1950s and 1960s. Figure 11.3 plots gross and net emigration of U.K. and Commonwealth citizens from 1964 to 1998. Gross emigration rates fell steadily from a peak of more than 4 per thousand in

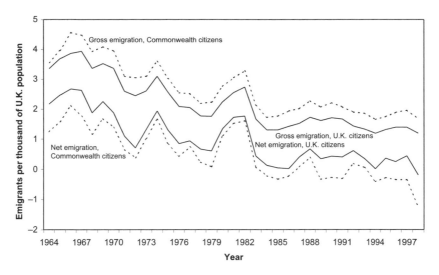

Figure 11.3
Gross and net emigration, U.K. and Commonwealth Citizens, 1964–1998. *Source:* Hatton 2004b.

the late 1960s, and by the late 1990s, net emigration rates were not far above zero for U.K. citizens and negative for Commonwealth citizens. Most U.K. emigrants continued to flow to the four traditional destinations. About two-thirds of the decline in U.K. emigration over the period is accounted for by declines in immigration to those four regions.

Figure 11.4 shows profiles of gross U.K. emigration to the principal destinations. The United States may have been the leading destination for U.K. emigrants before 1914, but Australia accounted for 53 percent of the four-country total in the early postwar period. Australia's emigration campaign and its heavy subsidization of passage must have diverted many British emigrants from the shorter and cheaper trip across the Atlantic. Furthermore, the discontinuation of these travel subsidies must also help explain why after the 1960s, British emigration to Australia fell so much more dramatically than it fell for the other countries combined. British emigration to Canada fell after its sharp, but less-sustained, peak in the mid- to late 1960s, that to Australia fell after the late 1960s, and that to New Zealand fell after the early 1970s, turning negative in the early 1990s. The United States was the only country of the four to which British emigration increased between the early 1970s and the late 1990s, but even to the United States, it did not increase by much.

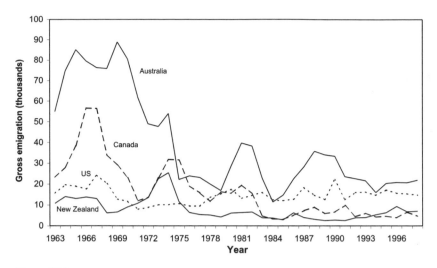

Figure 11.4
Gross U.K. emigration to the United States, Canada, Australia, and New Zealand. *Source:*
Hatton 2004b.

Can this striking late-twentieth-century decline in British emigration
be explained by the emergence of overseas policies that no longer favored the British? Or can it be explained instead by economic and demographic fundamentals? Or by both? We attack these questions from
two directions. The first is to predict what would have happened after
the mid-1960s if emigration had been determined in the same way as it
was before 1913, *without* immigration restrictions (Hatton 2004b). Using a model estimated for the different destinations before 1913 during
the free immigration period, figure 11.5 shows how U.K. emigration to
the four countries would have evolved after 1965 in the absence of immigration restrictions (the broken lines). The counterfactual suggests
that, after declining through the mid-1970s, emigration rates would have
surged through the late 1980s and then dropped sharply in the 1990s.
More to the point, actual emigration (conditioned by restrictive immigration policy abroad) and counterfactual emigration (under assumed
neutral immigration policy abroad) move pretty much the same way
through the mid-1970s and after the early 1990s, but their movements
differ dramatically in between. This pattern certainly suggests a role
for overseas immigration policy, as it changed over the period.

The second approach to the question is to estimate a migration
model for the late twentieth century that includes dummy variables to

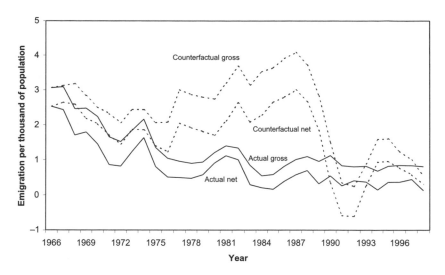

Figure 11.5
Actual and counterfactual U.K. emigration, four-country total, 1966–1998. *Source:* Hatton 2004b.

reflect decisive shifts in immigration policy in the key destination countries. Two insights emerge from this second approach. First, explanatory variables such as the share of population in the migration-sensitive age group, real wages, and unemployment rates (the latter two taken as a ratio of home to abroad) all have smaller effects after the mid-1960s than they did before World War I. While these labor market variables still influenced emigration, their effects were attenuated by the filter of tougher immigration policies. Second, policy dummies account for most of the fall in the level of emigration. Between 1966–1970 and 1980–1984, the gross emigration rate to the four countries fell by 1.6 per thousand. Policy shifts in Australia and Canada accounted for about 1.4 per thousand of the fall, or about 88 percent. Overseas immigration policy mattered a lot, and we can identify the impact.

The points systems imposed on immigration in the three former British dominions increasingly selected skilled immigrants. British manual workers had been heavily recruited in the 1950s and 1960s, but they subsequently faced points systems which made emigration much harder for them. While British unskilled workers were being squeezed out by immigrant policy, economic conditions at home made skilled workers lose interest in migration. That is, those who were higher up the British skill ladder had less incentive to emigrate, since the return to their skills increased dramatically at home. Between the late 1970s and the late 1990s, the Gini coefficient of household income increased in Britain from 0.25 to 0.32, an increase that reflected growing wage inequality and rising returns to human capital. Rising immigration barriers to the unskilled abroad and increasing returns to the skilled at home combined to account for a substantial share of the decline in British emigration in the postwar period (Hatton 2003). These variables also appear to account for the fact that British emigration to the United States did not fall after the early 1970s. U.S. immigration policies were less skill selective than those in Canada, Australia, and New Zealand, *and* the returns to skills increased in the United States just as much as they did in Britain. Once again, policy mattered a lot, and we can identify its impact.

Explaining U.S. Immigration

The United States was the leading destination country during the age of free migration, and it has held that position during the current age, when world migration has been constrained by policy. After falling from a spectacular pre–World War I flood to a restricted trickle in the 1930s, U.S. immigration surged from a low annual average of 252,000 in the 1950s to an impressive 916,000 in the 1990s. Chapter 10 showed how this growth was accompanied by a radical shift in the source country composition. Europeans accounted for more than half of all immigrants in the 1950s, and these were overwhelmingly from western Europe. The share from relatively rich western Europe declined to a mere 5.7 percent by the 1990s, while the share from relatively poor eastern Europe nearly doubled. The counterpart to the western European decline was the Asian rise: by the 1970s and 1980s, the Asian share of U.S. immigrants exceeded a third, a dramatic late-twentieth-century surge. The share from the American hemisphere also increased, particularly that from relatively poor countries in Central America and the Caribbean, and especially that from Mexico. Africa, the poorest continent, accounted for only a small share of U.S. immigrants although that share has grown rapidly.

The central feature of this late-twentieth-century evolution in U.S. immigration composition is the dramatic shift in source from rich to poor countries. What role has policy played in accounting for this shift? Did policy simply accommodate underlying demographic and economic forces that were causing immigrant sources to shift to poorer countries, a shift that mimicked the same forces which prevailed in the late nineteenth century? Or did policy provoke the shift?

The appropriate verb here is "accommodate," and the critical date is 1965, when U.S. legislation abolished the pro-European quotas that had prevailed since the 1920s and opened the door for immigration from the poorer parts of the world. The 1965 legislation produced a much larger pool of potential immigrants for whom the potential income gains from migration vastly outweighed any required compensating differential. Given their lower skills compared to the average U.S. resident, the new immigrants that resulted from the 1965 policy change were located farther down the U.S. income distribution than were previous immigrants, certainly compared with pre-1965 immigrants from favored western Europe, but even compared with the pre-1914 immigrants. That is, relative to average U.S. skills, post-1965 immigration became *less* positively selected, because of the shift toward poor country sources. We are less sure about changing skill selectivity *within* sending countries. To the extent that the return to skills was greater in sending countries than in the United States, there would have been negative selection within each source country, reinforcing the downward trend in the skills of the average U.S. immigrant (compared with the average U.S. citizen) driven by the shift toward poorer country sources. Earlier postwar waves of European immigration came from countries with income distributions similar to that of the United States and thus should have been more positively selected. We are less sure about income distributions in the poor countries that send migrants to the United States today.

One thing is certain: the 1965 immigration legislation, which favored family reunification, gradually lowered the costs of immigration for successive cohorts of migrants from new source countries. While the friends-and-relatives effect may have delayed the shift away from European immigrants, it quickly began to compound the flows from the poor Third World. It also fostered illegal immigration. In the long run, therefore, the change in U.S. immigration policy since 1965 has had an effect quite the opposite from that anticipated by most of its supporters.

Several studies have found that income gaps, inequality, policy, and the migrant stock all matter in accounting for immigration flows to the United States over the past half century (Borjas 1987; Yang 1995; Jasso, Rosenzweig, and Smith 2000; Karemera, Oguledo, and Davis 2000), just as part II reported was the case for the nineteenth century. However, none of these studies of modern world migrations has explored the role of these fundamentals *while controlling for policy*. We have dealt with this shortcoming by developing and estimating a model that explores both policy and fundamentals simultaneously (Clark, Hatton, and Williamson 2002). The data are a panel of migration rates to the United States from eighty-one countries over the years 1971–1998, and one variant of the model is shown in table 11.1.

The relative income variable is purchasing-power-parity-adjusted per capita income, and for that reason, relative skill levels, as proxied by years of education, are also included.[2] These variables produce significant coefficients with negative and positive signs, respectively, and the coefficients matter quantitatively. For example, the net effect of lower levels of income and education in South America as compared with lower levels of income and education in western Europe is to raise the typical South American country's migration rate to the United States by 25 percent over that of the typical country in western Europe. The relative return on skills is proxied by the ratio of source to destination income inequality. The Roy (1951) model suggests that the relationship between relative skills and the migration rate should be nonmonotonic, and hence the squared term is also included. The signs are positive and negative as expected, with a maximum when the ratio of inequality of source country relative to that in the United States is 1.33. These inequality effects raise the immigration rate from the typical (inegalitarian) South American country by 46 percent over the typical (egalitarian) western European country. Because South America has far higher skill premia and more-unequal incomes than Europe, the gains resulting from migration to unskilled South American immigrants would be greater than those to Europeans, even if the average income in South America and Europe was the same. Hence, South American immigrants should be less positively selected than European, or even Asian.[3]

Other variables also have the expected effects. The share of source country population in the age group fifteen to twenty-nine has a positive effect that raises migration rates from South America by 11 percent over those from western Europe. Adding a thousand miles to the distance from Chicago to the source country reduces the migration rate by about a fifth; the source country's being landlocked reduces it by more than a third; the source country's being predominantly

Table 11.1
Regression estimate for U.S. immigration, 1971–1998

$$LnMigRate = -11.95 - 1.80\ Ypc(f/h) + 2.61\ Sch(f/h) + 4.17\ Gini(f/h) - 1.57\ Gini(f/h)^2$$
$$\quad\quad (35.9)\quad (9.5)\quad\quad (12.7)\quad\quad\quad (7.1)\quad\quad\quad\quad (6.5)$$
$$+ 2.71\ Sp15\text{–}29 - 0.18\ Dist + 1.11\ Englp - 0.31\ Landlk + 42.91\ ImStck$$
$$\quad (2.7)\quad\quad\quad\quad (12.3)\quad\quad (15.4)\quad\quad (7.0)\quad\quad\quad (10.7)$$
$$- 182.94\ (ImStck)^2 - 0.36\ Pov + 0.06\ WH71\text{–}6 - 0.42\ EH71\text{–}6 - 0.01\ D92\text{–}8$$
$$\quad (6.5)\quad\quad\quad\quad (3.9)\quad\quad (0.8)\quad\quad\quad (6.3)\quad\quad\quad\quad (0.1)$$
$$+ 0.14\ D92\text{–}8 * Sch + 0.05\ IRCA$$
$$\quad (0.8)\quad\quad\quad\quad (2.9)$$
$$R^2 = 0.77$$

Source: This is a variant of the model presented in Clark, Hatton, and Williamson 2002. Further details concerning data sources and methods are available there.

Note: Robust t statistics in parentheses.

Sample: Balanced panel of number of immigrants to the United States by country/year, 1971–1998. Regional composition (number of countries): Western Europe (16), Eastern Europe (6), East Asia (14), Middle East (5), North America (2), Caribbean (4), Central America (6), South America (11), Africa (14), Oceania (3).

Definitions of variables: $LnMigRate$ = log of the ratio of immigrants admitted by country of birth per thousand of source country population; $Ypc(f/h)$ = ratio (source country to United States) of GDP per capita at 1985 purchasing-power parity; $Sch(f/h)$ = ratio (source country to United States) of years of schooling for those aged fifteen and over; $Sp15\text{–}29$ = share of source country population aged fifteen to twenty-nine; $Gini(f/h)$ = ratio (source country to United States) of Gini coefficient of household income; $Dist$ = great-circle distance from Chicago (in thousands of miles); $Englp$ = dummy, equals 1 if source country is predominantly English speaking; $Landlk$ = dummy, equals 1 if source country is landlocked; $ImStck$ = stock of immigrants in the United States from source country per thousand of source country population; Pov = source country Gini coefficient/source country income per capita squared; $WH71\text{–}6$ = dummy that equals 1 for Western Hemisphere countries times dummy that equals 1 for 1971–1976; $EH71\text{–}6$ = dummy that equals 1 for Eastern Hemisphere countries times dummy that equals 1 for 1971–1976; $D92\text{–}8$ = dummy, equals 1 for 1992–1998; $D92\text{–}8 * Sch$ = $D92\text{–}8$ times years-of-schooling ratio; $IRCA$ = estimated number of illegal immigrants residing in the United States in 1980 per thousand of source country population, times dummy that equals 1 for 1989–1991.

Method: Pooled ordinary least squares regression on 2,268 country/year observations. Dummies for Canada, Mexico, and eight regions (with Western Europe as the excluded group) included but not reported.

English-speaking raises it by a factor of three. The stock of previous immigrants from a source country enters nonlinearly. Evaluated at the mean, the coefficients imply that an addition of 1,000 to the migrant stock increases the annual immigrant flow by 26—an order of magnitude comparable with the that of the friends-and-relatives effect found for nineteenth-century European emigration. The migrant stock effect raises migration from the typical South American country by 49 percent (a high stock-to-population ratio) compared with that from the typical East Asian country (a low stock-to-population ratio).

What about poverty? Here we use the ratio of the source country's Gini coefficient of household income to the square of its income per capita. For a given mean income, an increase in inequality increases the poverty rate, whereas for a given level of inequality, a rise in mean income reduces the poverty rate. Table 11.1 reports that a fall in the poverty rate at the source increases migration to the United States. Thus, an increase in source country income influences emigration to the United States in two offsetting ways: a negative effect operating through the relative income variable (improved domestic economic conditions keep potential emigrants at home) and a positive effect operating through the poverty variable (reductions in poverty release the constraint on potential emigrants). For a typical western European country, a 10 percent rise in GDP per capita (holding education constant) reduces migration to the United States by 12.6 percent. The income effect dominates the poverty effect in rich Europe. A 10 percent increase in income reduces migration from the typical East Asian country by 4.3 percent and that from the typical South American country by 3.7 percent. The income effect dominates the poverty effect even in poorer Asia and Latin America, but barely so. For the typical African country, however, a 10 percent rise in income per capita *increases* migration to the United States by 0.3 percent. The poverty effect dominates the income effect on the poorest continent. If income increases by 10 percent in both the source country and the United States, there is virtually no change in migration from western Europe, but a 2 percent increase in migration from Africa. With this in mind, the next chapter looks more closely at African emigration.

Recall that all of these effects are measured in the presence of a binding quota on total immigration (excluding immediate relatives). The effects reflect the economic and demographic fundamentals that determine the outcome of the competition for visas. Yet while they capture the effect of changing conditions in a single source country, they do not capture the effects of worldwide changes that might tighten the quota constraint on that country. Several variables are included to capture shifts in quota constraints as intended by U.S. immigration policy. Merging the quotas for the Eastern and Western Hemispheres after 1976 sharply relaxed the constraint on immigration from Eastern Hemisphere countries. By contrast, the 1990 Immigration Act had marginal effects—even when its interaction with relative schooling levels is measured to reflect the shift toward a more-skill-selective policy. The largest effects are found to be those stemming from the legalization program under the Immigration Reform and Control Act, largely concentrated in 1989–1991, effects that doubled the Mexican immigration rate.

Although there are not enough data to allow us to compare precisely the span of years before and after the 1965 amendments to the Immigration and Nationality Act became effective, there is enough information to understand why the composition of U.S. immigration changed so dramatically over the late twentieth century. Rapid income growth and slow population growth in postwar Europe would by itself have reduced the numbers coming from Europe relative to other regions. Before the Asian miracle spread from east to south, conditions in Asia also served to crowd out Europeans in U.S. labor markets. After the introduction in the United States of a worldwide immigration quota, Asians competed directly with immigrants from South and Central America and the Caribbean. As the Asian economic miracle began to keep the more mobile at home, immigration pressure increasingly switched to south of the U.S. border. But the numbers from the poorest continent, Africa, still do not rival those of any other continent. As we show in chapter 12, this is because the poverty constraint has limited long-distance migration from Africa; the costs (including policy costs) of migration from Africa are high, and as a result, the African migrant stock in the United States is still too small to help overcome those costs.

South-to-West and East-to-West Migration within Europe

Guestworkers from the South

As chapter 10 noted, several European countries began in the late 1950s to recruit workers on a temporary basis from countries in southern and eastern Europe and North Africa. Guestworker agreements were made bilaterally with source country governments. The first (West) German *gastarbeiter* agreement was that with Italy in 1955, and it was followed by agreements in the early 1960s with Greece and Spain, the later in the decade by those with Turkey, Morocco, Portugal, Tunisia, and Yugoslavia. Similar agreements were made between France and the Netherlands with the same source countries, and Belgian *contingenten-systeem* workers were recruited, mainly from Italy, from the late 1940s to the early 1960s.

These blue-collar migrants worked mainly in manufacturing and construction. They were recruited through government agencies and were given work and residence permits for fixed periods, after which they were required to return to their home countries. Initially, they could not bring their families or gain permanent residency, were not entitled to state welfare benefits, and could not acquire political rights. During the 1960s, however, guestworkers became increasingly perma-nent through repeat migration and with the admission of families and dependants. Germany imposed the *anwerbestopp* (recruitment stop) in 1973, and the other main receiving countries followed suit in the following year. Even so, a large share of the existing guestworker migrants were permitted to stay (although with limited rights), and family reunification continued.

It is said that there is nothing more permanent than a temporary mi-grant (Martin 1998). Still, policy *was* effective in dramatically reducing migrant inflows into these countries. The number of foreigners resident in Germany rose from about 700,000 in 1960 to over four million in 1974 and then remained almost constant until the late 1980s (figure 11.6). Tighter immigration policies in other EU countries also reduced their net immigrant inflows after the mid-1970s. As we have seen in so many cases since the 1890s, abrupt changes in immigration policy re-flect long-run fundamentals that are galvanized by a sudden shock. The sudden shock in the EU case was the OPEC-induced rise in the price of oil that threw the world economy into recession and generated an immigrant backlash in the EU. The underlying fundamentals were an accumulating stock of unskilled foreign residents, a progressive weakening in the demand for unskilled labor, a rising unemployment rate, and greater welfare dependence among immigrants. Had immi-grants been more positively selected in the 1960s and 1970s, it seems likely that the policy backlash that resulted from the changes in these fundamentals would have been less dramatic.

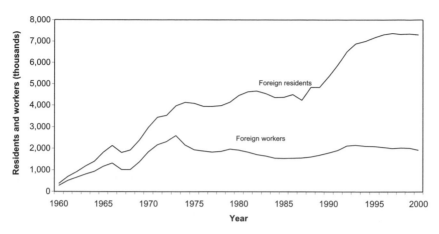

Figure 11.6
Foreign residents and workers in Germany (1960–1990: Federal Republic of Germany; 1991–2000: united Germany). *Source:* Data kindly supplied by Philip Martin.

Crumbling Iron Curtains

Growing economic disparities between East and West in postwar Europe revived old migration pressures along the same pre-1914 axis. These included older migrations from Poland and East Germany to the industrial heartland of the Ruhr, from the Jewish Pale to Germany, France, and England, and from eastern parts of the Austro-Hungarian Empire to urban industrial areas in northern Italy, France, Austria, and Germany. Between 1945 and the erection of the Berlin wall in 1961, about twelve million ethnic Germans moved to East and West Germany from Poland, Czechoslovakia, and Yugoslavia, and another four million moved from East Germany to West Germany.

As figure 11.6 shows, German controls reduced immigration from the mid-1970s until the collapse of the Warsaw Pact, that is, until the fall of the Berlin Wall opened the door to the east. Workers were recruited from eastern Europe during the 1990s, particularly from Poland and Romania, under guestworker-type schemes that included special-project employment (*werkvertragsarbeitnehmer*) and seasonal agricultural work. There was also a renewed inflow of about 650,000 ethnic Germans in the early 1990s. But much of the immigration surge from the east was in the form of asylum seekers fleeing conflicts in the former Yugoslavia and Soviet republics, as well as those from even farther afield, who often arrived as illegals on routes through eastern

Europe. In the aftermath of unification, German immigration policy tightened sharply, even against ethnic Germans, but especially against asylum seekers. Chapter 13 shows that policy seems to have been effective in reducing the inflow of asylum seekers, but its effect can be identified only once other influences are taken into account.

Mass Migration and EU Enlargement

Policy has been decisive in shaping the volume and structure of late-twentieth-century European immigration. But as this chapter has shown, the effects of policy changes are often difficult to separate from those resulting from other influences, and the outcomes often differ from what was anticipated. Nowhere is this better illustrated than by the debate over the mass migration consequences of the EU enlargement that took place in 2004. As a result of the process that began with the meeting of the European Council of Ministers in Copenhagen in 1993, agreement to admit 10 new countries was reached in 2002. The accession countries—Cyprus, the Czech Republic, Estonia, Hungary, Latvia, Lithuania, Malta, Poland, Slovakia, and Slovenia—have a combined population of a little over seventy-five million, about 20 percent of the fifteen-member EU population (call it the "west"). The effect of the abolition of migration barriers on emigration from these accession countries (call them the "east") is highly uncertain. In anticipation of a flood, the agreement allows existing EU member states to restrict worker immigration from the accession countries for two years, with the option of a further three years, and in exceptional circumstances an additional two years.

What east-west migrations do we expect from the EU enlargement? One approach to the question has been to look at the stated intentions of those in the accession countries. Among the five east European accession countries surveyed in 1998, the percentage of the population anticipating short-run migration ranged from 18 percent in Poland and Slovenia to 36 percent in the Czech Republic, while the percentage anticipating permanent migration ranged from 7 percent in Slovenia to 21 percent in the Czech Republic and Poland (IOM 1998). Not all of those anticipating a move to other EU countries will do so, but the surveys suggest that the number of permanent movers could be substantial, perhaps on the order of ten million. An alternative approach to determining enlargement's migration effects is to predict magnitudes using estimated models and forecasts of the postenlargement evolution of east-west income gaps (Bauer and Zimmermann 1999; Boeri and Brücker 2000; Fertig 2001; Sinn and Werding 2001). These forecasts are typically based on models of east-west per capita income convergence. The forecasts of net east-west migration for the 2005–2015 decade range from one to four million, implying average annual rates of outflow of 1.3 to 5.3 per thousand (Dustmann 2003, 32). These forecasts also predict that about four-fifths of the east-west migrants will flow to Germany and Austria, with two-thirds to Germany alone.

These forecasts are well within the range of late-nineteenth-century experience, and the income gaps inducing the forecasted migrations are also similar in size: as a group, the accession countries have per capita incomes about 45 percent of the EU-15 average. Nevertheless, most observers believe that the flows will be modest because of significant offsets. One offset is demography: the accession countries have aging populations and small numbers in the migration-sensitive age group (Schmidt 2000). Indeed, a significant share of those in this age group may have already left. Another offset is the integration in goods and capital markets that joining the European Union will bring: since the accession countries are labor abundant relative to the EU-15, trade deepening should increase unskilled employment and wages in the east. In addition, past history suggests that poor countries that previously have joined the European Union have experienced only modest emigration in the long run (Bauer and Zimmermann 1999). That was true of Italy after 1957, Greece after 1981, Spain and Portugal after 1986, as well as the smaller than expected east-west flows within Germany after unification. Furthermore, restrictions on immigration from accession countries in the years after accession are likely to remain in place until the migration pressures have eased, as they did when Greece, Spain, and Portugal joined the EU.

In the longer run, the east-west migration magnitudes resulting from the latest round of accessions are much more uncertain. The youngest cohorts (those under twenty) are larger than those who are currently in the migration-sensitive age group. And if economic convergence is slower than expected or if there is political instability in the new member countries, then east-west migration rates could be larger than anticipated. Even with some degree of economic convergence, the flows might be bigger than anticipated, for two additional reasons. First, some of the smaller estimated responses to income gaps are based on migrations in the presence of restrictive immigration policies, and hence they may be too small to reflect the free migration response.

As we showed for Britain, emigration responses tend to be smaller when restrictive policy filters are in place. Second, the friends-and-relatives effect may cause migrations to persist far into the future, despite declining income gaps.

Policy Coda

Both policy and underlying fundamentals matter. The same economic and demographic fundamentals that explained so much of the free world migrations before 1914 still explain much of the world migrations we observe today, and in the same way. Even in the presence of restrictive immigration policy, these fundamentals still help explain both the volume of the migrations and the sources of the migrants. However, immigration policy makes the influence of the fundamentals somewhat less powerful, and policy change has itself had a potent effect on both the volume of world migrations and the source of the migrants over the past half century.

12   Where Are All the Africans?

Africa is the world's poorest continent by far, and it is home to 12 percent of the world's population. Sub-Saharan Africa is the poorest of all the world's regions, and it contains 10 percent of the world's population. Per capita incomes there are typically between 10 and 20 percent of those in the high-income OECD countries and less than a half of those in middle-income Asian and South American countries. Wage gaps are similar: an unskilled laborer in Uganda earns only a fifth as much as one in Uruguay and only a fifteenth as much as one in the United Kingdom. These wage and income gaps are much larger than those that drove the mass migrations from Europe to the New World a century ago. Thus, Africans today have even more to gain from intercontinental migration than did Europeans on the eve of the First World War. As we have seen, however, Africans make up only a small minority of those who manage, one way or another, to become permanent residents in the more-developed parts of the world, particularly Europe and North America.

So why has African intercontinental migration been so modest until quite recently? Is migration pressure from Africa building up as some believe and others fear? And if so, what are the forces that are pushing migrants out of Africa, and what are the countervailing forces that hold the vast majority of Africans back?

Apart from the coerced migrations of the eleven million Africans who were transported across the Atlantic as slaves in the seventeenth, eighteenth, and early nineteenth centuries (chapter 2), free migration from Africa has always been modest in relation to the prospective gains. This chapter argues that this is not because institutions and culture make Africans any less mobile than those from other continents. In fact there is considerable mobility within and among the countries and regions of Africa. But migration out of Africa to other continents has been constrained by three key forces that should now be very familiar from earlier chapters. First, poverty constrains migration more in Africa than elsewhere in the world simply because there is more of it. According to the World Bank (2000), 46 percent of the population of sub-Saharan Africa is living on less than one U.S. dollar a day, the same proportion as in 1987. Second, immigration policies in the developed world have made it particularly difficult for Africans to gain access to high-wage labor markets, except as asylum seekers or as illegal immigrants. Third, as a consequence of poverty and policy, the African migrant stock overseas is still too modest to produce a friends-and-relatives effect sufficiently powerful to loosen the poverty constraint. However, two countervailing forces have recently strengthened the push out of Africa. First, a demographic transition—common to all late-twentieth-century Third World countries—has generated a booming cohort of young, mobile Africans with poor prospects at home. That boom is being deflated by the AIDS epidemic, an offset we take seriously at the end of the chapter. Second, civil wars, interethnic violence, and political oppression have driven many Africans to seek refuge, not only in neighboring countries, but also in the safe havens of the developed world.

African Migration and Mobility

A large literature testifies to high rates of mobility within and among African countries. Indeed, that mobility has served as a laboratory for numerous studies of rural-urban migration and migration across international borders. These studies suggest no lack of mobility among Africans. Two excellent examples are offered by rural-urban migration within Botswana as well as migration between that country and South Africa (Lucas 1985). This migration experience documents elastic responses to differences in wages and employment conditions (following Harris and Todaro 1970). Both the Botswana study and one dealing with rural-urban migration in Kenya (Agesa 2001) find that migration in Africa selects the young and educated adult from among the source populations. Like most European migration streams a century ago, African migrants today are often single and often male, and they tend to be young, typically ranging from fifteen to twenty-nine years of age. African migrants are also educated, a fact that strongly suggests some underlying positive selection, but it is so largely because of the greater economic return to education in the cities compared with the countryside.

African migrants often view their move as temporary. Surveys indicate that most intend to return to their rural (or, increasingly, urban) origins within a few years of migrating or upon retirement. This pattern is reminiscent of southern European emigrations at the turn of the twentieth century, and they have been interpreted as part of family-based strategies to maximize income and minimize risk (Stark 1991). Most African migrants send remittances back to their families in their homelands, funds that provide a vital addition to subsistence incomes from farming or casual labor. These remittances are large; in Kenya they have been estimated to account for 10–20 percent of all family incomes in the major cities (Oucho 1996, 16–17).

The literature is divided regarding the extent to which poverty restricts migration in Africa. One study explored rural households in the Senegal River valley in Mali whose members migrated, some to other locations in West Africa, but about 40 percent went to France (Findlay and Sow 1998). The authors found that the poorer the family, the more likely its migrants would remain in Africa. Thus, poverty restricted emigration out of Mali to Europe, despite the greater potential gains involved in such migration compared to those for migration within West Africa. The study also found that households with previous emigration experience in France were more likely to send new migrants to France, suggesting that the friends-and-relatives effect was more important for long-distance moves. Another study of international migrants from Egypt to neighboring countries found that laborers without land were the most likely to migrate (Adams 1993). The study's author concluded that "despite considerable travel and opportunity costs associated with international migration, males who are both poor *and* landless are able to find or borrow the money they need" (Adams 1993, 162). Plausible theory plus two conflicting anecdotes do not make the case for poverty constraints on emigration out of Africa. Later in this chapter, we try to bring more evidence to bear on the hypothesis.

Restrictive barriers to migration within the African continent are generally far lower than those between it and high-wage labor markets in the OECD. The treaty that formed the Economic Community of West African States (ECOWAS) in 1975 included a protocol providing for the free movement of capital and labor among the signatories.[1]

Agreements for trade and economic cooperation in other regions, such as the Common Market for Eastern and Southern Africa (COMESA), the Southern African Development Community (SADC), and the Eastern and Southern African Preferential Trade Area (PTA) were set up with free factor mobility as an objective but contained no explicit protocols for ensuring it.[2] Nevertheless, cooperation between groups of African countries has facilitated labor migration on an informal level—indeed, the effective barriers to cross-border migration in East Africa may actually be lower than in the western part of the continent (Akande 1998, 346). But such agreements and understandings have often followed rather than led growing cross-border labor migration. With completely porous borders between most contiguous African countries, a large amount of undocumented migration takes place, and attempts to control cross-border migration have been modest at best (Adepoju 1995, 93).

Although it may involve longer distances than moving to the nearest town, movement across borders in Africa is often very little different from migration within a given country. Most of it involves migration between neighboring states, in particular, between the more-populous or less-developed sending countries such as Burkina Faso, Uganda, Lesotho, Mozambique, Mali, Rwanda, and Burundi, and receiving countries like Côte d'Ivoire, Gabon, Equatorial Guinea, Nigeria, and above all, the Republic of South Africa. Thus, 30 percent of the foreign nationals in Benin in 1992 were from Nigeria, 25 percent were from Togo, 15 percent from Niger, 11 percent from Côte d'Ivoire, and 9 percent from Ghana. Similarly, migrants in the Republic of South Africa in the early 1990s were overwhelmingly from Botswana, Lesotho, Malawi, Mozambique, and Swaziland. These migrations have undergone booms and busts, usually in response to volatility in the export prices of minerals, cotton, coffee, oil, and other primary products.

Can the ebb and flow of cross-border migration in Africa be explained by the same variables that we have seen operating elsewhere today and in earlier centuries? We think so, although the data confirming it are limited to net cross-border migrations inferred from demographic accounting. Furthermore, the sources for these data make it impossible to distinguish between cross-border migrations within Africa and those out of Africa. Despite these limitations, the evidence strongly supports the view that net emigration in Africa is driven by much the same forces as we have observed for other times and places. Table 12.1 offers such support, based on net emigration from twenty

Table 12.1
Regression estimate for African net migration, 1977–1995

$$NetMigRate = -58.45 + 0.47\ NetRef + 10.02\ LnWRatio(f/h) + 2.11\ Sp15\text{–}29 - 0.53\ grY(h)$$
$$\quad\quad (2.4)\quad (3.1)\quad\quad\quad (2.9)\quad\quad\quad\quad\quad (2.4)\quad\quad\quad (2.0)$$
$$+ 0.04\ grY(f) - 1.46\ Pov$$
$$\quad (0.2)\quad\quad\quad (1.7)$$
$$R^2 = 0.53$$

Source: This is a variant of the model presented in Hatton and Williamson 2003. Further details concerning data sources and methods are available there.

Note: Robust t statistics in parentheses.

Sample: Unbalanced panel of countries and years comprising Angola (1982–1995); Burundi (1980–1985); Cameroon (1980–1995); Central African Republic (1989–1995); Chad (1980–1995); Côte d'Ivoire (1989–1995); Gabon (1977–1990); Ghana (1977–1995); Lesotho (1981–1995); Malawi (1987–1995); Mali (1987–1995); Nigeria (1977–1995); Rwanda (1979–1995); Senegal (1989–1995); Sierra Leone (1991–1995); Sudan (1984–1995); Swaziland (1978–1995); Togo (1982–1993); Zambia (1981–1995); Zimbabwe (1983–1995).

Definitions of variables: $NetMigRate$ = net out-migration per thousand of population; $NetRef$ = net outflow of refugees per thousand of population; $LnWRatio(f/h)$ = log ratio of real unskilled wage rates at 1990 purchasing-power parity (foreign to home), where the foreign index is a weighted average of wage rates in the region (0.9) and the OECD (0.1); $Sp15\text{–}29$ = share of population aged fifteen to twenty-nine; $grY(h)$ = growth rate of real GDP per capita in home country; $grY(f)$ = index of growth rate of GDP in the region (west, east, middle, and south); Pov = inverse of home real wage squared.

Method: Pooled ordinary least squares regression on 265 country/year observations. Dummies for Ghana (1983 and 1985) and Nigeria (1983 and 1985) included but not reported.

sub-Saharan countries between the late 1970s and the mid-1990s. The net emigration rate ($NetMigRate$) is explained by refugee outflows ($NetRef$), the ratio of real unskilled wages abroad to those at home ($LnWRatio$), the share of the population who are young adults ($Sp15$–29), GDP per capita growth at home and in the surrounding region ($grY(h)$ and $grY(f)$), respectively, and "poverty" (Pov, proxied by the inverse of the home real wage squared). The table confirms that demographic forces are particularly important in explaining net African emigration: a rise of five percentage points in the share of young adults in the population (say, from 25 percent to 30 percent) increases net emigration by one per thousand. Economic growth at home sharply reduces net emigration, consistent with the notion that successful development attracts foreign immigrants across porous borders and keeps more potential native emigrants at home. Income growth in the rest of the region has the opposite effect, but the influence appears to be weak. We also allow separately for the net movement of refugees, a topic to which we return later in the chapter.

The relative income variable in table 12.1 is the purchasing-power-parity-adjusted unskilled wage rate abroad (including a component representing high-wage destinations outside Africa) relative to the unskilled wage at home. The table reports that a 10 percent increase in the foreign-to-home wage ratio raises net emigration by about 1 per thousand—an impact similar to that for European emigration a century ago. What about the poverty constraint that kept so many poor Europeans at home in the late nineteenth century, something we also think severely constrained African migration to the United States in the late twentieth century? Our proxy for poverty suggests at first glance that the constraint has not been very binding: an increase in the home wage increases net emigration by 0.2 per thousand, an effect that only partially offsets the 1-per-thousand negative effect operating through the wage ratio. This result from table 12.1 appears to be in contrast with the chapter 11 finding that for international migration from Africa to the United States, the poverty constraint more than offset the relative income effect. The contrast may be more apparent than real. Most of the net migration explained in table 12.1 is across borders *within* Africa, and the poverty constraint is likely to be less binding for those shorter moves. It seems reasonable to suppose that poverty is a more-important constraint on long-distance migration out of Africa than on cross-border migration within Africa and thus the friends-and-relatives effect is more important for long-distance moves.

Inter-African Migration Currents and Policy Shocks

Within Africa, cross-border migration has responded to wage gaps and demographic forces, and it has waxed and waned with each commodity price boom and bust in host countries. This cross-border migration confirms that Africans are very responsive to economic opportunities, but its magnitude, averaged over these booms and busts, has not been very large. The explanation is pretty clear. Most African countries have neighbors who are at similar levels of development. Thus, the incentives for cross-border migration have not been large enough in most of Africa to induce any secular migrant floods. The biggest exception to this rule is South Africa, where living standards and job quality are far higher than in neighboring countries. Not surprisingly, therefore, South Africa has much tougher and more-comprehensive immigration controls than the rest of Africa. But politics influence migration elsewhere in Africa too.

At its independence in 1957, Ghana (formerly the Gold Coast) was one of the more-advanced African economies. It had a well-developed mining sector producing gold, diamonds, and manganese, a timber and logging industry, and above all, a cocoa-producing sector which accounted for two-thirds of export revenues.[3] The economy grew rapidly from 1957 to 1965 and again from 1970 to 1975, but it faltered thereafter. In particular, the cocoa-producing sector suffered a severe decline due to falling world prices, an artificially high exchange rate, and an export tax. Economic policy and performance was closely tied to political developments. The Nkrumah government pursued ambitious plans for industrialization through import protection and expansionary government spending, financed in part by revenues generated by the cocoa sector. After Nkrumah's removal in a 1966 coup, a policy of gradual liberalization ensued, especially under the Acheampong government (1972–1978), but this liberal trend was reversed after a 1979 coup that installed Jerry Rawlings. The late 1970s and early 1980s saw droughts, deficits, negative economic growth, raging inflation (128 percent in 1983), and sharply declining real wages (Frimpong-Ansah 1992). Growth resumed in the late 1980s, although Ghana has since still experienced a somewhat bumpy economic ride.

These swings in political and economic conditions in Ghana greatly influenced migration movements, both internal and international. Strong growth in the 1950s and 1960s drew immigrants from neighboring countries, particularly Nigeria, to work in the cocoa sector as well as in the expanding urban sector. But in 1969, the Ghanaian government issued the Aliens Compliance Order, which effectively deported foreign labor, equivalent to about 5 percent of the labor force. Labor shortages resulted (Addo 1987, 293). When the country's economic situation worsened in the 1970s, urban unemployment and underemployment rose, and increasing numbers of Ghanaians emigrated (figure 12.1). Most moved to Nigeria, where booming export revenues from oil and expanding manufacturing and services produced an average growth rate of 6.7 percent in the 1970s. According to one account, "in Ghana, the migration was gradual and clearly targeted: people fled an economy brought near to collapse by a combination of economic and political factors" (Arhin 1994, 268). But the Nigerian oil sector slump in the early 1980s, coupled with political upheaval, soon changed the climate for migrants in that country.

The ECOWAS treaty permitted relatively free movement of documented migrants, but only about half the Ghanaians in Nigeria had

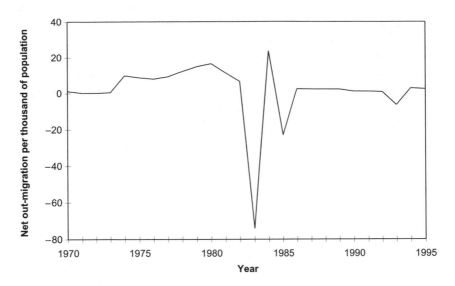

Figure 12.1
Net out-migration from Ghana, 1970–1995. *Source:* Data appendix in Hatton and Williamson 2003.

legal immigrant status. In 1983 the Nigerian government ordered the removal of those who had migrated across the border without obtaining official papers. One estimate puts the number returning in 1983 at 900,000, with another 90,000 returning following a further order in 1985. This sudden injection of labor occurred at a time when Ghana least needed it, but unemployment did not rise. Instead, something else changed to clear the market: the unskilled wage (in 1990 U.S. dollars) fell to 50 percent of its 1976 level by 1983 (figure 12.2).

The economic recovery program introduced in Ghana in 1983 eliminated price subsidies, corrected the external imbalance, and reduced the rate of inflation. This was followed by a structural adjustment program beginning in 1987 which introduced further financial, structural, and institutional reforms.[4] The gradual recovery of the Ghanaian economy reversed the downward trend in real wages and reduced the incentives for Ghanaians to out-migrate: by 1999, the unskilled wage was a bit above its 1976 level. Meanwhile slow growth in Nigeria and elsewhere in West Africa produced a downward trend in the region-wide unskilled wage (a regional index in which Nigeria takes on a weight of 62 percent). As figure 12.2 shows, the foreign wage available to potential out-migrants from Ghana declined from its peak at

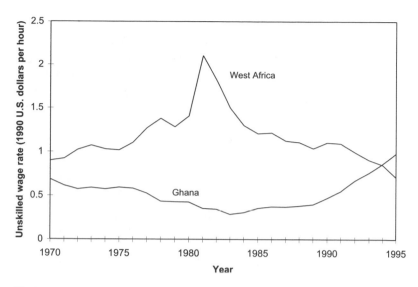

Figure 12.2
Unskilled wage rates in Ghana and West Africa, 1970–1995. *Source:* Data appendix in Hatton and Williamson 2003.

the height of the oil boom in the early 1980s (Bevan, Collier, and Gunning 1999, 135). By the mid-1990s, real wages in Ghana exceeded those in West Africa. The powerful incentives to emigrate from Ghana in the mid-1980s had evaporated a decade later. No wonder net out-migration from Ghana has exhibited such volatility over the past three decades.

South Africa provides a particularly interesting example in terms of how labor market forces effect migration in that country and how South African policy responds to it, under circumstances in which there is a much bigger gap in living standards between the sending African neighbors and the receiving African host. For more than a century, migrants have been recruited from all over southern Africa to take South African farm, service, and above all, mining jobs, the last including jobs mining coal, gold, and other minerals. A dualistic labor market developed under the apartheid regime that became known as the South African labor system. Immigrant workers from Botswana, Lesotho, Malawi, Mozambique, and Swaziland were recruited to the mines on short-term contracts in a series of bilateral agreements dating from the 1960s. Males were recruited for periods ranging from six months to two years, and since they were obliged to return home at the end of the contract, they could not gain permanent residence in South Africa. The incentive to return was strengthened by a system of compulsory remittances amounting to a significant share of total income. Increasingly, however, these migrants became a quasi-permanent labor force, much like the guestworkers in postwar Germany (Milazi 1998). Meanwhile, black South Africans were increasingly concentrated in "homelands," regulated by strict pass laws, and either commuting or migrating temporarily to work in the industrial sector.

Recruitment to the mines has been determined partly by the fortunes of the mining industry (especially gold mining) and partly by policy. In the wake of political independence around South Africa and a toughening in the apartheid system within it, the source countries withdrew from the arrangement: Tanzania in 1962, Zambia in 1966, Malawi in 1974, and Zimbabwe in 1981 (de Vletter 1985). It has also been suggested that the arrangement began to fall apart because of pressure from land owners in the sending-country border regions, which faced increasingly scarce agricultural labor (Lucas 1987). Figure 12.3 shows the numbers of foreign and South African workers employed by the members of the South African Chamber of Mines in the 1970s through 1990s. When the foreign labor supply fell sharply in the

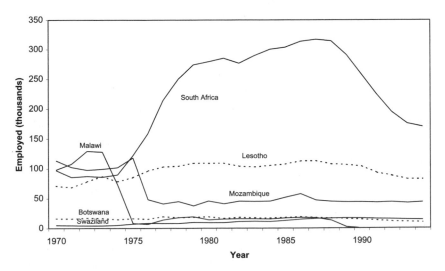

Figure 12.3
Employment in the South African Mines, 1970–1994, by nationality. *Sources:* de Vletter 1985; ILO 1998.

1970s, more South Africans were employed to fill the gap, so that
the share of foreigners in the labor force fell from 80 percent in the
early 1970s to less than half in the 1980s. The South African mining
industry stopped recruiting workers from Malawi in 1988 because a
considerable number had tested positive for HIV, but there were also
deeper causes, such as the collapse of apartheid and increased job competition between domestic and foreign workers (Chirwa 1997). Above
all, expulsion orders were promulgated against immigrants, and immigrant recruitment stops were imposed mainly in response to worsening employment conditions, such as those prevailing in the late 1980s
(Adekayne 1998).

Despite the advent of democratic government in South Africa after
the demise of apartheid, a two-tier system enshrined by the 1991 Aliens Control Act remained in place throughout the 1990s. Permanent
immigration, previously restricted to those who were deemed "assim-
ilable" in a white society, continued to be tightly restricted, while
bilateral agreements for contract labor to the mines and agriculture
continued on a reduced scale. But liberalization of the South African
labor market widened employment opportunities for black Africans
and improved working conditions, further increasing the incentive to
immigrate to South Africa. This incentive was reinforced by the deterioration of economic conditions in some of South Africa's neighbors. As
a result, the number of illegal immigrants in South Africa is thought to
have grown to between 2.5 and 5 million by the late 1990s. Three other
factors help explain the rise in South African immigration. One is that
migration over longer distances has increased, as documented by the
arrival of migrants from West and Central Africa. It seems likely that
this has been driven largely by falling transport costs within Africa.
Another is the growing number of asylum seekers following South
Africa's accession in 1993 to the Geneva Convention on Refugees. A
third is the opportunities for permanent residence that were given to
temporary and illegal immigrants in 1995–1996 (ILO 1998).

Violence, Persecution, and African Refugees

One type of African migration that hits the headlines more often than
most is that of refugees fleeing conflict and persecution. While Africa
has a little more than a tenth of the world's population, more than a
third of the world's stock of refugees originates there in most years.
But refugees, who by definition have fled their country of origin, are

only the tip of the iceberg. International agencies estimate that 2.5 percent of the African population is in a refugee-like situation, but about three-quarters of these are internally displaced; that is, they remain in their country of origin. The overwhelming majority of those who do manage to leave their home country in search of a safe haven are displaced across international borders mainly to neighboring African states. Despite press coverage about rising numbers of African asylum seekers beating on the doors of the developed world, these represent only a very small proportion of the total displaced by war and violence (chapter 13).

The analysis of African migration in table 12.1 took refugee flows to be an exogenous factor helping explain overall net migration. What we did not stress earlier in the chapter, however, is that the coefficient on *NetRef* is less than one. This has a very important implication. If the net refugee movement had a one-for-one effect on net migration, then the coefficient would be one. The fact that the coefficient is substantially less than one implies that refugee flows generate offsetting movements by "economic" migrants in the opposite direction. Thus, it appears that refugees crowd out others and that the crowding out is very significant—for every two refugees, one local is pushed out of the home labor market, or one foreigner who would have otherwise entered the home labor market does not.

Not surprisingly, refugee movements are an important component of cross-border African migration, and so it is worth examining the causes of these displacements a little further. The causes of refugee flight include coups, government and political crises, civil wars, guerilla campaigns, and invasions from hostile neighbors. These are among the many variables that have been used to explain the total number of refugees that fled from forty sub-Saharan countries between 1987 and 1992 (Hatton and Williamson 2003, table 2). Coups d'état during that time typically created an efflux of thirty-eight per thousand of the country's population, government crises almost nineteen refugees per thousand, and guerilla warfare twenty-two per thousand. The advent of a civil war generated more than thirty-six refugees per thousand, and each military death in a civil war generated an additional twenty-five refugees per thousand. Civil wars were found to be by far the most important cause of refugee displacements, which accords with casual observation as well as with the results of other studies. By contrast, economic (and demographic) variables add little to the explanation, a result that might be taken to mean that refugee flows are not influenced by economic forces. We prefer a different interpretation: refugees are pushed across borders by civil wars and political upheavals; these events also cause poverty and destitution, which adds to the pressure to migrate.

The evidence also suggests remarkably little persistence in the effects of wars and upheavals on refugee flows. As soon as a war ends, the stock of refugees from the warring country declines very quickly. Rates of repatriation are higher in Africa than elsewhere in the world. These high rates could perhaps be explained by the fact that resettlement programs of international agencies such as the office of the United Nations High Commissioner for Refugees (UNHCR) have been particularly effective; between 1970 and 1990, however, only about one in ten Africans who were repatriated returned home under an organized scheme (Rogge 1994, 17, 29). Even among those who remained displaced for long periods, such as those from southern Sudan (1955–1972) or those exiled from Burundi (1972–1994), mass returns took place as soon as conditions permitted. Many returned even before it was safe to do so and against the advice of the UNHCR. Thus, at least 100,000 refugees from Burundi returned early in 1994 as soon as the fighting there receded, despite continuing instability in the country (U.S. Committee on Refugees 1994, 48).

In other cases, refugees have been pushed back by hostile populations, unwelcoming governments, or the outbreak of hostilities in the host countries. Thus, when civil war erupted in Zaire in 1996, resulting finally in the overthrow of the Mobutu regime, an estimated 600,000 to 700,000 exiled Rwandans were pushed back across the shared border (U.S. Committee for Refugees 1998, 84). It may be that political motives, tribal and kinship ties, the loss of culture and identity all make refugees keen to return as soon as possible (Makanya 1994). But there may be a more-important economic motive at work: African refugees, often displaced into camps in rural parts of bordering states, experience even greater deprivation there than they do at home. One exception is the Mozambican refugees in South Africa. At the height of the civil war in Mozambique in the mid-1980s there were about 350,000 Mozambican refugees in South Africa; in 2000, eight years after the conclusion of the conflict, 200,000 remained in South Africa, mainly in the northeast near the Mozambique border. Very few took advantage of the UNHCR's free repatriation program in the mid-1990s, and some of those who did subsequently returned to South Africa.[5] This serves to illustrate the point that the better the conditions under which the displaced find refuge, the less likely they are to return to their home countries.

Rising Emigration Pressure in Africa?

Demographic Transitions versus AIDS

While conflict and policy certainly matter, African international migration is driven chiefly by demographic forces and economic incentives. Africa's poor long-run economic performance has increased the latent pressure on emigration, and it has been powerfully reinforced by a demographic transition that has produced an increasingly large cohort of young adults with the greatest incentive to leave. In fact, demographic forces have been one reason that real wages have grown so slowly in Africa. Analysis of real wage determinants across Africa reveals that population density and the population share aged fifteen to twenty-nine have a powerful negative impact on an African country's real wage (table 14.3). From this we calculate that growing demographic pressure reduced the real wage by 17 percent in sub-Saharan Africa between 1976 and 1995. Improvements in underlying labor productivity were barely enough to offset the negative demographic effects. Malthusian pressure seems to be particularly acute in Africa, even though the region is not very densely populated. This implies that demographic pressure on migration out of Africa is especially strong. Not only does this pressure create large emigration-age cohorts full of those most susceptible to emigration, but it also adds to the emigration incentive by pressing down the home wage facing prospective migrants.

African international migration is mostly *within* low-wage Africa rather than between Africa and the high-wage developed world. Yet it seems likely that if demographic and economic pressures continue to mount, some part of Africa's international migration will spill over into intercontinental migration. The data necessary to permit a direct measure of future spillover effects are not available. However, it is possible to generate plausible estimates of emigration pressure by invoking different assumptions about those spillover effects. Our projections for the future are driven entirely by demographic forecasts constructed by the United Nations and the U.S. Bureau of the Census. Demography has two effects in our projections: *directly* influencing emigration by increasing the number of young adults and *indirectly* influencing emigration by reducing the home wage through a labor supply glut.

Table 12.2
Projected emigration pressure in sub-Saharan Africa

	2000	2010	2020	2030
Per thousand of population in sub-Saharan Africa (per annum)				
5% spillover	0.20	0.48	0.57	0.59
10% spillover	0.20	0.76	0.92	1.00
15% spillover	0.20	1.03	1.15	1.40
Millions of migrants from sub-Saharan Africa (per annum)				
5% spillover	0.13	0.48	0.57	0.59
10% spillover	0.13	0.62	0.91	1.07
15% spillover	0.13	0.83	1.03	1.50

Note: These projections are an updated version of those presented in Hatton and Williamson 2003 (table 5). They are based on the 2002 revision (United Nations 2003) rather than the 1998 version (United Nations 1999) of the United Nations' *World Population Prospects*, which we used in our earlier study.

Some illustrative projections are provided in table 12.2. They begin with the estimated net emigration from sub-Saharan Africa in 2000. On the assumption that 10 percent of the increase in migration pressure spills over into emigration out of Africa, the emigration rate increases from 0.2 per thousand in 1995 to 0.8 per thousand in 2010, rising more slowly to 1.0 per thousand by 2030. With an assumed 5 percent spillover into intercontinental migration, projected emigration accumulates to a more-modest figure of 0.6 per thousand from 2020 onward. These out-of-Africa emigration rates, if actually attained by 2020, would be modest by the standards of the pre–World War I mass migrations from western Europe: the figure was 2.2 per thousand for the 1870s and 5.4 per thousand for the 1900s. Yet these out-of-Africa emigration projections still imply sizable numbers. Under the 10 percent spillover assumption, the total number of African emigrants per annum rises by about 800,000 over twenty years. These significant increases follow from the rise in the young-adult population share from 27.7 in 2000 to 29.6 in 2020 and the rise in population density from 27.4 to 41.5 per square kilometer over the same period. These calculations are only illustrative, but they indicate that demography matters in Africa today, just as it did in Europe a century ago.

Demographic predictions for Africa have become especially uncertain because of the HIV/AIDS pandemic. About twenty-five million are infected in Africa, and the prevalence rate among adults in sub-Saharan Africa is 8.6 percent. The disease is particularly pervasive in southern Africa, where the adult prevalence rates are 37 percent in Botswana, 25 percent in Zimbabwe, and 20 percent in South Africa. The demographic forecasts underlying table 12.2 were constructed in 2002 and anticipated the effects of the epidemic. According to these forecasts, a large proportion of the population increase induced by demographic transition will be decimated by the epidemic, and to the extent that HIV/AIDS is a young-adult disease, the epidemic will also alter the African population's age structure.[6] Indeed, UN population forecasts for Africa have been revised downward substantially over the last decade. Our estimates of migration pressure are accordingly smaller than earlier ones based on forecasts made in 1998.[7] Future revisions could increase or decrease the estimated effects. If, as is happening in Uganda, the spread of HIV/AIDS is controlled early, then UN population forecasts could be much too low. If, on the other hand, the disease spreads rapidly, as in Botswana and South Africa, and the rate of infection is not stabilized quickly, then the UN projections could be much too high.

The implications of HIV/AIDS for migration in Africa extend far beyond its effects on population numbers. The deteriorating health status of a significant section of the population must surely impede mobility both within and out of Africa—effects that would be reinforced by health checks that are increasingly part of host country immigration policy. There are also indirect effects that work through the effects of HIV/AIDS on economic well-being. The evidence suggests that there are important negative effects on individual productivity. AIDS could conceivably increase the incentive for those not directly affected by the disease to emigrate to escape exposure to the disease, but surely families hit by AIDS will slip farther down into poverty, making it harder for them to finance the escape of the very healthy.

Alternative Economic Scenarios

From the mid-1970s to the mid-1990s, the real wage grew at 1.35 percent per year in OECD countries while it stagnated in Africa. A 1.35 percent growth gap in real wages over twenty years increases the relative wage gap by 30 percent. Surely the growing pressure on Europe's southern borders must be one manifestation of Africa's falling behind economically. Our estimates for the late nineteenth century (table 4.3) suggest that had the wage gap between Europe and its emigrant destinations increased by 30 percent, the (gross) emigration rate would have increased by 2.2 per thousand, other things constant. Applied to Sub-Saharan Africa, this experiment implies that African emigration would increase to more than a million per annum. Additional productivity growth that served to raise African wages at 1.35 percent per annum would keep the wage gap between Africa and the OECD constant, thus stemming some of the emigration pressure from relative wages, but easing the poverty constraint. Underlying productivity growth would need to be greater still in order to offset the downward pressure on the real wage that would be caused by the mounting demographic burden previously discussed. Is any of this likely?

Over the last twenty years, structural adjustment programs have been launched in a number of countries, of which Ghana was one of the pioneers. So far the results for economic growth have been modest or at best, mixed. But there are other possible effects too. Such programs typically include the realignment of overvalued exchange rates and the liberalization of restrictions on trade in the hope that the gains from increased trade will lever up living standards. Indeed, the standard two-good, two-factor Heckscher-Ohlin trade model suggests that opening an economy up to trade should raise the income of the relatively abundant factor in that country. Thus, trade and migration could be substitutes, but more-general models that include more factors, specific factors (such as land), or differences in technology generate ambiguous results. One such analysis suggests that in low-income countries like those in sub-Saharan Africa, trade liberalization increases the pressure to emigrate (largely because of the fall in the real exchange rate). On the other hand, agricultural trade liberalization by developed countries or worldwide liberalization would stem the flow of emigrants (Faini, Grether, and de Melo 1999).

It seems unlikely, therefore, that policy-induced changes will greatly alter the incentive for Africans to emigrate. The wage gaps between Africa and the developed world are now more than twice as large as those that gave rise to mass migration from Europe to the New World in the late nineteenth century. Furthermore, in absolute terms, living standards in Africa today are roughly equivalent to the levels of western Europe in the 1820s—before mass migrations took off. If living standards were to rise at the same rate in Africa as in the developed world over the next twenty years, then although the incentive to emigrate would remain unchanged, the poverty constraint would be gradually eased, and emigration pressure would *increase*, not decrease.

Immigration policy in the developed world makes it hard for Africans to enter legally in large numbers, and as a result, the African migrant stock in the OECD is still relatively small. But it is increasing. From 1981 to 2001, the number of African nationals living in the European Union increased by about 70 percent, from 700,000 to 1.2 million. It seems likely that the rise will continue, loosening through remittances the poverty constraint and enabling larger numbers to migrate through family reunification schemes. Thus, as the stock of the African-born living abroad increases, the emigration rate will rise as well, through the same family network effects that have been such a powerful force behind world mass migration since 1820.

13   The Rise (and Fall?) of
Asylum Seeking

The numbers of people seeking asylum in the industrial world
increased tenfold between the early 1970s and the late 1990s, from
about 50,000 to about half a million per annum, while the increase for
the European Union alone was about 200,000 between 1981 and 1999.
Indeed, applications for asylum in the European Union have matched
or even exceeded the numbers admitted as immigrants for permanent
settlement. Almost all of those seeking asylum in the European Union
apply either at land borders, seaports, and airports or from within the
country, and a large share of the latter have already entered illegally.
The vast majority of the asylum claims are rejected, but a large share
of those who apply for asylum nevertheless remain in the countries
to which they apply. Not surprisingly, fierce political debate about
asylum policy broke out in the European Union in the 1990s. Governments responded to the rising political temperature with a range of
measures aimed at deterring asylum applications. The policy packages
introduced in each country have led over the past decade to a gradual
harmonization across the EU in various policy dimensions.

Debate over asylum seekers and asylum policies often generates
more heat than light. Some see asylum seekers principally as "economic migrants," a phrase that has acquired a rather negative connotation in part because such migrants are viewed as abusing the system
and attempting to jump the queue. Others argue that most asylum
seekers are genuine refugees fleeing conflict and persecution, implying
that the growth in their numbers reflects either growing worldwide
oppression or an increasing ability to flee from it. But posing the question as a sharp dichotomy is at best unhelpful. The UNHCR puts it this
way: "Many people leave their home for a combination of political,
economic and other reasons. The mixture of motives is one factor creating a perception of the widespread abuse of asylum systems, which is

often manipulated by politicians and the media" (UNHCR 2001, 156). Yet the factors that drive so many to claim asylum are not well understood, at least in quantitative terms.

Has tougher asylum policy within any given industrial country really deterred applications? What about the effect of the progressive toughening of asylum policy in *all* industrial countries collectively, particularly in Europe? Answers to these questions should form an important background for policy. To some observers it may seem obvious that the increasing numbers of asylum applications observed after the 1970s could not possibly be consistent with the position that tougher policies—individually or collectively—have had the deterrent effect intended. An alternative interpretation of recent asylum history must also be considered, namely, that without the deterrent policies, the surge in asylum applications would have been even greater. In this interpretation, tougher policies may have been quite effective in deterring asylum seekers, but their effects have been overwhelmed by other forces operating to increase the upward pressure on asylum claims.

Is the mounting number of asylum applications simply a reflection of war and oppression in source countries? Do economic incentives account for some of the upward trend? The same questions have been raised about the impact of Jewish pogroms in the Pale settlement of Tsarist Russia after the 1870s. As chapter 4 has shown, economic historians find it difficult to sort out the independent influence of the pogroms on mass emigration, since the Jews responded to economic and demographic fundamentals in exactly the same way as did the economic migrants of that time. Given what we know about the past, we expect to face similar problems in extracting answers from the present.

The Surge in Asylum Seeking

Asylum applications to industrialized countries in the late-twentieth and early-twenty-first centuries are plotted in figure 13.1. The figure shows the total number of new applications filed in thirty-seven industrial countries based on data collected by the UNHCR. These are applications rather than individuals, and the number of individuals they represent would be 20 or 30 percent higher than the number of applications, since some applications represent families. The figure documents an enormous surge from about 150,000 in the early 1980s to a peak of 850,000 in 1992, with the number falling sharply to 380,000 in 1997 before rising again more recently. The bulk of these applicants claimed

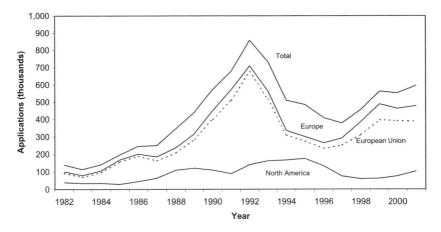

Figure 13.1
Asylum applications to industrialized countries, 1982–2001. *Source:* UNHCR 2002 (113–114).

asylum in Europe, principally in the fifteen countries of the European Union, which by itself accounted for 68 percent of all applications over the two decades, with North America accounting for most of the remainder. The EU share of the European total has fallen since the mid-1990s, largely because some eastern European countries, particularly the Czech Republic, Hungary, Poland, and Turkey, have emerged to take up the slack left in the wake of tougher policies in western Europe. There has also been a decline in the number of people seeking asylum in North America, partly as a result of a decline in the number of applicants from Central and South America.

The source of the asylum applicants is plotted by region in figure 13.2. The sharp spike in the early 1990s is accounted for by applications from eastern Europe, following the disintegration of the Soviet Union and the Balkan conflicts that attended the breakup of the former Yugoslavia. But there is also a clear upward trend in asylum applications from Africa and Asia as well as in those from eastern Europe.

The left panel of table 13.1 breaks down the top twenty sources of asylum applicants by country for the decade 1992–2001. Eastern Europe is well represented on the list, with three countries near the top (Yugoslavia, Romania, and Bosnia), as is the Middle East (Iraq, Iran, and Afghanistan), both being regions where violent conflict has been endemic. But some of the poorest countries which have been engulfed in violence, such as Angola, Rwanda, and Ethiopia/Eritrea, did not

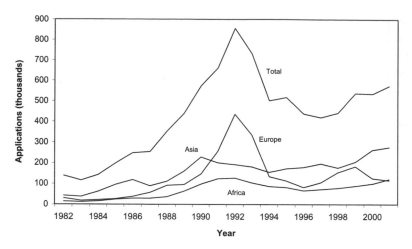

Figure 13.2
Asylum applications by source region, 1982–2001. *Source:* UNHCR 2002 (116–117).

generate as many asylum seekers as might have been expected given
the scale of the conflicts in those countries. As we have seen, African
refugees fleeing conflict at home generally do not get much farther
than a neighboring country, if they manage to leave at all. It is also notable that according to the figures for 1982–1991 provided in the table,
countries which generated large numbers of asylum applications in
1992–2001 typically generated significant numbers in the previous decade as well. Indeed, there is a striking and distressing historical persistence in the list of countries that generate the largest numbers of
asylum applications. There were powerful historical persistence forces
at work on the nineteenth-century mass migrations too, and we argued
earlier in this book that the friends-and-relatives effect explained most
of it. We suspect that the same argument applies to the asylum seeker
trends over the past three decades, and our suspicions are confirmed
at the end of this chapter.

The right panel of table 13.1 documents the chief destination countries to which asylum seekers applied over the decade 1992–2001. The
list is headed by Germany, with a massive 1.6 million applications, followed by the United States and the United Kingdom. Not surprisingly,
nine other EU countries also appear on the list. More notable still is
the appearance of Turkey, the Czech Republic, Hungary, and Poland
on the list, countries that were major sources of asylum seekers in the
1980s. These countries might have become more-attractive havens in

Table 13.1
Top twenty sources and destinations of asylum seekers, 1982–2001

Source country	1992–2001 Number	Per thousand	1982–1991 Number	Per thousand	Destination country	1992–2001 Number	Per thousand	1982–1991 Number	Per thousand
Yugoslavia Federal Republic	817.2	77.5	269.8	17.0	Germany	1,597.3	19.6	996.9	16.6
Iraq	310.8	15.4	52.1	3.4	United States	869.0	3.2	437.7	1.8
Turkey	308.8	4.9	499.3	9.6	United Kingdom	576.6	10.0	164.5	2.9
Romania	304.7	13.1	195.4	8.6	Netherlands	358.6	23.2	95.0	6.6
Afghanistan	204.1	10.6	54.0	4.0	Canada	286.3	9.8	239.4	9.3
El Salvador	196.5	34.7	69.6	14.6	France	281.0	4.8	347.4	6.3
Bosnia and Herzegovina	186.1	54.4	—	—	Switzerland	243.5	34.2	170.2	26.0
Sri Lanka	168.9	9.5	176.8	11.3	Sweden	228.6	25.9	183.2	21.9
Islamic Republic of Iran	161.1	2.6	195.5	4.0	Belgium	219.5	21.7	69.7	7.1
Guatemala	154.8	15.5	38.1	4.9	Austria	128.0	15.9	134.0	17.7
China	149.7	0.1	21.9	0.0	Denmark	97.4	18.6	45.3	8.9
Somalia	147.6	20.1	51.1	7.7	Australia	89.2	4.9	30.1	1.9
India	124.4	0.1	63.2	0.1	Spain	84.2	2.1	37.5	1.0
Pakistan	113.2	0.9	67.9	0.7	Italy	83.4	1.5	55.0	1.0
Russian Federation	105.2	0.7	25.0	0.2	Norway	71.1	16.3	32.3	7.8
Democratic Republic of Congo	103.9	2.3	97.5	3.0	Turkey	54.5	0.9	27.8	0.5
Algeria	92.6	3.3	—	—	Czech Republic	48.1	4.7	3.8	0.4
Bulgaria	91.2	10.8	47.5	5.3	Ireland	39.7	11.0	0.03	0.0
Nigeria	77.1	0.8	33.0	0.4	Hungary	37.5	3.7	4.4	0.4
Mexico	74.5	0.8	—	—	Poland	25.0	0.6	2.4	0.1

Source: Asylum seeker numbers from United Nations High Commissioner for Refugees 2002 (112–113, 115–116); population totals for 1985 and 1995 from United Nations 2002a (various tables).

the post-Soviet period, but the shift in these countries from sources of to destinations for asylum seekers may also reflect the increasing difficulty of gaining entrance to western Europe. While most destination countries experienced an increase in the number of applications between the 1980s and 1990s, the amount of growth in those numbers varied widely. In western Europe, large percentage increases occurred in the United Kingdom, the Netherlands, Belgium, and Ireland (from a base close to zero), while modest increases or small declines occurred in France, Switzerland, Sweden, and Austria.

These trends must have been influenced by changing policy in the destination countries, but they must also reflect distance and historic ties between source and destination. In addition, they may also be driven by exactly the same forces that we isolated for economic migrants in chapter 11. Almost all the applicants from South American countries such as El Salvador, Guatemala, and Nicaragua applied in the United States and Canada. By contrast, the bulk of applicants from eastern Europe applied somewhere in western Europe. During the 1990s, three-fifths of asylum applicants to the European Union from elsewhere in Europe applied in Germany, although these formed only half of all applications to Germany; indeed, compared with other destination countries, Germany also received the largest number of applications from Asia and Africa. More than half of the applications to Austria, Belgium, Finland, and Sweden came from elsewhere in Europe. For other countries with strong colonial and thus language ties outside Europe, like France and the United Kingdom, the share from Europe was less than one-fifth, while almost all of the rest came equally from Africa and Asia. Clearly, proximity, colonial inheritance, language, and the size of the foreign-born population all must have helped to determine both the total number of asylum applications to any host country and their source country composition.

What Happens to Asylum Seekers?

Are asylum seekers mostly accepted or mostly rejected, and if rejected, are they subsequently removed or do they become illegals? The answers are important, because the vast majority of those seeking asylum apply from within the country in which they are seeking it, having previously gained admission on a nonpermanent visa or by illegal entry. Four-fifths of all Danish applications for asylum in 1995–1999 were submitted from within the country, while the figures for the United

Kingdom were 68 percent in 1999 and 59 percent in 2001. Since most of the remainder apply at ports of entry, asylum seekers are almost all located within the country in which they are seeking asylum (or at the border) when their applications are lodged. Indeed, it is not possible to submit an asylum application to most countries from abroad, and those that do are rarely have their applications approved.

While annual asylum applications to the industrial world increased from 140,000 to 575,000 between 1982 and 2001, the number of applicants actually granted recognition as refugees under the 1951 Geneva Convention on Refugees increased much less, from 54,000 to 91,000. Some asylum seekers who are not recognized under the convention have nevertheless been given residency on humanitarian grounds, a number that increased over the period from 1,400 to 57,000. But the gap between applications and acceptances widened from about 85,000 to 427,000. About 20 percent of all applications lapse or are withdrawn before a decision is made, and hence acceptances should be compared with the total number of claims on which there are decisions.[1] Figure 13.3 plots the share of all first-instance decisions that result in acceptances, both under the convention and in total. The share of total acceptances fell sharply in the 1980s, from more than half in 1982 to less than one-fifth in 1990; among EU countries (the dashed lines in the figure) it fell even faster. In the 1990s total acceptances averaged 25 percent of decisions in the European Union, while those recognized as

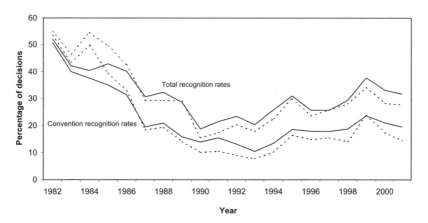

Figure 13.3
Recognition rates of asylum claims in industrialized countries, 1982–2001. *Source:* UNHCR 2002 (121–122, 124–125).

refugees under the convention accounted for a mere 14 percent of all decisions.

Since the majority of all asylum applications are rejected, what happens to the rejected applicants? The question is good, but the published statistics are not. The vast majority of applicants who apply within a country have to wait for their claims to be adjudicated under conditions that differ according to the policies of the receiving country. Based on press reports, this can take quite a long time. In the late 1990s, the median time to a first-instance decision was typically between six months and a year (IGC 1997), although waiting times have decreased as a result of recent initiatives to speed up the process. But for a significant minority, the process can still drag on for years, especially when there are appeals. Those whose claims are ultimately successful usually gain the right to long-term residency in the accepting country, while those who are rejected are obliged to leave.

Information on departures of rejected applicants generally refers only to those who are removed or who leave "voluntarily" once enforcement procedures are initiated. Notably, removals and voluntary departures from the United Kingdom were less than half the number of the claims that were rejected in the late 1990s, leaving us to ponder what happened to the other half. It is hard to avoid making the inference that most either went underground or simply remained in a state of limbo because there was no possibility for legal migration elsewhere. It is generally believed that only around a third of applicants to EU countries whose claims are rejected ultimately leave, although there is little hard evidence to confirm this estimate.[2] It is also possible that the rising rejection rates have deterred some potential asylum seekers from making any claim at all, with these individuals preferring instead to remain underground rather than to risk rejection and removal. This is especially likely for those with relatively weak asylum claims and in countries where the flourishing underground economy makes it relatively easy to live and work undetected.

Even more difficult to assess are the skills, labor market performance, welfare dependency rates, and overall economic outcomes for asylum seekers who do gain access to EU labor markets. As was true of the nineteenth century, those arriving as refugees today are not *lumpenproletariat* but rather appear to have skills that are of value in the labor market, although the evidence is admittedly rather thin on this important point. In a small sample of refugees admitted to the United Kingdom in the mid-1990s, one-third had university degrees, postgraduate training, or professional qualifications, and two-thirds of those formerly employed had been in professional, managerial, or business occupations (Carey-Wood et al. 1995). While such skills may not be easily transferable to labor markets in Europe given receiving countries' nonrecognition of overseas qualifications as well as refugees' inadequate documentation of their prior training or employment and lack of fluency in the host country language, they do indicate very strong positive selection among asylum seekers. If confirmed, this result would hardly be surprising. Where poverty constrains the emigration of the poor from sending countries, one would expect that war devastation would push poor, disadvantaged families still further down into poverty, since their assets are not mobile and thus easier to destroy or expropriate. Those with mobile financial assets and education are better equipped to leave, a relative advantage over the poor that increases in wartime. Our guess is that asylum seekers obey strong positive selection rules.

Still, employment rates among refugees are very low, even among those who have obtained the right to work. For example, the employment rate for prime-age male refugees in Denmark is half that of other immigrants. While that employment gap diminishes after five to ten years of residence, a significant wage penalty remains (Husted et al. 2000). Part of refugees' labor market disadvantage seems to be due to country-of-origin effects rather than to refugee status per se. In the United Kingdom, immigrants from refugee-sending countries have wage rates some 20 percent lower than immigrants with similar characteristics from non-refugee-sending countries (Lindley 2002). The disadvantage is even greater for those who are illegal and working in the underground economy. Undocumented workers suffer a wage penalty of 14–24 percent in the United States, largely because they are confined to the least skilled jobs where their human capital is not rewarded (Kossoudji and Cobb-Clark 2002).

Has the World Become a More-Dangerous Place?

Any assessment of the numbers of people seeking asylum must consider the population at risk. Do the trends in asylum applications simply reflect rising numbers of those displaced from their country of origin, or has the propensity to seek asylum increased, or have asylum seekers increasingly targeted the developed world for asylum, or is it all of the above? One key fact needs to be stressed: only about 5

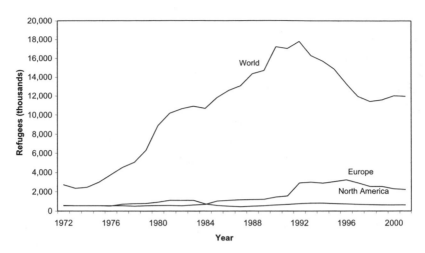

Figure 13.4
Worldwide stock of refugees. *Source:* UNHCR 2001 (annex 3).

percent of those displaced actually emerged as OECD asylum seekers in 2000. Figure 13.4 plots the total number of refugees as estimated by the UNHCR. This is the total worldwide number of those who are living outside their country of origin in refugee-like situations (a stock rather than a flow), situations that make them "of concern" to the UNHCR. The number increased dramatically from the early 1970s to a peak of eighteen million in 1992, and although the 2002 figure had fallen from that peak, it was *still* almost six times that of thirty years ago. Trends in world refugee stocks (figure 13.4) correspond pretty closely with trends in the flow of asylum applications (figures 13.1 and 13.2). Refugees in Europe and North America are a small share of the world stock, dominated as it is by those from Africa and Asia. Still, the European share increased from 14 percent in the 1980s to 23 percent in the 1990s. The rising European share can be attributed largely to two factors. The first is that refugees from eastern Europe were more likely to seek asylum in western Europe than elsewhere. The second is that those who do reach western European countries are less likely to return to their home countries. This shows up as persistence in the European total after 1992. In contrast, as we saw in the last chapter, large-scale displacements within Africa are often followed by wholesale repatriations once conditions permit.

One could easily argue that the upward trend in both the flow of asylum seekers and the world stock of refugees reflects the growing

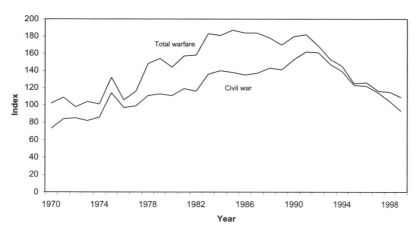

Figure 13.5
Global warfare index. *Source:* Hatton 2004a.

ability of the victimized and oppressed to flee across borders and to gain refuge in host countries, not just that the world has become a more-dangerous place, causing more refugee flights. One measure of the underlying causes of refugee flight is the number and intensity of armed conflicts in the world. Indices of worldwide conflict are plotted in figure 13.5. Each episode is given a score ranging from one to seven that reflects the scale of the conflict and its societal impact. A score of one denotes "sporadic or expressive political violence"—that is, low-level violence by small militant groups. A score of seven denotes "pervasive warfare"—that is, full-scale wars that consume the entire society. The index reflects the total of these scores.

The total conflict index trended upward from 1965 to the late 1980s, although the increasing trend dates back to the late 1940s. Contrary to widespread belief, the cold war witnessed a secular increase in violence associated with proxy wars, independence struggles, and postcolonial civil wars. The independence wars of the 1960s and 1970s gave way in the 1980s to intercountry wars, often involving newly independent states. But while intercountry wars declined beginning in the late 1980s, civil wars, which account for the bulk of worldwide violence, continued to increase until the early 1990s. These local conflicts often reflect long-standing ethnopolitical tensions, such as in the former Yugoslavia, where they were unleashed at the end of the cold war. We have already noted that these civil wars have been a powerful source of refugee displacement in Africa and a strong influence on total cross-border migration there. The central point is that the levels of violence escalated to a peak between 1984 and 1992 and have since declined substantially.

These profiles of world violence bear a fairly close resemblance to the patterns observed in the flows of asylum seekers and in the stock of refugees. The number of new conflicts breaking out declined in the 1990s, and more old ones were either contained or settled (Gurr, Marshall, and Khosla 2000). Note, however, that while the level of conflict fell in the 1990s back to that of the 1970s, the numbers of refugees and asylum seekers did not return to their former levels. This may be because the number of refugees generated per conflict increased as a result of the growth of populations affected and the accessibility of more-destructive weapons (Weiner 1997). It may also reflect an increased ability to escape conflicts at lower cost.

The percentage of all governments that were autocracies fell gradually from the 1970s and more sharply after the collapse of the Soviet Union and the end of the cold war (Marshall 1999). Although the number and share of countries under democratic government increased, the greatest rise was in what we have come to call transitional regimes. The evidence suggests that these transitional regimes are almost as prone to conflict as autocracies, but a chaotic transitional regime is also easier to escape than an autocratic police state. The easier-to-escape hypothesis is consistent with the experience of eastern Europe after 1989, the region which accounts for most of the recent increase in the number of states that are labeled transitional. Finally, distance and persistence matter. The Balkans and the previous Soviets are close to western Europe, and they also have a long historical tradition of east-west migration, both of which must have served to raise the refugee-to-conflict ratio in the 1990s.

The European Policy Backlash

The great surge in asylum applications at the end of the twentieth century was mainly felt in western Europe and particularly in the European Union. Asylum has, as a result, been high on the European Union's policy agenda since the late 1980s. The fundamental basis for EU policy toward asylum seekers is the Convention Relating to the Status of Refugees, signed in 1951 by twenty-nine countries in Geneva. A refugee is defined under the convention as someone who is outside his or her country of origin and who is unable or unwilling to return owing to a "well founded fear of persecution." The convention definition excludes internally displaced persons and those who have committed serious crimes. It also provides that refugees may not be forcibly returned to a situation in which they would face the threat of persecution (*nonrefoulement*). The convention does not guarantee refugees permanent right of residence in the host country, except insofar as this is provided by the *nonrefoulement* clause.

Since the convention obliges governments to assess all asylum claims and to accept those that are valid, the only way to control the numbers is to influence the volume of applications. This can be done cooperatively, as has happened with EU policy harmonization of late, or it can be done competitively, as we have seen was true of country immigration policy in the late nineteenth and early twentieth century. Chapter 8 has shown that when the United States chose liberal or restrictive immigrant policy between 1870 and 1930, countries with smaller numbers of immigrants followed suit, fearing that immigrants deflected from America would end up on their doorsteps. Furthermore, some of these countries, like Argentina, took their policy cues from the behavior of a closer neighbor, like Brazil. Similar competitive behavior can be observed in recent EU asylum policy, although policy coordination among EU countries has gradually increased. That fact makes it easy to understate the deterrent role of tougher asylum policy, as we show subsequently.

In the face of an increase in the number of asylum seekers, a series of agreements and resolutions were adopted, either formally as EU policy or through intergovernmental conferences.[3] Most of these agreements and resolutions were not strictly binding on EU member governments, but policy was closely harmonized in areas such as visa requirements and carrier sanctions. The 1990 Dublin Convention sought to put an end to "asylum shopping" by providing that an asylum claim would be dealt with by one EU state only, specifically, the state of first entry. Following this, a meeting of EU ministers produced three key (but nonbinding) principles known as the London Resolutions. The first involves the "safe third country" concept, which allowed member states to refuse to consider an asylum claim if the applicant had transited through a country deemed "safe" where he or she could have sought asylum. The second determined that "manifestly unfounded" asylum claims could be summarily rejected without right of appeal.

The third designated "safe countries of origin" in which there is a presumption of no serious risk of persecution and for which an expedited procedure could be used.

The European Council of Ministers produced a number of recommendations in the mid-1990s that built upon this existing framework. Among the most important were the recommendations on readmission adopted in 1994 and 1995.[4] The most recent developments follow from the 1997 Treaty of Amsterdam and the European Council meeting in Tampere, Finland, in 1999. Under the former, the commission gained the sole right to propose legislation, starting in 2002. At the latter, EU ministers reaffirmed that any common European asylum regulations would be based on a "full and inclusive" application of the Geneva Convention, and in particular that the convention's *nonrefoulement* clause would be honored. These EU-wide initiatives have certainly brought a degree of harmonization to member state policy, but they are best seen as evolving from the succession of ad hoc policy developments that took place at the national level in the various member countries during the 1980s and 1990s. Finally, while considerable policy harmonization has been achieved in the European Union, repeated efforts to promote "burden sharing" have met with only limited success, particularly with regard to the distribution of refugees across member states.

Prior to policy harmonization and in the absence of a single EU-wide asylum policy, individual EU member countries responded to mounting asylum pressure by passing more-restrictive asylum legislation. Legislation of this type had four goals: to tighten access to the country's borders by potential asylum seekers, to toughen asylum procedures, to toughen the treatment of asylum seekers during processing, and to toughen treatment of rejected asylum seekers. Policies to limit access included carrier sanctions, the designation of airports as international zones, and tighter visa requirements for visitors from countries likely to generate asylum seekers. Among the earliest to introduce carrier sanctions were Germany and the United Kingdom, both in 1987, and by the late 1990s such sanctions had become universal in EU countries. Visa restrictions were applied more gradually, and by 1993 the signatories shared a joint list that included 73 countries, with the figure exceeding 150 by 1998.

The most important reforms to the processing of asylum applications were the implementation of procedures for manifestly unfounded claims and the establishment of safe-third-country lists that followed the Dublin Convention. The most notable case was Germany, where the measures introduced in 1993 required an amendment to the constitution, which guaranteed the right to asylum. Particularly contentious in Germany was the list (sometimes called a white list) of safe countries of origin, countries deemed sufficiently safe to be unable to give rise to legitimate claims for asylum.[5] Similar sets of policies were introduced in most other EU countries between 1991 and 1998. In addition there were reforms that affect the outcomes of asylum procedures. These include the speed at which asylum claims are processed and an increase in the toughness of deportation policies in the event of an unsuccessful claim. Some countries also moved to limit the granting of humanitarian status to those denied full convention status.

Finally, some reforms related to the treatment of asylum seekers during processing, including dispersal and detention, access to welfare benefits, and the right to seek employment. During the 1980s a number of countries permitted asylum seekers to work while their applications were being processed, but this right was largely withdrawn during the 1990s. A number of countries also restricted asylum seekers' access to welfare benefits, providing only in-kind subsistence generally available only at designated reception centers. Such measures were often reinforced by the dispersal of asylum seekers to centers outside the major metropolitan areas and by increasingly restrictive detention rules.

Measures of toughness in these different policy dimensions are displayed in figure 13.6. The figure graphs averages across fourteen EU countries of variables that take the value zero before, and one after,

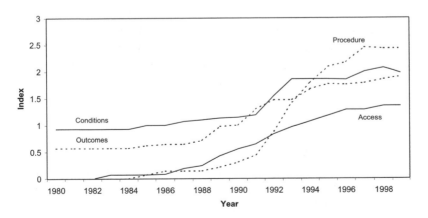

Figure 13.6
Asylum policy index, EU average, 1980–1999. *Source:* Hatton 2004a.

the introduction of a restrictive measure. The "access" index includes two components, whereas those for "procedure," "outcomes," and "conditions" each include three components. All four dimensions of policy show a steep increase in restrictiveness, particularly in the first half of the 1990s. Most marked is the toughening of asylum procedures between 1991 and 1994 associated with safe-third-country policies and procedures for manifestly unfounded claims. Converting each policy component into a crude binary indicator often involves a judgment call, and it cannot take account of smaller gradations of policy or of the way specific policies are implemented and enforced. Nevertheless, the policy index is likely to be a reasonable reflection of the overall toughness of a country's policy stance compared with that of other countries and with its own in the past.

Econometric analysis of this policy index indicates that the most important explanatory variable is its own lagged value, reflecting a high degree of policy persistence (Hatton 2004a, table 7), just as we found for nineteenth-century policy toward all immigrants (chapter 8). The average policy stance of the other EU countries, lagged one year, also has a positive influence, suggesting some degree of spillover from policies introduced elsewhere, yet another repetition of nineteenth-century experience. In addition, a country's policy is more responsive to increases in asylum applications to the European Union as whole than it is to increases in its own application numbers. Strong economic growth tends to postpone increases in policy restrictiveness, since buoyant labor markets ease fiscal pressure, modern policy behavior that again repeats that of a century ago. Finally, and somewhat surprisingly, there seems to be little relationship, either positive or negative, between the restrictiveness of asylum and immigration policy. Of course, immigration policy may have a powerful *indirect* impact on asylum policy to the extent that a smaller number of economic immigrants, shut out by tougher immigration policy, improves labor market conditions, thus easing tough attitudes toward asylum seekers.

Motives and Mechanisms

What motivates asylum seekers? Does their decision-making process differ from that of other migrants? Are they driven by fear of persecution only, or do the benefits and costs of migration enter into their calculations? What discretion do they have in regard to the destination and timing of migration?

Studies find that civil wars and political genocide are the most important causes of refugee flight, while government crises, ethnic fractionalization, and lack of political rights have weaker effects (chapter 12; Schmeidl 1997). The separate role of economic conditions in the sending country is usually hard to identify, since these conditions are so intertwined with conflict and violence: while violence at home triggers a refugee flow, it also creates economic hardship, making it more difficult for a poor family to finance the move. In any case, the same fundamentals that influence immigration may also explain the numbers seeking asylum and the countries to which they apply.

How do asylum seekers choose their destinations? One way to seek an answer is to ask the asylum seekers themselves whether their destination was the result of choice or chance. Dutch experience suggests that conscious choice dominated anywhere from one-third to two-thirds of the cases. One survey found that asylum seekers in the Netherlands, Belgium, and the United Kingdom were influenced in their choice of destination by historic ties with the host country, language, migrant networks, transportation costs, ease of access, and economic and social conditions. Such findings would encourage the belief that home violence dictates the *timing* of an asylum-seeking move, while destination choice is dictated by the same factors that influence the economic migrant's decision, a characterization that held in exactly the same way for the Jews fleeing pogroms in Tsarist Russia. Thus, the degree of deliberation preceeding asylum seeking must depend on factors like the urgency and unexpectedness of the flight and individual resources. In short, destination is determined by a combination of choice and constraint (Böcker and Havinga 1997, 89).

The major constraint on an asylum seeker is the cost of gaining access to the host country. The vast majority of potential asylum seekers have found it more and more difficult to enter as a legitimate visitor or immigrant. Since it is necessary to reach the destination before claiming asylum, candidates often enter illegally using the services of migrant traffickers and smugglers. It is estimated that about half of those claiming asylum in Germany and two-thirds of those in the Netherlands are smuggled in. It has been suggested that payments to smugglers by or on behalf of asylum seekers ranged from $4,000 to $5,000 in the mid-1990s.[6]

Three implications follow from the previous paragraph. First, potential asylum seekers who come from low-income countries and who finance their own moves are unlikely to be from the bottom of the

income distribution (Morrison and Crosland 2001, 21). The poor cannot
finance a costly move. This, of course, is consistent with the positive
selection that has characterized global migration for the past two centuries and even longer (part I). Second, migrant networks are likely to
be particularly important in providing information about destinations,
advice about routes, and financial support (Koser and Pinkerton 2002).
Again, this implication is consistent with what we know about global
migration over the past 200 years. Third, the expansion of people-
smuggling networks, particularly on routes through eastern Europe,
has probably contributed to the level and persistence of asylum seeker
flows.[7] One wonders how similar the economics of people smuggling
is today compared with those of Asian contract labor in the nineteenth
century (chapters 2 and 7).

Which policy elements matter most and how? Consider the debate
over why the numbers of asylum seekers fell from its peak in the early
1990s. A 1997 report issued by the Inter Governmental Consultations
on Asylum and Migration commented that the likelihood of shorter
screening periods and shorter procedures in general, along with "considerable reductions and even suppression of entitlements usually
associated with an asylum application (right to social and cash entitlements, housing) might have had a dissuasive effect on those considering departure from countries of origin on economic grounds. In
addition, safe country declarations may have similarly led to a reduction in the number of unjustified claims" (IGC 1997, 22). This report
assumes that policy mattered. But did it, and if so, how? And how do
we explain the fact that asylum applications continued to increase during the 1990s in some countries *in spite of* the introduction of restrictive
measures similar to those enacted elsewhere in the European Union?

Explaining Asylum Seeker Trends

Country policies reacted strongly (but with a lag) to the rapid growth
in asylum applications during the 1990s. Furthermore, asylum policies
converged across European countries. Although the number of asylum
applications fell sharply between 1992 and 1997, it did not come close
to falling to the levels observed in the early 1980s, when policy was
much less restrictive. This has led some to conclude that the tightening
of asylum policy that took place in the 1990s has not been very effective in achieving its goal of deterring asylum applications. However,
measures of global conflict rose through the late 1980s and early 1990s,

after which they declined. So to what extent can changes in the number of asylum applications, particularly in Europe, be explained by policy and to what extent by the rise and fall of source country conflict? What role is there, if any, for changing economic conditions in source and destination countries? And how far can these variables explain the long-run upward trend in asylum applications?

Such questions cannot be answered without a multivariate framework that accounts simultaneously for the different influences and, in addition, allows a country's policy itself to respond to the number of applicants for asylum in that country and to developments in other destination countries. Despite the intensity of the popular debate about asylum policy, very few studies have done so, and thus very few can be confident that they have isolated the role of policy. For example, a recent survey concluded (somewhat prematurely) that no consistent policy influence could be found, partly because policy effects could not be separated from other determinants, partly because policy itself is endogenous, and partly because the requisite data were absent (Zetter et al. 2003).

One excellent case study examined the determinants of asylum applications to Germany from seventeen countries in Africa and Asia over the years 1987–1995 (Rotte, Vogler, and Zimmermann 1997). The level of political terror in the source countries was found to raise the number of asylum applications, but so did source country improvements in political rights and civil liberties. Economic incentives and constraints were found to be important: the bigger the income gap between Germany and the source country, the greater the number of asylum applications; in addition, source country income by itself had a positive effect, confirming that poverty constraints are important. Furthermore, after other influences are controlled for, tougher German asylum policy had a large negative impact on the numbers seeking asylum.

These are useful findings to be sure, but Germany is only one country. More recently, another study examined trends in the share of asylum applications across twenty OECD countries from 1985 to 1999, focusing only on destination country effects (Thielemann 2003). The key variables at work here were labor market conditions (as reflected in the unemployment rate), the existing stock of foreign nationals (the friends-and-relatives effect), and the country's reputation for generosity (as measured by overseas development aid). Asylum policy, as measured by a composite index of deterrence policies (similar to that

Table 13.2
Explaining asylum applications to the European Union, 1981–1999

$LnAs/Pop_t = -2.12\ LnYRatio(s/d)_{t-1} - 7.17\ Unem(d)_{t-1} + 17.17\ Conflict_t + 0.51\ PolRts_t$
    (4.4)   (3.6)   (2.9)   (2.7)
    $+ 0.26\ Mstock81 + 0.77\ EEur90 - 0.09\ Policy_t + 0.20\ Time$
    (5.8)   (1.9)   (2.0)   (8.9)
    $R^2 = 0.78$

Source: This is a variant of the model presented in Hatton 2004a (table 8). Further details concerning data sources are available there.

Note: Robust *t* statistics in parentheses.

Sample: Balanced panel for 1981–1999 of asylum applications from each of three source regions (Africa, Asia, and eastern Europe) to each of fourteen EU countries (Austria, Belgium, Denmark, Finland, France, Germany, Greece, Ireland, Italy, Netherlands, Portugal, Spain, Sweden, and the United Kingdom).

Definitions of variables: LnAs/Pop = log ratio of applications from source region to destination country per thousand of source region population; *LnYRatio(s/d)* = log ratio of purchasing-power-parity-adjusted GDP per capita (source region to destination country); *Unem(d)* = unemployment rate in destination country; *Conflict* = index of the number and intensity of wars in the source region; *PolRts* = Freedom House index of political rights (higher value = fewer rights); *Mstock81* = log source region nationals in destination in 1981; *Eur90* = dummy for eastern Europe from 1990; *Policy* = asylum policy index for destination country; *Time* = time trend.

Method: Pooled ordinary least squares regression on 798 source/destination/year observations. Fixed effects for each destination and each source and dummy for Italy (Asia and Africa only) from 1990 included but not reported.

displayed in figure 13.6), was found to be significantly negative but not very important in explaining application trends.

Studies like these fail to agree on the effectiveness of asylum policy, and they offer no assessment of exactly what difference the escalating toughness of such policy has made to the flow of asylum applications. They also focus either on one destination country or on the distribution of asylum claims among countries, excluding source country effects. However, table 13.2 shows results of a panel analysis of asylum flows from three source regions to fourteen EU countries between 1981 and 1999. According to these results, asylum flows are highly responsive to economic forces, consistent with other findings in this book, including those of the last two chapters dealing with economic migrants over the last half century. An increase of 1 percent in the ratio of source to destination GDP per capita reduces the number of asylum applications by 2.2 percent, while an increase in the destination unemployment rate by the same amount reduces the number of asylum seekers by 7.2 percent. A 10 percent increase in the source country's conflict index raises the

Table 13.3
Decomposition of change in asylum applications by source region, 1981–1999 (thousands)

	Africa	Asia	Eastern Europe	Total
Source region population	18.1	28.6	2.7	49.4
GDP per capita ratio, source to host	30.1	−79.1	17.7	−31.3
Unemployment in destination	−7.7	−28.6	−23.6	−59.9
Conflict index	−11.7	−28.3	51.3	11.3
Political rights index	−14.2	−11.6	−138.5	−164.2
Eastern Europe from 1990	—	—	70.9	70.9
Asylum policy	−25.5	−66.4	−63.4	−155.3
Total above effects	−10.9	−175.6	−82.8	−269.3
Actual change, 1981–1999	53.0	80.4	69.5	202.9

Source: Hatton 2004a (table 10).
Note: Decomposition based on the coefficients in table 13.2.

number of asylum claims by 7.5 percent, while a 10 percent improvement in the source country's index of political rights reduces asylum claims by 25 percent. Finally, the effect of the asylum policy index confirms the view that more-restrictive asylum policy deters asylum seekers and reduces the number of applications. Toughening policy has a powerful impact on asylum flows.

So how much have policy, violence, and other variables contributed to the twenty-year trend in asylum applications? Table 13.3 reports the contributions of the key forces which account for the change in the absolute number of asylum applications to fourteen EU countries from three source regions between 1981 and 1999, which amounted to an increase of 202,900. About 50,000 of the increase (about 25 percent of the change to be explained) was due to population growth in the source region. Changing levels of war and conflict reduced the numbers coming from Africa and Asia but increased the number from eastern Europe. The total effect of conflict across all three regions was to increase applications by 11,300, a small share (about 6 percent) of the total increase to be explained. Finally, the effects of opening up the borders between eastern and western Europe gave a very strong boost to asylum applications despite the fact that improving political rights was increasing the incentive to stay home. Opening up the eastern-western European borders accounted for 70,900 of the increase in applications, or almost 35 percent. These three forces combined accounted for two-thirds of the rise in asylum applications between 1981 and 1999. If these were the only forces at work, the surge would have been quite a bit more modest.

Furthermore, there were powerful forces at work *reducing* asylum applications. Relative income trends had negative effects overall (−31,300), since the impact of Asian economic growth catch-up outweighed the relatively poor growth performance in Africa and eastern Europe. Since the economies of Africa and eastern Europe fell further behind those of the EU, the number of asylum claims from those regions increased as a result that force alone. If significant growth catch-up were to start in these two economically troubled regions in the future, the rise in applications should slow down (controlling for the poverty constraint). Because unemployment was higher in most EU countries in 1999 than it was in 1981, the overall effect of changing employment conditions in EU destinations was also negative (−60,000): softening labor markets tended to make the European Union less attractive to asylum seekers as time went on. Improvements in political rights in sending regions also served to reduce the number of asylum applications dramatically, especially from eastern Europe (−164,200). So far, it appears that these offsetting negative forces were large enough to have caused a *decline* in asylum applications (131,600 − 255,400 = −123,800), not the 202,900 rise we observe.

Now consider asylum policy. Table 13.2 identifies the effect of tougher asylum policy after having controlled for these other important influences. For the European Union as a whole, the impact of the tougher asylum policy was enormous. While EU applications over this period increased by 202,900, the effect of policy was to *reduce* them by 155,300. Without the tougher policy, then, the number of applicants would have increased by 358,200. The tougher policy served to reduce asylum applications by 43 percent.

When asylum policy effects are added to all other effects in table 13.2, the combined impact should have been to *reduce* applicants by about 270,000, not to *increase* them by about 200,000. If country asylum policy and the other influences captured in table 13.3 were serving to reduce asylum applications, why did the actual numbers reported in table 13.2 increase so much? Consider four candidates omitted from the table.

First, it is sometimes suggested that more-restrictive immigration policies spill over into asylum applications. For example, a crude measure of country immigration policy suggests that the more restrictive the policy, the *lower* the number of asylum applications, perhaps as a result of signaling: that is, tougher immigration policy may signal tougher asylum policy to potential applicants (Hatton 2004a). A second omitted candidate might be some "deflection effect" whereby a toughening of asylum policy in one EU country deflects asylum seekers to other EU countries. Since there was a general increase in policy restrictiveness across the EU from the late 1980s, the deterrent effect of policy toughening by one country could be partially undone if other countries also enacted tougher policies. There is some evidence favoring this view, and if the view reflects reality, the EU-wide policy effect was probably much smaller than the sum of the marginal country effects reported in table 13.3. A third candidate might be that we have not fully controlled for changing source country conditions. These could include an easing of the poverty constraint as source country incomes increase. They could also include improvements in source country infrastructure and education levels that facilitate refugee flight, as well as changes in demographic structure. These forces are hard to quantify, but they probably account for some of the upward trend.

A final and, we think, more-important omitted candidate is the cumulative effect of past inflows of asylum seekers. This book has shown that the friends-and-relatives or network effect has had a powerful impact on global migration for two centuries, but it turns out to be a very powerful influence even on asylum seekers: indeed, it has been estimated that every hundred added to the existing refugee stock in a country generates a further eight applications to that country for asylum per year (Hatton 2004a). This effect probably accounts for the entire remaining upward trend in asylum applications that the other variables in table 13.2 fail to explain. It seems likely that this network effect has strengthened over time with an increasing density and more-efficient network of people smugglers. Migrant trafficking has grown since the late 1980s as smugglers have become more professional and expert, developments that have been coupled with the opening up of a variety of routes into western Europe from eastern Europe.

These findings help resolve any apparent inconsistency between the literature on immigration and asylum policy; in both cases tougher policy reduces immigration. But the powerful effects of asylum policy have been obscured by the strong upward trends in the numbers seeking asylum and by the fact that policy trends have been similar across countries. They have been obscured even more by the cumulative effect of asylum seeker flows, the building of family networks, and more-efficient people-smuggling networks. These forces have made, and will make, it very difficult to reduce the flows once these networks are in place. Had European asylum policy toughened a decade earlier, the cumulative effects would have been attenuated, and the flows in the 1990s might have been far smaller.

14　　　　The Labor Market and Fiscal Impact of Immigration

Most developed countries moved decisively to restrict immigration during the twentieth century. We have argued that the introduction of highly restrictive controls from the turn of the century to the 1930s was the result of a combination of factors: public assessment of the impact of immigration on the labor market, growth in the political participation of those who felt that impact most keenly, and as a triggering mechanism, the sudden shocks delivered by world war and depression. Part IV of this book shows that when public opinion has been negative toward immigration, this has often been interpreted as a response to the imagined or real economic threats immigration has brought. Nineteenth-century U.S. history shows that this response is hardly new. Nor is it solely a response to labor market effects, since fiscal effects matter in the debate too, although they matter far more today than a century ago when governments and their social welfare programs were so much smaller. Nevertheless, the labor market effect of immigration has always been the key focus in debate over immigration policy, and a large research effort has been devoted to measuring its effects over the century since the U.S. Immigration Commission reported its findings in 1911.

The debate can be motivated by reference to the textbook picture of labor supply and demand in figure 14.1, in which we simplify by assuming for the moment only one type of output and one type of labor. As usual, labor demand (D_1) is downward sloping to the right, capital and technology are taken to be fixed, and exogenous changes in immigration serve to increase total labor supply from S_1 to S_2. Immigration lowers the wage rate from W_1 to W_2 while it raises total profits from the area X to the area $X + Y + Z$ (the area under the demand curve down to the wage). The total loss to resident wage earners is area Y, and the net gain to society, excluding the immigrants themselves, is Z.

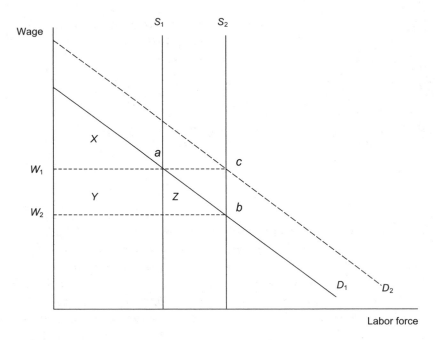

Figure 14.1
Economic effects of immigration

Two points emerge immediately from figure 14.1. First, the overall collective gain from immigration to all native-born residents is likely to be very small. One modern estimate for the United States puts the annual gain (Z) from the accumulated stock of immigrants at 0.1 percent of national income (Borjas 1999a, 1701). Second, distributional effects are unambiguous—wage earners lose while their employers gain—and those effects are likely to be large. Immigration therefore has a different impact on different interest groups, but if wage earners are the voting majority, and if immigration policy reflects majority preference, then policy is likely to be restrictive.

Things get more complicated the farther we depart from the assumptions underlying the simple textbook analysis underlying figure 14.1. Five complications are particularly important to the final assessment. First, if labor markets fail to clear through wage adjustment (in the short run at least), then immigrants will add more to the labor force than to employment. If immigrants are first hired and last fired, then they rob jobs from native-born residents, pushing some of them into unemployment or out of the labor force entirely. If, on the other hand, immigrants are last hired and first fired, then they dominate the unemployed and/or the "informal" sector, where wages are more flexible and productivity lower. Second, labor market effects may be attenuated by adjustments in goods or capital markets. For example, if capital is the only other input and if it is perfectly mobile internationally, then the new equilibrium in figure 14.1 will be at c rather than b as capital chases after the migrants in response to the incipient rise in returns (shifting the labor demand curve to the right from, say, D_1 to D_2). Under perfect world capital mobility, and thus completely elastic capital supplies, the incomes of the domestic owners of capital and the wages of resident workers remain unchanged: native-born residents are neither better nor worse off, and the immigrants have been absorbed without a hitch. Third, suppose there are two or more types of labor. If the immigrants are mainly unskilled, then unskilled residents may lose as a result of the increased job competition, but skilled workers may gain. The more are skilled and unskilled workers complements in production (and the less they are substitutes), the more likely skilled workers will gain from unskilled immigration. Fourth, perhaps unskilled immigration can induce a skilled labor market supply response in both the short run and the long run. In the long run, higher wage gaps and skill premia induced by unskilled immigration may trigger a schooling response among future native-born generations, an effect that chapter 9 suggested was operating a century ago. In addition, Michael Kremer and Stanley Watt (2004) have recently suggested that unskilled female immigrants may release skilled workers from home work (child and elderly care) to do market work. Finally, some of the economic effects of immigration may come through fiscal transfer rather than labor market adjustment. If immigrants have low wages, low labor market participation, high unemployment, and/or high dependency rates, then they are likely to be supported by native-born residents through redistributive tax and welfare systems. If immigrants do not have those attributes, then they are likely instead to be net fiscal contributors.

These are some of the more-obvious effects immigration has on the incomes of resident populations. Listing them is easy enough; measuring them is not.

Looking at Local Labor Markets

One obvious way to measure the impact of immigration is to look across local or regional labor markets within a given country that have different rates of immigration from abroad to see whether those with higher rates of immigration also have slower wage or employment growth (or higher unemployment growth) among resident workers. One advantage of this so-called spatial-correlation approach is that focusing on local labor markets *within* a country holds country-specific shocks and institutions constant. Because of these attractive features, a number of studies have employed this methodology to investigate the effects of immigration. The results of a representative sample of these are summarized in table 14.1, covering four OECD countries over the last four decades. The penultimate column reports the percentage impact on wages from an immigrant-induced 1 percent change in the labor force. The last column reports the impact, in percentage points, of the same immigrant-induced labor force change on employment, unemployment, or both.

Table 14.1 makes it clear that there is little consensus among economists regarding the amount by which an immigrant influx (equivalent to 1 percent of the resident workforce) reduces the wage. In some cases, wages of native-born residents (and of previous immigrant cohorts) are reduced; in other cases, they are not. Lack of strong negative wage and crowding-out effects might be explained by the fact that in the short run, immigration serves to increase unemployment, as immigrants either "rob jobs" from locals or remain unemployed themselves. This impact would be expected if wage rates were sticky downward, as we think they are in the short run. However, there is no consistent evidence confirming adverse effects on employment or unemployment in local labor markets.

Findings like these contributed to a consensus by the mid-1990s that the effects of immigration on host country labor markets are small (Borjas 1994; Friedberg and Hunt 1995). Yet two nagging doubts suggest that the small-impact conclusion may be premature. First, the finding that immigration neither reduces the wage nor raises unemployment is blatantly inconsistent with the standard labor demand curve depicted in figure 14.1. It seems justified to insist that analysts offer an explicit explanation for any finding that rejects such a powerful weapon from the standard economist's arsenal—demand curves are downward sloping to the right—and is inconsistent with decades of empirical work by labor economists, who have estimated the labor demand curve to have elasticities well above -0.5 (Hammermesh 1993; Borjas 2003). Second, there is little consistency across these different studies, even for the same country. As Borjas (1999a) puts it: "One could easily argue that this literature has failed to increase our under-

Table 14.1
Estimated effects of immigration on wages and employment of natives

Study	Country/region/time	Effect on earnings of immigration equivalent to 1% of the labor force (in percent)	Effect on employment and unemployment of immigration equivalent to 1% of the labor force (in percentage points)
Altonji and Card 1991	U.S. cities, 1970–1980	−1.2 (low skilled)	Employment: negligible Unemployment: −2.3
Borjas, Freeman, and Katz 1997	U.S. states, 1960–1990	0.59 (1960–1970); 0.07 (1970–1980); −0.01 (1980–1990)	Employment: −0.03 (1960–1970); 0.13 (1970–1980); −0.05 (1980–1990)
Card 2001	U.S. cities, by occupation, 1985–1990	−0.15	Employment: −0.05
De New and Zimmermann 1994	German industries, 1984–1989	−4.1	
Pischke and Velling 1997	German counties, 1985–1989		Employment: 0.05 Unemployment: 0.2
Addison and Worswick 2002	Australian states by occupation, 1982–1996	1.5 (all); 2.7 (less educated)	No effects on unemployment
Dustmann et al. 2003	U.K. regions 1983–2000	1.9 (all); 2.2 (skilled); 1.2 (semiskilled); 2.2 (unskilled)	Unemployment: 0.2 (all); 0.1 (skilled); 0.4 (semiskilled); 0.03 (unskilled)

Note: The estimates reported here are based on regression coefficients that are often not significantly different from zero. Many of the authors offer a range of estimates using different specifications, and the ones presented here are considered the most representative. Since the model specifications also vary among studies, the estimates from different studies are not strictly comparable. The estimates are for males.

standing of how labor markets respond to immigration. If we take the empirical evidence ... at face value, the implications are disturbing: either we need different economic models to understand how supply shocks affect labor markets in different periods ... or the regression coefficients are simply not measuring what we think they should be measuring" (1740).

So what has gone wrong? There are a couple of reasons why the spatial-correlation approach could be biased against finding large crowding-out effects. One reason is simply that the annual flow of immigration is usually small relative to the size of the labor market. Since immigrants gravitate toward a few major urban centers, most regions in most countries that make up the bulk of the observations in local area studies have immigrant inflows that are very small relative to local labor demand and supply. Nearly a third of the U.S. foreign-born live in just three metropolitan areas (New York, Los Angeles, and Miami), and 60 percent of all U.S. legal immigrants entered through two "gateway" states: California and New York (Borjas, Freeman, and Katz 1996). About 40 percent of immigrants to Britain go to London, and the same share of immigrants to Australia go to Sydney, while more than a third of those arriving in France locate in Île-de-France (the greater Paris area). Under these real world circumstances, systematic immigration effects are hard to assess anywhere but in the few gateway areas where new immigrants concentrate. To make matters worse for the econometrics, immigrants tend to locate in areas where economic conditions are favorable—where unemployment is low and wages are high and possibly rising. Where immigration is endogenous—as it almost always is—the direction of causation is reversed and of the opposite sign. When this endogenous effect and the "true" labor market impact are both present, the net result is to bias estimates of the labor market impact downward, possibly very substantially.

A more important reason still is that the markets for labor and goods are likely to be very well integrated within developed countries—*much* more so than between countries. Suppose the goods market adjusts quickly: as immigrants are absorbed in one region, that region expands its output of goods that use most intensively the skills that immigrants bring to it. In short, a boom in the region's export sector absorbs the immigrants. This is what international economists call the Rybczynski (1955) effect. Labor markets are also far better integrated within a country than they are between countries. As immigrants enter a local labor market, they induce interregional migration by the native-born and previous immigrant cohorts with whom they compete. As a result, the labor market impact of immigration cannot be observed accurately at the local level. Indeed, it may not be observed there at all. Integrated national goods and labor markets imply that the effects of immigration will be spread across the entire country—all boats rise and fall together as the immigrant tide ebbs and flows, regardless of the shore upon which immigrant waves lap. The better integrated are the markets for goods and labor across regions within a country, the less will an immigration shock be reflected in local wage rates, even though the effects of immigration could still be large for the country as a whole.

If regional markets are well integrated, then the effects of immigration can be observed only at the national level. But how? Borjas (2003) has argued recently that if different types of labor defined by schooling and labor market experience are not good substitutes for each other, then the effects of immigration can be inferred by estimating the relative wage impacts of changes in the supply of different types of labor at the national level. One advantage of this approach is that mobility between these skill groups is limited. Intercensal changes between 1960 and 2000 reveal strong effects consistent with labor demand elasticities ranging between −0.3 and −0.4. Thus, the 11 percent increase in labor supply brought about by immigration between 1980 and 2000 must have reduced the wage of the average nonimmigrant worker by 3.2 percent. Not surprisingly, these impacts vary across education and experience groups: immigration reduced the wage by 8.9 percent for high school dropouts, by 2.6 percent for high school graduates, and by almost nothing for those with some college education (Borjas 2003, 1370). Thus, to the extent that immigrants cluster in the group competing with high school dropouts, the crowding-out impact will be very big. This result is consistent with assessments of immigration's impact on host labor markets during the age of mass migration before World War I, summarized in chapters 6 and 8.

An alternative approach is to look across countries whose labor markets are only very loosely linked. One recent study examined the short-run impact of immigration on native-born employment rates in eighteen European countries between 1983 and 1999, using the "shock" of asylum immigrants from eastern Europe to better identify the effects (Angrist and Kugler 2003). The study found that adding 100 immigrants to a country's labor force reduced employment among the native-born by between 35 and 85. These job losses were largest among young males. Furthermore, overall job loss was greatest in countries with the least flexible labor markets and with the highest benefit replacement rates. It seems reasonable to conclude that the initial effects of immigration on employment in countries with less-flexible labor markets would eventually translate into wage effects, with the adjustment process depending on the degree of labor market flexibility.

These new findings seem to have solved the riddle of why the modern, spatial-correlation approach so often fails to find big negative immigration effects either on wage rates or on resident employment. Immigrants *do* lower the incomes of those residents with whom they most directly compete, just as they did a century ago.

Immigration and Regional Integration within Host Countries

Why does the spatial-correlation approach fail to find big labor market effects when in fact such effects are present? Is it goods market integration, labor market integration, or something else that accounts for this failure? Let us begin with the goods market.

Recall that the Rybczynski theorem implies that a globally integrated region can absorb changes in relative factor supply without changes in relative factor prices (in this case, wages relative to other factor prices).[1] When unskilled immigrants arrive in a local market, the theorem predicts a relative expansion of industries that use the additional unskilled labor most intensively and a shift in the pattern of external trade toward the export of those goods that use the newly abundant factor most intensively. A recent study isolated these effects by looking at the skill composition across forty industries in fourteen U.S. states. The study found that a significant part of the difference across states in their skill mix was accounted for by changes in their output mix "consistent with the hypothesis that state-specific factor-supply shocks do not trigger large state-specific wage effects" (Hanson and Slaughter 2003, 19).[2] While these results offer an impressive confirmation of market integration among U.S. states, they do not tell us whether it is the goods market or the labor market that does the adjusting. So let us turn to the labor market.

In April 1980 Fidel Castro declared that Cubans were free to emigrate from the port of Mariel. In just a few months, 125,000 took Castro up on his offer, and about half of these settled in Miami. The Cuban influx added 7 percent to the Miami labor force, and these immigrants were mainly unskilled. In his celebrated study of the Mariel boat lift,

David Card (1990) found that the large influx of Cuban immigrants resulting from the boat lift had almost no effect on unskilled wage rates relative to skilled wage rates in Miami or relative to unskilled wage rates in other states. Even previous cohorts of Cubans and other Hispanics did not seem to have suffered from competition with the Mariels. The reason appears to be displacement. Immigration of the native-born (or of previous immigrants) from other parts of the United States into Miami slowed down dramatically in the early 1980s, so much so that interregional migration accounted for most of the adjustment.

How general are the Mariel findings? Is the effect of interregional displacement of natives by immigrants substantial at the economy-wide level? One post-Mariel study found that an influx of immigrants in 1975–1980 equivalent to 1 percent of standard metropolitan statistical area's labor force displaced native workers equivalent to 1.2 percent of the labor force (Filer 1992). This huge displacement—more than one for one—seems consistent with the Miami experience following the Mariel boat lift. Looking at intercensal *changes* in the growth of native and foreign-born populations in U.S. states, another study also found a crowding-out effect close to one (Borjas, Freeman, and Katz 1997). Other studies have reported more-modest effects. Thus, Card (2001) found that an inflow of immigrants in a particular occupation group has little effect on outflows of natives and earlier immigrant cohorts in the same occupation group.

This variation in the reported impact of immigration on native-born displacement is hardly unique to U.S. labor market studies, and it may be due in part to some of the same problems that beset the spatial-correlation studies of local employment and wage rates. That is, when immigration to most of the regions in a sample is very small, measurement error or idiosyncratic shocks to regional labor supply or demand may obscure the immigration crowding-out effect. To illustrate this point, consider the regression in table 14.2, explaining net interregional migration to six booming regions in the southern United Kingdom from 1982 to 2000. In the regression, interregional migration is determined by regional vacancy rates, earnings, and house prices, as well as by the net immigration rate to the region. The coefficient estimate of −0.43 for net immigration (lagged) suggests that for every 100 foreign immigrants, 43 residents are displaced from the region, a powerful displacement effect indeed. But when the same regression is estimated for all eleven U.K. regions—not just those six in the booming

Table 14.2
Regression results for U.K. interregional migration, 1982–2000

$NetMigR_t = -0.43\ NetImR_{t-1} + 0.44\ LogVacs_t - 0.13\ LogUnR_t + 2.78\ LogEarn_{t-1}$
$\quad\quad\quad\quad(2.1)\quad\quad\quad\quad\quad\quad(2.3)\quad\quad\quad\quad\quad(0.3)\quad\quad\quad\quad\quad(2.4)$
$\quad\quad\quad - 0.83\ LogHseP_t + 0.94\ \Delta LogHseP_t$
$\quad\quad\quad\quad(2.2)\quad\quad\quad\quad\quad(1.7)$
Adj. $R^2 = 0.92$

Source: Hatton and Tani 2005 (table 5). Further details concerning the specification and the data are given there.

Note: t statistics in parentheses.

Sample: Balanced panel of regions/years. Regions are Greater London, Rest of the Southeast, East Anglia, East Midlands, West Midlands, and South West.

Definitions of variables: NetMigR = net migration rate into the region from elsewhere in the United Kingdom, per thousand of the region's population; *NetImR* = net immigration from abroad of foreign citizens per thousand of the region's population; *LogVacs* = log of the region's vacancy inflow rate; *LogUnR* = log of the region's unemployment rate; *LogEarn* = log average earnings of full-time-equivalent workers in the region; *LogHseP* = log of average house price in the region; $\Delta LogHseP$ = change in log house price.

Method: Ordinary least squares regression; fixed region effects and year dummies included but not reported. Note that because year dummies are included, this is equivalent to defining the logs of vacancies, unemployment, lagged earnings, and house prices as log ratios to the U.K. mean.

south—the coefficient falls from -0.43 to -0.3 *and* becomes insignificant. This result appears to be consistent with the arguments offered above: the additional five regions received relatively few migrants, and so the total immigration effect is harder to discern when those regions are included.

Substantial displacement effects can be observed for other times and places provided that the regions studied are ones in which immigration has also been large. Between 1870 and 1910, the bulk of immigrants to the United States moved into the New England, Mid-Atlantic, and East North Central census regions. An analysis of the intercensus flows of native-born from the fourteen states that those three regions comprise showed that crowding out occurred there too. Indeed, nineteenth-century westward migration in the United States was powerfully influenced by the influx of foreign immigrants into the east. For every net inflow of 100 immigrants, the out-migration of native-born increased by 40 (Hatton and Williamson 1998, 168). This late-nineteenth-century estimate is very close to the late-twentieth-century estimate reported for contemporary southern Britain in table 14.2 (100 immigrants crowding out 43 residents). The similarity serves to reinforce the point that immigration's crowding-out effects can be observed only by focusing on times and places in which immigration has been sufficiently large that its effects can be clearly assessed.

Immigration Shocks and Labor Market Absorption: Three Modern Examples

Another way to assess the effects of immigration on the host economy is to look at what might be called natural experiments: cases—like the Mariel boat lift—in which changes in immigration have been sudden and unambiguously exogenous (and thus not a response to conditions at the destination) and are large enough to leave a clear imprint on the whole country's labor market. This section considers three modern examples: the migration of Soviet Jews to Israel in the early 1990s after Soviet emigration policy became liberal; the return migration of French Algerians to metropolitan France in 1962 following Algerian independence; and the return migration of Portuguese from Angola and Mozambique when the independence struggle in those nations reached a climax in 1974–1976.

The dramatic influx of immigrants into Israel in the early 1990s offers a classic example of an exogenous immigration shock of significant economy-wide proportions. Late in 1989 the government of what was then the Soviet Union shifted its policy to permit Soviet Jews to emigrate. Most of those who left went to Israel. The dramatic surge in Israel's aggregate immigration rate is shown in figure 14.2. In the decade before 1990, Israel's immigration rate averaged 3.7 per thousand of the Israeli population. The rate surged to more than 35 per thousand in 1990–1991 and then continued at 10–15 per thousand for the rest of the decade. There was an inflow of 610,000 immigrants in the first two years following the liberalization of the Soviet policy, equivalent to 7 percent of the Israeli population, and by the mid-1990s, the influx amounted to a million immigrants, or about 12 percent of the population before the liberalization. The effects on the labor market were equally dramatic: the working-age population increased by 8 percent between 1990 and 1992 and by 16 percent through 1997.

An exogenous immigration shock of this magnitude should have left a clear mark on Israel's labor market, and figure 14.3 confirms that it did. The figure plots percentage deviations from logarithmic trends calculated for the preshock period, 1980–1989. The labor force was more than 15 percent above trend by the mid-1990s. Employment rose more slowly at first, but by the mid-1990s, it was more than 20 percent

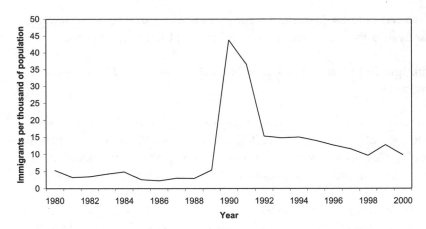

Figure 14.2
Immigration to Israel, 1980–2000. *Source:* Central Statistical Bureau, Israel, http://
194.90.153.197/reader/shnatonenew.htm.

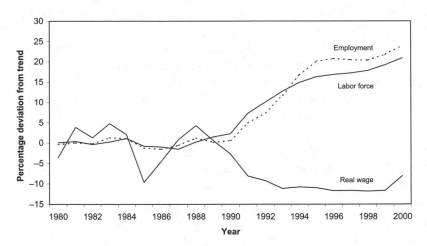

Figure 14.3
Labor supply and the real wage in Israel, 1980–2000. *Source:* Bank of Israel, http://
www.bankisrael.gov.il/publeng/dataeng.htm.

above trend. Relative to its preshock trend, the real wage plunged in the early 1990s and then hovered at about 10 percent below trend for the rest of the decade. There were other short-run adjustments as well. The unemployment rate was 10.6 percent in 1991, compared with an average of 6.1 percent over the 1980s. Furthermore, the unemployment rate was 37.3 percent among immigrants, as compared with 9 percent among nonimmigrants. This difference evaporated over the 1990s, and by 2000 it was just two percentage points: the rate was 10.4 percent for immigrants and 8.4 percent for nonimmigrants.

The Israeli evidence seems stark and clear: the real wage fell by around 5 percent for every 10 percent immigration-induced increase in the labor force. But there were other forces at work that helped ease the labor market adjustment. One was an impressive capital accumulation response. The sudden increase in labor supply reduced the capital-to-labor ratio and increased the return to capital; as a result, gross investment in machinery and equipment increased from 12 percent of the stock in the 1980s to 19 percent in 1994–1996. This accumulation response was financed largely from abroad; as a share of GDP, the current account deficit increased by about eight percentage points between 1990 and 1996 (Cohen and Hsieh 2000, 19). In contrast, adjustments through induced changes in the composition of output and the structure of trade (Rybczynski effects) do not seem to have been important. Although immigrants were more highly skilled than natives, no shift in the output composition toward skill-intensive sectors took place (Cohen and Hsieh 2000, 15).

Given that immigrants *appeared* to enter with much higher skill levels than natives, and given the lack of adjustment in output mix, one might have anticipated a big fall in the premium for skill. Appearances can be deceiving. Among those Soviet Jews arriving in the first wave, 60 percent were college educated and 25 percent were college graduates, as compared with 30 percent and 12 percent, respectively, of Israeli Jews. They also had much higher occupation-specific skills. Of those arriving in 1990–1993, 57,000 had been engineers and 12,000 had been physicians; by comparison, the numbers in the much bigger 1989 Israeli labor force were 30,000 and 15,000, respectively. Thus, given the higher skills of the immigrants, one might have expected the skill premium to fall.[3] In fact, it *increased* (very slightly) to the mid-1990s, before it fell back, largely because the Russian immigrants entered occupational grades that were considerably below those in which they had worked previously. Looking across occupations, there is a negative correlation between the number of Russian entrants and wage growth between 1989 and 1994: every 10 percent added to employment reduced the wage by 3–6 percent. But there is no correlation between the number of Russians classified by *former* occupation and wage growth in that occupation (Friedberg 2001). Thus, in 1994 a Russian immigrant in Israel earned 45 percent less than an Israeli, despite having an average of one more year of schooling. There are two important explanations for the downgrading. First, education and skills acquired by Soviet immigrants in Russia were not easily transferable to the Israeli labor market, and second, many of the immigrants had poor Hebrew language skills. The process of assimilating the Soviet immigrants took time (as is discussed further in chapter 15), but they did move up the Israeli occupational ladder, and by 1997 they had about the same occupational distribution as the Israeli labor force as a whole.

The second example is offered by the inflow into metropolitan France following Algeria's independence. These immigrants were very largely French-born expatriates fleeing the regime change, and about 900,000 flooded into France in the year 1962. They added about 1.9 percent to the population and 1.6 percent to the labor force, but they located largely in southern France. These repatriates were slightly younger and better qualified on average than the host labor force, but the differences were not large. An analysis of changes in average earnings across French *départements* between 1962 and 1967 (using the spatial-correlation approach) showed that an influx of repatriates equivalent to 1 percent of the French labor force reduced the wage by 0.5–0.8 percent (Hunt 1992, 567). The overall effect of the Algerian repatriation was to reduce the French wage by 1.3 percent and to increase unemployment rates by 0.3 percentage points. In short, the Algerian immigration shock was sufficiently large to have a clear effect on French labor markets.[4]

Larger still was the repatriation of Portuguese from Angola and Mozambique (*retornados*) when independence struggles came to a climax in 1974–1976. Like the Algerian repatriates, these *retornados* were somewhat more educated and skilled than the host country population. The 600,000 *retornados* added about 7 percent to the Portuguese population, a huge effect that was enhanced still further by the abrupt halt in the guestworker flows from Portugal to France and Germany in 1974–1975. As figure 14.4 shows, net immigration to Portugal spiked in 1975, reaching a peak of forty per thousand. The figure also shows

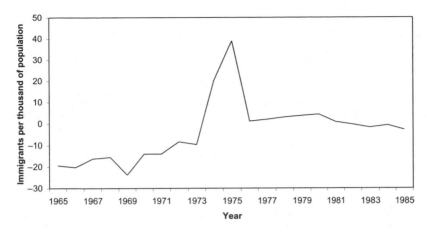

Figure 14.4
Net immigration to Portugal, 1965–1985. *Source:* Council of Europe 2001.

that net immigration was negative during the period of guestworker outflows up to 1973. It has been estimated that the influx of *retornados* reduced the real wage in Portugal by 5–9 percent for every 10 percent addition to the population (Carrington and de Lima 1996, 344). Thus, it seems that the bigger an immigration shock, the clearer and the larger are its observed effects.

The effects of these immigrants on the Portuguese labor market are more difficult to discern in the economy-wide data, since the gross immigration shock occurred just at the time of the first oil crisis and was followed very soon after by rising unemployment and slower productivity growth (Carrington and de Lima 1996). That is, while gross immigration of the *retornados* was certainly exogenous, the gross emigration of Portuguese guestworkers to the north surely was not. Perhaps the net immigration impact could be identified more clearly if we compared Portugal with its closest neighbors. Figure 14.5 therefore shows Portuguese employment and real wages relative to those of Spain and France. The surge in Portuguese employment relative to that in the other two countries in the mid-1970s is clear, but it is exaggerated relative to that in Spain because of Spain's deep recession at that time, and hence the comparison with France may be more useful. Both relative real wage series also show a decline after the early 1970s. As with the Soviet Jews immigrating to Israel fifteen years later, the Portuguese *retornados* suffered higher unemployment for a number of years; in 1981 their unemployment rate was 14 percent, whereas for

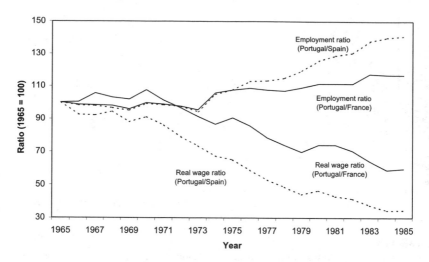

Figure 14.5
Employment and real wages in Portugal relative to Spain and France. *Sources:* OECD
1993 (various tables). Nominal wage index for Portugal kindly supplied by Pedro Lains.

other Portuguese workers, it was 6 percent. These differences eroded
gradually over time as the *retornados* were absorbed into the Portuguese labor market.

The Wider Picture

What are the longer run impacts of immigration? How has it affected
incomes and income distributions in the larger economies, such as the
United States, that have received the bulk of migrant flows from the
less-developed parts of the world? And how do these effects compare
with those we have observed for the age of mass migration before
1914? The examples presented in the preceding section suggest that
when the impact on the host country labor supply is large enough to
be observed clearly, the effects of immigration accord with the simple
model of labor supply and demand depicted in figure 14.1. Given that
accordance, the wider effects of immigration can be easily calculated.

Assuming a standard production function that combines capital
with different types of labor by skill, the effects on the earnings of
workers of different skill levels arising from immigrant-induced
changes in labor supply by skill can be estimated (Borjas, Freeman,
and Katz 1997). Assuming capital to be fixed, the effect of U.S. immigration between 1979 and 1995 was to reduce the earnings of skilled

native-born by 2.5 percent and of unskilled native-born by 4.6 percent. Immigration therefore contributed to a rise in U.S. earnings inequality, the ratio of skilled to unskilled earnings having increased by 2.1 percent as a result of immigration. If instead perfect world capital mobility is assumed, such that capital is allowed to flow freely into the U.S. economy in response to immigration and at a rate which keeps the return on capital constant, then earnings of skilled natives are found actually to have increased (although only slightly) while those of unskilled natives are found to have fallen by 4.6 percent as before. Thus the ratio of skilled to unskilled earnings is increased by even more (5 percent) when there is perfect world capital mobility and thus elastic capital supplies. Because the bulk of the U.S. labor force is skilled, and capital and skilled labor are assumed to be complementary, the average wage falls only marginally when there is perfect world capital mobility. The gain to the economy as whole (area Z in figure 14.1) is at most 0.1 percent of GDP.

How do these estimated modern labor market impacts compare with the late-nineteenth-century estimates discussed in chapter 6? Had there been no immigration from 1870 to 1910, the unskilled real wage in the United States would have been higher in 1910 by 34 percent, a figure that falls to 9.2 percent if perfect world capital mobility is assumed. While these late-nineteenth-century impact estimates are, at a minimum, double those for the late twentieth century (9.2 versus 4.6), the former covers a much longer period when the contribution of immigration to the labor force was much higher too. Suppose we focus instead on 1870–1890, a shorter period with a lower immigration rate. In this case, the 1890 real wage would have been higher by 14.4 percent in the absence of immigration, and by only 3.7 percent if perfect world capital mobility is assumed (Hatton and Williamson 1998, 212). While the estimates for the late nineteenth century are derived differently from those for the late twentieth century, they appear to be in the same ballpark (3.7 versus 4.6), at least when perfect world capital mobility is assumed.

This analysis of two U.S. immigration periods separated by a century ignores some important differences in the character of the immigration and in the structure of the economy—differences that are likely to have mattered to the economy-wide impact. First, as we show in the next chapter, the skill gap between immigrants and natives was much larger in the late twentieth century than in the late nineteenth century (for the policy-related reasons explained in chapter 10), and hence their influence on the U.S. skill mix has been greater in more-recent times. Added to that, the unskilled are now a much smaller share of the U.S. labor force than they were a century ago, and so a given immigrant inflow makes a proportionately larger contribution to the unskilled labor supply. This suggests that the effect of immigration on the unskilled wage is even greater today than a century ago.

On the other hand, what about the absorptive capacity of the U.S. economy? After all, agricultural employment—in which labor was unskilled—accounted for 50 percent of the U.S. labor force in 1870 and 27 percent in 1913, but only 3 percent in 1999. How does this fact speak to the labor absorption issue (Williamson 1982)? Land was a much more important factor of production a century ago—and land is a quasi-fixed factor. As we showed in chapter 6, relative to wages, immigration raised the rent on and the price of land in the New World and reduced it in Europe. There were much stronger economy-wide diminishing returns to unskilled labor in the nineteenth century compared with today—given the importance of a quasi-fixed factor, land—and this influence was only partly weakened by international capital mobility. For this reason, the same immigrant inflow probably had larger effects on unskilled earnings in the nineteenth century than it does today. Which of these offsetting forces dominated? Was it immigrant skills or was it absorptive capacity?

A century ago, there was some symmetry between the effects of mass transatlantic migration on source and destination. Even primary-product-importing Europe had large resource-based sectors, although levels of industrialization and economic specialization differed. But the economic gaps between Europe and the New World were much smaller a century ago than they are today between the OECD and the Third World. In Asia, Africa, and even Latin America, land and natural resources are far more important than they are in the OECD. This fact suggests that today the size of emigration effects on source countries may be bigger than the size of immigration effects in destination countries. In spite of this predicted asymmetry, economists have devoted remarkably little attention to understanding the effects of emigration on modern source countries.

Consider the world's poorest region, Africa. The regression in table 14.3 explains differences in the unskilled real wage among a panel of sub-Saharan countries. The data are far from perfect, but the results are strong enough to support the view that demographic supply side pressure pushed down the wage in a manner reflecting classic dimin-

The Labor Market and Fiscal Impact of Immigration

3

Tabl 14.3
Determinants of African real wages, 1977–1995

$$LnRWage = 4.06 - 0.002\ Pop/km^2 - 0.13\ Sp15\text{–}29 - 0.01\ Illit$$
$$\quad\ \ (6.1)\quad (5.1)\qquad\qquad\ (5.3)\qquad\qquad (5.3)$$
$$R^2 = 0.31$$

Source: Hatton and Williamson 2003. Further details concerning data sources and methods are available there.

Note: t statistics in parentheses.

Sample: Unbalanced panel of countries and years comprising Angola (1982–1995); Burundi (1980–1985); Cameroon (1980–1995); Central African Republic (1989–1995); Chad (1980–1995); Côte d'Ivoire (1989–1995); Gabon (1977–1990); Ghana (1977–1995); Lesotho (1981–1995); Malawi (1987–1995); Mali (1987–1995); Nigeria (1977–1995); Rwanda (1979–1995); Senegal (1989–1995); Sierra Leone (1991–1995); Sudan (1984–1995); Swaziland (1978–1995); Togo (1982–1993); Zambia (1981–1995); Zimbabwe (1983–1995).

Definitions of variables: $LnRWage$ = real unskilled wage rates at 1990 purchasing-power parity; Pop/km^2 = population per square kilometer; $Sp15\text{–}29$ = percentage of population aged fifteen to twenty-nine; $Illit$ = percentage of adult population illiterate.

Method: Pooled instrumental variables regression on 265 country/year observations. $Sp15\text{–}29$ (the migration age group) is instrumented using the share aged ten to fourteen five years earlier. A dummy for southern Africa is included but not reported.

ishing returns. Population density matters in modern Africa: an increase of ten persons per square kilometer pushes down the wage by 2 percent. The share of population aged fifteen to twenty-nine also has a negative effect on the wage: a one-percentage-point increase pushes the wage down by nearly 13 percent. Not surprisingly, human capital matters too: a one-percentage-point fall in the rate of adult illiteracy increases the real wage by 1 percent. These results suggest that when very poor countries lose population through emigration, the wage gains for those left behind might be substantially larger than the wage losses for the rich host countries that receive immigrants. This assertion needs further exploration if mass migration is to be assessed from a world perspective. We think it should be, so we return to this issue in chapter 17.

Fiscal Effects of Immigration

A deleterious labor market effect from immigration is not the only reason that residents in host countries might take an anti-immigration stance. If immigrants pay lower taxes and receive higher benefits (or consume more public services) compared with nonimmigrants, then even those who suffer least from competition with immigrants in the labor market might have good reason to oppose immigration if it involves substantial fiscal transfers. There has been considerable dispute about the fiscal effects of immigration, and it has been compounded by differences in methodology and measurement.

The most common approach to measuring immigration's fiscal effects is simply to examine the balance between taxes and expenditures associated with the stock of immigrants and natives at a point in time. Immigrant households in the United States are more likely than native households to receive benefits from one or more public welfare programs: 19.7 versus 13.3 percent, respectively, in 2000 (Boeri, Hanson, and McCormick 2002, 235). The public assistance incidence is particularly high for Mexican, Central American, and Caribbean immigrants, and the gap between immigrants and natives in the use of public welfare programs in the United States has been on the rise partly as a result of shifts in immigrant source country composition toward this region. Since Latin immigrant households also tend to have larger families, they also receive larger public education benefits. To compound the immigrant fiscal burden in the United States, immigrants who are poor also pay lower taxes. A study commissioned by the U.S. Congress calculated that the net fiscal burden per immigrant-headed household in 1996 was between $1,613 and $2,206, representing a fiscal cost of between $166 and $226 per nonimmigrant household (Smith and Edmonston 1997, 293).

This fiscal accounting includes both state and federal government. Since immigrants are so unevenly distributed across the United States, the state fiscal burden is also very uneven. Thus, the burden on the average nonimmigrant household in California is estimated to exceed $2,000 per annum, about ten times the U.S. average. This fact makes it less surprising that in 1995, California residents approved Proposition 187, whose purpose was to deny public benefits (including education) to illegal immigrants. Although the proposition was struck down by a court ruling, the federal government responded to the signal sent by the passage of the legislation by introducing reforms in 1996 which restricted access to certain welfare programs for recent immigrants (not just illegals).

This episode, and the debate that surrounded it, serves to illustrate two points. The first is that the fiscal impact of immigration genuinely concerns voters. The second is that states with generous benefit systems act as welfare magnets, attracting immigrants who are most likely to depend on welfare.

The fiscal concerns surrounding immigration are all the more acute in the European Union, where welfare support systems are more comprehensive than those in the United States and vary widely among countries. Table 14.4 shows the difference between the incidence of adult immigrants and that of natives in the receipt of three kinds of welfare benefits: generally, immigrants in the European Union are more likely to receive unemployment and family benefits than EU nationals and less likely to receive public pensions. But there are also enormous differences among countries: for example, the difference between immigrant and native unemployment benefit incidence is very large for Denmark, the Netherlands, Belgium, Austria, and Finland, but very small or even negative for Germany, the United Kingdom, Greece, Spain, and Portugal. These differences across the European Union largely reflect two forces. First, welfare states differ widely in the benefits offered and in the conditions they impose on eligibility for those benefits, with the northern European countries being the most generous. Second, access to and use of welfare benefits depends on the characteristics of the immigrants. As the right panel of table 14.4 shows, where immigrants are less educated than natives, the gap in the immigrant-native unemployment benefit incidence is larger. Similarly, in France, where immigrants have more children than natives, the gap in the immigrant-native family benefit incidence is larger.

Much of the difference between immigrants and natives in the overall net fiscal burden they impose can therefore be accounted for by differences in their characteristics, and age is one of the most important. Over the past two centuries, immigrants have tended to be considerably younger than natives, and the EU sample in table 14.4 confirms this fact once more. Since younger adults are obviously less dependent on pension benefits than are older adults, it is hardly surprising that the immigrant-native gap in pension benefit use is negative. The same is probably true of health services. Thus, the net fiscal claim of a person evolves over the life cycle—from a net burden as a child, to a net contribution as a working adult, to a net burden again as a retired adult. Since life cycle conditions are so important, the appropriate way to evaluate the overall fiscal impact of an immigrant, permanent or otherwise, is to calculate the discounted net present value over the net contribution stream from arrival to death or return migration.[5] This approach implies that age differences matter only because immigrants arrive part of the way through their life cycles.

Table 14.4
Welfare dependency and personal characteristics in the European Union, 1994–1996 (differences between immigrants and EU nationals)

Country	Percentage-point difference between immigrants and EU nationals in receipt of			Difference in characteristics between immigrants and EU nationals			
	Unemployment benefits	Family benefits	Pensions	Low educated	High educated	Age (years)	Number of children
Germany	1.6	—	—	21.2	-5.5	-8.6	0.54
Denmark	24.5	5.3	-17.9	14.7	0.6	-7.8	0.47
Netherlands	7.0	7.9	-14.9	22.7	5.3	-7.7	0.65
Belgium	6.7	1.1	-6.1	10.6	-14.1	-2.5	0.12
France	4.9	16.7	-12.8	22.5	-7.2	-3.6	1.10
United Kingdom	0.6	0.6	-23.4	-15.4	21.2	-8.7	0.85
Greece	-0.6	1.9	-2.2	-9.8	6.1	0.6	0.07
Spain	-1.6	3.2	-10.9	-27.4	14.2	-7.3	0.34
Portugal	-2.2	-9.7	-6.4	-34.9	20.1	-6.3	0.35
Austria	8.9	8.1	-18.0	7.8	12.2	-10.6	0.35
Finland	31.7	0.2	-12.7	-12.3	17.5	-7.4	0.04

Source: Boeri, Hanson, and McCormick 2002 (74–75).
Notes: Data for those aged sixteen and above are from the European Community Household Panel. The first three columns refer to differences between non-EU citizens and EU citizens in the percentage receiving the benefit. The next two columns show differences in the percentage with less-than-completed secondary school education and the percentage with college degrees.

The net present value approach also implies that any long-run assessment of the net fiscal contribution of immigrants depends crucially
on their lifetime earning capacity, not their age. One estimate puts the
net present value in 1996 of an immigrant to the U.S. tax coffers at
−$89,000 if the immigrant has less than a high school education (Boeri
et al. 2002, 246). Although still representing a burden, this figure falls
to −$31,000 for immigrants with no more than a high school degree,
but it becomes a positive benefit of $105,000 for those with more than
a high school degree. Other studies have come to different conclusions
about the overall net fiscal contribution of immigrants, both in the
cross section and over the life cycle.[6] But they all agree on one thing:
the net contribution is much more positive the more skilled and educated the immigrant. The precise magnitude of the difference depends,
of course, on tax-benefit structures, on the way the labor market
rewards skills, and on differences in family structure between the
skilled and unskilled. It also depends on how well immigrants assimilate into the host country labor market and their postimmigration accumulation of human capital. Assimilation is a central focus in the next
chapter.

15

**Migrant Selection,
Immigrant Assimilation,
and Emigrant Brain Drain**

One of the most contentious and widely researched migration issues over the last thirty years has been the performance of immigrants in OECD labor markets. Do immigrants catch up with, or even overtake, the native-born in these markets in terms of earnings, employment rates, and other dimensions of labor market success? Is immigrants' host country labor market performance related to country-of-origin characteristics? Are migrants positively or negatively selected from source country populations? The reader should appreciate that these questions are not new, since part II already showed they were just as much a part of the debate over immigration in the late nineteenth century as they are today. Now as then, the answers to these questions—right or wrong—have guided policy, and the search for these answers has always been most intense in the United States.

The literature on the economics of the brain drain adds another important dimension to the world migration debate. To what extent does emigration to the developed world deprive developing countries of their best and brightest and their skilled and schooled? Does this imply economic loss, and does it therefore have negative implications for growth and development in the Third World? Because it focuses on experience at the source rather than at the destination, the brain drain literature has until recently developed independently of the literature on immigrant assimilation and selectivity. Yet the two are closely related. If, by luck or through policy, rich countries manage to attract those who are likely to produce the greatest net economic benefits for the host country, shouldn't it follow that the source country suffers a net loss? As we show in this chapter, the answers are not quite as obvious as they might seem.

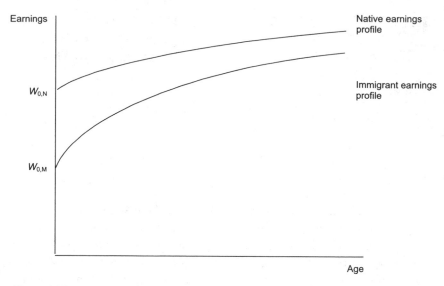

Figure 15.1
Economic assimilation of immigrants

How to Think about Immigrant Assimilation

When immigrants arrive at their destination, they typically suffer a dis-advantage in the labor market relative to similar native-born workers. In the late-nineteenth-century United States, that initial disadvantage eroded as time in the United States increased, and hence immigrants caught up with the native-born. This economic assimilation process is depicted in figure 15.1. An immigrant arriving as a young adult starts with earnings $W_{0,M}$, which subsequently increase over his remaining working life. The earnings of a native-born worker at a similar age starts at $W_{0,N}$, which also increases over his working life. These profiles can be thought of as averages for a given cohort, and they reflect both wage rates when working and the probability of not being at work. In this example, the gap between native-born and immigrant earnings declines over time but it does not evaporate: immigrants catch up with but do not overtake native-born workers.[1]

Immigrant earnings at arrival, $W_{0,M}$, are determined by a number of factors. The immigrant's initial level of human capital matters, and it may be lower than that of the native-born with whom the immigrant competes. Lack of knowledge of the host country labor market, limited access to networks, and above all, lack of fluency in the host country language also matter. These initial disadvantages imply that the immigrant's human capital has a lower value in the host country than at home. Immigrant characteristics reflect conditions in the country of origin, but they also reflect how immigrants are selected from the origin population. The more positive the selection from a given source, the higher will be $W_{0,M}$. Selection may be in terms of observable skills and education, or it may be in terms of unobserved qualities such as raw ability, motivation, energy, and enterprise. Finally, if after arrival new immigrants invest heavily in the acquisition of more human capital, and if they do it largely at the expense of earnings foregone, then we have another reason that earnings might be lower at arrival compared with those of the native-born. Thus, the initial wage disadvantage immigrants face reflects some combination of factors which will vary across immigrant group depending on host country, origin country, and route of entry.

Figure 15.1 makes it appear that the higher is $W_{0,M}$, the more likely it is that the immigrant will ultimately catch up with a comparable native-born individual. This would certainly be true for a parallel upward shift in the age-earnings profile. But there are reasons for thinking that the *slope* of the age-earnings profile might also differ among immigrants in some systematic way that will influence the degree of convergence of immigrant to native-born earnings. Immigrants who arrive with little initial human capital may find the return to postarrival human capital investments so high that they invest heavily early in their stay. Earnings profiles will be steeper for this group than for those who arrive with higher initial levels of human capital: the lower the starting point, the steeper the slope. One might expect this catching up to be all the more important the younger the new immigrant. Now suppose instead that low initial earnings capacity reflects characteristics produced by negative selection, in which case the incentive to invest in human capital upon arrival will be weak. In this case, the lower the starting point, the flatter the slope. Alternatively, suppose that the human capital acquired at the origin is complementary with human capital at the destination. In that case, those with high initial endowments will invest more postarrival and may have a steeper earnings profile subsequently than those with low initial endowments. Thus, the degree to which the earnings of immigrants converge on or overtake those of natives depends on the immigrants' characteristics upon arrival, and these will differ depending on where they come from and how they are selected from the source population.

Immigrant assimilation experience may also differ across destinations as well as across origins. Different countries select immigrants from different origins because of policy, distance, historic ties, and the friends-and-relatives effect. Labor market outcomes also differ across destinations, because some host countries have labor markets that are more flexible and have fewer restrictions and thus absorb immigrants more easily than others. And finally, where discrimination against ethnic minorities is strongest, some immigrants may find it harder to gain employment and to climb up the job ladder, blunting the incentives for postimmigration human capital investment and impeding the process of labor market assimilation. This may not matter for immigrants who are unlikely to accumulate human capital upon arrival, but it matters for immigrants who intend to do so. Thus, host countries that discriminate against immigrants will negatively select immigrants. Indeed, host countries that discriminate against immigrants because they think immigrants are "poor quality" will have their views confirmed.

Labor Market Assimilation in the United States

The United States has long been the leading laboratory for studies of immigrant assimilation, and the very large literature on the subject can be surveyed only briefly here.[2] Barry Chiswick's (1978) pioneering work used microdata from the 1970 U.S. census to estimate age-earning profiles for native-born and foreign-born males. The number of years since migration was included as a variable in the foreign-born analysis and had a strong positive impact on earnings, as in figure 15.1. Male immigrants had earnings upon arrival that were about 10 percent lower than those of comparable native-born males. However, they had caught up after thirteen years, and after twenty years they had earnings 6 percent *higher* than the comparable native-born (Chiswick 1978, 906). Chiswick argued that this impressive immigrant labor market performance could be attributed to positive selection on unobserved characteristics. One piece of evidence supporting this positive selection hypothesis is that the sons of immigrants, who inherit some of their parents' characteristics but do not inherit their immigrant status, outperform the sons of native-born parents (Chiswick 1977).

Since Chiswick reported his findings, others have argued that his picture of rapid immigrant assimilation is too optimistic. After all, immigrant cohorts may change their composition such that their average

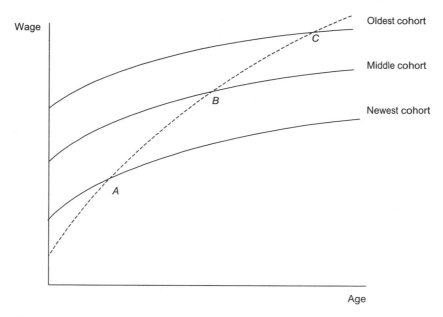

Figure 15.2
Wage profiles for different immigrant cohorts

quality, and thus $W_{0,M}$ in figure 15.1, may decline over time. This possibility is illustrated in figure 15.2, in which the most recent immigrant cohort has an average lifetime earnings profile that is below that of the preceding cohort and lower still than the earliest cohort. Since immigrants typically arrive at their destination as young adults, the most recent cohort will be clustered around point A in the figure. Those from the middle cohort will be clustered around B, while those from the earliest cohort will be clustered around C. If we simply observe a cross section of immigrants, as did Chiswick with the 1970 census, it is impossible to distinguish movements along the age-earnings profile (an assimilation issue) from shifts in the profile associated with different immigrant cohorts (a selection issue). As a result, the estimated profile will look something like the broken line in the figure, which has a steeper upward slope than any of the profiles for the individual cohorts.

George Borjas (1985, 1995) tried to overcome this problem by using observations from two successive censuses, thus estimating the earnings growth of a given cohort over time. Estimated this way, the wage profiles of individual cohorts are somewhat flatter than when the observations are taken from a single census cross section. Different studies have produced a range of results, but they all confirm significant immigrant catching up with the earnings of the native-born. According to one study, male immigrants who arrived in 1965–1969 increased their earnings by 9 percent relative to the native-born in the decade 1970–1980 (Lalonde and Topel 1992, 89). Another finds that male immigrants from the same cohort increased their earnings relative to the native-born by 10 percent between 1970 and 1990 (Borjas 1995, 216). A third study finds that those arriving in the late 1970s increased their earnings relative to those of the native-born by 14 percent between 1980 and 1990 (Antecol, Kuhn, and Trejo 2003, 24). These estimated rates of wage catch-up all cluster around something like 1 percent per year over the first twenty years, and they are strikingly similar to those observed for U.S. immigrants in the years before World War I (chapter 5).

A wide range of variables have been found to influence the earnings of immigrants. These include education, English language fluency, age at arrival, route of entry, and above all country of origin. The positive effect of years since migration on earnings diminishes when variables that reflect dimensions of the assimilation process itself, such as language fluency and postmigration skill acquisition, are included. Although there has been debate about magnitudes, none of the subsequent studies have radically altered the picture of substantial immigrant economic assimilation in the United States (Jasso and Rosenzweig 1986; Yuengert 1994; Chiswick and Miller 1998; Friedberg 2000).

However, it appears that the economic assimilation rate of U.S. immigrants has fallen over the past fifty years. While the immigrant cohorts of the 1950s and 1960s caught up with, and sometimes overtook, the native-born in regard to earnings, more-recent cohorts have suffered a much larger initial disadvantage and have failed to assimilate rapidly enough to catch up with native-born. Differences across immigrant cohorts or immigrant country of origin might be less troubling if those with lower earnings initially experienced faster earnings growth. Under those conditions, there would be earnings convergence among immigrants as well as between immigrants and the native-born. Sad to say, there seems to be no overall negative correlation between an immigrant's initial earnings and subsequent earnings growth. However, once education acquired before migration is taken into account, two offsetting forces are revealed: the positive effect of initial education and the negative effect of initial earnings (Duleep and Regets 1997; Borjas 2000). Thus, education acquired before migration and education acquired afterward are complements. Immigrants who receive low initial rewards on their education raise the return on their human capital endowment as they accumulate host country experience and as they invest in language skills. Still, each successive U.S. immigrant cohort has brought lower human capital endowments with it *relative to the native-born*.

The Decline in Immigrant "Quality"

There has been much discussion in recent years about the apparent decline in the labor market "quality" of U.S. immigrants as reflected by their skills, education, and earning power. While immigrant males earned 4.1 percent more than native-born men in 1960, they earned 16.3 percent *less* in 1990 (table 15.1). Some of this decline in relative earnings was due to a decline in immigrant educational attainment relative to native-born: "on average, . . . immigrants have fewer years of

Table 15.1
Relative wage and relative education of immigrants in the United States, 1960–1990

	1960	1970	1980	1990
Percentage earnings differential relative to the native-born				
All immigrants				
Earnings unadjusted	4.1	−0.1	−9.7	−16.3
Earnings adjusted	1.3	−1.7	−7.1	−10.0
Recent immigrants				
Earnings unadjusted	−13.9	−18.8	−32.8	−38.0
Earnings adjusted	−16.2	−19.8	−24.1	−26.9
Percentage-point difference in educational attainment relative to native-born				
All immigrants				
Education > 16 years		3.5	2.4	0.0
Education < 12 years		3.2	14.3	22.1
Recent immigrants				
Education > 16 years		12.9	7.5	4.9
Education < 12 years		5.6	13.1	20.4

Sources: Borjas 1999a (1724), Borjas 1995 (208).
Note: Recent immigrants are those who arrived in the five years preceding the census date. Adjusted earnings are obtained after controlling for age, educational attainment, and region of origin.

schooling than natives—*a difference that has grown over the past two decades*, as the mean years of schooling in the immigration population increased less rapidly than the mean years of schooling of natives. As a result, *the immigrant contribution to the supply of skills has become increasingly concentrated in the lower education categories"* (Borjas, Freeman, and Katz 1997, 6, italics added). Thus, immigrants have reduced the educational quality of the U.S. labor force, and they have reduced it more and more over time. Although the average educational attainment of immigrants has improved since the 1960s, reflecting an education revolution that has taken place in the Third World, it has *deteriorated* relative to that of the native-born. As the lower panel of table 15.1 shows, those with sixteen years of education (equivalent to college graduates) make up a larger percentage of immigrants than of natives, but that advantage has been decreasing. More notably, the percentage with less than twelve years of education (equivalent to less than high school) is greater among immigrants than among the native-born, and that gap increased dramatically between 1970 and 1990. For newly arrived immigrants, that share was 5.6 percentage points higher than that for native-born in 1970, but 20.4 percentage points higher in 1990, an increase of almost *four times*.

But that is not all: even when we control for the rising education gap, the adjusted relative wage *still* fell by 13.3 percent over these thirty years, suggesting that immigrant quality has declined over time (relative to the U.S. labor force) in addition to their deteriorating relative educational achievement.[3] Recent immigrants always suffer an earnings disadvantage in comparison to the native-born, and that was true even in 1960, when so many came from western Europe under the old quota system. But this initial relative wage disadvantage deteriorated by twenty-four percentage points over those thirty years.

Most of this decline in immigrant quality is accounted for by changes in the source country composition of U.S. immigrants (table 10.2). The current debate over the impact of shifting immigrant source on the labor market quality of immigrants has its parallel in controversy in the pre-1914 years that culminated in the country-of-origin quotas in the 1920s. This is an ominous comparison, perhaps, but it provides an obvious benchmark. So how do the two eras match up? In 1909 the wage for the average male immigrant in industry was 6.4 percent lower than that for native-born males, a figure comparable with the late 1970s. Newly arrived male immigrants earned 20.4 percent less than natives in 1909, a figure that is also similar to that for the

1970s. But note this important fact: the variation in immigrant earnings by source is *five times greater in modern times* than it was in the past. The standard deviation of the log wage across twenty-six nationalities was 0.056 in 1909, compared with 0.295 across forty-one nationalities in 1980 (Hatton 2000, 525). Much of the source country differences in labor market performance of pre-1914 immigrants were accounted for by the wage gap between old and new immigrants. The wage gap in 1909 between immigrants from northwestern Europe (old) and those from southern and eastern Europe (new) was 6.7 percent. By contrast, the wage gap in 1980 between European immigrants (old) and those from Africa, Asia and South America (new) was 30.7 percent, again five times the 1909 figure. Since wage gaps among recently arrived immigrants are much wider in more-recent times, the effects of changing nationality mix are potentially much more powerful.

The implication, of course, is that any shift in immigrant source away from high-quality toward low-quality origins will have a much bigger impact on the average quality of immigrants today than was true a century ago. Chapter 5 reported that the effect of changing source country composition was to reduce the immigrant wage by 4.7 percentage points between 1873 and 1913 (2.3 percentage points after 1893). Between 1940 and 1980, source country composition shifts reduced the immigrant wage by 27 percentage points (17 percentage points after 1960). Thus, while immigrants experienced an earnings disadvantage in 1980 similar in magnitude to that prevailing at the eve of the First World War, the decline that preceded it was *much* larger in the modern era. Our guess is that a similar decline in immigrant quality would characterize the twenty-five years since 1980. Furthermore, these calculations seriously understate the true size of the downward drift in immigrant quality to the extent that it considers only *legal* immigrants. *Illegal* immigrants tend to be less skilled than legal ones, and they have increased in relative importance over the past half century.

In the first global century, shifts in the source country composition of U.S. immigrants were the result of rising incomes and demographic booms in Europe combined with falling transport costs between sending and receiving regions—forces that were amplified by the friends-and-relatives effect. These tended to reduce positive selection of immigrants, but only slowly. The same forces have also been at work in the modern era, but the fundamentals reducing positive selection have changed *much* more dramatically, and as chapters 8 through

11 have argued, changes in U.S. immigration policy have enhanced the effect of those fundamentals. The dramatic changes in fundamentals have included the growth miracles in Asia (which released the constraint on emigration from that region) and demographic transitions everywhere in the Third World. The accommodating changes in U.S. immigration policy have included the abolition of the country-of-origin quotas that favored Europe, the shift to a worldwide immigration quota, and the emphasis on family reunification over skills as the key criterion for admission. Other OECD countries have also opened their doors more widely and experienced shifts in immigrant composition and in immigrant quality, but the effects have not been as dramatic. In Canada, for example, the sources of immigration widened from the 1960s, but the quality of immigrants fell by less than it did in the United States (Baker and Benjamin 1994). Furthermore, most of that fall can be accounted for by deteriorating conditions in Canadian labor markets (McDonald and Worswick 1998). Some have argued that the difference in the experiences of these two North American countries can be explained by policy, with the Canadian points system selecting immigrants with higher average labor quality (Borjas 1993). No doubt policy mattered, but note how much of the difference is accounted for by one dominant fact: while Latin Americans account for 47 percent of U.S. immigrants, they are only 14 percent of Canadian immigrants, and Mexicans account for most of that disparity (Antecol, Cobb-Clark, and Trejo 2003). While this Latin difference may be partly due to immigration policy, it also reflects location. Distance matters enormously in explaining who migrates to the United States (table 11.1). Because of its greater proximity to Latin America and its long land border with Mexico, the United States would need an even more skill-selective immigration policy than Canada (or even quotas for Latin Americans) in order to raise immigrant quality to the Canadian level. The United States serves as a buffer, making it easier for Canadian policy to select higher quality immigrants.

What about the selection of immigrants from a given country? According to the Roy model illustrated in figures 11.1 and 11.2, immigrants should be more negatively selected the higher is the return to skills at the origin and thus the greater is earnings inequality there. Given that Mexican earnings inequality exceeds American earnings inequality, Mexican emigrants should be relatively unskilled. However, in terms of observable skills, late-twentieth- and early-twenty-first-century immigrants from Mexico have been drawn predominantly from the *middle* of the Mexican distribution, not from the bottom (Chiquiar and Hanson 2002).[4] It appears that this is because migration costs decrease sharply as a share of income with rising skill levels, offsetting the selection effects of greater income inequality at the source. In contrast, migrants from Puerto Rico (also with more income inequality than the United States) were found to be strongly negatively selected from the source population (Ramos 1992). This suggests that the most important difference is the costs associated with policy. Puerto Ricans can migrate freely to the United States without going through the immigration process, so they face far lower migration costs than do Mexicans (especially the low-skilled), and hence Puerto Rican selection is influenced more by incentive than by cost. Negative selection from Puerto Rico and positive selection from Mexico can be easily reconciled by reference to relative migration costs.

Although Latin American emigrants are not, on the whole, negatively selected, it seems likely that they are less positively selected than migrants from poorer and more-distant sources. As we have noted previously, high migration costs favor positive selection, and Mexico, Central America, and the Caribbean are all close enough to the United States to imply lower migration costs and thus poorer immigrants. Although we do not have definitive evidence, the costly policy hurdle, greater distances, lower source country inequality, smaller friends-and-relatives effect and (for the poorest regions) the poverty constraint all imply that migrants from further away will be more positively selected than are Latin Americans.[5] One implication of this is that the brain drain must be more serious the poorer, the more distant, and the more egalitarian the sending nation. Some aggregative evidence supporting this proposition can be seen in table 15.2: the 1990 share of U.S. immigrants with tertiary schooling was more than three times higher for Asians and Africans than it was for Mexicans and Central Americans.

Immigrant Assimilation in the Rest of the OECD

The United States has long served as the benchmark for immigrant assimilation studies, but there are good reasons to suppose that labor market outcomes may be quite different for immigrants elsewhere in the OECD. Such differences in outcomes might arise for two reasons. The first relates to the structure of the host country labor market, taken to include such features as wage flexibility, employment protection, welfare benefits, training programs, and education systems, as well

Table 15.2
Education of U.S. immigrant stock by source region, 1990

| Region | Percentage of immigrants with schooling level | | | Total number (millions) |
	Primary or less	Secondary	Tertiary	
Mexico	13.4	73.9	12.6	2.74
Central America	6.7	62.8	29.5	1.02
South America	2.6	51.1	46.3	0.30
Asia and the Pacific	4.0	34.5	61.5	2.38
Africa	1.6	24.0	74.4	0.13

Source: Carrington and Detragaiche 1998 (table 1).
Note: Educational attainment levels of foreign-born adults aged twenty-five and over in 1990.

as whether these labor market features discriminate, overtly or not, against immigrants. The second relates to the demographic and economic characteristics of the immigrants themselves, and these are determined by migration incentives that the labor market offers, by the selection effects of policy, by the impact of distance, and by the legacies of the past. Let us consider each in turn.

Do host country labor market features make a difference for immigrant outcomes? Immigrant assimilation along two dimensions—wage rates and unemployment—has been compared across three countries: the United States, Canada, and Australia (Antecol, Kuhn, and Trejo 2003). Allowing for cohort effects, relative growth of total immigrant earnings over twenty years was greatest in the United States, followed by Canada. In Australia's more-regulated labor market, all of the immigrant earnings growth was due to the increasing probability of employment, mainly within the first ten years after arrival. In the more-flexible U.S. labor market, less than half of that growth came from increasing employment probabilities, while more than half came from increasing wage rates. This suggests that a more-egalitarian wage structure with greater labor market regulation serves to restrict new immigrant access to good jobs but delivers higher initial wage rates and thus slower relative wage growth for those lucky ones who get the good jobs such an economy offers (Gregory, Anstie, and Klug 1992). The less-egalitarian but more-flexible U.S. wage structure lowers initial wages but raises relative wage growth (Miller and Neo 2003).

Table 15.3
Participation rates and unemployment rates of natives and foreigners, 1998

	Participation rate				Unemployment rate			
	Men		Women		Men		Women	
	Natives	For-eigners	Natives	For-eigners	Natives	For-eigners	Natives	For-eigners
Austria	79.8	84.3	62.4	63.4	4.8	10.3	5.3	8.9
Belgium	72.9	69.0	55.1	40.7	6.5	18.9	10.9	24.1
Denmark	84.1	69.4	76.0	51.6	3.8	7.3	6.1	16.0
Finland	76.0	81.0	70.2	57.8	12.7	36.0	13.3	43.7
France	75.0	76.1	62.5	49.0	9.6	22.0	13.5	26.8
Germany	79.4	77.3	63.4	48.7	8.5	17.3	10.1	15.9
Greece	79.1	91.4	49.1	61.2	6.9	9.7	16.5	18.8
Ireland	77.1	73.3	52.1	50.9	8.0	12.4	7.3	10.4
Italy	73.6	89.1	44.4	54.0	9.6	5.1	16.7	17.6
Netherlands	83.2	66.5	63.5	40.8	3.1	11.6	5.6	14.1
Portugal	83.5	77.4	65.5	56.1	3.8	1.4	5.6	17.4
Spain	75.9	84.0	47.7	52.2	14.0	10.9	26.6	24.0
Sweden	79.1	70.5	73.4	52.7	9.3	23.2	7.5	19.4
United Kingdom	83.0	78.1	67.4	56.1	6.8	10.7	5.2	9.4
Australia	74.8	70.8	57.1	48.7	8.3	8.6	6.9	8.2
Canada	73.8	68.4	60.2	52.7	10.3	9.9	9.5	11.6
United States	74.2	79.7	60.8	52.7	4.3	4.9	4.5	6.0

Source: OECD 2001a (173).

Access to employment becomes even more important for the assimilation process when EU countries are added to the analysis. Table 15.3 reports that EU unemployment rates are much higher among immigrants than among natives, nearly twice as high on average, whereas the unemployment rates for immigrants and natives in Australia, Canada, and the United States are much closer together. The EU employment gaps would be even bigger if the comparison was restricted to *recent* immigrants, given the evidence that gaps in unemployment rates decline with years in the host country.[6] The gaps are especially large in France, Germany, the Lowland countries, and the Nordic countries, all members of continental northern Europe. While it is now widely accepted that labor market institutions have contributed to higher European unemployment (Nickell 1997; Blanchard and Wolfers 2000), it also appears that labor market rigidities make access to jobs particularly difficult for immigrants. Although European immigrants are marginalized indirectly by high overall unemployment rates, their access to jobs may also be directly limited by employment protection legislation and by restrictions on the employment of foreigners in certain sectors such as government service. The employment gaps in southern Europe are much smaller, since opportunities for self-employment and informal-sector employment are greater.

Some of the more-successful immigrant groups worldwide have been those that suffered a downgrading of occupational status when they migrated from which they subsequently recovered. The Ugandan Asians who formed a middle class business elite before they were expelled in the early 1970s by Ugandan leader Idi Amin are a case in point (Robinson 1994). Another is the Russian Jews who migrated to Israel in the early 1990s. As we saw in chapter 14, a change in Soviet emigration policy produced a flood of Jewish emigrants, many of whom had high levels of education and occupational skills. Their earnings were initially only 70 percent of those of Israeli natives, with relatively little dispersion. These Jewish immigrants received almost no return on their human capital initially, but its value increased over the ensuing decade, accounting for about half of the convergence of their earnings with those of the native born (Eckstein and Weiss 2003).[7] Thus, their average earnings increased relative to those of the native-born as did their earnings dispersion, while their share in white-collar and professional occupations rose from 12 to 31 percent. No doubt much of this was due to the steep increase in Hebrew language fluency that has been observed among non-Hebrew-speaking immigrants (Chiswick 1998). This and other postarrival investments served to unlock the earnings potential of the skills these immigrants brought with them from the Soviet Union.[8]

Like that of United States immigrants, the experience of EU immigrants is conditioned by the skills they bring and the labor markets they enter. It is also powerfully influenced by country of origin, and immigrant composition by source varies widely across Europe as a result of colonial history, the legacy of guestworker policies, and more recently, the flood of asylum seekers. Thus, the income of U.K. immigrants coming from elsewhere in the European Union or from other Western countries exceeds that of the native-born, while those coming from Africa, the Caribbean, Pakistan, and Bangladesh do significantly worse than U.K. natives. Similarly, German immigrants coming from elsewhere in the European Union or from other Western countries do as well as or better than natives, while the *ausseidler* from eastern Europe do less well, and those from the guestworker countries of the past or the asylum seeker countries of the present do even worse. Some western European countries have experienced long-run changes in the source country composition of their immigrant pool which have led to immigrant quality decline, although the decline is not nearly as dramatic as in the United States (Hayfron 1998; Bauer, Lofstrom, and Zimmermann 2000, 16). Indeed, much of the decline in the economic status of European immigrants is due to the long-run deterioration in labor market conditions rather than to the declining quality of the immigrants themselves (Bevelander and Nielsen 2001). Comparisons among countries indicate that the more depressed and the less flexible is the receiving country labor market, the more immigrants are marginalized (Schultz-Neilsen and Constant 2004).

It is sometimes argued that immigrants are attracted to some European countries by generous state welfare provisions, particularly where immigrant unemployment rates are especially high. Since choice of destination depends on the whole package of earnings, taxes, and benefits, weighted by the probabilities of receiving them (or paying them, in the case of taxes), countries with generous welfare systems might attract those least likely to be successful in the labor market. That is, those host countries with generous welfare systems should cause more negative selection among immigrants. Yet the evidence supporting this otherwise plausible view is limited (Boeri, Hanson, and McCormick 2002, 87–89; Constant and Schultz-Neilsen 2004), perhaps because more-generous welfare benefits are also often associated with labor markets that make immigrant access to employment difficult. These offsetting effects on immigrant selection help explain why generous welfare alone is not strongly correlated with immigrant quality.

Measuring the Brain Drain

The possibility that migration to the OECD robs less-developed countries of their best and brightest has long been a matter of concern, just as it was in nineteenth-century Ireland, Sweden, and other European countries sending emigrants overseas. The recent debate often cites losses of qualified doctors, engineers, and information technology specialists from the Third World, but for a full assessment, we need more-comprehensive data. Indeed, what we need are data measuring the skill mix of emigrants relative to those who stay behind. Such data are now available for emigration to the OECD from low- and middle-income countries (Carrington and Detragaiche 1998; Adams 2003),[9] and they are summarized in table 15.4. The "Total" column reports, for each source country, the proportion of the population aged twenty-five and over that was living in the OECD in 1990. This figure can then be compared to the "Tertiary" column, which shows the proportion of those in the source country in the higher-education category (i.e., having equivalent to thirteen or more years of education) that was also living in the OECD.

As the table shows, for most source countries, the proportion of adults who have emigrated is small (5 percent or less), but for a few the numbers are much larger. These are mainly small countries that are close to the major receiving regions—particularly those in the Caribbean, Central America, North Africa, and the Middle East. Whether they record high or low total emigration rates, however, all of the sixty-one poor nations in table 15.4 report larger emigration rates for those with tertiary education than for all citizens. Fifteen of those listed had lost more than 20 percent of their highly educated manpower through emigration but far smaller proportions of their total workforce. The ratio of the highly educated emigrating to the total emigrating averages about twenty to one for those fifteen countries. Even those countries with total emigration rates of 5 percent or less report average ratios about fourteen to one. The loss of the highly qualified through emigration exceeds 40 percent for Turkey, Algeria, Gambia, Senegal, Jamaica, Trinidad and Tobago, and Guyana. And these losses are all the more striking considering the small shares of the highly educated in the source country population, ranging from 3 percent in Turkey and Tunisia down to less than 1 percent in Gambia.

OECD immigrants have 7.2 more years of education than the adults they left back home. True, these data are not adjusted for the fact that immigrants are considerably younger than the average adult back home or for the fact that immigrants may have received some education in host countries after their arrival. However, it is very clear that there is a big gap between mover and stayer, implying a brain drain.

These data confirm a large loss of qualified manpower in the Third World, and they also show where to look for the biggest brain drains. But even the measurement of net emigrations of "brains" per capita can be clouded by the demographic transition. Younger adults emigrate from the Philippines in large numbers, but older adults also re-

Table 15.4
Migration rates from poor nations to the OECD: Total and high education, 1990

Country	Total	Tertiary
Asia and Pacific		
Bangladesh	0.1	2.5
China	0.1	3.0
Fiji	3.6	21.3
India	0.2	2.6
Indonesia	—	1.5
Iran	1.5	25.6
Korea	4.2	14.9
Malaysia	1.2	22.7
Pakistan	0.3	6.9
Papua New Guinea	—	2.2
Philippines	3.1	9.0
Sri Lanka	0.8	23.6
Syria	0.7	3.0
Taiwan	1.6	8.4
Thailand	0.2	1.5
Turkey	8.5	46.2
Africa		
Algeria	6.3	55.0
Benin	—	0.4
Cameroon	—	3.2
Central African Republic	—	1.7
Congo	—	0.5
Egypt	0.5	5.0
Gambia	0.2	61.4
Ghana	0.4	25.7
Kenya	0.1	10.0
Lesotho	—	2.9
Malawi	—	2.0
Mali	—	0.9
Mauritius	0.2	7.2
Mozambique	—	8.6
Rwanda	—	2.2
Senegal	2.4	47.7
Sierra Leone	0.3	24.3
South Africa	0.4	7.9
Sudan	—	1.8
Togo	—	1.3
Tunisia	8.6	63.3

Table 15.4
(continued)

Country	Total	Tertiary
Uganda	0.1	15.5
Zambia	0.1	5.0
Zimbabwe	0.1	4.7
Americas		
Costa Rica	2.4	7.1
Dominican Republic	6.5	14.7
El Salvador	11.3	26.1
Guatemala	3.4	13.5
Honduras	3.0	15.7
Jamaica	20.3	77.4
Mexico	7.7	10.3
Nicaragua	4.7	18.8
Panama	6.7	19.6
Trinidad and Tobago	9.5	57.8
Argentina	0.6	2.7
Bolivia	0.7	4.2
Brazil	0.2	1.4
Chile	1.1	6.0
Colombia	1.1	5.8
Ecuador	1.9	3.8
Guyana	14.5	77.5
Paraguay	0.2	2.0
Peru	1.0	3.4
Uruguay	1.1	3.8
Venezuela	0.4	2.1

Source: Carrington and Detragaiche 1998 (table 3).
Notes: Numbers represent shares of the stock of total and highly educated population aged twenty-five and over born in the origin country but living in an OECD country. Dashes indicate no information available.

turn to the Philippines in large numbers, following life cycle patterns (Yang 2004a). Furthermore, the large drain we observe today is due in part to the large cohort of young adults found in the middle of the demographic transition. As Third World sending countries pass through the demographic transition, the pressure on young-adult exits will fall while the pressure on older adult return migration will rise. Thus, a brain drain today may become a brain gain tomorrow.

However, confirming the magnitudes is not the main problem; rather, it lies with interpretation. We need to answer counterfactual questions such as, Would skill levels in source countries have been higher or lower in the absence of emigration? While emigration of the highly skilled certainly increases short-run skill scarcity at home, it also provides an incentive for others to acquire skills and education, replacing those who have left. Better emigration opportunities for the highly skilled raises the expected *total* return to skills. The expected total return is calculated as a weighted average of low returns at home and high returns abroad, where the weight on the latter is the probability that a migration opportunity will arise (Mountford 1997). Thus, an increase in OECD migration opportunities (or a fall in the cost of reaching the education threshold set by immigration policies abroad) has two offsetting effects. One increases the total number of brains produced by the domestic economy (the brain effect); the other reduces, through emigration, the share of those brains available to the domestic economy (the drain effect). Which of these effects dominates? One recent study used the data in table 15.4 to infer that the brain effect dominates in some countries, particularly those with low total emigration rates and low shares of highly educated in the source population (Beine, Docquier, and Rapoport 2003). The drain effect dominates for other countries, particularly for those with high total migration rates and large shares of highly educated in the source population. These findings have been criticized on both theoretical and empirical grounds (Commander, Kangasniemi, and Winters 2003; Faini 2003a), but at least they caution that brain drain might not be the disaster that popular writing often suggests.

It may also be the prospect of gaining admission to higher-education programs abroad that boosts education at home, rather than just the prospect of emigrating when fully trained. Many foreign-born OECD residents have received some of their education at their destinations rather than in their home countries. For example, male immigrant employees in the United Kingdom have an average of fourteen years of education, of which nearly three were acquired in the United Kingdom. Among foreign citizens staying in the United Kingdom for more than a year, the proportion who were incoming students rose from 23 percent in 1975–1979 to 32 percent in 1995–1999 (of a much larger total [Dobson et al. 2001]). Of all students enrolled in OECD institutions, 37 percent are foreign, and more than half of these are from outside the OECD (OECD 2001a). Four-fifths of these Third World students are from Asia and Africa, and four-fifths of them are located in five main education-providing countries: Australia, France, Germany, the United

Kingdom, and the United States. All of this may help explain the finding that greater numbers of highly educated emigrants living abroad offer incentives to younger cohorts to complete secondary education at home (Faini 2003a).

Much of the education acquired by immigrants at their destinations might not have been undertaken at all if those immigrants had stayed at home. And some of it may be returned to the source country if those who emigrate as students take their skills back home. Here the evidence is mixed. Only 12.5 percent of the foreign students who enrolled in the United States in the late 1970s transferred from student visas to work permits (Bratsberg 1995). The share emigrating for educational reasons has increased dramatically since then, and partly as a result of changes in foreign student immigration policy, the proportion of those staying has also increased. Despite the rise in the *share* of students staying in the host country after completing their educations, the *absolute* number who return has also risen. Many of them would have received less education (fewer years and/or lower quality per year) had they stayed at home, and this provides some offset to the human capital loss associated with the permanent movers.[10] Still, the greater a student's educational investment in the host country and the longer his or her stay, the less likely that the student will return home after completing his or her education.

Does Emigration Impede Development at Home?

Economists have been debating the impact of the brain drain on developing economies since the 1970s. Theory suggests certain conditions under which brain drains might not be harmful. If skilled labor is underemployed or unemployed at the source, then its emigration cannot be too harmful. Under these circumstances, the brain drain is simply a symptom of other economic problems in the sending country, and whatever is suppressing growth potential is also suppressing the derived demand for skills. The same theory suggests that when these other problems are solved, the demand for skills will rise, and potential emigrants will stay home. Until then, emigration might raise the expected earnings of skilled workers by reducing their unemployment and, if labor markets are flexible, raising their wages. This benign conclusion becomes more complicated when three additional questions are added to the agenda: First, who pays for the education at home and abroad? Second, do migrants remit more surplus from abroad than they would generate if they stayed home? Third, how many return, and when?

So what does the evidence suggest? While there is an unambiguous positive correlation between educational levels and per capita incomes across countries, there is no consistent relationship between growth rates in per capita income and educational levels. The absence of such a correlation may be explained by the fact that the growing educational stock has failed to find productive use in cases where supply has outpaced demand (Pritchett 2001). Thus, brain drains should be important mainly to countries in which the educational stock has grown slowly and skills remain scarce.

This evidence speaks to the role of human capital but not to brain drain. Brain drain issues are even more complicated, for at least three reasons: emigration is selective, even within education levels; education of workers who leave almost certainly is subsidized by those who stay; and emigrants probably remit more surplus than they would have generated had they stayed home.

Do Remittances Compensate?

We know that emigrants remit some of their earnings to relatives at home and that these remittances have a powerful impact on the Third World households and villages that receive them. Consider, for example, one recent study of households in El Salvador, 15 percent of which received such remittances. The study found that these remittances raised school retention rates much more than for an equivalent amount of income from other sources: one hundred dollars of remittances (the mean amount for households receiving remittances) reduced by a quarter in rural areas the probability of children's leaving school and by even more in urban areas (Cox Edwards and Ureta 2003). Of course, this rise in school retention rates could have been driven either by the prospects of future emigration or by remittances from emigrants per se, but in either case it suggests mechanisms though which emigration might lead to greater educational effort in the emigrants' origin country. Additional examples from other household and village studies can easily be cited. For instance, remittances received by Mexican households are positively correlated with better schooling attendance rates and lower infant mortality rates (Córdova 2004). Remittances to

Philippine households are also linked with improved child schooling rates, reduced child labor participation rates, and increased education expenditures (Yang 2004b).

One would have thought that this knowledge about household impact would be sufficient, but the literature on the effects of emigrant remittances also asks whether these remittances are large enough to make a difference to the *economies* that receive them. Indeed, it asks whether remittances contribute to economic development (e.g., Buch and Kuckulenz 2004; Chami, Fullenkamp, and Jahjah 2003).

Emigrant remittances totaled seventy-three billion dollars in 2001, double the figure (in real terms) of the late 1980s. Furthermore, this figure captures only that portion of remittances that flows through official banking channels, and hence it understates the true total, perhaps by a margin of 10 to 90 percent (Puri and Ritzema 1994, table 4). Even so, the understated 2001 figure was 85 percent as large as capital inflows (including foreign direct investment) to developing countries, and it was 2.6 times the value of official development assistance. For low-income developing countries, remittances amount to nearly 2 percent of GDP, to about 6 percent of imports, and to nearly 10 percent of domestic investment (Ratha 2003, 157). These are very big numbers indeed, but the scale of remittances varies widely across countries. Four of the thirty-seven Third World countries listed in table 15.5 report remittance inflows at more than 10 percent of GDP: El Salvador, Jamaica, Jordan, and Yemen. For four more, the share ranges between 5 and 10 percent of GDP: the Dominican Republic, Nigeria, Egypt, and Sri Lanka. For fourteen more, the share ranges between 1 and 5 percent of GDP. For the remaining fifteen, among them Brazil, Peru, Ghana, Indonesia, and the Philippines, the share is less than 1 percent of GDP.

How do these remittance shares in GDP compare with the numbers who have emigrated? Consider the twenty-four emigrating countries in table 15.4 that also report remittance shares in table 15.5. Those with high emigration rates (equal to or greater than 3 percent) reported remittance shares averaging 3.9 percent in the mid-1990s, and those with low emigration rates (less than 3 percent) reported remittance shares averaging 2.1 percent. The size of the emigration rate obviously matters, and big brain drains yield big remittance shares. Are remittances big enough to offset the drain?

Consider this back-of-the-envelope calculation regarding brain drain versus remittance gain. For the countries documented in table 15.5, the stock of emigrants living in the OECD averages 3.3 percent of the

Table 15.5
Flows of remittances to developing countries in the mid-1990s

Country	Official remittances (US$ millions)	Percentage of source GDP
Latin America		
Bolivia	2	0.03
Brazil	2,891	0.41
Colombia	739	0.80
Costa Rica	122	1.03
Dominican Republic	914	7.13
Ecuador	382	2.13
El Salvador	1,084	11.22
Honduras	128	3.12
Jamaica	636	11.46
Mexico	3,673	1.28
Nicaragua	25	1.47
Panama	16	0.20
Paraguay	200	2.21
Peru	472	0.96
Trinidad and Tobago	6	0.12
Sub-Saharan Africa		
Ghana	7	0.12
Madagascar	11	0.35
Mali	103	4.43
Mauritania	5	0.47
Namibia	8	0.25
Niger	6	0.32
Nigeria	1,920	6.37
Senegal	73	1.71
North Africa & Middle East		
Algeria	1,101	2.63
Egypt	3,279	5.45
Iran	1	0.01
Jordan	1,655	23.08
Morocco	1,336	4.24
Tunisia	551	3.71
Yemen	1,018	28.48
East Asia		
Bangladesh	1,217	3.16
India	7,685	2.17
Indonesia	796	0.39
Nepal	101	2.30
Pakistan	1,409	2.19
Philippines	443	0.62
Sri Lanka	790	6.06

Source: Adams and Page 2003 (annex table A1).

home population. The (unweighted) ratio of remittances to home GDP for the same group is 3.6 percent. If we assume an emigrant labor participation rate of 0.8 and an emigrant impact on home GDP at 0.7,[11] then the 3.3 percent population loss implies a 1.8 percent GDP loss, smaller than the 3.6 remittance gain. Thus, remittances *overcompensate* for brain drain. The calculation is, of course, crude, and there is also very wide variance among countries which reflects differences in migration patterns. Most of the remittance flows to Latin America originate from emigrants who have settled permanently in the United States. By contrast, most of the remittances to the Middle East and much of Southeast Asia come from temporary migrants to Gulf States, particularly Saudi Arabia and Kuwait. Where migration is temporary, remittances are larger. Where migration is permanent, remittances are smaller. Furthermore, much depends on how the remittances are used. If they are used to finance the travel and living expenses of new migrants—as was true of remittances from European immigrants in the nineteenth century—then the long-run impact of remittances on GDP back home will be less.

Is there a link between remittance flows and the brain drain? The causality could go both ways. Higher-skilled emigrants will be more successful in the host country labor market and might be expected to remit more than lower-skilled emigrants. However, the facts seem to suggest the contrary: other things equal, the larger the share of a source country's emigrants with tertiary education, the smaller is the return flow of remittances (Faini 2003b). Perhaps this weak remittance rate by more highly educated migrants can be explained by their longer stay in the host country and by their lower dependence on family loans during their education abroad, thus implying weaker links with friends and relatives at the origin.

Emigration opportunities abroad generate remittances that in many cases exceed any brain drain losses. In addition, emigration opportunities provoke private and public educational investment responses in sending countries, just as they did in late-nineteenth-century Europe.[12]

The Bottom Line

Immigrants still ascend host country economic ladders after arrival, just as they did in the first global century. The more highly educated rise faster as they acquire additional human capital (especially language skills) that complement the human capital endowments they have brought with them. Relative to the native-born in the OECD, the economic quality of immigrants has deteriorated over time as a result of a combination of the changing source country composition—shifting to poorer and poorer sources—and worsening host country labor market conditions. Still, while immigrants typically have less human capital (and increasingly so) than the natives in the host countries to which they migrate, they have vastly more human capital than the populations in their countries of origin. This enormous gap between the skills of sending-country migrants and nonmigrants has led to a renewed interest in the economics of the brain drain. The new interest has spawned a new view: when education responses at home and remittances from abroad are considered, it is not at all clear that migration from poor to rich countries always generates a brain drain, but it is clear that this migration has generated a big brain gain for the world as a whole.

IV

The Future of World Mass Migration

In most of the OECD, anti-immigration attitudes have been on the rise since the 1960s. They have reached high levels of hostility, spilled out onto the streets, influenced political outcomes, and attracted considerable media attention. However, the intensity of the public hostility to immigration has varied considerably over time, across liberal democracies absorbing immigrants, and across citizen groups within those democracies. Why? Finding the answer is crucial to policy formation, and it motivates this chapter. The search is organized around three underlying fundamentals: public concern about immigrant competition in the labor market; fears that immigrants are a net fiscal burden given their high demand for public goods, their high use of the welfare safety net, and their low tax contributions; and cultural prejudice. These three fundamentals—labor market competition, fiscal burden, and cultural prejudice—exhibit very different relative power over time, across countries, and across individuals.

Public hostility toward immigration and immigrants appears to be at odds with mainstream academic views that immigration has only modest effects on labor market and net welfare burdens and, furthermore, that both of these tend to dissipate as immigrants assimilate and as their time in the host country increases. Thus, it is often argued that the public is being misled by hysterical rhetoric from the right into erroneous beliefs about immigration's effect on host country economies and that it lacks the knowledge to counter that rhetoric with evidence. There may be some truth to this. After all, rational citizens may wish to avoid the costs of learning about immigration and therefore rely on their political representatives to do that learning for them. Still, informed debate about immigration is more limited than about most issues, official data are scarcer for this issue than for most, and official judgment about the evidence is more ambiguous than for most. As

Gary Freeman (1995) and others have pointed out, since the labor market and welfare impacts of immigration policies tend to be lagged, "the short-term benefits [are] oversold and the long-term costs denied or hidden" (883). The same can be said, of course, about many policies, but there are several characteristics of immigration policy that makes it especially prone to political illusion.

One reason that politicians skirt open debate about immigration is the fear of being labeled racists. Another reason is that their positions on immigration policy have been influenced by special-interest groups, and they would rather not let that secret be known to the voting public. Still, we argue in this chapter that there is no great contradiction between public attitudes toward immigration and the evidence. Consider, for example, labor market impact. Most academic research has shown that increased immigration has not been the most important force accounting for the rise in earnings inequality in most countries after the 1970s. Nor is it the principal cause of persistently high unemployment among the unskilled in countries in which this earnings inequality has increased less. The public seems to see it differently, however, believing that the presence of more immigrants has mattered in both respects. As we just noted, this does not necessarily imply any inconsistency between public attitude and evidence, and Kenneth Scheve and Matthew Slaughter (2001b, 10–11) list three reasons it does not. First, small effects aren't zero effects. Second, the public may agree with academics that technological change is the main driving force in labor markets, but it may also believe that while policy has little impact on technical change, it can have a big impact on immigration. Third, the public is forward-looking and anticipates big effects in the future. We do not deny that all three matter in explaining the divergence between public attitudes toward immigration and what the evidence seems to show, but we think a fourth reason is playing an even bigger role. That is, the public may have a counterfactual in its head when it expresses anti-immigrant attitudes. Even though immigration may not account for much of observed labor market experience over the past three decades, a world without immigration might have improved that experience quite a bit.

Most people have heard the phrase "we have lost control of our borders" so often—especially as it is liberally sprinkled in political speeches—that it is no wonder they have come to believe that myth. We join most analysts in believing that we *do* have control of our borders, but that we choose not to control them. This chapter has much more to say about this issue, but it argues that much of the illegal migration we observe is produced by legislation and its implementation (or its nonimplementation), resulting in an apparent tolerance for illegal migration that suits lobbying interests just fine. We think it better to explore attitudes and policies toward immigration as the rational result of political economy in the liberal democracies, although we grant that the outcomes can vary with the liberal democracy, its history, its institutions, and its neighbors.

We argue in chapter 17 that there are substantial gains to the world as a whole from freeing up international migration. In this sense world mass migration is not big enough. Here, however, we ask a very different question: Why aren't immigration policies even *more* restrictive than they are? Or why does the OECD accept unwanted immigration, and thus why does it exhibit what some observers call an "expansionary bias" (Joppke 1998; Freeman 1995)? The next section begins by documenting the evolution of public attitudes toward immigration and immigrants. We then ask what economic theory has to say about these public attitudes, using that theory to explain why there are asymmetries in policy and attitude between immigration, on the one hand, and trade and capital markets, on the other. Economics can't explain everything, of course, so the chapter goes on to explore the relation between cultural preference, falling immigrant quality, and rising anti-immigrant prejudice.

The Evolution of Public Attitudes toward Immigration

Attitude surveys toward globalization are now common, but one of the better ones was the 1995 International Social Survey (ISSP), a national identity survey conducted in twenty-four countries.[1] Some of these are the well-known New World countries with two centuries of significant immigration experience (Australia, Canada, New Zealand, and the United States). Some are countries in western Europe with two centuries of immigration experience, absorbing European migrants from the east and south (Austria, western Germany, and the Netherlands). Some have become immigrant nations only in recent decades after having experienced long histories of emigration (Ireland, Italy, Norway, Spain, and Sweden). Some are major emigrating countries but also serve as destinations for immigrants from poor countries, some in transit, and many illegal (Bulgaria, the Czech Republic, eastern Germany, Hungary, Latvia, Slovakia, Slovenia, Poland, and Russia).

And some have little or no immigration experience at all (the Philippines and Japan).

The survey asked respondents questions about their attitude toward immigrants and refugees: should the number of immigrants in their economy be increased a lot (1), be increased a little (2), remain the same (3), be reduced a little (4), or be reduced a lot (5)? The survey also asked respondents about their attitudes toward trade—should their country limit the imports of foreign products in order to protect their domestic industries?—and their answers could range from very protrade (1) to very antitrade (5).

Table 16.1 displays the results. Four of the survey's findings are common to most other globalization attitude surveys as well. First, attitudes toward immigration were found to be the most intensely negative of the three attitudes surveyed. On average, the answers ranged between "immigration should be reduced by a little" and "immigration should be reduced by a lot" (3.9). Nine of the countries recorded answers approaching "reduced by a lot" (above 4) and these included three important EU immigrant countries—Britain, Germany (divided into East and West in the survey and table), and Italy—as well as a number that have recently experienced immigration from the east. Twenty of the countries reported scores above 3.7. Thus, anti-immigrant feelings are not limited to fringe groups of the sort that took to the streets in Genoa, Göteborg, and Seattle or that splash ugly graffiti across European mosques. On the contrary, public anti-immigration feelings are widespread and in the mainstream. Second, anti-immigrant sentiment was found to be stronger than antitrade sentiment (3.9 versus 3.6), even when the sample omits the recently autarchic and centrally controlled countries in eastern Europe (without them, the comparison is 3.7 versus 3.5). Third, attitudes toward refugees among respondents were much more benign than those toward immigrants, with most feeling that genuine refugees should be allowed to stay. Finally, no significant correlation was found at the country level between antitrade and anti-immigration sentiment, especially when the eight eastern European countries are excluded.[2] That is, median-voter antiglobal and antiimmigration sentiments are not interchangeable. Anti-immigration attitudes appear to be driven by independent influences.

There is much to be said for focusing attention on ISSP anti-immigrant attitudes in those OECD countries where immigrants loom large in populations and labor markets, that are also included in the

Table 16.1
Attitudes toward immigrants, refugees, and imports, 1995

Country	Anti-immigrant	Antirefugee	Antitrade
Hungary	4.402	2.838	4.047
East Germany	4.338	1.961	3.563
West Germany	4.226	2.049	3.083
Bulgaria	4.219	2.661	4.190
Latvia	4.182	3.757	4.042
Czech Republic	4.158	2.463	3.415
Italy	4.151	2.846	3.571
Britain	4.052	2.820	3.723
Slovakia	4.004	3.021	3.488
Sweden	3.961	2.275	3.228
Slovenia	3.939	3.565	3.465
Poland	3.888	2.535	3.787
United States	3.873	2.748	3.707
Norway	3.847	2.340	3.144
Netherlands	3.826	2.366	2.912
Austria	3.804	2.095	3.873
Philippines	3.796	3.708	3.624
Australia	3.768	2.954	3.997
New Zealand	3.742	2.807	3.406
Russia	3.717	2.698	3.670
Spain	3.401	2.460	3.813
Japan	3.391	3.014	2.919
Canada	3.317	2.404	3.264
Ireland	3.071	2.163	3.650
Unweighted average	3.878	2.690	3.567

Sources: O'Rourke and Sinnott 2004 (table 1) and O'Rourke 2003 (table 1), based on data from the 1995 ISSP module on national identity. See text for discussion of questions asked and rating scales employed.

1997 Eurobarometer survey. For the eight included in both surveys (Austria, Britain, Germany, Ireland, Italy, the Netherlands, Spain, and Sweden), the ISSP anti-immigrant response was 3.9, and for the two with the highest foreign-born population shares (Austria and Germany), the ISSP 1995 anti-immigrant score was 4.1, well above the average anti-immigrant sentiment. A recent analysis of the 1997 Eurobarometer survey offers some interesting stylized facts for the thirteen EU member states surveyed (Boeri, Hanson, and McCormick 2002, 107–122). First, one-third of the respondents openly described themselves as quite racist or very racist, suggesting that culture matters as a determinant of anti-immigration sentiment. Furthermore, the highest number of racist responses came from respondents in countries where the foreign-born share is highest (Austria, Belgium, France, Germany, and Sweden), in contrast with lower numbers of racist responses in countries where the foreign-born share is lowest (Finland, Italy, Portugal and Spain). In addition, anti-immigration sentiment is also strongest where the foreign-born share is highest. Second, the prevalence of racist feelings is unrelated to economic variables, suggesting to some observers that culture has an influence independent of economics, a view we challenge later in the chapter. Third, while there was a positive correlation between unemployment and immigration concerns, the correlation was weak. As we show subsequently, this correlation is generally far stronger in countries with flexible labor markets (like the United States) than in those that protect jobs (like France, Germany, and the Scandinavian countries). Fourth, education moderated ethnic hostility, racism, and anti-immigrant sentiment, in a correlation that has its roots in standard theory, as we show in the next section. Finally, one of the strongest correlations in the data was between the foreign-born share and the view that "immigrants abuse the system of social benefits," at least in this EU sample where the welfare state loomed so large. In summary, the 1997 Eurobarometer survey confirmed "that both welfare and labour market concerns matter for the expressed opinion toward further immigration, but racially motivated concerns are the most important factors" (Boeri, Hanson, and McCormick 2002, 120).

This might be a good place to raise an issue of causality. Our interest in this chapter is in exploring the connection between public attitudes and policy outcomes. However, policy can also have a powerful influence on public attitudes. Consistent with the theme of chapter 15, it has been emphasized recently that

nearly all significant receiving countries [have] recently experienced a decline in the quality of immigrants, as measured by the wage differential on arrival between immigrants and natives. In all cases, the decrease in the quality of migrants comes together with a significant change in the country-of-origin mix of the immigrants ... even though all countries face a decline in the quality of migrants, an assimilation of immigrants to natives can be observed only in those countries that select immigrants on the basis of their labour market characteristics.... [Thus], it is difficult to separate the extent to which sentiments of the population are in line with policy or policy is in line with sentiments. (Boeri, Hanson, and McCormick 2002, 121–122)

In short, public anti-immigration attitudes may be at least partially endogenous with respect to policy: countries which give preference to potential immigrants with "good" labor market attributes will get immigrants who assimilate more quickly (thus exhibiting less-extreme departures from the native cultural mainstream), crowd out fewer natives, and are a smaller burden on the welfare state. Public attitudes toward immigrants are likely to be more benign in such countries and during such times. In contrast, those countries which accept immigrants with "poor" labor market attributes will get immigrants who assimilate more slowly, crowd out more unskilled natives, and place heavier demands on the welfare state. Immigrant quality is, of course, the result of more than policy. For example, it can be influenced by the quality of a country's neighbors—as in the case of the United States and its southern neighbor, Mexico, or that of Austria and Germany and the eastern European countries nearby. As chapter 11 has shown, immigrant quality has also been influenced by economic and demographic factors that have served to push more Third World emigrants toward the OECD in recent decades. In any case, we are forewarned that public attitudes toward immigration are not likely to be fully exogenous.

How have public attitudes toward immigrants evolved through time? Let us start with the biggest immigrant country with the longest immigrant history, the United States. Chapter 8 devoted considerable space to the connection between public attitudes and policy in the United States before the 1920s and the imposition of immigration quotas. In that first global century, anti-immigrant attitudes were highly correlated with rising immigrant numbers and with declining immigrant quality. The rise in anti-immigrant sentiment came in two bursts.

The first burst was during the initial surge in U.S. immigration during the 1840s and 1850s, when immigration rose from modest rates before the mid-1840s (four or five per thousand) to levels a decade later that have never been exceeded since (fifteen per thousand). Furthermore, the new immigrants were much poorer than those who had come before, and many were actually fleeing European famines. Thus, these individuals were of much lower quality than those who had been so strongly positively selected earlier, they assimilated more slowly, and they contrasted more markedly with the mainstream Anglo-Saxon culture. Anti-immigration feelings dominated, spilled out on to the streets, and appeared in the popular press. Nativist political organizations became more powerful and louder, and organized labor rebelled,

sometimes violently. Much like the contemporary parties and factions led by Jean-Marie Le Pen in France, Jörg Haider in Austria, Pim
Fortuyn in the Netherlands, Pauline Hanson in Australia, and Pat
Buchanan in the United States, the Order of the Star Spangled Banner
(popularly known as the Know-Nothings) spouted a nativist creed.
The Know-Nothings grew from a secret band of forty-three in 1852
to a national political organization boasting one million members in
1854, and as chapter 8 documented, they had a very big impact at the
polls.

The second burst started in the mid-1890s after U.S. immigration
had resumed its secular boom over the three decades following the
Civil War, an epoch during which the quality of U.S. immigrants had
declined once again. New immigrants arrived from the poor east and
south of Europe, clashing with the native-born mainstream culture,
and undergoing slower assimilation. Public anti-immigration attitudes
again were rife. Recall from chapter 8 that almost 63 percent of those
Kansas workingmen interviewed in 1895 felt that immigration should
be restricted, and another 24 percent thought it should be suppressed, leaving only a handful happy with free immigration. The
anti-immigrant feeling actually became even worse as the 1890s wore
on, and we also recall from chapter 8 how congressmen in the nation's
capital responded to this sentiment: they voted overwhelmingly to restrict immigration by imposing a literacy test that they hoped would
screen out low-quality immigrants.

Figure 16.1 brings anti-immigrant attitudes up closer to the present.
The figure plots the percentage of the U.S. population favoring less immigration from 1953 (when the foreign-born were a minor presence in
the United States and most current immigrants were European) to 1997
(when the foreign-born were a major presence and most current immigrants were from the Third World) (Fetzer 2000, table A1.4, 165–166).
First, note that for most of the past fifty years, at least half of the Americans surveyed thought there were too many immigrants, and this was
true even before the great immigrant surge and the decline in immigrant quality of the 1970s and afterward. Even during the more tolerant 1950s and 1960s, more than 40 percent thought that immigration
should be reduced. Second, those numbers rose to as high as 60 and 70
percent in the 1980s and 1990s. Indeed, "some polls [revealed] that a
large minority—about 20 [percent]—favor[ed] the extreme solution of
a complete moratorium on immigration" (Lee 1998, 22). Despite its
reputation as a land of immigrants, one can hardly say that the United

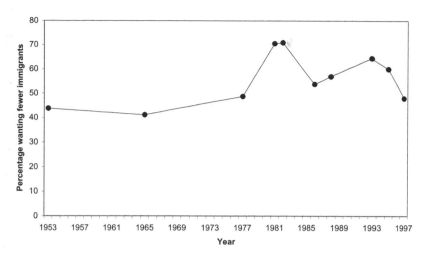

Figure 16.1
Opposition to immigration, United States, 1953–1997. *Source:* Fetzer 2000 (table A1.4, 165–166).

States has had a proimmigration attitude over the last half century. Indeed, the United States entered a period of neorestrictionist sentiment in the early 1980s, and polls taken in "gateway" states—like Texas and California—were consistent with national trends. These trends have been positively correlated with deteriorating conditions in labor markets, including the unemployment rate, and the same correlation can be seen for Canada (Espenshade and Hempstead 1996, 538–539). However, Kenneth Lee (1998) has pointed out that a 1984 poll already revealed a chink in this anti-immigrant public armor. It showed "how Americans, despite their restrictionist views, are supportive of immigration if it is framed in terms of family reunification because most Americans regard the family as paramount.... [I]mmigration supporters have effectively used this 'soft spot' for the family to their advantage" (25).

What about the intensity of these opinions? While most Americans think the immigration issue is important, it is not at the top of their political agenda, having about the same priority as environmental issues, well below inflation and unemployment, and certainly below national security. Still, immigration has moved up in the ranking of issues important to the American public: by 1994, 72 percent of those surveyed thought that mass immigration constituted a critical threat to the vital interests of the United States (Lee 1998, 27–28).

A more recent study brings this survey of U.S. anti-immigrant attitudes even closer to the present. In this survey, those who thought immigration should decrease averaged more than 51 percent of all U.S.
respondents between 1994 and 2000. Furthermore, more than three-
quarters thought that immigrants robbed jobs from natives, and almost
85 percent thought they were a net welfare burden (Boeri, Hanson, and
McCormick 2002, 251–254). Americans have both labor market and
welfare concerns in regard to immigrants, it seems.

Among the European countries that now have large foreign-born
population shares, Britain, France, Germany, Belgium, and the Netherlands have all undergone particular (unintended) postcolonial and
(unintended) guestworker experiences that make anti-immigration
attitudes especially intense and complicated. These experiences started
with a post–World War II welcome to Asians, Africans, and Caribbeans who had been colonials and now found British, French, German,
and Low Country labor markets now open to them. This created a
racial aftershock which is still being felt, and it is related to low-
quality immigrants, slow assimilation, and cultural gaps. Furthermore,
as Freeman has so eloquently put it, "The politics of immigration in
these states today is haunted by the mistakes, failures, and unforeseen
consequences of the guestworker era and by the social conflicts associated with the new ethnic minorities created during that time. Perhaps
the most powerful legacy is the conviction that temporary labor programs will inevitably turn in to processes of permanent migration"
(Freeman 1995, 890). As a result, the public attitude toward immigration is much less positive in these European countries than in the "settler societies" like Australia, Canada, New Zealand, and the United
States, as table 16.1 confirms (4.1 versus 3.7). The asylum crisis that
followed the collapse of the Berlin Wall exacerbated anti-immigrant
attitudes still further. In France, this anti-immigrant attitude has been
manifested by the steady support of Jean-Marie Le Pen and his anti-
immigrant Front National party. Since December 1983, the proportion
of French respondents who have a positive opinion of the party has
varied between 10 and 25 percent (Fetzer 2000, 84–85, 166–169), with
no trend. In Germany, the share opposing the presence of immigrants
reached as high as 50 percent in the fall of 1991, while the share intending to vote for the anti-immigrant Die Republikaner party ranged from
6 to 8 percent in 1992–1993. Again, there is no apparent long-run trend.
As another example, results from the British Social Attitudes Survey,
taken eight times between 1983 and 1991, show that anti-immigration

attitudes in Britain during that time were far more intense toward
West Indians and Asians than they were toward Europeans, Australians, and New Zealanders (Dustmann and Preston 2000, table 2, 12;
2001). Attitudes in Britain toward immigrants are formed by three
familiar factors: opinions about welfare abuse, labor market impact
and racial prejudice. It appears that "racial prejudice is by far the most
important component explaining negative inclinations toward immigration of ethnically different populations" in Britain (Dustmann and
Preston 2000, 24). These attitudes can be traced back to the 1940s,
and they reached a peak in the 1960s and 1970s. From the 1962 Commonwealth Immigrants' Act to the 1971 Immigration Act, a series of
measures to tighten restrictions on immigration marched in lockstep
with a series of measures aimed at improving race relations (Hatton
and Wheatley Price 2005, 128). British immigration policy was "about
as restrictive as it can possibly be" in the following two decades (Hansen 2000, 222). Despite these increasingly tight regulations, however,
immigration from New Commonwealth countries—principally that
from the West Indies, India, Pakistan, and Bangladesh—actually
increased. Thus, family reunification generated persistent immigration
long after primary migration had been shut down by more restrictive
policy.

Finally, what about the new EU immigration countries? Greece,
Italy, Portugal, and Spain have only recently made the transition from
heavy emigrating countries in the past to heavy immigrating countries
in the present. Returning Italians exceeded emigrating Italians for the
first time in 1972, for Spaniards and Greeks it was 1975, and for Portuguese it was 1981 (Freeman 1995, 893). Over the quarter century since,
these four countries have been receiving increasing (low-quality) numbers of immigrants from their poor neighbors in North Africa, sub-
Saharan Africa, and the Balkans. These immigrants have been pulled
to these high-wage Mediterranean countries by their rapid economic
growth, extensive informal sectors, modest immigration controls, and
a demographic slowdown in the growth of their adult populations
(Venturini 2004, chap. 2). All of this presents a huge challenge to these
new immigrating countries along the northern edge of the Mediterranean as they try to master their borders and to develop a policy that reflects the national interest. It appears that benign public attitudes offer
their governments some breathing space to the extent that respondents
report "modest racial feelings" (Boeri, Hanson, and McCormick 2002,
109), "little concern over immigrants" (Boeri, Hanson, and McCormick

2002, 111, 113), and very low levels of anti-immigrant attitudes (in Spain, but not in Italy: table 16.1).

What Does Economic Theory Predict about Public Attitudes toward Immigration?

What explains public attitudes toward immigration? How much of these attitudes does economics explain, and how much is left for culture, prejudice, and racism? When searching for answers, it is important to distinguish between the short run, when macroeconomic shocks influence the timing of changes in anti-immigrant attitudes, and the long run, when economic and demographic fundamentals explain secular trends and differences among nations.

Of the three familiar forces influencing public attitudes toward immigration—labor market competition, fiscal burden, and cultural prejudice—it is the first that exhibits macro instability. Booms and busts in labor markets have a clear impact on changes in public attitudes toward immigration. Bad times breed immigrant hostility (even if the immigrants have nothing to do with the bad times), and good times breed the opposite. This can be seen from U.S. time series experience since the liberal immigration legislation of 1965. U.S. immigration rose after 1965, but so did inequality and unemployment, and the unskilled worker failed to share in the prosperity. Anti-immigration attitudes surged (figure 16.1; see also Scheve and Slaughter 2001b, 87–93), even though most economists agree that less-restrictive immigration and trade made only a modest contribution to these labor market trends (Lindert and Williamson 2003). During the rapid growth of the 1990s, employment rates were high again, and anti-immigration attitudes dropped back to the levels of the 1970s. The same correlation has characterized much of European experience, in which "there is a 'good times/bad times' dynamic in which migration is tolerated or even encouraged during expansionary phases, but becomes the focus of anxieties when unemployment rises. Immigrants during bad times are targeted as scapegoats for conditions they may have no part in causing" (Freeman 1995, 886; see also Kindleberger 1967; Hollifield 1992).

This correlation between levels of economic prosperity and attitudes toward immigrants was also evident in the first global century, at least as revealed by policy. Chapter 8 showed that proimmigration policy was introduced (or anti-immigration policy was choked off) during good labor market times in the nineteenth and early twentieth centuries in Argentina, Australia, Brazil, Canada, and the United States, while anti-immigration policy was introduced (or proimmigration policy was choked off) during bad labor market times. The best historical example of the correlation is offered by the surge in anti-immigration attitudes and the start of the U.S. congressional debates over immigrant restriction in 1895 and 1896, years which marked the depths of a serious and protracted depression, and a debate which concluded a quarter of a century later with the passage of the Literacy Act in 1917 and the imposition of quotas on immigration in the 1920s.

None of these observations about how labor market conditions influence the timing of public attitudes toward immigration and the development of immigration policy should come as a surprise. The more contentious issue is what explains the fundamentals driving public attitudes in the longer run or differences among voters at any given time. Voters may reject immigration for two reasons.[3] The first reason is noneconomic: racism, xenophobia, nativism, and goals of cultural homogeneity can all generate anti-immigrant attitudes. The second reason is economic: voters' attitudes toward immigrants can also be driven by economic self-interest. The standard view on how democracies work (challenged later in the chapter) has it that these various interests are aggregated such that policy reflects the view of the me dian voter (Benhabib 1996).

If economic self-interest matters, who should favor immigration and who should oppose it? Standard Heckscher-Ohlin trade theory offers explicit answers, and a number of economists have used it recently to explore empirically the sources of public attitudes toward immigration (Mayda and Rodrik 2001; Mayda 2003; O'Rourke 2003; O'Rourke and Sinnott 2004; Scheve and Slaughter 2001a, 2001b). The relative wages of skilled workers, according to Heckscher-Ohlin theory, should be lower in rich, skill-abundant countries, while the opposite should be true in poor, labor-abundant countries. The theory predicts that rich countries export skill-intensive products, import labor-intensive products, host unskilled immigrants, and send skilled emigrants abroad. Poor countries export labor-intensive products, import skill-intensive products, send unskilled emigrants abroad, and host skilled immigrants. It follows that if economic self-interest matters, the skilled and educated voter should favor free trade and liberal immigration policy in the rich country, while the unskilled and poorly educated voter should oppose those policies there. In contrast, the skilled and

educated voter should oppose free trade and liberal immigration policy in the poor country, while the unskilled and poorly educated voter
should favor those policies there (assuming, of course, that he or she
has the vote). What is true of voters within countries should also be
true of median voters across countries. Thus, anti-immigrant and antitrade sentiment should be correlated with GDP per capita: rich nations,
dominated by educated and skilled median voters, should favor open
trade and immigration policies, but unskilled voters in those nations
should resist them; poor nations, dominated by poorly schooled and
poorly skilled median voters, should also favor open trade and immigration policies, but skilled voters in those nations should resist them.

There are other theories besides Heckscher-Ohlin theory that offer
additional predictions regarding anti-immigration attitudes. For example, while we have assumed so far that migration from poor to rich
countries is always unskilled, we know that this assumption is often
violated. Indeed, we have already used the Roy model to deal with
issues of positive and negative selection in chapter 15. We can use it
again here to explore anti-immigration attitudes. According to the Roy
model, if income is very unequal and skill scarcity is very high in one
country (compared with another), the first will send unskilled immigrants to the second (high-wage, rich) country. So far there is no
conflict between the Roy and the Heckscher-Ohlin predictions. But if
income is very equal and skill scarcity very modest in the first country
(again, compared with the host country), the Roy model predicts that it
will send *skilled* migrants to the second (rich) country (where returns to
skills are high). Thus, the highly educated and highly skilled voter will
have less-liberal immigration attitudes in a rich country with unequal
incomes and high skill premia. The same is true of the median voter in
such countries.

The factor-proportions analysis model, used by labor economists,
assumes an integrated national market just as does the Heckscher-
Ohlin model (Scheve and Slaughter 2001a, 136; 2001b, 51–53). However, the former assumes a single aggregate output sector, while the
latter does not. Yet the factor-proportions analysis model makes
the same predictions regarding anti-immigrant attitudes as does the
Heckscher-Ohlin model.

In assessing immigrant impact on labor markets, chapter 14 pointed
out that some economists favor what has come to be called the area
analysis or the local labor market model, one that appeals to the premise that regional labor markets are segmented and that truly national

labor markets are absent. While the area analysis model is unlikely to hold in the long run, it may well be relevant in the short or medium run (Scheve and Slaughter 2001a, 137; 2001b, 51–53; Money 1997, 690–691). In any case, the model implies that anti-immigrant attitudes will be far stronger in gateway communities in which immigrants tend to enter and perhaps even concentrate.

Empirical results have strongly favored all of these economic predictions except the gateway predictions of the area analysis model. Let us begin with the U.S. results, then move on to the ISSP 1995 country cross section. The work of Scheve and Slaughter (2001a, 2001b) has found that less-skilled workers in the United States are much more likely to favor immigrant restriction and have anti-immigrant attitudes than more-skilled and more-educated workers. Thus, there is a strong skills and education "cleavage" in anti-immigration attitudes in America. There is also no evidence supporting the view that the connection between unskilled labor and anti-immigrant attitudes is stronger in gateway communities—such as California, New York, and Texas—than in the nation as a whole. Others have offered additional evidence confirming these U.S. findings (Boeri, Hanson, and McCormick 2002, 255–262). As we show subsequently, this result can be explained by the fact that public reaction to increasing immigrant numbers is driven by two opposing forces.

Public attitudes toward immigrants are consistent with economic models of the labor market, but are they also consistent with models of fiscal effects and welfare burdens? It turns out that voters believe that immigrants are a net burden on the welfare system. They also believe that the more unskilled, unschooled, and poorer the immigrant, the bigger the welfare burden, and there is evidence to support these opinions. In addition, voters appear to understand that the quality of an immigrant is correlated with the GDP per capita of the sending country. It is not surprising, therefore, that public attitudes vary "substantially with the geographic origin of immigrants. Although immigrants from different parts of the world may differ in many characteristics, one difference that is well documented is their skill levels.... [T]he evidence suggests that the U.S. public is more receptive to immigration from countries whose immigrants have been relatively more skilled" (Boeri, Hanson, and McCormick 2002, 258). This is an important addendum to the standard labor-market-driven finding that skilled and well-educated U.S. voters are less anti-immigration, while unskilled and poorly educated voters are more anti-immigration. After

all, if the skilled and educated median voter in rich countries has nothing to fear from unskilled immigrant workers, then the median voter
ought to be happier the more unskilled the immigrant. Happier, that
is, if only labor markets matter, but much less happy if welfare
burdens matter. Indeed, welfare burdens offer one explanation for the
secular rise in anti-immigration feeling in the United States, a rise that
is highly correlated with the decline in immigrant skill levels (relative
to those of the native-born) and the shift in immigrant origins as poor
Third World countries have increasingly come to dominate U.S. immigration (chapter 15). However, that shift in immigrant origin may also
touch off anti-immigrant attitudes based on culture and race. This issue
is revisited later in the chapter, but it is relevant to note that first, the
same rise in U.S. anti-immigrant attitudes took place in the late nineteenth century, when immigrant quality fell as new immigrants from
poorer parts of Europe increased in importance, and second, all of this
took place when there was no welfare state for the immigrant to abuse
or exploit. If race and culture were at work a century ago, before the
rise of the welfare state, it seems very likely that they are at work today, although motives may be masked by the presence of the welfare
state.

Anna Maria Mayda (2003) and Kevin O'Rourke (2003; O'Rourke and
Sinnott 2004) have extended these findings for the United States to the
world at large, or at least to the twenty-four countries underlying the
1995 ISSP sample. Both scholars confirm the Heckscher-Ohlin and
factor-proportions analysis predictions: the more educated and skilled
are median voters in rich countries, the more liberal are country attitudes toward immigration; the more educated and skilled are median
voters in poor countries, the less liberal are country attitudes toward
immigration. They also confirm predictions of the Roy model:[4] ceteris
paribus, the more unequal are incomes in a rich, high-skilled country,
the more anti-immigrant are median voters; the less unequal are
incomes in a rich, high-skilled country, the less anti-immigrant are median voters (O'Rourke 2003; O'Rourke and Sinnott 2004).

Attitude and Policy Asymmetries: Migration versus Trade and Capital Markets

These empirical studies offer powerful support for the view that
economic interests matter in determining anti-immigrant attitudes. But
they also reveal a puzzling attitude and policy asymmetry. The bar-

riers to trade are far lower than are the barriers to migration, and barriers to international capital movements are lower still (Hillman and Weiss 1999, 77; Bordo, Taylor, and Williamson 2003), even though trade, migration, and movements of international capital are all relevant to a nation's economic interests. This asymmetry seems all the more puzzling given that standard Heckscher-Ohlin trade theory predicts that trade is a substitute for factor mobility and that "free trade has the same consequences for wages ... of rich countries as a direct movement of workers between poor and rich countries" (Wellisch and Walz 1998, 1596). Voters who are protectionist should also be anti-immigration, and free trade voters should also be proimmigration. Indeed, the theory implies that "protection without immigration restrictions will not work, since protection without immigration restrictions will simply lead to more immigration; immigration barriers without protection will not work, since immigration barriers on their own will simply lead to more trade" (O'Rourke 2003, 6, following Mundell 1957).

So why is there such an asymmetry in public attitudes toward trade and migration? Table 16.1 suggests that anti-trade sentiment today is less intense than anti-immigrant sentiment. While she finds that anti-trade and anti-immigration sentiments are correlated when she controls for other influences, Mayda (2003) has shown that voters are more protrade than proimmigration and less antitrade than anti-immigration: "the country-specific percentages of respondents in favor of trade are much higher than for immigration. [Yet] the two variables are also positively and significantly correlated.... This evidence is consistent with the intuition that a few common factors affect both types of preferences, while some of the forces at work in anti-immigration attitudes are absent or softened in the case of trade" (29). The OECD has become staunchly free trade since World War II, but it remains restrictionist regarding immigration. Furthermore, the European settler countries in the Americas and in Oceania were among the most protectionist in the world between 1860 and World War I (Williamson 2005), yet they all maintained open and unrestricted immigration policies.

Why the asymmetry in policy regarding immigration and trade? There are three answers to this question. First, the Heckscher-Ohlin model greatly oversimplifies the labor market issue in regard to immigration. Some goods (or, more accurately, services) are not traded, and this fact influences public attitudes. Thus, "workers in non-traded sectors feel shielded from foreign competition working through trade but not from labor market competition from immigrants" (Mayda 2003, 29). Some observers feel that this is likely to be an important factor explaining asymmetry in attitudes toward trade and immigration (Faini 2002), and Mayda offers some evidence in support of this view. Second, culture, prejudice, and nativism may also tip the median voter toward greater hostility toward immigrants, adding to the gap between attitudes toward trade and immigrants. (We save the role of culture for the next section. We also save for the last section an explanation for the gap between immigration policy and immigration attitudes in which we examine whether the median-voter model really reflects the way democracies always resolve conflicts in attitudes across voters and interest groups.) Third, labor market competition is only one of two economic factors that matter in regard to immigration attitudes and immigration policy, the other, of course, being fiscal burden.

Apparently the addition of the fiscal burden dimension tips the median voter toward more anti-immigrant views: "The basic difference between free trade and free migration is that the former ... does not change the international allocation of skilled residents as recipients of welfare programs while the latter increases the number of unskilled residents in rich countries.... Hence, the costs of redistribution programs for rich countries are higher in the free migration case. It is therefore not surprising that [voters in] rich countries prefer free trade over free migration" (Wellisch and Walz 1998, 1597). Analysts have shown that the new (low-quality) immigrants have relatively high rates of welfare reliance and thus that immigration places a net fiscal burden on host countries (Borjas 1999b, 190). Voters seem to understand this fact. According to the 1997 Eurobarometer survey, from 40 to 70 percent of respondents in eight countries believed that immigrants abused the welfare system (Austria, Belgium, Britain, Denmark, Finland, France, Germany, and Sweden), while the percentage ranged from 30 to 40 in the remaining five (Ireland, Italy, the Netherlands, Portugal, and Spain). This welfare burden belief also rose with the foreign-born share (Boeri, Hanson, and McCormick 2002, 113–114). American respondents felt the same way when interviewed in 1992, especially toward new immigrants from Asia and Latin America: 89 percent of respondents thought it was likely that Hispanic immigrants would raise respondents' taxes through an increase in immigrant demands for public services, and 79 percent thought this was also true of Asian immigrants (Boeri, Hanson, and McCormick 2002, 254).

Finally, note that the addition of the welfare burden issue helps explain why anti-immigration attitudes are harsher in Europe than in the United States (table 16.1). While there is a degree of anti-immigrant attitude everywhere in the OECD, the attitude appears to be most hostile in the more-committed welfare states, just as one would expect.

Cultural Preference, Immigrant Quality, and Prejudice

As noted earlier in the chapter, culture, racism, and nativism influence anti-immigrant attitudes too. Indeed, existing studies find that prejudice against those of a different race and culture is the *most* important influence on attitudes toward immigrants (Boeri, Hanson, and McCormick 2002, 120; O'Rourke and Sinnott 2004, 19; Mayda 2003, 24–28), especially when immigrants are concentrated within communities rather than being dispersed. Thus, when the sources of increasing European anti-immigration attitudes between 1988 and 1997 are decomposed, only about 12 percent of the increase can be attributed to changing economic characteristics of the respondents over time, that is, to a changing share of unemployed, skilled, and educated (Gang, Rivera-Batiz, and Yun 2002, 23–25). The residual, a very big 88 percent, can be attributed to rising anti-immigrant hostility on the part of all respondents across all economic attributes. Regardless, then, of education, skill, and employment status, Europeans collectively underwent rising anti-immigrant sentiment over the decade between the late 1980s and the late 1990s. The educated displayed increasing hostility toward immigrants. Employed and salaried workers displayed increasing hostility. Even the self-employed and retired displayed increasing hostility.

The correlation between ethnic concentration (in gateway communities) and anti-immigrant attitudes has been a favorite hypothesis in the literature for some time. As Christian Dustmann and Ian Preston (2001) remind us, the association is theoretically ambiguous "since high ethnic concentration may, by way of creating a perception of threat and alienation, exacerbate hostility towards minorities. Intergroup contacts may, on the other side, reduce intergroup conflicts, by way of reducing unrealistic negative perceptions of one another" (370). On the other hand, when immigrants move into a locality, they tend to push others out, and those pushed out are most likely to be those least tolerant of immigrants. When the empirical analysis is done properly (controlling for mobility), high concentrations of ethnic minorities in

England (Asian and West Indian minorities in particular) are shown to
lead to more hostile attitudes. The debate has yet to be resolved, however, since quite the opposite has been shown to hold for the United
States, where "regional-level contact [in gateways] seems to decrease
...dislike for immigrants" (Fetzer 2000, 106). Until more studies consistently control for the selectivity of interregional mobility, the debate
will probably remain unresolved.

This so-called contact and concentration literature faces many problems. It is important, for one thing, to distinguish between workplace
and neighborhood proximity (Fetzer 2000, 135). It is also important,
for another, to control for immigrants' length of time in the host country, quality, and assimilation experience, a set of controls that suggest
how economic factors may indirectly influence race, culture, and nativism. Natives tend to welcome warmly immigrant groups whose origin,
culture, and quality approximate those of the host country population.
Natives tend to be more hostile toward immigrant groups which are
different. This was certainly true of U.S. immigration experience over
the century before the 1920s: the rising share of new immigrants and
the decline in their quality provoked increasingly hostile attitudes that
eventually produced the quotas that were instituted to keep out low-
quality immigrants (and succeeded in doing so). It appears that the
same has been true in the United States over the past four decades.
When U.S. respondents were asked in 1965 which immigrant groups
they preferred (revealingly, Africans were not on the list), 28 percent
answered Canadian, another 28 percent answered English or Scottish,
17 percent answered German, 7 percent answered Italian, and some
answered other old immigrant groups. Those from Mexico were named
only 5 percent, and those from Asia and the Middle East were hardly
mentioned at all. As immigrant origin shifted toward Mexico, Central
America, South America, and Asia and as the quality of immigrants
declined, the cultural gap between foreign migrants and the native-
born became larger and larger. Assimilation became increasingly difficult, and anti-immigrant attitudes were correlated with it. Britain
seems to have experienced the same problem with Asian and West
Indian immigrants, not unlike similar race and culture problems witnessed on the European continent.

If our interpretation is correct and if rising ethnic prejudice is closely
related to shifting sources of immigrants, then the future of immigration attitudes does not look too bright, since what has been happening

to immigrant quality over the past quarter century is likely to persist over the next quarter century.[5]

Why Does the OECD Have an Expansionary Bias?

Immigration policy does not seem to reflect public opinion. When the U.S. Congress passed the 1990 Immigration Act—a liberal act which increased legal immigration by almost 40 percent—a Roper poll taken just four months earlier had reported that the majority of American voters opposed increased immigration (Lee 1998, 4). Senator Alan Simpson's restrictive immigration bills of 1996 had strong popular support, but they were defeated in Congress (Lee 1998, 78). As figure 16.1 shows, between 1953 and 1997, the share opposing immigration among U.S. voters surveyed never fell below 40 percent, and at one point the share rose above 70 percent. Why do rich countries accept so many immigrants when their citizens do not want them? How is it possible for a democracy to aggregate over voters' strong anti-immigrant preferences and enact policies that still admit large and rising immigrant numbers (Boeri, Hanson, and McCormick 2002, 262)?

One view believes that the answer lies in the political structure itself. The proponents of this view argue that the executive and especially the public service bureaucracy tends to be more educated, more liberal, and thus less anti-immigrant than the median voter. The argument is most compelling for countries where the executive is powerful relative to the legislature. For Australia, it has been suggested that the lack of policy toughening in the face of the dramatic increase in anti-immigrant sentiment between 1961 and 1988 was due to the rise of the educated (and largely public sector) elite (Betts 1988). For Britain, it has been argued that "throughout the postwar period British policymakers were, taken as a whole, more liberal than the public to which they owed their office" (Hansen 2000, vi). There are, however, two reasons for thinking that this factor can explain little of the apparent proimmigration bias. One has to do with a time series argument. The steep increase in Australian anti-immigrant sentiment between 1968 and 1972 was followed by sharp cuts in the immigration target by the incoming Whitlam government in response to pubic opinion in key marginal electorates (Money 1999, 192). Similarly, in the French election of 1974 and the British election of 1979, the rise of anti-immigrant sentiment and the associated rise of minority parties caused the mainstream parties to respond by toughening their immigration policies sharply.[6] As we have argued throughout this book, such shifts in opinion take time to influence policy, and they are often driven by the rise of fringe parties whose policies subsequently become absorbed into the mainstream. The second reason for doubting that greater liberality of public servants explains proimmigrant bias arises from a cross-section. Where immigration quotas or work permits are controlled by administrative order, immigration policies should be more open than in countries where control lies with the legislature. Yet this does not seem to be the case. Policy in France, Germany, and the United States is no less proimmigration than it is in Britain, Canada and Australia.

The standard resolution of the gap between voter attitudes and government policy comes from the theory of collective action and interest group or client politics (Olson 1965; Wilson 1980; Freeman 1995). Thus, if the benefits from a given policy are concentrated in a small group and if the cost of monitoring each member's contribution to lobbying is low, then this group will be much more successful in its lobbying efforts than any large group with diffuse interests for whom there is a free-riding problem (Boeri, Hanson, and McCormick 2002, 263). Groups of taxpayers (concerned about the welfare implications of additional low-quality immigrants), unskilled workers (who feel threatened in their labor market), racists (who dislike foreigners), and nativists (who place high value on cultural homogeneity) (Hillman 1993; Hillman and Weiss 1999) are all too diffuse and beset with free riders. Interest groups with strong lobbying commitments will dominate under those circumstances, and the interest groups favoring immigration are quite obvious: labor-intensive business interests in agriculture, manufacturing, and services (Lee 1998; Boeri, Hanson, and McCormick 2002, 262–272).

One would think that the theory of interest group politics could be applied to *any* political issue, but the evidence is quite clear that the gap between public attitude and government policy is far greater for immigration issues than it is for war, inflation, unemployment, gun control, and abortion. What makes immigration so different? The answer lies in three additional realities: family reunification, asylum seekers, and illegal immigrants.

Family reunification is a cornerstone of most if not all OECD immigration policies, but nowhere is it more generous or is "family" defined more broadly than in the United States. Chapter 8 showed that this has been true since the Quota Acts of the 1920s. Thus, family reunification serves to augment total immigration by a large factor, softening much of the restrictive intent of immigration legislation. Family reunification has also been skillfully exploited by proimmigration interests to deflect the political impact of anti-immigration public attitudes or even to suppress anti-immigrant political debate. Consider three excerpts from speeches given by the proimmigration forces that defeated Senator Simpson's restrictionist immigration bills in 1996 (quoted in Lee 1998, 132–133):

In a Congress which heralds family values as its prevailing theme, this bill is extreme antifamily legislation. Restrictions to family reunification in this bill ensure that American families may be forever separated from their loved ones. (Representative Nancy Pelosi).

[The proposed bill will] hurt family reunification efforts and show the hypocrisy of a Congress that promotes family values. (Representative Robert Menendez).

At a time when strong family bonds are more important than ever, restrictions in family based immigration will hurt legal immigrant families in America. (Representative Sheila Jackson-Lee).

Since even anti-immigration voters are lenient when it comes to family reunification (Lee 1998, 134), the proimmigration interests use it to deflect debate away from primary immigrant quotas without fear of backlash at the polling place. In contrast, family immigration in Europe has always been a right rather than the result of a quota. Immigrants who entered the country to reunite with family members may have been unanticipated and unwanted, but they were given the legal right to enter in the postcolonial era decades ago (Joppke 1998, 280–290).

Attitudes are even more positive toward genuine refugees: those who have a "well founded fear of persecution" in the origin country (table 16.1). The 1951 Geneva Convention on Refugees defines what could in principle be an unlimited number of genuine refugees and provides them with rights of access to countries of refuge. But the convention was signed under circumstances that are very different from those prevailing today. The surge of asylum seekers can be seen as the long-term (and unintended) consequence of a policy that was framed at a time when the few who managed to escape from communist eastern Europe were welcomed by the West. Even in 1967, when protection was extended to asylum seekers from outside Europe, policymakers could not have anticipated the flood of asylum applications that rose to a crescendo in the early 1990s. As chapter 13 showed, the policy backlash was dramatic, but by the time a tougher regime came into effect, the cumulative forces pushing the number of asylum seekers upward had gained a momentum of their own. As a result, asylum policy ended up being tougher than it would have been had it been introduced before these cumulative effects had gained the upper hand.

While attitudes toward genuine refugees remain strongly positive, attitudes toward those *claiming* to be refugees have become increasingly negative as the number has increased—and for three familiar reasons. First, many Europeans believe that the majority of those who apply for asylum are economic migrants, an opinion that is increasingly validated by policies which reject the overwhelming majority of applicants for asylum. Second, the perception has been growing that a significant proportion of asylum seekers, whether they are given refugee status or not, end up as a burden on the welfare state. An April 27, 2000, headline in the British *Daily Star*—"Hello Mr Sponger...Need Any Benefits?"—is just one example of the backlash in popular attitudes that has resulted from this perception. Third, the fact that about half of those applying for asylum in a given country have entered the country illegally and that about half of those whose applications are rejected end up staying illegally add further fuel to the unpopularity of asylum seekers. This result is, of course, at least partially self-fulfilling, as the progressive toughening of policy has driven more potential asylum seekers underground and converted a refugee issue into an illegal immigrant issue.

Illegal immigration offers the third explanation as to why immigrants are "unwanted". It is a myth that Europe and the United States have lost control over their borders. Illegal immigration in the United States is the endogenous result of three policy-related forces set in motion in the 1960s and 1970s (Joppke 1998, 272–280; Lee 1998, 13, 28–31, 55–59): the ending in 1964 of the *bracero* guestworker program, which had since World War II supplied western states with cheap foreign fruit and vegetable pickers; the setting of a ceiling of 120,000 on visas for immigrants from the Western Hemisphere in 1965, when the region had been exempt from immigration quotas before; and, also in 1965, the 20,000 annual limit on visas to those from Western Hemisphere countries, thereby creating enormous excess demand from contiguous Mexico. This was the first of four ingredients of a recipe ensuring an inevitable surge in illegal immigration. The second ingredient was to impose only modest sanctions on employers of illegals and then to fail to enforce even those. The third ingredient was to offer amnesties to previous illegal immigrants who wished to become legal, thus giving incentive for more illegals to follow. The fourth ingredient was to reject national identity cards as inconsistent with democracy. All four of these ingredients contributed to soaring illegal immigration, in addition to the fundamentals pushing up the demand for emigration from the Third World. They also gave the proimmigration groups another opportunity to deflect needed debate away from the size of the desired immigrant flow and focus it instead on the illegals that were cheating the system, jumping the queue, stealing jobs, and becoming a public burden.

There is a large gap between the number of immigrants that the OECD voters want and the number their governments accept, and the gap is widening (Cornelius, Martin, and Hollifield 1994). Family reunification, asylum, and illegal immigration, together with interest group politics, make it difficult to have a public debate about the number of immigrants voters want and how to achieve it, especially when those who favor smaller numbers and higher-quality immigrants have to face rhetorical charges of racism, antifamily values, and lack of humanitarian conscience.

Debate over immigration policy has gotten more intense in recent years, and much of it seems to adopt the view that policy is failing in the face of mounting migration pressure. Debate about asylum policy has become especially fierce. These policy debates have been more polarizing than most, and they have been exploited by extremist parties. Meanwhile, centrist governments have responded to the rising political temperature with increasing policy activism. The volume of new migration legislation increased fourfold between the 1970s and the 1990s (United Nations 2002a, 22). While much of this new legislation has aimed at restricting immigration—particularly of asylum seekers and illegal immigrants—some of it has dealt with the development of new entry channels for both highly skilled permanent migrants and unskilled temporary migrants.

In the last chapter, we emphasized the political constraints on international migration. But consider for a moment what might happen if those constraints were relaxed and a significant liberalization took place. How much migration would there be? How much would the liberalization of immigration policies advance the welfare of the world as a whole? What immigration policies would need to be adopted to achieve the highest welfare? How would the benefits and costs of such policies be distributed between workers and employers in source and destination countries and the migrants themselves? Political realities suggest an additional question: what policies would maximize the gain for the winners, but minimize the pain for the losers, in the host country? Our ultimate aim here is to canvas a number of policy alternatives, but to restrict the discussion to those alternatives that past and present realities tell us are feasible. To equip us for the discussion, we start by returning to a question raised many times in this book, namely, who gains from migration, who loses, and by how much?

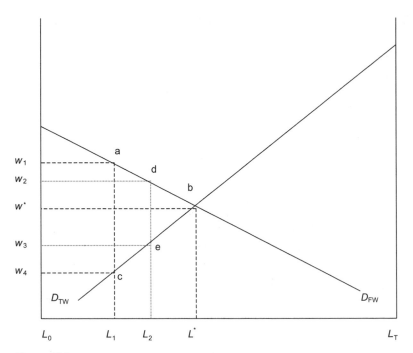

Figure 17.1
Global gains from migration

Winners and Losers: How Big Are the Stakes?

In a classic paper written more than twenty years ago, Bob Hamilton and John Whalley (1984) argued that more-permissive immigration policies could deliver massive welfare gains to the world as a whole. Their analysis is captured in figure 17.1, in which the world is assumed to have just two parts, say, the First World and the Third World. The labor demand curve for the First World (D_{FW}) slopes downward to the right, while the labor demand curve for the Third World (D_{TW}) slopes downward to the left. Total world labor supply is the width of the open box where $L_1 - L_0$ are those located in the First World and $L_T - L_1$ are the remainder located in the Third World. Wages are much higher in the First World (w_1) than they are the Third World (w_4). Now consider reallocating labor from the Third World to the First World until the point L^* is reached where wages are equated at w^*. First World wage earners each lose an amount $w_1 - w^*$, while Third World emigrants *and* those who stay behind each gain $w^* - w_4$. Assuming for the moment no world capital mobility, profits (or rents) rise in the First World and fall in the Third World. The welfare gain for the world as a whole is the area marked out by the triangle *abc*.

Figure 17.1 leads to a number of economic inferences worth noting. Consider first some important policy implications of the geometry. First, suppose that instead of moving to the free migration equilibrium allocation L^*, the First World retained enough immigration controls so that the world moved only halfway to the free migration point, that is, to L_2. The gains for the world as a whole would certainly be smaller, but they would amount to *three-quarters* of the total gains in this simple two-region model with linear demand curves (the area *adec* is three-quarters of the area *abc*). Moving just a tenth of the way to L^* yields almost a fifth of the total available welfare gain. Thus, even a marginal loosening in immigration controls could have very large payoffs for the world as a whole. Immigration restrictions do not have to disappear completely for significant world income gains to be achieved.

Second, note that the biggest gainers by far are the migrants themselves, and they have no vote over immigration policy in the host country. In the loosening-only-halfway (L_2) scenario, each migrant gains $w_2 - w_4$. The nonemigrating Third World stayers gain something too, $w_3 - w_4$, and they don't have a vote in the host country either. Employers in the Third World end up losing profits of w_3ecw_4, but they also don't have a vote. So who has the vote? Native-born workers in the First World do, and they end up losing $w_1 - w_2$. Employers in the First World do, and their profits increase by w_1adw_2.

Third, note the political implications of the slope of the demand curves. The flatter is the derived labor demand curve in the First World, the smaller are the losses to the native-born residents there as a result of immigration and the bigger are the gains to the migrants; conversely, the steeper is the derived labor demand curve in the Third World, the greater are the gains resulting from emigration for the stayers left behind and the bigger the gains to the migrants. This geometry is central to any policy assessment. The smaller are the losses to First World workers and the larger are the gains to movers from and stayers in the Third World, the more likely some compensation mechanism can be found that could bribe First World workers to accept more immigrants. So is there an asymmetry in the absorptive capacity for labor between host First World and source Third World? Are the derived labor demand curves in fact anything like what this asymmetry implies, or are they pretty much the same as they are drawn in figure 17.1? It matters.

How big is that triangle? Hamilton and Walley set out to estimate the welfare gain from migration that changes the world distribution of labor from L_1 to L^*. They estimated for 1977 that with perfect labor mobility, where wage rates are everywhere equalized, world GNP would have doubled from such migration. If such estimates seem huge, it is largely because they are based on ludicrously infeasible migrations patterns. Figure 17.1 makes that clear, since at L^* the population in the First World is dramatically increased. Furthermore, this simple experiment ignores the very real costs associated with long-distance moves. Even a return to the unrestricted migration policies of the first global century would not serve to equalize real wages worldwide.

More-recent research has qualified the experiment and thus produced smaller gains. Thus, Jonathan Moses and Bjørn Letnes (2003) estimate 1998 world net gains from migration that would have changed the world distribution of labor from L_1 to L^* at 3.4 trillion dollars or 9.6 percent of world GNP. How is it that Hamilton and Whalley estimate a doubling for 1977 while Moses and Letnes estimate only a tenth of that for 1998? Some of the difference has to do with the underlying models (e.g., a two-region versus a three-region world), and some of it has to do with underlying data, but most of it has to do with the assumed attributes of the migrants: Moses and Letnes assume that the migrants' labor participation rates are smaller and that the labor efficiency gains from their move are much smaller. Still, the Moses and Letnes three-region calculation implies a fall of 3.1 percent in the wages of First World nonmigrants, a rise of 2.1 percent in those of Second World nonmigrants, and a rise of 11.4 percent in those of Third World nonmigrants. Thus, liberal immigration policies like this would contribute quite a bit to worldwide wage convergence.

It is important, however, to emphasize that maximizing welfare gains for the world as a whole would require an enormous transfer of labor, the likes of which the world has never seen and is likely never to see. Recall that during the height of the unrestricted mass migration between 1870 and 1910, the immense emigration from Europe served to lower population there by "only" 11 percent and the labor force by "only" 13 percent. The same mass migration served to raise populations in the New World by "only" 29 percent and labor forces by "only" 40 percent over those four decades (table 6.2). To imagine a modern counterfactual mass migration greater than 40 percent of the OECD population or greater than 13 percent of the Third World population seems silly, even giving the world four decades to do it. History simply will not support such policy counterfactuals: even returning to the free and unrestricted mass migrations of a century ago would not get the modern global economy even halfway to L^* by 2050.

Still, it is worth stressing that the gains from moving only a small part of the way to a fully integrated world labor market could be very large, as we have already illustrated by reference to figure 17.1. To illustrate with another example, a partial liberalization that reduced the wage gaps by just 10 percent would deliver 23 percent of the maximum gains—or 774 billion U.S. dollars, a figure that is 11.8 times the world's official funding for development (e.g., unilateral and mulitlateral aid in 2000; Moses and Letnes 2003, 13). However, to reduce wage gaps by "only" 10 percent would still require the transfer of 432 million people to the First World, numbers that would almost double the First World population, requiring a transfer that would be about three times what took place in the age of free migration a century ago.

These estimates are based on very simple models of the world economy, and it is easy to criticize them as naïve and their counterfactuals as politically unrealistic and inconsistent with history. The models assume only two factors, capital and labor; they ignore skills, land, and natural resources; they assume world capital immobility; and they do not account for adjustments through international trade. Using instead a general equilibrium model that distinguishes between skilled and unskilled labor, allows for intermediate goods, and permits international trade, Terrie Walmsley and Alan Winters (2004) estimate that a transfer of sixteen million workers (eight million skilled and eight million unskilled) from the rest of the world to the OECD (adding about 3 percent to the OECD labor force[1]) would raise world GDP by $156 billion, or about 0.6 percent.[2] That is hardly a doubling, but it is still a substantial amount, given that it involves a transfer of only half a percent of the world's labor force. Such a transfer would precipitate a 1 percent fall in skilled wages and a 0.6 percent fall in unskilled wages in the OECD, while it would precipitate a 5 percent rise in skilled wages and 0.1 percent rise in unskilled wages in the less-developed source countries. The 0.1 percent gain to the unskilled nonmovers in source countries may seem tiny, but remember that eight million unskilled migrants would also be a tiny share of the unskilled workforce in Africa and Asia.[3]

Could not the same (or perhaps even greater) world efficiency gains be achieved through trade, without involving all the social and financial costs associated with massive migrations? In the simple two-good, two-factor trade model, migration and trade are perfect substitutes. Under that extreme assumption, all the gains could be reaped through free trade without either migration or capital flows. But reality is very different (Collins, O'Rourke, and Williamson 1999): given transport costs and nontradables, "free" trade cannot be achieved even through the most liberal policy; there are specific factors such as land and natural resources involved that matter; and there are very large world differences in total factor productivity. Total factor productivity in the First World is about five times that of the Third World and about three times that of the Second World (Acemoglu and Zilibotti 2001; Hendricks 2002). Even with unified world prices, trade cannot do as much work as migration can, essentially because productivity differences are country-specific. The gains from migration arise largely from shifting people from places where their productivity is low to places where their productivity is high—something that trade cannot achieve.[4] In their multiregion general equilibrium model, Walmsley and Winters (2004, 19) estimate that the world income gains from removing all remaining trade restrictions would be $104 billion. Thus, the gains from abolishing *all* trade barriers would be only two-thirds as large as those that would flow from a much more modest liberalization in the barriers to migration.

What about capital mobility? All economic models predict that immigration will raise the return on capital in the host countries, where labor is scarce compared to capital, while emigration will reduce it in sending countries, where labor is abundant compared to capital. In the absence of restrictions, therefore, capital should chase after labor from the Third World to the First (as it did from Europe to the New World in the nineteenth century). This would attenuate the losses to native labor in the First World and to local capital in the Third World, and it would attenuate the gains to local capital in the First World and to nonmigrant labor remaining in the Third World (Klein and Ventura 2003). For the world as a whole, the gains would be much larger if capital is mobile than if it is not. If there are only two factors, then world gains would be maximized only when the Third World had emptied out and all labor and all capital had migrated to the First World where productivity is highest.

The discussion so far has assumed that the removal of restrictive immigration policy in the OECD would be sufficient to yield a new distribution of world labor in which wages were everywhere the same. Yet we know this would not be true, as history has shown. Even in the

absence of immigration controls, migration is not sufficiently responsive to wage gaps to cause wage equalization. Most people require
Smithian compensation to move away from home, and many additional factors mute any migration response: transport costs, poverty
traps, and the size of the young-adult cohort who do most of the moving, among others. Still, more-liberal immigration policies would produce greater responses over time as poverty traps were gradually
unlocked in the sending countries and the cumulative impact of
friends-and-relatives networks was allowed to magnify the effects of
the fundamentals.

Three main lessons can be seen clearly from these global calculations. First, the gains from liberalization of immigration policies are
potentially large for the world as a whole, but so are the migrations
necessary to realize them. Second, substantial gains could be reaped
from smaller migrations, but even these involve much higher migration rates than current ones and, in many cases, rates even higher than
those achieved a century ago when mass migrations were unrestricted
by policy. Third, and perhaps most important, the losses suffered by
existing workers in the developed world would be small relative to
the worldwide gains and especially relative to the gains that would be
realized by the migrants themselves.

OECD Population Aging and Replacement Migration

One of the most pressing problems facing OECD countries is population aging. The first column of table 17.1 uses UN forecasts to provide
some sense of the magnitude of the problem as it will evolve over the
next half century in the United States and the European Union. The
elderly support ratio, calculated as the ratio of the population aged fifteen to sixty-four to the population aged sixty-five and over, is a useful
statistic for summarizing those demographic trends. Unless behavior,
institutions, and policy all change, the elderly support ratio in the European Union will fall to half of its 2000 level by 2050, a spectacular decline. Furthermore, more than half of that fall will have taken place by
2025, just two decades away. Again, unless behavior, institutions, and
policy all change, the fall will be equally dramatic in the United States,
and once again, more than half of that decline will have taken place
only two decades from today.

While aging populations have produced and will produce a variety
of important economic effects, the main concern emerging from public

Table 17.1
UN estimates of replacement migration, 2000–2050

Year	Actual forecast	Zero immigra- tion	Constant total population	Constant age group 15–64	Constant ratio 15–64 to 65+
European Union (15 countries)					
Total population (millions)					
2000	375.3	372.4	372.4	372.7	400.1
2025	367.3	354.5	372.4	394.6	641.1
2050	331.3	310.9	372.4	418.5	1228.3
Elderly support ratio (population aged 15–64/population aged 64+)					
2000	4.08	4.06	4.06	4.06	4.31
2025	2.73	2.66	2.78	2.94	4.31
2050	1.96	1.89	2.21	2.41	4.31
Total support ratio (population aged 15–64/population aged 0–14 and 65+)					
2000	3.02	3.02	3.02	3.02	3.05
2025	2.68	2.66	2.69	2.72	2.98
2050	2.31	2.28	2.39	2.47	2.89
Immigration per annum (thousands)					
2000–2025	210	0	612	1380	8556
2000–2050	270	0	1287	1795	18404
United States					
Total population (millions)					
2000	278.3	274.3	274.3	274.3	274.5
2025	325.6	296.6	296.6	308.4	566.9
2050	349.3	290.6	297.8	315.6	1065.2
Elderly support ratio (population aged 15–64/population aged 64+)					
2000	5.28	5.21	5.21	5.21	5.21
2025	3.34	3.09	3.09	3.20	5.21
2050	2.82	2.57	2.63	2.74	5.21
Total support ratio (population aged 15–64/population aged 0–14 and 65+)					
2000	2.94	2.93	2.93	2.93	2.93
2025	2.70	2.64	2.64	2.66	2.92
2050	2.58	2.50	2.52	2.56	3.02
Immigration per annum (thousands)					
2000–2025	760	0	255	288	14309
2000–2050	760	0	218	359	11851

Source: United Nations 2000b (75, 88).
Note: Forecasts are based on the medium variant forecasts of the UN Population Division's 1998 revision of *World Population Prospects* (United Nations 1999).

debate seems to be a growing fiscal burden on a dwindling working population. It has been suggested by many that one way to mute the economic impact of OECD aging would be to let in more immigrants, thereby supplying more labor to the nontradable service sector consumed by the elderly and helping to avert the pension crisis that looms large for those countries with pay-as-you-go systems. Even for those countries with more-solvent pension systems, public expenditures on health, social security, and other entitlements are also projected to increase, raising the tax burden on a shrinking share of those working. Based on its 1998 population forecasts, the United Nations (2000b) has assessed the effects of different migration scenarios on the size and age structure of OECD populations. Its estimates for the European Union and the United States are reported in table 17.1. If net immigration is assumed to remain much the same as in the recent past, the elderly support ratio in the European Union falls from 4.1 in 2000 to 2.0 in 2050 and that in the United States falls from 5.3 to 2.8. If zero net immigration is assumed, implying a successful shutting down of OECD borders, the support ratio falls even more: to 1.9 for the European Union and 2.6 for the United States. A comparison of these two projections is itself revealing: current rates of immigration into the OECD will do very little to erase the spectacular impact of aging over the next half century. Thus, the fall in the elderly support ratio would be pretty much the same with current immigration rates continuing as it would be in a future without any immigration at all. An anti-immigration backlash even bigger than that of the interwar years would hardly make the fall in the elderly support ratio any bigger. And *much* bigger immigration rates would be necessary for immigration to have a significant impact on what has come to be called "replacement."

What immigration policies *would* stem the aging crisis? To maintain a constant total population at its projected peak over the half century (reached in 2000 for the European Union and in 2030 for the United States), net immigration would need to increase substantially above that forecast for the European Union, but the net immigration needed would be lower than that forecast for the United States. More to the point, to keep the fifteen-to-sixty-four age group constant in absolute numbers, immigration to the European Union would need to be 1.4 million per annum in 2000–2025 and 1.8 million per annum in 2025–2050, *six to eight times* the actual forecasts. The required immigration needed to keep the numbers of people aged fifteen to sixty-four constant in the United Sates, however, would still fall below the actual forecast. So far, it appears that the EU faces a far more pressing aging problem, for which feasible immigration trends will offer far less effective solutions, than the United States. Now consider the most relevant measure of the aging problem, the elderly support ratio. In order to keep the elderly support ratio constant at its 2000 level—4.3 for the European Union and 5.2 for the United States—a massive influx of immigrants would be required. Net U.S. immigration would need to be 14.3 million per annum in 2000–2025 and 11.9 million per annum in 2025–2050, roughly *fifteen times* that based on current rates. Net EU immigration would have to be even higher, 8.6 million and 18.4 million per annum, *forty to almost seventy times* the immigration flows projected according to current rates. The implied replacement immigration is certainly very high in both cases, but also note that it must *increase* over time for the European Union. There are two reasons for this: the immigrant arrivals need to be a multiple of the rapidly growing over-65 cohorts, and immigrants themselves age, so that ever larger injections are necessary to keep the elderly support ratio constant.

The OECD's demographic future seems much less dire if we look instead at the *total* support ratio—the population aged fifteen to sixty-four relative to the sum of those under fifteen and over sixty-five—since while the share over sixty-four rises, the share under fifteen falls. Thus, the UN forecasts have the EU total support ratio falling from 3.0 to 2.3 over the fifty years and the U.S. ratio falling from 2.9 to 2.6. It is commonly believed that the elderly support ratio is more relevant than the total support ratio from a fiscal point of view, since it is believed that the public cost of an elderly person is two to two-and-a-half times larger than that of a child. On the other hand, while the elderly can reduce their public cost by postponing retirement and working part-time after retirement, children have no way of reducing their public cost. In any case, immigration does not help diminish the fall in the total support ratio much either, except in the most extreme immigration scenario, depicted in the last column of table 17.1.

These forecasts have been interpreted to imply that immigration is not and will not be the solution to population aging. Certainly it cannot be the *only* solution, but it can make a significant contribution as part of a wider set of solutions that include pension reform, later retirement, and higher part-time labor participation by the older cohorts. In addition, declining child cohorts will reduce the demand for non-market household labor, an event that should help counterbalance the expansion of the elderly-care sector. Furthermore, unskilled immigrants caring for young children and elderly parents could serve to release skilled native-born labor from home to market work (Kremer and Watt 2004), an event which could have a positive fiscal effect.

Some immigrants help more than others. The effects of different immigration scenarios on fiscal balance have been estimated up to 2040 for the United States (Storesletten 2000; see also Lee and Miller 1997), while they have been estimated up to 2100 for Japan, the European Union, and the United States combined (Fehr et al. 2003; Fehr, Jokisch, and Kotlikoff 2004a, 2004b). The simulations through which these estimate have been obtained use a dynamic, overlapping-generations, general equilibrium framework that takes into account the effects of immigration on wage rates, interest rates and accumulation rates as well as its net fiscal effects.

Let's consider the U.S. studies first (Storesletten 2000). Immigration could in principle avert a tax hike of 4.4 percent of GDP that would otherwise be required on current fiscal projections. Averting such a tax increase would require an annual intake of 1.8 million high-skilled emigrants, although the number could be somewhat fewer if they entered without families. Chapter 14 showed that the fiscal effects of immigration depend on who the immigrants are; it is not just their numbers, but also their attributes, that matter. The more children permanent immigrants bring with them (or subsequently acquire), the lower is the long-run fiscal benefit to the host economy. And no amount of unskilled and illegal immigrants could make a positive contribution to the fiscal balance in the long run, except if unskilled and illegal immigration allows skilled native-born workers to shift from home to market work, as we suggested earlier.

The United States has a more-favorable demographic structure than does the European Union. Hence, while the immigration levels required to plug the fiscal gap are large, they are not implausibly large (table 17.1). The United States also has a much smaller welfare state than the European Union. EU countries with much larger welfare states will not close their demographically induced fiscal gaps through any politically plausible levels of immigration. Domestic reforms will therefore be more urgent in reducing these gaps. Nevertheless, even a country like Sweden could get significant net fiscal benefits from immigration, especially if the immigrants are temporary, are aged between twenty and thirty, have few children, and return home well before their retirement years (Storesletten 2003). They will help even more if they have high expected earnings and low unemployment probabilities. Where the welfare state is large, as in much of the continental European Union, benefits and taxes are more sensitive to age and income, and so the positive selection of immigrants is more important for fiscal balance. Where the welfare state is small, as in the United States, positive selection is less important for fiscal balance.

We conclude with the work on the developed world more generally by Laurence Kotlikoff and his collaborators (Fehr, Jokisch, and Kotlikoff 2004a, 2004b), who agree that offsetting forces turn out to minimize the ability of immigration to erase much of the projected fiscal crisis:

> More immigrants increase the number of workers and, therefore, the taxable wage base. [But] more immigrants, particularly low skilled immigrants, demand public goods as well as transfer payments, neither of which is cheap. According to our model, the costs of additional immigrants, assuming they have the same distribution of skills as the current immigrants, roughly equal the revenue gains they engender. On balance, such a uniform expansion of immigration makes essentially no difference to the developed world's demographic transition path. [And] if immigration is expanded primarily among the low skilled, fiscal conditions will significantly deteriorate. (Fehr, Jokisch, and Kotlikoff 2004b, 3)

As the authors point out, the developed world's future economic prospects would be significantly improved only by an immense increase in the levels of high-skilled immigration from the Third World. Unfortunately, it is not even clear that the available number of potential skilled emigrants from the Third World sending regions will grow fast enough in the future to match the needs of the First World host countries. After all, the Third World is *also* working its way through a demographic transition. With the exception of Africa, every sending region will undergo a major fall in the growth rate of its economically active population between 1965–1990 and 1990–2025: a 2.19-percentage-point fall in East Asia, a 1.24-percentage-point fall in Southeast Asia, a 0.63-percentage-point fall in South America, and a 0.40-percentage-point fall in South Asia (Bloom and Williamson 1998, 442, 444). The secular decline in Third World growth rates is even sharper for young adults, those who have been and will be the first to achieve higher levels of education, and those most likely to emigrate.

Immigration Policy Options

While the economic gains from a massive world population redistribution would be large, political realities are unlikely to permit more than a modest movement in that direction, at least over the next few decades. But as long as potential migrants respond to wage gaps as they have over the past two centuries, there will be an immense demand for immigration into high-wage countries, and thus there will be a need for fair, efficient, and effective immigration policies. It follows that immigration policies in the host countries will matter for most of this century. The relevant question, therefore, is what should those policies be? And how can they be developed in ways that would yield more of the gains associated with increased international migration? In the last chapter, we reviewed the connection between immigration policy and its three most important determinants: the threat of immigrant competition in the labor market, concern about the fiscal costs of immigration, and prejudice against immigrants from cultures significantly different from the host country culture. We have seen earlier in this chapter that there are gains to the world as a whole from freer migration, and some of those gains could be captured by OECD nationals. So what might host countries do to exploit more of the potential gains while reducing the labor market and fiscal effects that larger numbers of immigrants might engender?

Selective Immigration Policy

Selective immigration has become an increasingly important component of immigration policies in the developed world, in part because the cost of migration no longer serves as the powerful positive selection device that it did in the first global century. The clearest examples of selective immigration policies are offered by countries like Canada, Australia, and New Zealand, all of which have adopted, and subsequently refined, points systems for ranking potential immigrants that stress qualifications and skills as well as age. A significant share of the annual immigrant inflow comes under the points system in those countries, so each exercises a significant degree of selectivity in regard to immigrants. By the mid-1990s, nearly half of immigrants to Canada, more than a third of immigrants to Australia, and nearly two-thirds of immigrants to New Zealand were admitted on labor market characteristics. Employment-based immigration accounts for a smaller proportion of the total and is less skill-selective in the United States and other Western countries.

The Australian points system provides an example of the way in which different immigrant characteristics can be rewarded (table 17.2).

Table 17.2
Australian points system, 2004

Characteristic		Points
Skill	Occupations with specific training	60
	General professional occupations	50
	General skilled occupations	40
Age	18–29 years	30
	30–34 years	25
	35–39 years	20
	40–44 years	15
English language ability	Competent English (IELTS 6.0 on each component)	20
	Vocational English (IELTS 5.0 on each component)	15
Work experience	Three of four preceding years in a 60-point occupation	10
	Three of four preceding years in a 40- or 50-point occupation	5
Occupation in demand	Listed occupation and a job offer	20
	Listed occupation and no job offer	15
Australian qualifications	Doctorate	15
	Master's or honors degree	10
	Degree, diploma, or trade qualification	5
Regional residence	Two years' residence in a nonurban or low-growth area	5
Spouse skills	Spouse satisfies minimum points requirements	5
Bonus points	Capital, Australian work experience, listed language	5
Relationship	Sponsoring relative a citizen or permanent resident	5

Source: http://www.immi.gov.au/migration/skilled/points_test.htm#x2.

The pass mark for admission in 2004 was 120 points.[5] Note that the Australian points system rewards characteristics that are likely to maximize the employability of the immigrant and to minimize the fiscal burden he or she imposes on the Australian welfare system. Most prominent are the points awarded for skills, experience, and occupations in demand. Presumably, the stress on language ability and youth helps immigrants achieve easier assimilation. There are also certain requirements (e.g., age less than 45) that the immigrant must satisfy, even if the overall pass mark is exceeded. In the skilled migrant class, a few extra points are awarded for having relatives in

Australia and if the immigrant's spouse also fulfills the minimum requirements.

Points systems apparently shift the immigrant mix significantly toward those with better labor market characteristics. Deborah Cobb-Clark (2004) compared the outcomes for two cohorts of Australian immigrants, the first of which arrived in 1993–1995 and the second of which arrived in 1999–2000. Between these two cohorts, the points system was changed to give more weight to English language skills, youth, and experience, minimum thresholds and spouse points were introduced, and the numerical quota for points-tested immigrants was increased. In addition, immigrants were denied social welfare benefits for their first two years in the country. Not surprisingly, the proportion of skills-based immigrants rose from 35 percent in the first cohort to 49 percent in the second cohort, and the average skills of immigrants admitted improved substantially. Labor market outcomes (after eighteen months in Australia) also improved, with employment rates rising across the cohorts from 61 percent to 73 percent for men and from 31 percent to 45 percent for women. About two-thirds of the change in male and female employment rates was due to differences in cohort characteristics and hence largely due to the increased skill selectivity of the country's immigration policy.

If such improvements in immigrant performance can be observed in a country with a points system already in place, then the effects should be even greater if such a system is introduced where none has previously existed. Skill-selective policies such as a points system could be developed in other countries, but in order to be effective, they would need to cover the majority of immigrants admitted. Would a point system be politically feasible elsewhere? Recall that family reunification is a major plank of immigration policy in most Western counties, at least for permanent immigrants. As the experience of Canada showed in the early 1980s, if preferential treatment is given to family reunification immigrants, then the share of employment-based immigrants in the total falls as the quota is lowered. Indeed, chapter 9 has shown how the introduction of quotas in the 1920s served to diminish the quality of U.S. immigrants for precisely that reason, and the impact was very substantial. Sharply narrowing the family reunification preference will be essential where an increase in skill-based immigration is the goal, especially for countries like the United States, where nonimmediate relatives constitute a significant share of family reunification admissions.

One compromise would be to build a larger element of selection by skill, language fluency, and age into family reunification migration, particularly for nonimmediate relatives. This would be a way of extending the coverage of the points system while still maintaining a family-based migration stream. It should be added that *temporary* worker migration schemes may also offer a way to diminish the family reunification effect.

Another limitation to any policy shift toward greater skill selectivity is that it would screen out the least skilled from the poorer countries and thus reduce the gains to migration where they are greatest. This can be stated another way: increasing skill selectivity may produce greater competition between developed countries over a limited number of skilled migrants, yielding an OECD "churning" in which overall world gains would be small. Indeed, countries which have in recent years opened or widened their immigration doors for the very highest skilled have often failed to fill their targets. The Third World simply may not be able to produce enough young-adult skilled workers to satisfy a rising OECD demand, although good opportunities abroad will certainly give Third World youth a significant incentive for more schooling and language training at home.

One increasingly popular policy solution to this skilled-migrant-scarcity problem has been to admit for permanent residence those who come to the host country for higher education. Until recently, Australia, Britain, the United States, and other countries issued student visas that terminated at the end of the study period and could not be extended for employment and permanent residence. There are three advantages to a relaxation of this requirement. First, skills and language acquired in the host country are most useful there. Second, foreign students have already had several years in which to assimilate into the host country's culture and institutions. Third, students tend to be young and hence of greatest benefit to aging populations. Of course, making it easier for foreign students to become permanent immigrants means that their skills are lost to the origin country. Whether this matters or not depends on where the reader stands on the brain drain issue as it was laid out in chapter 15.

Taxing the Immigrants

Migration can have important distributional consequences for the host country. Part II showed how native workers, especially the lower skilled, suffered from immigrant competition in the first global century, and part III explored the same issue for the second global century. We used figure 17.1 to summarize those distributional issues. Our discussion in chapters 11 and 16 clearly implies that lower-skilled workers have more to fear from labor market competition if immigration policy remains less selective. Higher-skilled workers may have more to fear from labor market competition if immigration policy becomes more selective, although they will be less concerned if future growth favors skill-intensive sectors, as it surely will. High-skilled workers may have more to fear from the tax implications of a less-selective policy and might be willing to trade off increased labor market competition for lower fiscal burdens. Since labor earnings are the principal source of income for the majority of voters, and since median voters in the OECD would be roughly as skilled as immigrants under some more-selective future immigration policy, governments will have to persuade voters that a more-selective immigration policy will reduce fiscal burdens a lot. Governments will face less serious political resistance from median voters if they introduce more-liberal immigration policies that are less selective *and* offer fewer welfare services to immigrants.

One way to overcome voter resistance to more-liberal immigration policy would be to find an acceptable way for gainers to compensate losers. As figure 17.1 illustrates from the host country perspective, the big gainers from a liberalization are host country employers and the migrants themselves, while native labor loses. Any compensation scheme aimed at offsetting the distributional consequences of more immigration has two elements, one political and one economic. The politics are that migrants don't have a vote on immigration policy, whereas native workers and employers do. So the politics imply that some of the burden should fall on the immigrants. But the economics says that the capacity to make such transfers depends on the elasticity of labor demand in the host country. The lower is that elasticity, the greater is the potential wage fall from migration, and the less a tax on immigrants alone can be used to compensate native workers.[6] And the lower the elasticity, the more employers gain, and the greater the need to shift the burden of compensation toward capital.

Consider first a tax on immigrants that is used to compensate native labor. Such transfers would be difficult to achieve with an entry fee, since a lump sum tax that compensated native workers for losses to their future income streams might exclude all but the richest immigrants. Most prospective immigrants would find it impossible to pay such a lump sum tax upon arrival.[7] Furthermore, prospective immigrants might find it difficult to secure a loan in their sending country to cover such a lump sum tax and would be unable to pay such a tax without appealing to some illegal indentured contract or to home country governments, who are likely to demand that the borrower return at the end of some short stay (as many do now for their students abroad). This difficulty could be overcome if the entry fee were paid by the immigrant through the host country tax system. In that case, immigrants would in effect face higher tax rates than nonimmigrants, and the revenue collected could target those hurt most by immigration. Some equity could be built into the scheme by making the tax income contingent: migrants would pay only when their earnings exceeded some threshold. Systems like this already exist for financing higher education in an increasing number of countries (Chapman 2005). There is no reason why they could not be applied to migrants who, like young students, are also credit-constrained and are making significant long-term investments that yield very high returns in the long run. The scale of payments might also be linked to a points system: the higher the immigrant's score, the lower the entry fee.

An alternative or addition to an income-contingent tax on immigrants would be a tax on employers, but such a tax would have to be levied in a way that it did not shift the tax burden onto native labor. In practice, it could be levied on firms that employ immigrant labor in significant amounts. Schemes of this type have been introduced for skilled temporary workers in some Asian countries (e.g., Singapore and Malaysia; Manning and Bhatnager 2003). A tax on employers seems attractive, since those who hire cheap immigrant labor benefit by higher profits. Such a tax would also encourage preferential treatment for natives, who would be less likely to be crowded out by the now-less-cheap immigrants. Where the tax incidence falls on employers, it implies a search for an optimal tax: if the tax is large, few immigrants would be recruited; if the tax is small, not much revenue would be raised. If instead the tax incidence falls on the immigrants through lower wages, then the policy might be seen as undercutting native labor. Here, it would be up to the politician to show the voter that the total labor cost to employers would be the same whether they hired an immigrant or a native.

All of these schemes involve some reduction in the income gains to the migrant, and this fact implies a reduction in immigrants' remittances to families at home. Under plausible assumptions this income source (a fall in remittances per migrant) will be offset by the expansion in immigration (a rise in the number of migrants sending remittances).

Temporary Worker Schemes

Most observers feel that any scheme that significantly expands the rate of permanent immigration will heighten social tensions even if the economic effects are small. One way for high-income countries to deal with this concern is to expand temporary migration programs, much as the Europeans did with guestworkers up to the early 1970s and as the United States did with *braceros* up to 1964. Temporary migration schemes have been adopted in some Asian and Middle Eastern countries and, in a qualified way, are incorporated into Mode 4 of the General Agreement on Trade in Services (GATS). Temporary contracted migration has been suggested recently as a means of expanding immigration to Europe while avoiding some of the costs. If immigrants were resident in host countries only for a few working years, and if they were resident without family dependents, then the fiscal burden they imposed on the host country would be much smaller. Indeed, they would be much more likely to make a net contribution to host country tax coffers. Furthermore, temporary migration does not shift any fiscal burden back on to the immigrant's home country to the extent that poor sending countries are not yet welfare states.

How can temporary workers be prevented from disappearing into the illegal labor market and failing to leave the host country at the end of the contracted period? One possible device is to use a system of forced savings that would be returnable to immigrants only upon their departure (a provision reminiscent of the 1960s guestworker schemes). Alternatively, the employer could be required to post a bond, refundable only when the foreign employee has departed (Boeri, Hanson, and McCormick 2002, chap. 6).

While temporary worker systems might add an element of flexibility to a host country's immigration policy, they really do not offer a way to achieve a significant expansion of OECD immigration. First, such policies are aimed chiefly at unskilled workers who are in the least demand. Short-term contracts would not provide these immigrants (or their employers) with incentives to invest in skills specific to the firm or to the host country labor market. Second, while it is possible to regulate the inflow of temporary workers, past experience has shown that it is often impossible to resist the pressure to allow them to bring relatives and to settle permanently. Temporary immigration programs may be the worst of both worlds: they discourage the immigrant's acquisition of human capital during the period when his or her immigrant status is temporary (or at least uncertain), and they end up as gateways to permanent migration for those who might not have been admitted had their permanent status been anticipated from the start. Short contracts are also likely to lead to defection of immigrants into the illegal market, even if there are incentives to leave at the end of the contract.[8] As an immigrant's contract is lengthened to improve incentives, the more like permanent migration the arrangement becomes.

In short, temporary migration is unlikely to provide the magic bullet that many host countries seem to think it will provide as they search for the best way to liberalize immigration policy in the future.

Immigration and Asylum

Immigration policy may be highest on the long-run agenda, but the most pressing issue in recent years has been policy toward asylum seekers in the face of their rising numbers (chapter 13). Immigration and asylum policies have very different motivations. The best immigration policy is one in which the perceived net gains to society are largest and the losses to specific (voting) groups are smallest. The losers have some voting power, and they will try to use it to lobby for immigration restrictions. However, the losers—low-skilled and poorly schooled native-born—are diffuse and thus less effective as a lobby. The winners include employers in labor-intensive industries, and their concentrated lobby will work to keep restrictions loose. The winners also include those whose relatives join them from abroad, and naturalized citizens will use their voting power to lobby for the retention of comprehensive family reunification clauses. In contrast, asylum seekers are admitted on humanitarian grounds, where the motivation is the benefit to them, rather than economic gain to the host society. Recall that the *sole* basis on which asylum claims are judged is whether the individual has a "well founded fear of persecution," the 1951 Geneva Convention on Refugees language. Refugees gain by protection from persecution, and that benefit satisfies the host country voters' altruistic and humanitarian motives rather than self-interest. Furthermore, voters genuinely value the protection offered to refugees, as table 16.1 illustrates.

Asylum seekers and immigrants are two separate streams marked out by different admission criteria. The decision to admit an immigrant typically gives no weight to humanitarian considerations. By contrast, the decision to admit an asylum seeker is based solely on whether the individual has the required "well founded fear of persecution." Thus, the term "economic migrant" takes on a negative connotation when applied to asylum seekers but not when applied to other immigrants. Given that many asylum seekers have skills that would lower their cost to the receiving country, there is a case for combining the two streams under some common criteria.

Figure 17.2 illustrates a scheme in which the immigration and asylum streams are combined under a points system, analogous to that of Australia, in which points are awarded in a way that reflects the host country valuation of various immigrant attributes. As suggested earlier, such systems could be extended to cover family reunification migration. In addition, humanitarian points could be awarded that reflect society's altruism toward refugees, with the number of points

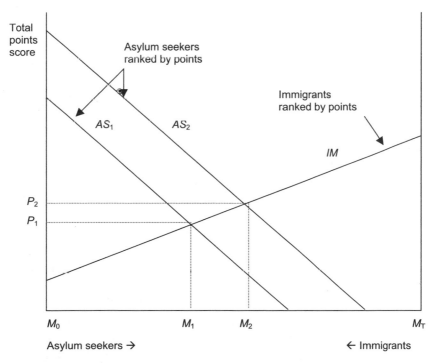

Figure 17.2
Combining asylum seekers and immigrants

awarded varying according to the gravity of the case. The only difference between those seeking asylum and those seeking admission as
immigrants is that the former receive some humanitarian points while
the latter do not. In figure 17.2, those counted as asylum seekers are
ranked in descending order of points (humanitarian plus economic)
from left to right (schedule AS_1), while those without any humanitarian claim are ranked by descending order of points from right to left
(schedule IM). The value of the marginal asylum seeker is equated to
that of the marginal immigrant at point score P_1. The total immigration
quota is the width of the box M_0 to M_T; those between M_0 and M_1 will
be asylum seekers, and those between M_1 and M_T will be economic
immigrants.

This scheme would have three major advantages. First, if the points
system employed truly reflected society's valuation of the different
immigrant characteristics, then total net benefit would be maximized
where the valuation of the marginal immigrant and that of the marginal asylum seeker are equated. Should that valuation fall (for instance, because of an economic recession), then the quota (the width of
the box) could be reduced, raising the equilibrium point score. Second,
even with a fixed quota, the system would be responsive to humanitarian crisis. An increase in the demand for asylum as represented by the
shift from AS_1 to AS_2 would crowd out some economic immigrants
and raise the equilibrium point score to P_2. Third, and perhaps most
important, there is a potential political payoff. Since attitudes toward
genuine refugees are generally positive, letting asylum seekers compete on equal terms with ordinary immigrants would help remove the
stigma attached to asylum seekers as economic migrants by another
name or as queue jumpers. Subjecting asylum seekers to the same economic test as other migrants might help allay suspicions that they
are subverting the system and are likely to be a burden on the host
country.

The scheme would certainly have its difficulties as well. One potential difficulty is that it seems to be inconsistent with current refugee
law, which requires that those judged to be genuine refugees must be
admitted on the basis of fulfilling that criterion alone. But current refugee law could easily be incorporated into the scheme by ensuring that
those who qualify as refugees under the 1951 Geneva Convention on
Refugees receive sufficient points on humanitarian grounds alone to
gain admission. Another potential difficulty lies with the translation of

the gravity of persecution into a point score. Yet similar judgments are already being made in decisions on whether to award full refugee status or a lesser humanitarian status or to reject an asylum application. A more-serious problem is that the scheme does not appear to address the issue of illegal immigration, the means by which many asylum seekers get to their destination in order to lodge a claim. Of course points could be deducted for illegal entry, although this would be inconsistent with the convention, which explicitly excludes illegal entry as a criterion for assessing an asylum claim. The only way to achieve a more-liberal refugee policy without generating additional illegal immigration is to make it possible to apply for asylum from outside the country receiving the claim, either at embassies and consulates or through refugee agencies like the UNHCR. However, a single country adopting an integrated asylum and immigration policy might find itself overwhelmed by asylum claims if such a policy was seen as easing access to that country compared with others.

Illegal Immigrants and Amnesties

Illegal immigration is seen as a major problem in most developed countries. Crude estimates indicate that the annual U.S. inflow of illegals is about a quarter of a million, while the EU inflows may be twice that. Public attitudes are strongly against illegal immigrants, and this spills over into negative attitudes toward immigrants generally. Illegal immigrants working in the underground economy are also seen as unfair competition for native unskilled labor and as an erosion in the tax base. Finally, the seeming inability of OECD authorities to control illegal immigration undermines the credibility of immigration policy, making it more difficult for governments to persuade their constituencies that an expansion in legal immigration is an attractive goal.

Illegal immigration is seen by some as the inevitable result of tough policies toward legal immigrants. To them, a social Bernoulli law is at work, since those who cannot enter legally choose the illegal route instead. While good estimates documenting the size of such an effect do not exist, the view certainly seems plausible. An induced rise in illegals is especially likely to appear when schemes for recruiting unskilled workers are cut off, leaving behind a well-developed friends-and-relatives network which is used to help future illegals. The moral is clear: while expanding legal immigration might reduce illegal immigration, it will not reduce it by much if it fails to open the door to those unskilled who are most likely to become illegals.

Others argue that illegal immigration is largely a failure of enforcement. But lack of coordination or even lack of resources allocated to border enforcement is not the main problem. Rather, it is political will. Studies of illegal immigration across the U.S.-Mexican border suggest that enforcement has been half-hearted as a result of political pressure applied by U.S. employers of unskilled illegal workers in the Southwest (Boeri, Hanson, and McCormick 2002, chap. 11). A more-coordinated border policy might help: applying more resources to patrols on just one part of the border has little effect, since illegals then choose routes that take them across other parts of the border. Similarly, employer sanctions legislated in the 1980s by the U.S. Congress under the Immigration Reform and Control Act (IRCA) have never been firmly enforced, again as a result of political pressure. Stronger employer sanctions and border control could solve much of the illegal immigration problem, but the political will is lacking and the cost too great, the latter all the more so since the channels of illegal immigration have now become firmly entrenched. As we have shown in chapter 13 with European asylum policy, once such flows get established, it is much harder for policy to reduce them.

A number of countries have introduced amnesties for illegal immigrants. U.S. legalizations under IRCA totaled some 2.7 million in 1986. Italian amnesties between 1987 and 1998 legalized a total of 800,000 immigrants, while 370,000 were legalized in Greece and 80,000 in France in 1997–1998 (OECD 2000b). These and similar amnesty programs in other countries have often been accompanied by increased border enforcement and legislated employer sanctions. Amnesty programs make it possible for immigrants to use their human capital more efficiently, to accumulate without constraint, and to augment government tax revenues, but they also serve to encourage future illegal immigration. Amnesties are also likely to enhance legal migration through the friends-and-relatives effect and to encourage further illegal immigration by raising the expectation of more amnesties in the future. The enhanced enforcement measures that have often accompanied amnesties seem to have had less-powerful effects in the opposite direction, especially in the absence of the implementation of serious sanctions against employers for hiring illegal immigrants.

Alessandra Venturini (2004) comments on the illegal immigration problem in southern Europe as follows:

The southern European countries, in the hope of improving their migration policy, have resorted to increasing checks and deportation and to a series of regularizations. Instead of correcting the illegal side of the phenomenon, these policies have had two effects. On the one hand, they have given potential immigrants the general expectation of further legalizations and so have created a continuous flow of illegal immigration. On the other hand, they have given those who employ illegal foreigners the conviction that such behaviour will go unpunished. Additionally, citizens have become less tolerant of irregular foreigners. (229)

A Final Word

There is not now, nor was there ever, too much global migration. The world would clearly be better off with more migration. The problem is therefore not that there is too much global migration, but rather that we do not yet have effective ways whereby the gainers from global migration can compensate the losers. The problem is not global migration. The problem is a lack of political will.

18   World Mass Migration: Past, Present, and Future

We have come to the end of our two-century tour of world mass migration. Along the way we have encountered recurrent themes: the forces that drive migration, the economic and social consequences of migration, and the policy responses to migration. We have tried to be clear about what is similar and what is different about the two global centuries. Subject to these qualifications, we have done our best to extract the policy lessons that can be derived from both the distant and the more-recent past. It is worth revisiting some of these lessons before ending our tour. But rather than simply marching through a recapitulation, we use this opportunity to raise additional questions that are relevant for the future of migration and migration policy. Let us first retrace our steps by thinking about world migration regimes.

World Migration Regimes

Migration regimes are often thought of in terms of typologies such as the slave trade, contract labor and guestworker systems, free settler migrations, high-skilled or business migrations, and refugee diasporas, to name but a few. These regimes have always been molded by two forces: deep economic and demographic fundamentals that differed across world regions and changed over time and policies that have sought to stem or encourage migrations. The interplay of these two forces have determined the size and character of world mass migrations, but the fundamentals have had a profound impact on policy as well.

Until the first half of the eighteenth century, the costs and uncertainties of long-distance migration were so great that all but the wealthy were, in the absence of slave coercion or indentured contract, deterred from migrating. A new regime began to evolve in the greater

Atlantic economy during the early decades of the nineteenth century. The early waves of free migration involved family groups from the more-developed European economies, farmers and artisans seeking to settle new lands. These were from the middle class of those times, but they gave way in the late nineteenth century to much larger flows drawn from the working class and from less-developed sending economies. The age of mass migration was the first to demonstrate clearly how economic and demographic fundamentals drive migration and how they determine immigration's selectivity. The first of these underlying fundamentals was the mid-nineteenth-century fall in transport costs, which made migration feasible for an ever-widening pool of potential migrants, combined with the large incentives that labor-scarce overseas economies offered potential European emigrants. The second fundamental was rising income at home, which further expanded the pool of potential immigrants by increasing the feasibility of migration even for the relatively poor. The third fundamental was the demographic transition that worked its way across nineteenth-century Europe, creating big cohorts of young adults who were most responsive to the migration incentives. The friends-and-relatives effect gave added momentum to these fundamentals and built persistence into the world migration system.

The greater Atlantic economy offered one migration environment, while the rest of the world offered another. Free mass migrations were delayed three or four decades in the southern half of the Atlantic economy, and they were delayed elsewhere for almost a century. Indeed, quite another world migration regime emerged in the poor part of the periphery. This part of the world was segmented from the Atlantic economy's labor market, and the new regime had parallels with the earlier Atlantic migration experience with indentured contracts. Migrants from India and China traveled to the plantation economies stretching from Southeast Asia to South America; the greater the distance from sending to receiving economy, the more often migration took the form of indentured servitude or contract labor. These mass migrations expanded as time went on, driven on the demand side by improving terms of trade for primary products from tropical estates and plantations and on the supply side by falling world transport costs.

Back in the Atlantic economy, mass migration peaked in 1913 and restrictive policy followed. War and depression played a key role in shutting down mass migration, but the forces of restriction had been gathering for three decades before that as migrants came increasingly from poorer countries and as migrations altered the relative unskilled labor scarcity in overseas host countries. This shift in fundamentals was pervasive across all host countries even though the United States assumed leadership in setting immigration policy. And what happened in the interwar Atlantic economy also happened elsewhere as the terms of trade for primary products fell, the world depression deepened, and political backlash against immigration intensified and solidified.

The immigration regimes that emerged in the postwar period were increasingly shaped by immigration policy. Guestworker programs recruited unskilled labor to feed the long OECD boom that lasted until 1973. These guestworker migrations connected specific sources to specific destinations, typically through bilateral agreements, and they eventually involved migrations within Asia and from Asia to the Persian Gulf. Yet the postwar migrations maintained the prewar segmentation for almost three decades. This segmentation began to break down in the 1960s as Asians moved westward to a widening array of OECD destinations and as Latin Americans moved north. By the end of the twentieth century, only the poorest were excluded from world migration currents. Even so, rapidly growing numbers from the poorest and most war-torn parts of the world were also finding their way to the West as asylum seekers—creating yet another migration regime.

Two Global Centuries of Mass Migration

It has become commonplace to compare the mass migrations before the First World War with those since the Second World War. Earlier chapters dwelt at length with these comparisons, but it might be useful to revisit them here. The similarities between the two are obvious. World migration grew and its scope expanded in both eras. The richer parts of the world were the magnets for long-distance migration from the poorer (but not too poor) parts in both eras. But the differences need to be stressed too. The principal destinations for European emigrants in the late nineteenth century were the Americas and Australasia. In the late twentieth century, Europe faded as a source of emigrants and grew as a destination for immigrants, while South and Central America did the opposite. This evolution is consistent with the economic and demographic fundamentals that drive mass migrations, in this case the European growth miracle and the Latin American growth failure.

Both eras shared another feature, a widening development gap between high-wage host countries and low-wage source countries. Falling transport costs and rising incomes at the source both contributed to augmenting the list of sending countries, pulling more immigrants from more-distant and poorer places. In both eras, the gap in labor market performance between new and old immigrants contributed more and more to the quality gap between immigrants and natives in the host countries. Some of that gap may have been due to the shift from positive to negative (or less-positive) selection of immigrants from any given country, but most of it was due to the changing mix of source countries from those with higher levels of education and skills and higher average incomes to those with lower levels of education and skills and average incomes. The gap progressively widened in both eras, but it widened much faster and became much larger in the half century after 1950 than it did in the half century after 1870. That, too, is consistent with changing fundamentals, especially the trickle down of economic development that has eased the poverty constraint all over the world, with the possible exception of places like sub-Saharan Africa.

The biggest difference between the two global centuries, however, lies in immigration policy. In the nineteenth century, host economies encouraged immigration, either implicitly through their open door policies or explicitly through subsidies. Their policies gradually became less proimmigrant as the period evolved, and openness ended in the 1920s with quotas on immigration and the first great policy backlash against it. The restrictions on international migration that arose all around the world have remained in place since then. Indeed, in many respects they have become even more prohibitive, especially since the 1970s. Furthermore, policy has changed its goals with regard to immigrant mix, and in two ways. First, it has become much less discriminatory. Policies that restricted immigrants to a few key source countries—as a result of racial animosity, ethnic affinity, proximity, or colonial past—have evolved into policies that, at least in principle, admit immigrants from anywhere in the world on the same basis. Second, policy has become increasingly skill selective. Some countries have developed points systems. Even countries that do not have points systems, like Germany and the United States, have shifted away from admitting low-skilled guestworkers toward admitting high-skilled permanent immigrants.

Trade and Migration Policy: Why the Difference?

If the difference in immigration policy between the two global centuries is curious, the contrast in trade policy is a real paradox. World exports grew faster than world output in both periods. But was the rise in the world trade share due to policy, or was it due to economic fundamentals? The answer, of course, is that it was shaped by both. But trade policy in the Atlantic economy was far more liberal in the half century following 1950 than it was in the half century following 1860. Tariffs were far higher (and rising) in the late nineteenth century than they were in the late twentieth century (when they were also falling) (Williamson 2004a, figure 1). The puzzle is that immigration policy was more proglobal than trade policy in the first global century, while the reverse has been true of the second. In 1860, a promigration and protrade legacy was in place, but a backlash pushed trade policy in an antiglobal direction long before it did the same to immigration policy. In 1950, an antitrade and anti-migration legacy was in place, but while a protrade policy reversed that legacy, no such reversal took place for immigration policy.

Why the policy difference? In a simple two-good, two-factor model, migration and trade are perfect substitutes: all the gains from globalization can be reaped by migration alone or by trade alone. If restrictions on trade are introduced to protect the scarce factor (labor), they will be unsuccessful unless restrictions are also placed on migration. The obverse is also true. Thus, according to the simple theory, restrictions on trade and restrictions on migration should go hand in hand. While the assumptions of the model may appear to be much too simple (Collins, O'Rourke, and Williamson 1999), it is a fact that voters in the OECD who tend to oppose immigration also tend to oppose trade. So why isn't fact consistent with theory? Why the difference between trade and immigration policy across the two global centuries?

There are many potential explanations for the apparent paradox. The spread of democracy and the decline of empires radically altered the political landscape between the two periods of global migration. No doubt social norms and attitudes toward foreigners also changed in ways that might alter the mix of trade and migration policies. Alternatively, it has been argued that trade is fundamentally an economic issue driven by group politics, while immigration is fundamentally a social issue driven by diffuse democratic politics (Greenaway and Nelson 2004). While these complications may matter as well, we think most of the policy paradox can be explained by three factors: discrimination and the labor market; government revenues, social expenditures, and the fiscal impacts of immigration and trade; and the presence or absence of international cooperation.

The first explanation involves varying attitudes toward discrimination among different groups of potential immigrants. At the start of the first global century, European emigration was conditioned by migration costs and the poverty trap, so that migrants came mainly from the relatively rich parts of Europe. If overseas host countries had a preference for western Europeans, there was no need to develop a discriminatory immigration policy to achieve that end, since the fundamentals that drove migration were barriers enough to poor sending countries. Although anti-immigration voices got louder as the century unfolded, outright restriction was simply not necessary for most of the period. Thus, the U.S. Congress did not debate immigrant restriction until the 1890s when the numbers from poor parts of Europe began to surge. When much poorer regions, such as China or India, began to offer an immigration threat, exclusion was swift and decisive.

In the second global century, things have been somewhat different. First, the edifice of exclusion gradually collapsed, to be replaced by nondiscriminatory immigration policies, of which the 1965 amendments to the U.S. Immigration and Nationality Act and the abolition of the White Australia Policy are but two examples. That alone might not have mattered much were it not for the gradual relaxation of the poverty constraints in poorer parts of the world and the compounding role of family reunification policies that permitted the friends-and-relatives effect to do its work. With the door having been opened wider to the poorer parts of the world, restrictions on all potential immigrants had to be tightened if the same aggregate rates of inflow were to be maintained. Thus, policy looks much tougher now simply because there are far more potential migrants to hold back. This offers one explanation for the fact that while trade policy has liberalized dramatically since the 1960s, immigration policy has not.

The second explanation for the apparent paradox lies in fiscal impact. Tariffs were a major source of central government revenue in the nineteenth century, including those in the labor-scarce immigration economies. Thus, protection and tariff rates were driven upward in part by rising revenue needs (Williamson 2004a). On the other hand, the fiscal impact of immigration mattered far less in the years before the twentieth-century welfare state, so threats to the treasury from immigration were almost irrelevant. In short, tariffs brought fiscal benefits in the first global century, while immigration brought no significant fiscal costs. Hence, high tariffs and low immigration restrictions coexisted for fiscal reasons before 1914. By contrast, social services and the welfare state expanded dramatically from the 1930s to the 1970s, while tax sources greatly diversified (Lindert 2003, 11–15). There was then less need for revenue-raising tariffs but a much greater need to control social spending. In short, the second global century produced an environment that was consistent with lower barriers to trade and higher barriers to migration.

The third explanation relates to international, and especially multilateral, cooperation. Beginning in 1948, successive rounds of negotiation under GATT reduced tariff levels through mutual agreement. Those agreements expanded in depth and coverage, and with the establishment of the World Trade Organization (WTO) in 1995, they increased in scope. While critics argue that political compromise on textiles and agriculture still makes for an illiberal trade policy, most observers believe that the secular decline in trade barriers over the last fifty years owes much to this process of multilateral agreement (Irwin 1995). There has been nothing remotely like this process for world migration. The International Organization for Migration (IOM) and its precursors have been in existence since 1951, but they have not established a track record anything like that of GATT. The IOM has assisted some eleven million migrants since its creation, but its mission has never been to broker multilateral migration agreements or to establish the architecture for international cooperation on migration issues.[1] Indeed, it is ironic that the only global agreement on migration has been made through the WTO,[2] rather than through the IOM.

Is There Scope for North-North Cooperation?

The last point invites another question: Why haven't international institutions developed to deal with world migration like those that have developed to deal with world trade? We know that the typical voter in the developed world is opposed to liberalizing both trade and migration. Yet while international trade negotiators seem to have been able to persuade nations to shed restrictions while ignoring voter preferences (Aaronson 2001; Deardorff and Stern 2002), nothing on the same scale has even been attempted for world migration. The asymmetry seems all the more paradoxical given that the potential gains to freer migration are so much larger than those to freer trade: "even a minor liberalization of international labor flows would create gains for the world economy that are much larger than the combined effect of all the post-Doha initiatives under consideration" (Rodrik 2002, 20).

So why the difference? Most economists agree that the gains to an individual country from free trade can be achieved by removing trade barriers unilaterally. Yet "countries seem willing to do themselves good only if others promise to do the same" (Krugman 1997, 113). While free trade may have won the battle of ideas (Irwin 1996), in practice it has been negotiated in a mercantilist spirit of exchanging concessions on market access. The principles upon which modern free trade has been built are those of reciprocity, nondiscrimination (most-favored-nation clauses), and fair treatment (a level playing field for foreign suppliers in domestic markets). These principles were well established in bilateral trade agreements that were achieved in the nineteenth century (notably the Cobden-Chevalier Treaty of 1860 between Britain and France), and subsequently they were built into multilateral trade agreements (Brown 2003).

The theoretical arguments for free trade are basically the same as those for free migration. But the basis upon which more-open trade has been negotiated differs sharply from the principles on which those arguments are based. So why hasn't more-open immigration been negotiated along the same lines? Some of the conditions analogous to trade are already present in the policies of individual countries. Major labor-importing countries have moved progressively toward nondiscrimination. Immigrants face the same rules for entry irrespective of their origin. And to a first approximation, immigrants are treated in domestic labor markets more or less the same way as are natives. But there is one big difference between trade and immigration policy: reciprocity. Migration is much more of a one-way street than is trade to the extent that bilateral migration balances are far more unequal than are bilateral trade balances. Consequently, there is much less scope for one country to bargain for its nationals to have access to a partner's labor market in exchange for the same access accorded to the partner's nationals in the first country's labor market. Thus, the pre-existing bilateral basis upon which multilateral trade agreements have been built hardly exists at all for migration.

This suggests that the scope for global agreement on migration liberalization is far more limited than it is for such agreement on trade liberalization. But it also suggests areas in which more-limited cooperation might advance. This would include blocks of countries among which there are significant migrant flows in both directions. Indeed, some agreements already exist among country clubs to open their labor markets to each other. The European Union's Schengen Convention of 1990 is perhaps the most well known, but others include the Nordic Common Labor Market of 1954 and the formation of ECOWAS in 1980. Thus, one potential process leading to freer migration would be to expand those blocks, especially within the developed world (which after all is where trade agreements originated) to embrace an ever-larger set of countries. To be sure, such negotiations are not always easy, a point illustrated by the reluctance of the fifteen existing EU members to open their labor markets to the ten newcomers in 2004. The main problem with the club approach, of course, is that expanding migration opportunities between countries with similar endowments and at similar levels of development will capture only a very small proportion of the potential gains from world migration.

Is There Scope for North-South Cooperation?

Most of the gains from freer migration would come from migration from poor to rich countries. Yet history shows that migration streams of this type are constrained by poverty traps, and when those traps are unlocked, the emigration surge often results in a host country backlash. The gradual widening of the sources of migration to include poorer countries and less-skilled migrants was a key force that led to the U.S. quotas on immigration in the 1920s, while macroeconomic shocks in the 1930s contributed to rising immigration barriers elsewhere in the greater Atlantic economy. The same was true of more-organized schemes. The contract worker regimes that persisted in parts of Africa, South America, and Asia until well into the twentieth century collapsed in the face of political backlash and macroeconomic shocks. The guestworker system that emerged in Europe in the early postwar years, the U.S. *bracero* program, and the more-recent migrations to the Gulf States have all entailed temporary worker arrangements that are not unlike the contract worker arrangements of the first global century. These modern regimes have focused on unskilled labor. They were intended to be schemes for importing needed workers temporarily, even though they often led to permanent migration.

Typically, they ended abruptly as a result of political backlash and macroeconomic shocks.

Such guestworker schemes do not provide a secure foundation for the liberalization of world migration, since they focus on the less-skilled segment of the labor market. And if that were not impediment enough, no international organization exists through which the terms of the bilateral agreements generally involved in guestworker schemes could evolve into a multilateral system. One alternative would be to extend the agenda of the multilateral trading organizations to cover migration issues. Rather than a new organization's being established (or the IOM's being transformed), the WTO could be expanded to include migration. Indeed, this has already happened in a limited form with the appearance of Mode 4 of GATS, which deals with "the temporary movement of natural persons" in the context of trade in services. It provides for the migration of professionals, managers, and specialists within service sector businesses in order to facilitate the supply of services to foreign markets. So far, the application of Mode 4 has been very limited, and serious obstacles remain. However, it has been suggested that both the momentum and the means exist to remove some of those obstacles and to expand the scope of the agreement to more occupations and more service sectors (Chanda 2001; Self and Zutshi 2002). Such developments could also build on existing provisions in individual countries, such as the H1B visas in the United States, by establishing a multilateral equivalent: a GATS visa. And although the present provisions apply only to temporary migration, they could form the basis for future agreements on permanent migration.

Potential also exists for multilateral cooperation in dealing with refugees and asylum seekers. The 1951 Geneva Convention on Refugees offers one international framework, but it has not evolved into an institution for multilateral cooperation. On the contrary, the original agreement has remained ossified as individual countries, while adhering to the letter of convention law, have introduced policies that have progressively undermined its spirit. The policy backlash described in chapter 13 might lead one to think that furthering international cooperation on refugees might be difficult. But as we argued in the previous chapter, refugees are valued by host country populations because they satisfy humanitarian and altruistic motives, and in this respect they can be viewed as public goods. It follows that people benefit from the knowledge that refugees find sanctuary in other countries as well as their own. It also follows that individual countries adopt policies that are too restrictive to maximize the joint welfare of the populations of refugee-receiving countries as a whole (Hatton 2004a, 2005; Hatton and Williamson 2004). Hence, there is scope for multilateral agreements among refugee-receiving countries that internalize these (positive) externalities through a coordinated expansion of refugee admissions. The greatest scope for such agreements is between countries that share similar characteristics and face similar demands for asylum. The obvious place to start would be with the European Union as it develops a common immigration and asylum policy. Furthermore, asylum policy could become integrated with immigration policy as part of an EU-wide points system, as suggested in the previous chapter.

One disadvantage of expanding asylum opportunities in the developed world is the cumulative effects that liberalization of such opportunities might have on the number of applications. The friends-and-relatives effect is particularly powerful for asylum seekers. Thus, even a small loosening of asylum policy in the West might lead to an even greater surge in applicants, a rise in the share who fail to qualify for admission, and thus a further increase in the numbers who remain as illegals. In its "convention plus" agenda, the UNHCR calls for greater cooperation, not only among Western countries and among countries in those regions of origin that serve as the first (and often the only) destination for refugees, but also between these two groups of countries. It recommends more-generous aid packages to improve the economic conditions of refugees in source regions, better access to procedures which determine refugee status, and more-generous quotas for resettlement in the West. Such provisions might be built into a protocol to the convention, but it would be a difficult sell, since any improvement in the severe poverty constraints that displaced populations face is likely to generate an even greater onward flow of asylum seekers to the West (Hatton and Williamson 2004). Any increase in refugee access to developed countries would have to be bought with measures that would help suppress the volume of flows at the source.

Looking to the Future

The gains from higher levels of world migration would be very large. Analysis of the current global century suggests this is so, and analysis of the first global century confirms it. But the obstacles to winning those gains are equally great. Thus, the second global century has recorded only a modest expansion in world migration compared with the immense surge in world trade and capital flows.

We must sound pessimistic about the future for world migration. After all, we have shown that the historical record does not offer any easy solutions to the world migration problems that face us today or tomorrow. Still, while history offers no silver bullet, it *does* furnish useful lessons to help guide a sequence of small liberalizations. If this book has been persuasive in pointing out those useful lessons of history, it will have achieved our objective.

Notes

2 Evolving World Migrations since Columbus

1. Immigration statistics tend to yield larger totals than emigration statistics. Hence, immigration totals recorded for the Americas are very similar to those for *all* European intercontinental emigration, despite the fact that the latter include such destinations as Australia, New Zealand, and South Africa.

2. A number of studies have examined the composition of European emigrant flows by country. What follows in the text draws on Carlsson 1976 for Sweden, Erickson 1972 for Great Britain, Fitzpatrick 1984 for Ireland, Hvidt 1975 for Denmark, and Swierenga 1976 for Holland.

3. Females were a higher share of emigrants from a few countries like Ireland, where they accounted for 48 percent between 1851 and 1913. These countries were, however, the exceptions to the rule.

4. This insight is often attributed to Sjastaad (1962), who was one of the first to suggest that migration could be analyzed using a human capital framework.

5. Cohn (1984, 297) estimates emigrant deaths on the passage to New York at 1.36 percent during 1836 to 1853, a large number for such a short trip and for a group dominated by adults. McDonald and Schlomowitz (1990, 90) estimate deaths on the longer passage to Australia at 1.45 percent between 1838 and 1892.

6. Less than 10 percent of the migration to Southeast Asia, the Indian Ocean, and the South Pacific was indentured, although a very large share was under contract or what was called *kangani* labor recruitment (McKeown 2004, 157).

7. U.S. slave imports had fallen off to low levels long before 1807, in part because slave mortality was far lower and slave fertility far higher on the mainland than in the Carribbean and other tropical areas in the Americas. However, and predictably, U.S. slave traders anticipated the 1807 legislation by recording large slave imports in the months before the deadline.

3 The Transition to Mass Migration: How It All Began

1. Almost exogenous, since it could be (and has been) argued that rising migration lowered steerage fares as a result of scale economies on the traditional trans-Atlantic

routes. It is also true that government subsidies in host countries were most often funded by export sector performance, another component of the nineteenth-century global boom. See subsequent discussion.

2. One of the best recent accounts that only the well-to-do could afford the expensive eighteenth-century trans-Atlantic move is in Wokeck 1999.

3. For an excellent description of the difficulty of reaching the European port of departure, see the eighteenth-century account in Wokeck 1999 (chap. 4).

4. Eastern European governments, however, did not. Russia, it will be recalled from chapter 2, restricted emigration until long after the 1860s.

5. In 1846–1850, the United Kingdom accounted for 78 percent of European migration overseas (Ferenczi and Willcox 1929, table 1, 230).

6. Emigration was sensitive to steerage and other costs of the move (Dunkley 1980, 356), and a large part of that sensitivity was reflected in destination choice. See also chapter 4.

7. Actually, until the 1860s the assistance scheme was implemented by the Colonial Land Office and the Emigration Commission in London.

8. Between 1835 and 1841, Australia experimented with a bounty system in which

the colonists ... themselves chose emigrants in England and [brought] them to the colony, receiving from the colonial Government a bounty equal to the cost of passage. From this scheme ... the colonists expected several advantages. They would import people whose occupations fitted them for colonial life and there would no longer be any danger of an over-supply of tradesmen for whom no demand existed. The cost of selecting the emigrants in England would disappear, for the colonists would bear the whole cost, as well as the whole responsibility for the selections. (Madgwick 1937, 150)

The system failed, since the bounties offered were not big enough for settlers who were averse to risk.

4   What Drove European Mass Emigration?

1. Australia and Brazil offer good counterexamples. Both went through periods when they offered generous subsidies to encourage immigration. To a lesser but still significant extent, the same was true of Argentina and Canada. Chapter 8 has far more to say about these issues.

2. Note that row B of table 4.2 reports Swedish figures of 36.7 and 59.9 for the 1870s and 1900–1913, a bit different than the figures of 33 and 56 reported in the text. The explanation, of course, is that not all Swedes went to the United States, which is the comparison reported in the text. To repeat, row B of table 4.2 reports the country wage relative to a weighted average of that in the most important destination regions for that country.

3. Taylor (1994) offers detailed evidence of this segmentation, and its impact on real wage convergence and divergence in the Atlantic economy was profound. While migration from Europe to the New World certainly closed the real wage gap between the two, it also served to widen the gap in real wages between Latin America and North America.

4. As noted previously, the share of the male labor force in agriculture was also included to serve as an inverse proxy for the level of industrialization, the expectation being that agrarian societies had lower mobility and emigration rates. It proved not to be significant.

5. A recent paper has argued that shipping cartels choked off emigration from north-western European ports, but only after 1909, pretty much at the end of the first global century (Deltas, Sicotte, and Tomczak 2004).

6. We stress the word "mass," since Iberians had been going to Latin America since 1492. However, as we noted in chapter 3, the Spanish emigrant flow was only 2,500 per year in the three centuries before 1800—a trickle (Sánchez-Albornoz 1994, 36).

7. The long-run effect of an increase of 1,000 in the migrant stock is to draw a further eighty to ninety migrants abroad each year. This is much larger than the effect obtained from cross-country estimation and is probably the result of using annual rather than decade average data.

5   Emigrant Origins and Immigrant Outcomes

1. Such temporary migration strategies are discussed at length in Gould 1980a, Cinel 1991, and Baines 1994.

2. Several older studies found that the earnings assimilation of these immigrants was slow and that in some cases they fell progressively further behind those of the native-born the longer the immigrants had been in the United States, but such findings appear to be an artifact of the particular specification used (Hatton 1997). All of these studies examined samples of blue-collar workers in Michigan, Iowa, and California. See Hannon 1982a and 1982b, Eichengreen and Gemery 1986, and Hanes 1996.

3. Paul Douglas (1919) made the same point in his critique of the commission's report: specifically, he argued that the proportion of skilled workers among the new immigrants in 1899–1909 was no lower than that among the old immigrants during the time when they formed the bulk of the inflow.

4. Similarities in the wage distributions are striking: in Canada, the log wage premia for operatives and craft workers over unskilled laborers were 0.14 and 0.39, respectively; in the United States, they were 0.19 and 0.40, respectively.

5. Among Italians who went to the United States between 1876 and 1930, 80 percent came from the south; among those who went to Argentina, only 47 percent came from the south (Klein 1983, 309).

6. Italians were pulled to Argentina by relatively high wages there, not by any gross domestic product (GDP) per capita differential. Indeed, since Argentina was labor scarce and Italy labor abundant, it is hardly surprising that the Argentina-to-Italy real wage ratio in 1913 was 1.7 (Williamson 1995, table A2.1), while the GDP per capita ratio was "only" 1.5 (Maddison 1995, table B).

7. It is sometimes suggested that the Italian flow to the United States was characterized by exceptionally high return migration rates. Although return rates for Italians were higher than those for most other immigrant groups in the United States, they were even higher for Italians who went to Argentina. Between 1861 and 1914, Italian repatriation rates were 47 percent for the United States and 52 percent for Argentina (Baily 1983, 296).

8. Among the northern Italian immigrants to the United States in 1899–1909, 88.2 percent were literate, whereas only 45.8 percent of the southern Italian immigrants were literate.

9. Note also that these gains are for a weighted average of destinations. The Italians and Spaniards who went to the United States gained far more on average than those who went to South America.

10. The term "shock troops" comes from Sidney Pollard (1978), who characterized the Irish in early industrializing Britain the same way. Williamson (1986) disagreed. The exchange between Pollard and Williamson over the impact of the Irish immigrants on British workers from the 1820s to the 1850s exactly parallels the debate over later immigrant impact in America.

11. Others have used more-formal time series methods to identify the wage effects of immigration. For example, using time series, Pope and Withers (1994) could find no consistent real wage effect of immigration for Australia over the whole period from 1860 to 1990. Australia *may* be an exception, but the correlation that should have been examined was that between immigration (a flow) and the change in the wage, not between immigration and the wage level, as was done by Pope and Withers.

6   The Impact of Mass Migration on Convergence and Inequality

1. In contrast, see two recent contributions by economic historians to this literature (O'Rourke and Williamson 1999, chap. 2; Bordo, Taylor, and Williamson 2003, chaps. 4 and 5).

2. The statistic C is defined as the variance divided by the square of the mean, which is equivalent to the coefficient of variation but easier to decompose.

3. C(17) includes Canada and the United States, while N(15) excludes them. North America bucked the convergence tide. I(13) excludes Portugal and Spain, which also bucked the tide.

7   Mass Migrations in the Poor Periphery

1. To keep the chapter within bounds, it ignores the Russian migrations to Siberia and the east, as well as the Chinese migrations to Mongolia and the north, but see chapter 2.

2. Here, we refer to a model in which factors are specific to given sectors. In this example, land is used only in agriculture and capital is used only in manufacturing. Labor is mobile between them. A summary of these models can be found in O'Rourke and Williamson 1999 (appendix, 289–294) and Williamson 2004 and 2005.

3. The "tyranny of distance" was the apt phrase that Geoffrey Blainey ([1966] 1982) used to describe its importance to Australian development in his excellent book of the same title.

4. This rise is computed over the fifteen years following 1858 (Huber 1971).

5. See Shah Mohammed and Williamson 2004 for more details on these long-run trends.

6. In contrast with the Atlantic economy real wage data (Williamson 1995), these wage comparisons around the periphery must assume that living costs were comparable, since we do not have the price information needed for purchasing-power parity adjustments. Still, we doubt that such adjustments would change the central conclusion: wage gaps were *much* bigger around the periphery than around the Atlantic economy core.

7. It has been estimated that some twenty million Indians were involved in long-distance migration *within* British India (Lai 2002, 241).

8. The average emigration rate from Kwangtung province (about the size of Italy) was at least 9.6 per thousand in the peak years of the 1920s (McKeown 2004, 160).

9. Calculated from Northrup 1995 (table 5.1), using four relevant observations: China to Hawaii, 1852 to 1881–1889; Japan to Hawaii, 1868 to 1885–1893; India to British Guiana, 1874 to 1907–1908; and India to British West Indies, 1847–1873 to 1909.

10. In the case of Japan, the net emigration rate was close to zero until late in the century.

11. Similarly, what accounts for the real wage fall from the 1880s to World War I in Indonesia and Siam (as well as Burma: Furnivall 1938, 93)? Was it the cumulative impact of immigration, or the fall in the terms of trade? We think it was the latter.

12. Although the Australia-wide policy was introduced in 1901, it had been preceded by similar legislation in some of the constituent colonies: Western Australia in 1897 and New South Wales and Tasmania both in 1898 (Huttenback 1976, 166).

13. This was less so in Britain itself. Indeed, the Committee on Indian Emigration chaired by Lord Sanderson argued in 1910 in favor of maintaining the system with only minor adaptations.

8 Political Debate and Policy Backlash

1. A focus on human rights developed after World War II, when most Western countries changed their immigration policies to provide special consideration for political refugees. Immigrant classifications for refugees did not exist prior to the 1930s, although the U.S. did let "displaced" Europeans in after World War I and just before the quotas were imposed.

2. Another strand of literature has recently developed which tries to tie the extension of the vote in Europe to inequality and the welfare state (Acemoglu and Robinson 2000; Lindert 2003).

3. The great migrations of Russian Jews to Israel in the 1990s offer an excellent modern example of a capital formation response that eased the absorption of a big immigrant shock (Cohen and Hsieh 2000). As we show later in the chapter, the United States in the 1850s offers another good example.

4. This, it turns out, is a reasonable assumption by the 1890s, at least for U.S. manufacturing (Hanes 1993).

5. In 1890, 54 percent of the U.S. labor force was involved in agriculture. The share was also 54 percent in Canada in 1891, but it was a bit lower in the rest of the overseas immigration regions like Argentina (21 percent in 1895), Australia (38 percent in 1901), and New Zealand (40 percent in 1896). See Mitchell 1983 (150–159).

6. In addition to the evidence presented earlier on this issue, Foreman-Peck (1992) concludes that they were substitutes after estimating a trans-log production function.

7. Indeed, the U.S. had the highest tariffs in the world for a number of decades after the early 1860s and the Civil War (Williamson 2004, 2005).

8. The Australia index is lagged two years, while the Canadian and United States indices are both lagged four years. These lagged indexes offered the best fits in the regression analysis.

9. Based on U.S. state labor bureau surveys at the site http://eh.net/databases/labor.

10. About 60 percent of the total emigration from Europe was to the United States (Hatton and Williamson 1998, chap. 2), and about 70 percent of the total emigration to our five-country New World sample was to the United States.

11. Furthermore, the econometric estimates of this effect are likely to be biased downward, since open immigration policy implies more immigrants and lower *WtoY*, as we have shown in chapter 6.

9   The Demise of Mass Migration and Its Impact

1. This section on U.S. quotas relies heavily on Gemery (1994, 179–183), who offers the best survey of what is a large literature.

2. Kirk's poor Europe sample includes Bulgaria, Estonia, Greece, Hungary, Italy, Latvia, Lithuania, Poland, Portugal, Yugoslavia, and, oddly, Belgium (Kirk 1946, table 12, 189).

10   Resurrection: World Migration since World War II

1. The proportion of the foreign-born in the population is influenced not only by immigration inflows but also by "exits," whether through return migration or death.

2. The rest of this section relies heavily on United Nations 2002a, a document devoted to cross-border migration in transition economies.

3. The coefficients estimated for the two periods are not strictly comparable because of differences in model specification. In particular, the pre-1914 model includes lags, while the post-1974 model does not. The range of magnitudes reflects the difference between using short-run and long-run coefficients from the pre-1914 estimates.

4. In the United States, the 1965 amendments to the Immigration and Nationality Act replaced the national-origins quota system with a system largely based on "kinship" to a U.S. citizen or permanent resident alien. The intention was to replace an obviously racist system with one that would appear racially neutral, yet would largely replicate the countries of origin of the immigrants who had come to the United States in previous decades (Daniels and Graham 2001, 43–44, 147–148). The actual effect turned out to be rather different, and Mexican and Asian immigrants, rather than European immigrants, have become the largest beneficiaries of the so-called kinship visas (Chiswick and Sullivan 1995).

5. The UN Declaration on Human Rights in 1948 and the International Convention on the Elimination of All Forms of Racial Discrimination in 1965 were followed by other agreements encouraging the protection of refugees and affirming the primacy of the family. From the 1960s onward, a series of ILO conventions provided for equal treatment of nonnationals. Not all countries subscribed to these declarations and conventions, but a number of regional associations such as the European Union, MERCOSUR (South America), NAFTA (North America), and ECOWAS (West Africa) enunciated rights for migrant workers. On these and other agreements, see United Nations 1997 (71–76).

6. Deteriorating labor market conditions may also explain why more than two-thirds of all German guestworkers had returned to their home countries by the mid-1980s (Bellemare 2004, 2).

7. Like those in other countries, such as Canada, changes in Australian immigration targets have usually been implemented by administrative action rather than by legislation

as in the United States. Even in the United States, administrative rules barring persons who were likely to become a public charge were tightened in the 1930s (and more stringently invoked to reduce the immigration of German Jews), and the requirements for labor certification for employment-based visas in the post–World War II period can be shown to be countercyclical.

11 World Migration under Policy Constraints

1. This phrase is associated with Arthur Calwell, who was Australia's minister for immigration in the Labor government of 1945–1949. Calwell initiated an immigration policy that would augment the Australian population by about 2 percent per year, a goal that was achieved between 1950 and 1970. But he stuck firmly to the position that the immigrants must be of European origin.

2. Relative GDP per capita is a much broader measure than the earnings gap for a given skill level. Among other things, it reflects differences in the per capita stock of human capital. Relative education is therefore included separately to adjust for differences in the human capital stock, and it is expected to take the opposite sign from GDP per capita.

3. Asia consistently records much lower levels of income inequality than Latin America (Higgins and Williamson 2002).

12 Where Are All the Africans?

1. ECOWAS includes Benin, Burkina Faso, Cape Verde, Côte d'Ivoire, Gambia, Ghana, Guinea Bissau, Liberia, Mali, Mauritania, Niger, Nigeria, Senegal, Sierra Leone, and Togo. Article 2(2) of the 1975 treaty states that "The Community shall by stages ensure the abolition as between member states of obstacles to the free movement of persons, services and capital" (Akande 1998, 347).

2. The agreements cover almost the whole of eastern and southern Africa. Members of the PTA are Angola, Botswana, Burundi, Comoros, Djibouti, Kenya, Lesotho, Malawi, Mauritius, Mozambique, Namibia, Rwanda, Somalia, Sudan, Swaziland, Tanzania, Uganda, Zambia, and Zimbabwe.

3. By 1970, manufacturing employed 12 percent of the labor force, commerce 14 percent, and services 10 percent. Agriculture employed 57 percent and included a large subsistence farming sector.

4. For an account of the success of these programs and their effects on the labor market, see Kapur et al. 1991 and European Commission and International Labour Organisation 1994.

5. This is despite the fact that they received no support (and sometimes harassment and deportations) from the South African government. These refugees did not gain the right of permanent settlement until 1999–2000 (SAMP 2001).

6. The present forecasts indicate that the proportion of young adults in the African population in 2000–2020 is *higher* than it would have been in the absence of AIDS, because AIDS-related deaths sharply reduce the numbers reaching middle age (United Nations 2003, vol. 3). Still, AIDS reduces the total population in the young-adult category.

7. Using the 10 percent spillover assumption, our earlier estimates suggested emigration pressure rising to 1.25 million in 2020, or 1.27 per thousand of the population (Hatton and Williamson 2003, table 5).

13 The Rise (and Fall?) of Asylum Seeking

1. The ratio of decisions to applications varies from year to year; when processing backlogs are accumulating, the number of decisions falls behind the number of applications, and it catches up when backlogs are falling. But over the period 1992–2001, the number of (first-instance) decisions was only 79 percent of applications; for the European Union alone, it was 85 percent.

2. In the United Kingdom, a recent parliamentary report noted with dismay that the government was not able to offer even a rough estimate of the number of asylum seekers whose claims had been rejected but who nevertheless remained in the country (U.K. Home Affairs Committee 2003, 12).

3. For wide-ranging accounts of European immigration and asylum policies, see Rasmussen 1997, Geddes 2000, and Noll 2000.

4. These are bilateral agreements with nonmember states that allow asylum seekers to be sent back to countries through which they had transited. They have been heavily criticized for opening the door to serial *refoulement*.

5. Related issues are whether convention status is accorded only to those under threat of persecution by agents of the state (as distinct from rebel factions or criminal groups) and whether there exists the alternative of internal flight (within the origin country).

6. The smuggling fees for passage from Asia are much higher. For example, according to Friebel and Guriev (2004), "China-U.S. smuggling fees reached U.S.D 35,000 in the mid-1990s and continued to rise [thereafter].... The fees for passage from China to Europe, or from India to the U.S. are lower but still above U.S.D 20,000" (5). Distance matters.

7. The process is well illustrated by a comment from an official of the Hungarian Border Guard:

In the beginning, only a few isolated individuals were involved in human trafficking, but as time passed they started cooperating, and step by step the business developed into an international one. Well-planned routes and well-organized groups have evolved, which are no longer coordinated from Hungary. Trafficking can be coordinated either from the destination country or from the migrants' country of origin. This is the result of a natural process of development; market demand and necessity have contributed to the development of certain branches of crime. (quoted in International Organization for Migration 2000, 196).

14 The Labor Market and Fiscal Impact of Immigration

1. The key assumptions of the theorem are that the individual region is a perfect competitor in the goods markets, that there are at least as many goods as factors of production, and that changes in factor supply are not sufficiently large to alter the set of goods that are produced.

2. A large part of the change in the skill composition was also accommodated by economy-wide skill-biased technical change, thus confirming that technology and factor supplies are always jointly at work.

3. The decrease in the skill premium should have been heightened by restrictions imposed after 1992 on the entry of Palestinian workers, who were overwhelmingly low-skilled. However, these were very largely replaced by an expansion in the number of temporary low-skilled workers from other countries (Cohen and Hsieh 2000, 13).

4. Hunt (1992, 569) also examined the effects of the influx of repatriates on internal migration but found a positive correlation between repatriate in-migration to a *département* and in-migration to a *department* from elsewhere in France. Were they driven by a third factor?

5. One might also wish to consider the fiscal impact of the children of immigrants, who are, of course, native-born but who would not be in the host country had their parents not immigrated.

6. See Liebfritz, O'Brien, and Dumont 2003 for a useful overview of recent estimates. A discussion of methodology and earlier studies can be found in OECD 1997 (part 3).

15   Migrant Selection, Immigrant Assimilation, and Emigrant Brain Drain

1. Since most of the literature compares the log of earnings for immigrants and natives, convergence of earnings is typically defined in relative rather than absolute terms.

2. Chapter 5 surveyed the equally large historical literature on U.S. immigrant assimilation. Here we focus on modern assimilation studies.

3. These results may also point to lower-quality schooling in the Third World, or to the inability of immigrants to use that schooling effectively when English is not their native language, or both.

4. For additional evidence supporting the Roy model taken from a large OECD sample, see Liebig and Sousa-Poza 2004.

5. One piece of evidence in favor of this hypothesis is that Latin American migrants in Canada have more schooling, better English language skills, and higher relative incomes than do those in the United States. While this may be partly due to different immigration policies in the two countries, the same Canadian-U.S. difference does not seem to apply to immigrants from other source regions (Antecol, Cobb-Clark, and Trejo 2003).

6. Among nonwhite adult male immigrants in the United Kingdom, unemployment rates fall from 41 percent for the most recent immigrants to 21 percent for those resident for ten years. The rise in the employment rate is even more dramatic: from 35 percent for the most recent immigrants to 66 percent for those resident for ten years. For white immigrants, the initial disadvantage is much smaller, and employment assimilation is much faster (Hatton and Wheatley Price 2004).

7. Rising returns on imported skills provided an added incentive for these immigrants to make investments in human capital immediately after their arrival because the foregone earnings cost was small relative to future expected earnings (Eckstein and Weiss 2003).

8. This may help explain the puzzle of why instrumental variables estimates of the effects of host country language on earnings are often so very large. What they reflect is not just the direct impact of language, but also the latent value of the human capital that host country language fluency helps unlock.

9. These data are subject to a number of qualifications. The most important of these is that the educational composition of immigrants from a given source country residing in the United States is assumed also to apply to immigrants from the same source residing in other OECD countries.

10. A key issue is who pays for the education received abroad. If the host country pays, then it is hard to view this as an investment lost to the sending country.

11. That is, we assume a labor output elasticity of 0.7 and that emigrants come from the middle of the skill distribution.

12. For a less-benign view, see Faini 2003b.

16   Policy and Prejudice

1. The details of the 1995 ISSP can be found in O'Rourke and Sinnott 2001, Mayda and Rodrik 2002, and Mayda 2003.

2. There is no gross correlation in the data. However, a correlation does emerge when we control for other factors that matter. See Mayda 2003.

3. Much of what follows in the next few paragraphs draws heavily on O'Rourke and Sinnott 2004 (1–4) and O'Rourke 2003 (1–3).

4. Mayda does not explore the Roy model, but she offers more detail than do O'Rourke and Sinnott, and she also documents the role of racist feelings.

5. Fetzer (2000, 153–154) disagrees.

6. In France the "threat" came from the National Front, while in Britain it came from the National Front. British Conservative Party leader Margaret Thatcher responded in a 1978 BBC current affairs program interview (*Panorama*) by saying that she would not see Britain "swamped by people of a different culture."

17   Policy and Performance

1. Does the immigrant-induced 3 percent rise in the OECD labor force seem large in terms of the annual rates recorded by the mass migrations a century ago? It certainly does not for Argentina, Australia, and Canada, although it would have taken a couple of years to produce that result for the United States.

2. Walmsley and Winters assume that the gain in labor efficiency that a migrant experiences by moving from sending to host country is only half of the observed gap between the two. Their making such a conservative assumption may be defended by the fact that their focus is on temporary rather than permanent migration. But if that assumption is changed from one-half to three-quarters, the world GNP gain rises to $235 billion, more than 50 percent higher (Walmsley and Winters 2004, 44).

3. It should be added that the transfer would serve to *improve* the terms of trade in the developing world by 0.5 percent (since skilled wages would rise relative to unskilled wages in sending countries, countries that export unskilled-labor-intensive products) and *deteriorate* by 0.2 percent in the OECD (since skilled wages fall relative to unskilled wages in host countries, countries that export skilled-labor-intensive products). The relative wage effects are the inevitable consequence of the assumption that emigrants (eight million each of skilled and unskilled) are more skilled than the stayers in the sending country *and* that immigrants are more skilled than residents in the host country. This second assumption seems unrealistic, especially given that it is inconsistent with two centuries of mass migration experience. In any case, the estimated terms-of-trade effects from immigration are more modest than those estimated by Davis and Weinstein (2002) for the United States using a different framework.

4. Of course, rapid development in the poor sending countries would eventually erase those productivity differences. Still, it took more than two centuries to produce these productivity differences between sending and receiving countries, and we assume that there is enough political urgency so that nobody wants to wait another two centuries to erase them.

5. There are slightly different cutoffs for other groups such as students and citizens of New Zealand. Those with a score of at least seventy points can enter a "pool" and have their applications held in reserve for up to two years.

6. For immigrants to be able to compensate native labor for immigration-related losses, the surplus that they gain by moving must be at least as large as the amount that native labor loses as a result of the immigration. This requires that the immigrant gain as a proportion of the host country wage must exceed the inverse of the elasticity of labor demand. If that elasticity is less than one, immigrants cannot compensate native labor even if the whole of the immigrant surplus is taxed away.

7. Indeed, it seems likely that those who were sufficiently rich in their home country to be able to afford the entry price would not wish to migrate anyway. Although some countries, such as Australia, offer visas to business owners or investors who can show that they have a certain minimum amount of capital, most do not require an entry fee even for these relatively rich migrants.

8. Indeed, forced savings that are deducted from the immigrant's earnings over the contract period increase the incentive to defect into the illegal market at the beginning of the contract rather than at the end. There will always be some rate of forced savings at which it pays the legal temporary to become a permanent illegal even if he or she takes a significant cut in pay to do so.

18 World Mass Migration: Past, Present, and Future

1. The same might be said of the International Labour Organization (ILO), which was founded in 1919 and became an agency of the United Nations in 1946. The focus of the ILO is industrial relations, social justice, and human rights, and although it has developed an interest in global governance, it does not provide a forum suitable for multilateral negotiations on migration.

2. The reference is to the agreement governing migration of personnel in specific service sectors under Mode 4 of GATS, an issue on which we elaborate later in the chapter.

References

Aaronson, S. A. 2001. *Taking Trade to the Streets: The Lost History of Public Efforts to Shape Globalization*. Ann Arbor: University of Michigan Press.

Abella, M. I. 1995. Asian Migrant and Contract Workers in the Middle East. In *The Cambridge Survey of World Migration*, ed. R. Cohen, 418–423. Cambridge: Cambridge University Press.

Abramovitz, M. 1961. The Nature and Significance of Kuznets Cycles. *Economic Development and Cultural Change* 9:225–248.

Acemoglu, D., and J. Robinson. 2000. Why Did the West Extend the Franchise? Democracy, Inequality, and Growth in Historical Perspective. *Quarterly Journal of Economics* 115:1167–1199.

Acemoglu, D., and F. Zilibotti. 2001. Productivity Differences. *Quarterly Journal of Economics* 116:563–606.

Adams, R. H. 1993. The Economic and Demographic Determinants of International Migration in Rural Egypt. *Journal of Development Studies* 30: 146–167.

Adams, R. H. 2003. International Migration, Remittances and the Brain Drain: A Study of 24 Labor-Exporting Countries. Policy Research Working Paper 3069, International Monetary Fund, Washington, DC.

Adams, R. H., and J. Page. 2003. International Migration, Remittances and Poverty in Developing Countries. Policy Research Working Paper 3179, World Bank, Washington, DC.

Addison, T., and C. Worswick. 2002. The Impact of Immigration on the Earnings of Natives: Evidence from Australian Micro Data. *Economic Record* 78:68–78.

Adekayne, J., Bayo. 1998. Conflicts, Loss of State Capacities and Migration in Contemporary Africa. In *Emigration Dynamics in Developing Countries*. Vol. I, *Sub-Saharan Africa*, ed. R. Appleyard, 165–206. Aldershot, UK: Ashgate.

Adepoju, A. 1995. Migration in Africa. In *The Migration Experience in Africa*, ed. J. Baker and T. A. Aina, 87–108. Stockholm: Nordiska Africainstitutet.

Addo, N. O. 1987. Population, Migration and Employment: The Case of Ghana. In *Population et Développement en Afrique* (Population and Development in Africa), ed. H. Jemai, 283–352. Dakkar: Codesria.

Agesa, R. 2001. Migration and the Urban to Rural Earnings Difference: A Sample Selection Approach. *Economic Development and Cultural Change* 49:847–865.

Akande, J. 1998. International Legal Treaties Relating to Migration in Sub-Saharan Africa. In *Emigration Dynamics in Developing Countries*. Vol. 1, *Sub-Saharan Africa*, ed. R. Appleyard, 338–362. Aldershot, UK: Ashgate.

Alesina, A., and R. Perotti. 1994. The Political Economy of Growth: A Critical Survey of the Recent Literature. *World Bank Economic Review* 8:351–371.

Allen, R. C. 2001. The Great Divergence in European Wages and Prices from the Middle Ages to the First World War. *Explorations in Economic History* 38:411–447.

Altonji, J. G., and D. Card. 1991. The Effect of Immigration on the Labor Market Outcomes of Less-Skilled Natives. In *Immigration, Trade and the Labor Market*, ed. J. M. Abowd and R. B. Freeman, 201–234. Chicago: University of Chicago Press.

Amjad, R., ed. 1989. *To the Gulf and Back: Studies on the Economic Impact of Asian Labour Migration*. New Delhi: International Labour Organisation Asian Employment Programme.

Anbinder, T. G. 1992. *Nativism and Slavery: The Northern Know Nothings and the Politics of the 1850s*. New York: Oxford University Press.

Anderson, E. 2001. Globalisation and Wage Inequalities, 1870–1970. *European Review of Economic History* 5:91–118.

Anderson, J. E. 1995. Tariff Index Theory. *Review of International Economics* 3:156–173.

Anderson, J. E., and J. P. Neary. 1994. Measuring the Restrictiveness of Trade Policy. *World Bank Economic Review* 8:151–169.

Angrist, J. D., and A. D. Kugler. 2003. Protective or Counter Productive? Labor Market Institutions and the Effect of Immigration on UK Natives. *Economic Journal* 113:302–331.

Antecol, H., D. A. Cobb-Clark, and S. K. Trejo. 2003. Immigration Policy and the Skills of Immigrants to Australia, Canada and the United States. *Journal of Human Resources* 38:192–218.

Antecol, H., P. Kuhn, and S. J. Trejo. 2003. Immigration Policy and the Skills of Migrants to Australia, Canada and the United States. Discussion Paper 802, Institute for the Study of Labor (IZA), Bonn.

Appleyard, R. T. 1988. *Ten Pound Immigrants*. London: Boxtree.

Arhin, K. 1994. The Re-accommodation of Ghanaian Returnees from Nigeria in 1983 and 1985. In *When Refugees Go Home*, ed. T. Allen and H. Morsink, 268–275. London: Africa World Press.

Baganha, M. I. B. 1990. *Portuguese Emigration to the United States, 1820–1930*. New York: Garland.

Baily, S. L. 1983. The Adjustment of Italian Immigrants in Buenos Aires and New York, 1870–1914. *American Historical Review* 88:281–305.

Baines, D. E. 1985. *Migration in a Mature Economy*. Cambridge: Cambridge University Press.

Baines, D. E. 1994. European Emigration, 1815–1930: Looking at the Emigration Decision Again. *Economic History Review* 47:525–544.

Baker, M., and D. Benjamin. 1994. The Performance of Immigrants in the Canadian Labor Market. *Journal of Labor Economics* 12:369–405.

Barro, R. J., and X. Sala-i-Martin. 1992. Convergence. *Journal of Political Economy* 100:223–252.

Barro, R. J., and X. Sala-i-Martin. 1995. *Economic Growth*. New York: McGraw-Hill.

Bauer, T. K., M. Lofstrom, and K. F. Zimmermann. 2000. Immigration Policy, Assimilation of Immigrants and Natives' Sentiments towards Immigrants: Evidence from 12 OECD Countries. Discussion Paper 187, Institute for the Study of Labor (IZA), Bonn.

Bauer, T. K., and K. F. Zimmermann. 1999. Assessment of Possible Migration Pressure and Its Labour Market Impact Following EU Enlargement to Central and Eastern Europe. Research Report No. 3, Institute for the Study of Labor (IZA), Bonn.

Baumol, W. J. 1986. Productivity Growth, Convergence and Welfare: What the Long-Run Data Show. *American Economic Review* 76:1072–1085.

Baumol, W. J., S. A. B. Blackman, and E. N. Wolff. 1989. *Productivity and American Leadership: The Long View*. Cambridge, MA: MIT Press.

Beine, M., F. Docquier, and H. Rapoport. 2003. Brain Drain and LDC's Growth: Winners and Losers. Discussion Paper 819, Institute for the Study of Labor (IZA), Bonn.

Bellemare, C. 2004. A Life-cycle Model of Outmigration and Economic Assimilation of Immigrants in Germany. Discussion Paper 1012, Institute for the Study of Labor (IZA), Bonn.

Benhabib, J. 1996. On the Political Economy of Immigration. *European Economic Review* 40:1737–1743.

Bernard, W. S. 1982. A History of U.S. Immigration Policy. In *Immigration*, ed. R. A. Easterlin, D. Ward, W. S. Bernard, and R. Ueda, 75–105. Cambridge, MA: Harvard University Press.

Bértola, L., and J. G. Williamson. 2005. Globalization in Latin America before 1940. Forthcoming in *Cambridge Economic History of Latin America*, ed. V. Bulmer-Thomas, J. Coatsworth and R. Cortés Conde. Cambridge: Cambridge University Press.

Betrán, C., and M. A. Pons. 2004. Skilled and Unskilled Wage Differentials and Economic Integration, 1870–1930. *European Review of Economic History* 8:29–60.

Betts, K. 1988. *Ideology and Immigration: Australia, 1976–1987*. Melbourne: Melbourne University Press.

Bevan, D. L., P. Collier, and J. W. Gunning. 1999. *Nigeria and Indonesia: The Political Economy of Poverty, Equity and Growth*. Washington: Oxford University Press.

Bevelander, P., and H. S. Nielsen. 2001. Declining Employment Success of Immigrant Males in Sweden: Observed or Unobserved Characteristics? *Journal of Population Economics* 14:455–471.

Bhagwati, J. N., and K. Hamada. 1974. The Brain Drain, International Integration of Markets for Professionals and Unemployment: A Theoretical Analysis. *Journal of Development Economics* 1:19–42.

Blainey, G. [1966] 1982. *The Tyranny of Distance: How Distance Shaped Australia's History*. Melbourne: Macmillan.

Blanchard, O., and J. Wolfers. 2000. The Role of Shocks and Institutions in the Rise of European Unemployment: The Aggregate Evidence. *Economic Journal* 110:C1–C33.

Blau, F. D. 1980. Immigration and Labor Earnings in Early Twentieth Century America. *Research in Population Economics* 2:21–41.

Bloom, D. E., and J. D. Sachs. 1998. Geography, Demography and Economic Growth in Africa. *Brookings Papers in Economic Activity* 2:207–273.

Bloom, D. E., and J. G. Williamson. 1998. Demographic Transitions and Economic Miracles in Emerging Asia. *World Bank Economic Review* 12:419–455.

Böcker, A., and T. Havinga. 1997. *Asylum Migration to the European Union: Patterns of Origin and Destination.* Luxembourg: Office for Official Publications of the European Communities.

Bodnar, J. 1985. *The Transplanted: A History of Immigrants in Urban America.* Bloomington: Indiana University Press.

Boeri, T., and H. Brücker. 2000. The Impact of Eastern Enlargement on Employment and Labour Markets in the EU Member States. Working Paper, Deutsches Institut für Wirtschaftsforschung, Berlin.

Boeri, T., G. Hanson, and B. McCormick, eds. 2002. *Immigration Policy and the Welfare System.* Oxford: Oxford University Press.

Bordo, M., A. M. Taylor, and J. G. Williamson, eds. 2003. *Globalization in Historical Perspective.* Chicago: University of Chicago Press.

Borjas, G. J. 1985. Assimilation, Changes in Cohort Quality and the Earnings of Immigrants. *Journal of Labor Economics* 3:463–489.

Borjas, G. J. 1987. Self Selection and the Earnings of Immigrants. *American Economic Review* 77:531–553.

Borjas, G. J. 1992. National Origin and the Skills of Immigrants in the Postwar Period. In *Immigration and the Workforce: Economic Consequences for the United States and Source Areas,* ed. G. J. Borjas and R. B. Freeman, 39–69. Chicago: University of Chicago Press.

Borjas, G. J. 1993. Immigration Policy, National Origin, and Immigrant Skills: A Comparison of Canada and the United States. In *Small Differences that Matter: Labor Markets and Income Maintenance in Canada and the United States,* ed. D. Card and R. B. Freeman, 21–43. Chicago: University of Chicago Press.

Borjas, G. J. 1994. The Economics of Immigration. *Journal of Economic Literature* 32:1667–1717.

Borjas, G. J. 1995. Assimilation and Changes in Cohort Quality Revisited: What Happened to Immigrant Earnings in the 1980s? *Journal of Labor Economics* 13:201–245.

Borjas, G. J. 1999a. The Economic Analysis of Immigration. In *Handbook of Labor Economics,* Vol. 3A, ed. O. Ashenfelter and D. Card, 1697–1760. New York: North-Holland.

Borjas, G. J. 1999b. *Heaven's Door: Immigration Policy and the American Economy.* Princeton: Princeton University Press.

Borjas, G. J. 2000. The Economic Progress of Immigrants. In *Issues in the Economics of Immigration,* ed. G. J. Borjas, 15–49. Chicago: University of Chicago Press.

Borjas, G. J. 2003. The Labor Demand Curve *Is* Downward Sloping: Reexamining the Impact of Immigration on the Labor Market. *Quarterly Journal of Economics* 118:1335–1374.

Borjas, G. J., R. B. Freeman, and L. F. Katz. 1992. On the Labor Market Impacts of Immigration and Trade. In *Immigration and the Work Force: Economic Consequences for the United States and Source Areas*, ed. G. J. Borjas and R. B. Freeman, 213–244. Chicago: University of Chicago Press.

Borjas, G. J., R. B. Freeman, and L. F. Katz. 1996. Searching for the Effect of Immigration on the Labor Market. *American Economic Review* 86:247–251.

Borjas, G. J., R. B. Freeman, and L. F. Katz. 1997. How Much Do Immigration and Trade Affect Labor Market Outcomes? *Brookings Papers on Economic Activity* 1:1–90.

Boustan, L. P. 2003. "America Was in Everybody's Mouth": An Economic Evaluation of Jewish Emigration from the Russian Empire, 1881–1914. Photocopy, Department of Economics, Harvard University, Cambridge, MA.

Boyer, G. R., T. J. Hatton, and K. H. O'Rourke. 1994. The Impact of Emigration on Real Wages in Ireland, 1850–1914. In *Migration and the International Labor Market, 1850–1914*, ed. T. J. Hatton and J. G. Williamson, 221–239. London: Routledge.

Brandt, L. 1985. Chinese Agriculture and the International Economy, 1870–1913: A Reassessment. *Explorations in Economic History* 22:168–180.

Bratsberg, B. 1995. The Incidence of Non-return among Foreign Students in the United States. *Economics of Education Review* 14:373–384.

Briggs, V. M. 1984. *Immigration Policy and the American Labor Force*. Baltimore: Johns Hopkins University Press.

Brito, D. L., and J. G. Williamson. 1973. Skilled Labor and Nineteenth Century Anglo-American Managerial Behavior. *Explorations in Economic History* 10:235–252.

Brown, A. G. 2003. *Reluctant Partners: A History of Multilateral Trade Cooperation, 1850–2000*. Ann Arbor: University of Michigan Press.

Buch, C. M., and A. Kuckulenz. 2004. Worker Remittances and Capital Flows to Developing Countries. ZEW Discussion Paper 04–31, Centre for European Economic Research, Mannheim, Germany.

Burds, J. 1998. *Peasant Dreams and Market Politics: Labor Migration and the Russian Village, 1861–1905*. Pittsburgh: University of Pittsburgh Press.

Burns, A. 1954. *The Frontiers of Economic Knowledge*. Princeton: Princeton University Press.

Butlin, N. G. 1994. *Forming a Colonial Economy: Australia, 1810–1850*. Cambridge: Cambridge University Press.

Cameron, R. 1989. *A Concise Economic History of the World from Paleolithic Times to the Present*. New York: Oxford University Press.

Canny, N. 1994. English Migration into and across the Atlantic during the Seventeenth and Eighteenth Centuries. In *Europeans on the Move: Studies in European Migration*, ed. N. Canny, 39–75. Oxford: Oxford University Press.

Card, D. 1990. The Impact of the Mariel Boatlift on the Miami Labor Market. *Industrial and Labor Relations Review* 43:247–257.

Card, D. 2001. Immigrant Inflows, Native Outflows, and the Local Labor Market Impacts of Higher Immigration. *Journal of Labor Economics* 19:22–64.

Carey-Wood, J., K. Duke, V. Kam, and T. Marshall. 1995. The Settlement of Refugees in Britain. Home Office Research Study No. 141, HMSO, London.

Carlsson, S. 1976. Chronology and Composition of Swedish Emigration to America. In *From Sweden to America; A History of the Migration*, ed. H. Rundblom and H. Norman, 114–148. Minneapolis: University of Minnesota Press.

Carrier, N. H., and J. R. Jeffrey. 1953. *External Migration: A Study of the Available Statistics, 1815–1950*. London: HMSO.

Carrington, W. J., and E. Detragaiche. 1998. How Big Is the Brain Drain? Working Paper 98-102, International Monetary Fund, Washington, DC.

Carrington, W. J., and P. J. F. de Lima. 1996. The Impact of 1970s Repatriates from Africa on the Portuguese Labor Market. *Industrial and Labor Relations Review* 49:330–347.

Chami, R., C. Fullenkamp, and S. Jahjah. 2003. Are Immigrant Remittance Flows a Source of Capital for Development? Working Paper 03-189, International Monetary Fund, Washington, DC.

Chanda, R. 2001. Movement of Natural Persons and the GATS. *World Economy* 24:631–654.

Chapman, B. 2005. Income-Contingent Loans for Higher Education: International Reform. Forthcoming in *Economics of Education Handbook*, ed. E. Hanushek and F. Welch. Amsterdam: Elsevier.

Ching-Hwang, Y. 1985. *Coolies and Mandarins: China's Protection of Overseas Chinese during the Late Ch'ing Period*. Singapore: Singapore University Press.

Chiquiar, D., and G. H. Hanson. 2002. International Migration, Self-Selection, and the Distribution of Wages: Evidence from Mexico and the United States. Working Paper 9242, National Bureau of Economic Research, Cambridge, MA.

Chirwa, W. C. 1997. "No Teba...Forget Teba": The Plight of Malawian Ex-Migrant Workers to South Africa. *International Migration Review* 31:628–654.

Chiswick, B. R. 1977. Sons of Immigrants: Are They at an Earnings Disadvantage? *American Economic Review* (Papers and Proceedings) 67:376–380.

Chiswick, B. R. 1978. The Effect of Americanization on the Earnings of Foreign-born Men. *Journal of Political Economy* 86:897–921.

Chiswick, B. R. 1988. Illegal Immigration and Immigration Control. *Journal of Economic Perspectives* 2:101–115.

Chiswick, B. R. 1992. Jewish Immigrant Skill and Occupational Attainment at the Turn of the Century. *Explorations in Economic History* 28:64–86.

Chiswick, B. R. 1998. Hebrew Language Usage: Determinants and Effects on Earnings among Immigrants in Israel. *Journal of Population Economics* 11:263–271.

Chiswick, B. R. 2000. Are Immigrants Favorably Selected? In *Migration Theory: Talking across Disciplines*, ed. C. B. Brettell and J. F. Hollifield, 61–76. New York: Routledge.

Chiswick, B. R. 2001. The Economics of Illegal Migration for the Host Economy. In *International Migration into the 21st Century*, ed. M. A. B. Siddique, 74–85. London: Elgar.

Chiswick, B. R., and T. J. Hatton. 2003. International Migration and the Integration of Labor Markets. In *Globalization in Historical Perspective*, ed. M. Bordo, A. M. Taylor, and J. G. Williamson, 65–119. Chicago: University of Chicago Press.

Chiswick, B. R., and P. W. Miller. 1998. English Language Fluency among Immigrants in the United States. *Research in Labor Economics* 17:151–200.

Chiswick, B. R., and T. A. Sullivan. 1995. The New Immigrants. In *State of the Union: America in the 1990s*. Vol. 2, *Social Trends*, ed. R. Farley, 211–270. New York: Sage.

Cinel, D. 1991. *The National Integration of Italian Return Migration, 1870–1929*. Cambridge: Cambridge University Press.

Clark, X., T. J. Hatton, and J. G. Williamson. 2002. Where Do U.S. Immigrants Come From? Policy and Sending Country Fundamentals. Working Paper 8998, National Bureau of Economic Research, Cambridge, MA.

Clemens, M., and J. G. Williamson. 2004. Wealth Bias in the First Global Capital Market Boom 1870–1913. *Economic Journal* 114:304–337.

Clingingsmith, D., and J. G. Williamson. 2004. India's De-industrialization under British Rule: New Ideas, New Evidence. Working Paper 10586, National Bureau of Economic Research, Cambridge, MA.

Coatsworth, J. H., and J. G. Williamson. 2004. Always Protectionist? Latin American Tariffs from Independence to Great Depression. *Journal of Latin American Studies* 36:205–232.

Cobb-Clark, D. A. 2004. Selection Policy and the Labour Market Outcomes of New Immigrants. Discussion Paper 1380, Institute for the Study of Labor (IZA), Bonn.

Cobb-Clark, D. A., and M. D. Connolly. 1997. The Worldwide Market for Skilled Migrants: Can Australia Compete? *International Migration Review* 31:670–693.

Cohen, S., and C.-T. Hsieh. 2000. Macroeconomic and Labor Market Impact of Russian Immigration in Israel. Unpublished manuscript, Tel Aviv University.

Cohn, R. L. 1984. Mortality on Immigrant Voyages to New York, 1836–1853. *Journal of Economic History* 44:289–300.

Cohn, R. L. 1992. The Occupations of English Immigrants to the U.S., 1836–1853. *Journal of Economic History* 52:377–387.

Collier, P., and J. W. Gunning. 1999. Why Has Africa Grown Slowly? *Journal of Economic Perspectives* 13:3–22.

Collins, W. J. 1997. When the Tide Turned: Immigration and the Delay of the Great Migration. *Journal of Economic History* 57:607–632.

Collins, W. J., K. H. O'Rourke, and J. G. Williamson. 1999. Were Trade and Factor Mobility Substitutes in History? In *Migration: The Controversies and the Evidence*, ed. R. Faini, J. DeMelo, and K. Zimmermann, 227–260. Cambridge: Cambridge University Press.

Commander, S., M. Kangasniemi, and L. A. Winters. 2003. The Brain Drain: Curse or Boon? Discussion Paper 809, Institute for the Study of Labor (IZA), Bonn.

Conselo Nacional de Estatistica 1957. *Annuario Estatistica do Brasil, 1957*. Rio de Janiero: Government Printer.

Constant, A., and M. L. Schultz-Neilsen. 2004. Immigrant Selection and Earnings. In *Migrants, Work, and the Welfare State*, ed. T. Tranæs and K. F. Zimmermann, 187–212. Odense: University Press of Southern Denmark.

Córdova, E. L. 2004. Globalization, Migration and Development: The Role of Mexican Migrant Remittances. Photocopy, Inter-American Development Bank, Washington, DC.

Cornelius, W., P. Martin, and J. Hollifield, eds. 1994. *Controlling Immigration*. Stanford: Stanford University Press.

Council of Europe. 2001. *Demographic Yearbook 2001*. http://www.coe.int/t/e/social%5Fcohesion/population/Demographic%5FYear%5FBook/.

Cox Edwards, A., and M. Ureta. 2003. International Migration, Remittances and Schooling: Evidence from El Salvador. Working Paper 9766, National Bureau of Economic Research, Cambridge, MA.

Crafts, N. F. R., and G. Toniolo. 1996. *Economic Growth in Europe since 1945*. Cambridge: Cambridge University Press.

Cross, G. S. 1981. *Immigrant Workers in Industrial France: The Making of a New Laboring Class*. Philadelphia: Temple University Press.

Cullen, L. M. 1994. The Irish Diaspora of the Seventeenth and Eighteenth Centuries. In *Europeans on the Move: Studies on European Migration, 1500–1800*, ed. N. Canny, 113–149. Oxford: Clarendon.

Daniels, R. 1995. The Growth of Restrictive Immigration Policies in the Colonies of Settlement. In *The Cambridge Survey of World Migration*, ed. R. Cohen, 39–43. Cambridge: Cambridge University Press.

Daniels, R., and O. L. Graham. 2001. *Debating American Immigration, 1882–Present*. Lanham, MD: Rowman and Littlefield.

Davis, D. R., and D. E. Weinstein. 2002. Technological Superiority and the Losses from Migration. Working Paper 8971, National Bureau of Economic Research, Cambridge, MA.

Davis, K. 1947. Future Migration into Latin America. In *Postwar Problems of Migration*, ed. L. J. Reed, 30–48. New York: Milbank Memorial Fund.

Davis, K. 1951. *The Population of India and Pakistan*. Princeton: Princeton University Press.

Deardorff, A. V., and R. M. Stern. 2002. What You Should Know about Globalization and the World Trade Organization. *Review of International Economics* 10:404–423.

Deininger, K., and L. Squire. 1996. A New Data Set Measuring Income Inequality. *World Bank Economic Review* 10:565–591.

Deltas, G., R. Sicotte, and P. Tomczak. 2004. Passenger Shipping Cartels and Their Effect on Trans-Atlantic Migration. Unpublished paper, Department of Economics, University of Illinois.

De New, J. P., and K. F. Zimmermann. 1994. Native Wage Impacts of Foreign Labor: A Random Effects Panel Analysis. *Journal of Population Economics* 7:177–192.

Department of Immigration and Multicultural Affairs, Australia. 2000. *Immigration: Federation to Century's End.* Canberra: Commonwealth of Australia.

de Vletter, F. 1985. Recent Trends and Prospects of Black Migration to South Africa. *Journal of Modern African Studies* 23:667–702.

Diaz-Alejandro, C. F. 1970. *Essays on the Economic History of the Argentine Republic.* New Haven: Yale University Press.

DIMA. *See* Department of Immigration and Multicultural Affairs, Australia.

Dobson, J., K. Khoser, G. McLaughlan, and J. Salt. 2001. International Migration and the United Kingdom: Recent Patterns and Trends. Research Development and Statistics Occasional Paper 75. London: UK Home Office.

Dole, T. 2003. The Great Migration and the Transport Revolution: The Influence of Transport Improvements on European Immigration, 1840–1913. Senior honors thesis, Department of Economics, Harvard University, Cambridge, MA.

Domar, E. D., and M. J. Machina. 1984. On the Profitability of Russian Serfdom. *Journal of Economic History* 44:919–955.

Dominion Bureau of Statistics. 1942. *Census of Canada, 1941.* Ottawa: Government Printer.

Douglas, P. H. 1919. Is the New Immigration More Unskilled than the Old? *Journal of the American Statistical Association* 16:393–403.

Douglas, P. H. [1930] 1966. *Real Wages in the United States, 1890–1926.* New York: Kelley.

Duleep, H. O., and M. C. Regets. 1997. Immigrant Entry Earnings and Human Capital Growth: Evidence from the 1960–80 Censuses. *Research in Labor Economics* 16:297–317.

Dunkley, P. 1980. Emigration and the State, 1803–1842: The Nineteenth Century Revolution in Government Reconsidered. *Historical Journal* 23:353–387.

Dunlevy, J. A., and H. A. Gemery. 1978. Economic Opportunity and the Responses of Old and New Immigrants in the United States. *Journal of Economic History* 39:901–917.

Dustmann, C. 2003. The Impact of EU Enlargement on Migration Flows. Online Report 25/03, UK Home Office, London. http://www.homeoffice.gov.uk/rds/pdfs2/rdsolr2503.pdf.

Dustmann, C., F. Fabbri, I. Preston, and J. Wadsworth. 2003. The Local Labour Market Effects of Immigration in the UK. Online Report 06/03, UK Home Office, London. http://www.homeoffice.gov.vk/rds/pdfs2/rdsolr0603.pdf.

Dustmann, C., and I. Preston. 2000. Racial and Economic Factors in Attitudes to Immigration. Discussion Paper 190, Institute for the Study of Labor (IZA), Bonn.

Dustmann, C., and I. Preston. 2001. Attitudes to Ethnic Minorities, Ethnic Context and Location Decisions. *Economic Journal* 111:353–373.

Easterlin, R. A. 1961. Influences on European Overseas Emigration before World War I. *Economic Development and Cultural Change* 9:331–351.

Easterlin, R. A. 1968. *Population, Labor Force and Long Swings in Economic Growth.* New York: National Bureau of Economic Research.

Easterlin, R. A. 1981. Why Isn't the Whole World Developed? *Journal of Economic History* 41:1–19.

Eckstein, Z., and Y. Weiss. 2003. On the Wage Growth of Immigrants: Israel, 1990–2000. Discussion Paper 710, Institute for the Study of Labor (IZA), Bonn.

Eichengreen, B. J., and H. A. Gemery. 1986. The Earnings of Skilled and Unskilled Immigrants at the End of the Nineteenth Century. *Journal of Economic History* 46:441–454.

Eldridge, H. T., and D. S. Thomas. 1964. *Population and Economic Growth: United States 1870–1950*, Vol. 3. Philadelphia: American Philosophical Society.

Eltis, D. 1983. Free and Coerced Transatlantic Migrations: Some Comparisons. *American Historical Review* 88:251–280.

Eltis, D. 2002a. Introduction. In *Coerced and Free Migration: Global Perspectives*, ed. D. Eltis, 1–31. Stanford: Stanford University Press.

Eltis, D. 2002b. Free and Coerced Migrations from the Old World to the New. In *Coerced and Free Migration: Global Perspectives*, ed. D. Eltis, 33–74. Stanford: Stanford University Press.

Eltis, D., S. D. Behrendt, D. Richardson, and H. S. Klein. 1999. *The Trans-Atlantic Slave Trade: A Database on CD-ROM*. Cambridge: Cambridge University Press.

Engerman, S. L. 1986. Servants to Slaves to Servants: Contract Labour and European Expansion. In *Colonialism and Migration: Indentured Labour before and after Slavery*, ed. E. van den Boogaart and P. C. Emmer, 263–294. Dordrecht: Nijhoff.

Engerman, S. L., S. Haber, and K. L. Sokoloff. 2000. Inequality, Institutions, and Differential Paths of Growth among New World Economies. In *Institutions, Contracts, and Organizations: Perspectives from the New Institutional Economics*, ed. C. Menard, 108–136. Cheltenham: Elgar.

Engerman, S. L., and K. L. Sokoloff. 2003. Institutional and Non-institutional Explanations of Economic Differences. Working Paper 9989, National Bureau of Economic Research, Cambridge, MA.

Erickson, C. 1972. Who Were the English and Scottish Emigrants in the 1880s? In *Population and Social Change*, ed. D. V. Glass and R. Revelle, 347–381. London: Arnold.

Erickson, C. 1990. Emigration from the British Isles to the U.S.A. in 1841: Part II; Who Were the English Emigrants? *Population Studies* 44:21–40.

Erickson, C. 1994. *Leaving England: Essays on British Emigration in the Nineteenth Century*. Ithaca: Cornell University Press.

Espenshade, T. J., and K. Hempstead. 1996. Contemporary American Attitudes toward U.S. Immigration. *International Migration Review* 30:535–570.

European Commission and International Labour Organisation. 1994. *Employment and Structural Adjustment in Ghana*. Brussels: European Union.

Faini, R. 2002. Development, Trade and Migration. *Revue d'economie et du développement*. 1–2:85–116.

Faini, R. 2003a. Revisiting the Growth Effects of the Brain Drain. Unpublished paper, University of Rome Tor Vergata.

Faini, R. 2003b. Is the Brain Drain an Unmitigated Blessing? UN-WIDER Discussion Paper 2003/64, World Institute for Development Economics Research, Helsinki.

Faini, R., J.-M. Grether, and J. de Melo. 1999. Globalisation and Migratory Pressures from Developing Countries: A Simulation Analysis. In *Migration: The Controversies and the Evidence*, ed. R. Faini, J. de Melo, and K. F. Zimmermann, 190–220. Cambridge: Cambridge University Press.

Faini, R., and A. Venturini. 1994a. Italian Migrations: The Pre-war Period. In *Migration and the International Labor Market, 1850–1939*, ed. T. J. Hatton and J. G. Williamson, 72–90. London: Routledge.

Faini, R., and A. Venturini. 1994b. Migration and Growth: The Experience of Southern Europe. Discussion Paper 964, Centre for Economic Policy Research, London.

Fehr, H., G. Halder, S. Jokisch, and L. J. Kotlikoff. 2003. A Simulation Model for the Demographic Transition in the OECD. Discussion Paper, University of Wurzburg, Wurzburg, Germany.

Fehr, H., S. Jokisch, and L. J. Kotlikoff. 2004a. The Developed World's Demographic Transition—The Roles of Capital Flows, Immigration, and Policy. Forthcoming in *The Politics and Finance of Social Security Reform*, ed. R. Brooks and A. Razin. Cambridge: Cambridge University Press.

Fehr, H., S. Jokisch, and L. J. Kotlikoff. 2004b. The Role of Immigration in Dealing with the Developed World's Demographic Transition. Working Paper 10512, National Bureau of Economic Research, Cambridge, MA.

Ferenczi, I., and W. F. Willcox. 1929. *International Migrations*. Vol. 1. New York: National Bureau of Economic Research.

Ferrie, J. P. 1999. *Yankeys Now: Immigrants in the Antebellum United States, 1840–1860.* New York: Oxford University Press.

Ferrie, J. P., and J. Mokyr. 1994. Immigration and Entrepreneurship in the Nineteenth Century U.S. In *Economic Aspects of International Migration*, ed. H. Giersch, 115–138. Berlin: Springer-Verlag.

Fertig, M. 2001. The Economic Impact of EU Enlargement: Assessing the Migration Potential. *Empirical Economics* 26:707–720.

Fetzer, J. S. 2000. *Public Attitudes toward Immigration in the United States, France and Germany*. Cambridge: Cambridge University Press.

Filer, R. K. 1992. The Effect of Immigrant Arrivals on Migratory Patterns of Native Workers. In *Immigration and the Workforce: Economic Consequences for the United States and Source Areas*, ed. G. J. Borjas and R. B. Freeman, 245–269. Chicago: University of Chicago Press.

Findlay, S., and S. Sow. 1998. From Season to Season: Agriculture, Poverty and Migration in the Senegal River Valley, Mali. In *Emigration Dynamics in Developing Countries*. Vol. 1, *Sub-Saharan Africa*, ed. R. Appleyard, 69–114. Aldershot, UK: Ashgate.

Fitzpatrick, D. 1980. Irish Emigration in the Later 19th Century. *Irish Historical Studies* 22:126–143.

Fitzpatrick, D. 1984. *Irish Emigration 1801–1921*. Dublin: Economic and Social History Society of Ireland.

Flam, H., and M. J. Flanders. 1991. *Heckscher-Ohlin Trade Theory*. Cambridge, MA: MIT Press.

Forbes, K. 2000. A Reassessment of the Relationship between Inequality and Growth. *American Economic Review* 90:869–887.

Foreman-Peck, J. S. 1992. A Political Economy of International Migration, 1815–1914. *Manchester School of Economic and Social Studies* 60:359–376.

Freeman, G. P. 1994. Can Liberal States Control Unwanted Migration? *Annals of the American Academy of Political and Social Science* 534:17–30.

Freeman, G. P. 1995. Modes of Immigration Politics in Liberal Democratic States. *International Migration Review* 29:881–902.

Friebel, G., and S. Guriev. 2004. Smuggling Humans: A Theory of Debt-financed Migration. Unpublished paper, Princeton University.

Friedberg, R. M. 2000. You Can't Take It with You: Immigrant Assimilation and the Portability of Human Capital. *Journal of Labor Economics* 18:221–251.

Friedberg, R. M. 2001. The Impact of Mass Migration on the Israeli Labor Market. *Quarterly Journal of Economics* 4:1373–1408.

Friedberg, R. M., and J. Hunt. 1995. The Impact of Immigrants on Host-Country Wages, Employment and Growth. *Journal of Economic Perspectives* 9:23–44.

Frimpong-Ansah, J. H. 1992. *The Vampire State in Africa: The Political Economy of Decline in Ghana*. London: Africa World Press.

Furnivall, J. S. 1938. *An Introduction to the Political Economy of Burma*, 2nd ed. Rangoon, Burma.

Gabaccia, D. 1996. Women of the Mass Migrations: From Minority to Majority, 1820–1930. In *European Migrants: Global and Local Perspectives*, ed. D. Hoerder and L. P. Moch, 90–111. Boston: Northeastern University Press.

Galenson, D. W. 1981. *White Servitude in Colonial America*. Cambridge: Cambridge University Press.

Galenson, D. W. 1984. The Rise and Fall of Indentured Servitude in the Americas: An Economic Analysis. *Journal of Economic History* 44:1–26.

Gang, I. N., F. Rivera-Batiz, and M.-S. Yun. 2002. Economic Strain, Ethnic Concentration and Attitudes towards Foreigners in the European Union. Discussion Paper 578, Institute for the Study of Labor (IZA), Bonn.

Geary, R. C. 1935–1936. The Future Population of Saorstát Eireann and Some Observations on Population Statistics. *Journal of the Statistical and Social Inquiry Society of Ireland* 15:15–32.

Geddes, A. 2000. *Immigration and European Integration: Towards Fortress Europe?* Manchester, UK: Manchester University Press.

Gemery, H. A. 1994. Immigrants and Emigrants: International Migration and the U.S. Labor Market in the Great Depression. In *Migration and the International Labor Market, 1850–1939*, ed. T. J. Hatton and J. G. Williamson, 175–199. London: Routledge.

General Register Office. 1906. *Census of the British Empire, 1901*. London: HMSO.

Gibney, M., and R. Hansen. 2002. Asylum Policy in the West: Past Trends and Future Possibilities. Unpublished paper, University of Oxford.

Girard, L. 1966. Transport. In *The Cambridge Economic History of Europe*, Vol. 6, *The Industrial Revolution and After: Incomes, Population and Technological Change* (Part I), ed. H. J. Habbakuk and M. M. Postan, 212–273. Cambridge: Cambridge University Press.

Godley, A. 2001. *Jewish Immigrant Entrepreneurship in New York and London, 1880–1914*. New York: Palgrave.

Goldin, C. 1990. *Understanding the Gender Gap: An Economic History of American Women*. New York: Oxford University Press.

Goldin, C. 1994. The Political Economy of Immigration Restriction in the United States, 1890 to 1921. In *The Regulated Economy: A Historical Approach to Political Economy*, ed. C. Goldin and G. D. Libecap, 223–258. Chicago: University of Chicago Press.

Goldin, C. 1998. America's Graduation from High School: The Evolution and Spread of Secondary Schooling in the Twentieth Century. *Journal of Economic History* 58:345–374.

Goldin, C., and L. F. Katz. 1998. The Origins of Technology-Skill Complementarity. *Quarterly Journal of Economics* 113:693–732.

Goldin, C., and L. F. Katz. 1999a. The Returns to Skill in the United States across the Twentieth Century. Working Paper 7126, National Bureau of Economic Research, Cambridge, MA.

Goldin, C., and L. F. Katz. 1999b. Egalitarianism and the Returns to Education during the Great Transformation of American Education. *Journal of Political Economy* 107:65–94.

Goldin, C., and L. F. Katz. 2001. Decreasing (and Then Increasing) Inequality in America: A Tale of Two Half-centuries. In *Increasing Income Inequality in America*, ed. F. Welch, 37–82. Chicago: University of Chicago Press.

Goldin, C., and R. A. Margo. 1992. The Great Compression: The Wage Structure in the United States at Mid-century. *Quarterly Journal of Economics* 107:1–34.

Gottschang, T. R. 2000. *Swallows and Settlers: The Great Migration from North China to Manchuria*. Ann Arbor: University of Michigan Press.

Gould, J. D. 1979. European Inter-continental Emigration, 1815–1914: Patterns and Causes. *Journal of European Economic History* 8:593–679.

Gould, J. D. 1980a. European Inter-continental Emigration: The Road Home; Return Migration from the U.S.A. *Journal of European Economic History* 9:41–112.

Gould, J. D. 1980b. European Inter-continental Emigration: The Role of "Diffusion" and "Feedback." *Journal of European Economic History* 9:267–315.

Green, A. G. 1995. A Comparison of Canadian and U.S. Immigration Policy in the Twentieth Century. In *Diminishing Returns: The Economics of Canada's Recent Immigration Policy*, ed. D. J. Devoretz, 31–64. Toronto: Laurier.

Green, A. G., and D. A. Green. 1995. Canadian Immigration Policy: The Effectiveness of the Points System and Other Instruments. *Canadian Journal of Economics* 28:1006–1041.

Green, A. G., and D. A. Green. 1999. The Economic Goals of Canada's Immigration Policy: Past and Present. *Canadian Public Policy—Analyse de politiques* 25:425–451.

Green, A. G., M. MacKinnon, and C. Minns. 2002. Dominion or Republic? Migrants to North America from the United Kingdom, 1870–1910. *Economic History Review* 55:666–696.

Greenaway, D., and D. Nelson. 2004. The Distinct Political Economies of Trade and Migration Policies through the Window of Endogenous Policy Models. Paper presented at the 2004 Kiel Week Conference, Kiel, Germany, June 21–22.

Gregory, R. G., R. Anstie, and E. Klug. 1992. Why Are Low Skilled Immigrants in the United States Poorly Paid Relative to Their Australian Counterparts? In *Immigration Trade and the Labor Market*, ed. J. M. Abowd and R. B. Freeman, 385–406. Chicago: University of Chicago Press.

Grubb, F. 1994. The End of European Servitude in the United States: An Economic Analysis of Market Collapse, 1772–1835. *Journal of Economic History* 54:794–824.

Grubb, F. 2003. Immigration and the Onset of Globalisation. Unpublished paper, University of Delaware.

Guinnane, T., C. Moehling, and C. ÓGráda, 2004. The Fertility of the Irish in the United States in 1910. Working Paper 2004/2, Department of Economics, University College, Dublin.

Gurr, T. R., M. G. Marshall, and D. Khosla. 2001. *Peace and Conflict, 2001*. College Park: Center for International Development and Conflict Management, University of Maryland.

Habakkuk, H. J. 1962. *American and British Technology in the Nineteenth Century*. Cambridge: Cambridge University Press.

Haines, R. F. 1997. *Emigration and the Labouring Poor: Australian Recruitment in Britain and Ireland, 1831–60*. New York: St. Martin's.

Hamilton, B., and J. Whalley. 1984. Efficiency and Distributional Implications of Global Restrictions on Labor Mobility. *Journal of Development Economics* 14:61–75.

Hammermesh, D. 1993. *Labor Demand*. Princeton, NJ: Princeton University Press.

Handlin, O. 1957. *Race and Nationality in American Life*. New York: Doubleday.

Hanes, C. 1993. The Development of Nominal Wage Rigidity in the Late Nineteenth Century. *American Economic Review* 83:732–756.

Hanes, C. 1996. Immigrants' Relative Rate of Wage Growth in the Late Nineteenth Century. *Explorations in Economic History* 33:35–64.

Hannon, J. U. 1982a. Ethnic Discrimination in a Nineteenth Century Mining District: Michigan Copper Mines, 1888. *Explorations in Economic History* 19:25–80.

Hannon, J. U. 1982b. City Size and Ethnic Discrimination: Michigan Agricultural Implements and Iron Working Industries, 1890. *Journal of Economic History* 42:851–876.

Hansen, R. 2000. *Citizenship and Immigration in Postwar Britain: The Institutional Origins of a Multicultural Nation*. Oxford: Oxford University Press.

Hanson, G. H., and M. J. Slaughter. 2003. Labor-Market Adjustment in Open Economies: Evidence from the U.S. States. *Journal of International Economics* 57:3–29.

Harlaftis, G., and V. Kardasis. 2000. International Shipping in the Eastern Mediterranean and the Black Sea: Istanbul as a Maritime Centre, 1870–1910. In *The Mediterranean Response to Globalization before 1950*, ed. Ş. Pamuk and J. G. Williamson, 233–265. London: Routledge.

Harley, C. K. 1988. Ocean Freight Rates and Productivity, 1740–1913: The Primacy of Mechanical Invention Reaffirmed. *Journal of Economic History* 48:851–876.

Harris, J. R., and M. P. Todaro. 1970. Migration, Unemployment and Development: A Two Sector Analysis. *American Economic Review* 60:126–142.

Hatton, T. J. 1995. A Model of UK Emigration. *Review of Economics and Statistics* 77:407–415.

Hatton, T. J. 1997. The Immigrant Assimilation Puzzle in Late Nineteenth Century America. *Journal of Economic History* 57:34–62.

Hatton, T. J. 2000. How Much Did Immigrant "Quality" Decline in Late Nineteenth Century America? *Journal of Population Economics* 13:509–525.

Hatton, T. J. 2003. Explaining Trends in UK Immigration. Centre for Economic Policy Research Discussion Paper 4019, London.

Hatton, T. J. 2004a. Seeking Asylum in Europe. *Economic Policy* 38:5–62.

Hatton, T. J. 2004b. Emigration from the UK, 1870–1913 and 1950–1998. *European Review of Economic History* 8:149–171.

Hatton, T. J. 2005. European Asylum Policy. Unpublished paper, Australian National University, Canberra.

Hatton, T. J., G. R. Boyer, and R. E. Bailey. 1994. The Union Wage Effect in Late Nineteenth Century Britain. *Economica* 61:435–456.

Hatton, T. J., and M. Tani. 2005. Immigration and Inter-regional Mobility in the UK, 1982–2000. Forthcoming in *Economic Journal*.

Hatton, T. J., and S. Wheatley Price. 2005. Migration, Migrants and Policy in the United Kingdom. In *European Migration: What Do We Know?* ed. K. F. Zimmermann, 113–172. Oxford: Oxford University Press.

Hatton, T. J., and J. G. Williamson. 1993. After the Famine: Emigration from Ireland, 1850–1913. *Journal of Economic History* 53:575–600.

Hatton, T. J., and J. G. Williamson. 1994a. Late-comers to Mass Emigration: The Latin Experience. In *Migration and the International Labor Market, 1850–1939*, ed. T. J. Hatton and J. G. Williamson, 53–71. London: Routledge.

Hatton, T. J., and J. G. Williamson. 1994b. What Drove the Mass Migrations from Europe in the Late Nineteenth Century? *Population and Development Review* 20:1–27.

Hatton, T. J., and J. G. Williamson. 1995. The Impact of Immigration on American Labor Markets Prior to the Quotas. Working Paper 5185, National Bureau of Economic Research, Cambridge, MA.

Hatton, T. J., and J. G. Williamson. 1998. *The Age of Mass Migration: Causes and Economic Impact*. New York: Oxford University Press.

Hatton, T. J., and J. G. Williamson. 2003. Demographic and Economic Pressure on Migration out of Africa. *Scandinavian Journal of Economics* 105:465–486.

Hatton, T. J., and J. G. Williamson. 2004. Refugees, Asylum Seekers, and Policy in Europe. Working Paper 10680, National Bureau of Economic Research, Cambridge, MA.

Hawkins, F. 1989. *Critical Years in Immigration: Canada and Australia Compared.* Toronto: McGill-Queen's University Press.

Hayfron, J. E. 1998. The Performance of Immigrants in the Norwegian Labor Market. *Journal of Population Economics* 11:293–303.

Hellie, R. 2002. Migration in Early Modern Russia, 1480s–1780s. In *Coerced and Free Migration: Global Perspectives,* ed. D. Eltis, 292–323. Stanford: Stanford University Press.

Hendricks, L. 2002. How Important Is Human Capital for Development? Evidence from Immigrant Earnings. *American Economic Review* 92:198–219.

Higgins, M., and J. G. Williamson. 2002. Explaining Inequality the World Round: Cohort Size, Kuznets Curves, and Openness. *Southeast Asian Studies* 40:268–302.

Hillman, A. L. 1993. The Political Economy of Migration Policy. In *Migration: A Challenge for Europe: Symposium 1993,* ed. H. Siebert, 263–282. Tübingen, Germany: Mohr.

Hillman, A. L., and A. Weiss. 1999. Beyond International Factor Movements: Cultural Preferences, Endogenous Policies and the Migration of People; An Overview. In *Migration: The Controversies and the Evidence,* ed. R. Faini, J. de Melo, and K. Zimmerman, 76–91. Cambridge: Cambridge University Press.

Hollifield, J. F. 1992. *Immigrants, Markets and States: The Political Economy of Postwar Europe.* Cambridge, MA: Harvard University Press.

Hourwich, I. 1922. *Immigration and Labor: The Economic Aspects of European Immigration to the United States,* 2nd ed. New York: Huebsch.

Huber, J. R. 1971. Effect on Prices of Japan's Entry into World Commerce after 1858. *Journal of Political Economy* 79:614–628.

Huff, W. G. 1994. *The Economic Growth of Singapore: Trade and Development in the Twentieth Century.* Cambridge: Cambridge University Press.

Hui, O. J. 1995. Chinese Indentured Labour: Coolies and Colonies. In *The Cambridge Survey of World Migration,* ed. R. Cohen, 51–56. Cambridge: Cambridge University Press.

Hunt, J. 1992. The Impact of the 1962 Repatriates from Algeria on the French Labor Market. *Industrial and Labor Relations Review* 45:556–572.

Huntington, S. P. 2004. *Who Are We? The Challenges to America's National Identity.* New York: Simon and Schuster.

Hurd, J. 1975. Railways and the Expansion of Markets in India, 1861–1921. *Explorations in Economic History* 12:263–288.

Husted, L., H. S. Nielsen, M. Rosholm, and N. Smith. 2000. Employment and Wage Assimilation of Male First Generation Immigrants in Denmark. Discussion Paper 101, Institute for the Study of Labor (IZA), Bonn.

Hutchinson, E. P. 1947. The Present Status of Our Immigration Laws and Policies. In *Postwar Problems of Migration,* ed. L. J. Reed, 82–94. New York: Milbank Memorial Fund.

Huttenback, R. A. 1976. *Racism and Empire: White Settlers and Colored Immigrants in the British Self-governing Colonies, 1830–1910.* Ithaca: Cornell University Press.

Hvidt, C. 1975. *Flight to America*. New York: Academic Press.

IGC. *See* Inter Governmental Consultations.

ILO. *See* International Labour Organization.

Inter Governmental Consultations. 1997. *Report on Asylum Procedures*. Geneva: Secretariat of the Inter Governmental Consultations on Asylum, Refugee and Migration Policies in Europe, North America and Australia.

International Labour Organization. 1998. Labour Migration to South Africa in the 1990s. Policy paper series 4, International Labour Organization, Geneva.

International Organization for Migration. 1998. *Migration Potential in Central and Eastern Europe*. Geneva: International Organization for Migration.

International Organization for Migration. 2000. *Migrant Trafficking and Human Smuggling in Europe* Geneva: International Organization for Migration.

International Organization for Migration. 2003. *World Migration Report: Managing Migration; Challenges and Responses for People on the Move*. Geneva: International Organization for Migration.

IOM. *See* International Organization for Migration.

Irwin, D. A. 1995. GATT in Historical Perspective. *American Economic Review* 85:323–328.

Irwin, D. A. 1996. *Against the Tide: An Intellectual History of Free Trade*. Princeton: Princeton University Press.

Issawi, C. 1966. *The Economy of the Middle East, 1800–1914*. Chicago: University of Chicago Press.

Jasso, G., and M. R. Rosenzweig. 1986. What's in a Name? Country of Origin Influence on the Earnings of Immigrants in the United States. *Research in Human Capital and Development* 4:75–106.

Jasso, G., M. R. Rosenzweig, and J. P. Smith. 2000. The Changing Skill of New Immigrants to the United States: Recent Trends and Their Determinants. In *Issues in the Economics of Immigration*, ed. G. J. Borjas, 185–225. Chicago: National Bureau of Economic Research.

Jenks, J. W., and W. J. Lauck. 1926. *The Immigration Problem*, 6th ed. New York: Huebsch.

Jerome, H. 1926. *Migration and Business Cycles*. New York: National Bureau of Economic Research.

Johnston, H. J. M. 1972. *British Emigration Policy, 1815–1830: "Shovelling Out Paupers."* Oxford: Oxford University Press.

Jones, M. A. 1992. *American Immigration*, 2nd ed. Chicago: University of Chicago Press.

Jones, R. W. 1971. A Three-factor Model in Theory, Trade, and History. In *Trade, Balance of Payments, and Growth*, ed. J. N. Bhagwati, R. Jones, R. A. Mundell, and J. Vanek, 3–21. Amsterdam: North-Holland.

Joppke, L. 1998. Why Liberal States Accept Unwanted Immigration. *World Politics* 50:266–293.

Jupp, J. 1991. *Australian Retrospectives: Immigration*. Sydney: Sydney University Press.

Kang, K. H., and M. S. Cha. 1996. Imperial Policy or World Price Shocks? Explaining Interwar Korean Living Standards. Paper presented at the Conference on East and Southeast Asian Economic Change in the Long Run, Honolulu, April 11.

Kapur, I., M. T. Hadjimichael, P. Hilbers, J. Schiff, and P. Szymczak. 1991. *Ghana: Adjustment and Growth, 1983–91*. Washington, DC: International Monetary Fund.

Karemera, D., V. I. Oguledo, and B. Davis. 2000. A Gravity Model Analysis of International Migration to North America. *Applied Economics* 32:1745–1755.

Karras, G., and C. U. Chiswick. 1999. Macroeconomic Determinants of Migration: The Case of Germany, 1964–1988. *International Migration* 37:657–677.

Keeling, D. 1999. The Transportation Revolution and Transatlantic Migration, 1850–1914. *Research in Economic History* 19:39–74.

Kero, R. 1991. Migration Traditions from Finland to North America. In *A Century of European Migrations, 1830–1930*, ed. R. J. Vecoli and S. M. Sinke, 111–133. Urbana: University of Illinois Press.

Kessner, T. 1977. *The Golden Door: Italian and Jewish Immigrant Mobility in New York, 1880–1915*. New York: Oxford University Press.

Kindleberger, C. P. 1967. *Europe's Postwar Growth: The Role of Labor Supply*. Cambridge, MA: Harvard University Press.

King, M., and S. Ruggles. 1990. American Immigration, Fertility and Race Suicide at the End of the Century. *Journal of Interdisciplinary History* 20:347–369.

Kirk, D. 1946. *Europe's Population in the Interwar Years*. Princeton: Princeton University Press for the League of Nations.

Klein, H. S. 1983. The Integration of Italian Immigrants into the United States and Argentina: A Comparative Analysis. *American Historical Review* 88:306–329.

Klein, P., and G. Ventura. 2003. Do Migration Restrictions Matter? Unpublished paper, Pennsylvania State University, University Park.

Korthals Altes, W. L. 1994. *Changing Economy in Indonesia*. Vol. 15, *Prices (Non-rice), 1814–1940*. The Hague: Royal Tropical Institute.

Koser, K., and C. Pinkerton. 2002. *The Social Networks of Asylum Seekers and the Dissemination of Information about Countries of Asylum*. London: UK Home Office.

Kossoudji, S. A., and D. A. Cobb-Clark. 2002. Coming Out of the Shadows: Learning about Legal Status and Wages from the Legalized Population. *Journal of Labor Economics* 20:598–628.

Kremer, M., and S. Watt. 2004. The Globalization of Household Production. Photocopy, Department of Economics, Harvard University, Cambridge, MA.

Krugman, P. 1997. What Should Trade Negotiators Negotiate About? *Journal of Economic Literature* 35:113–120.

Kuznets, S., ed. 1952. *Income and Wealth of the United States: Trends and Structure*. London: Bowes and Bowes.

Kuznets, S. 1955. Economic Growth and Income Inequality. *American Economic Review* 45:1–28.

Kuznets, S. 1958. Long Swings in the Growth of Population and in Related Economic Variables. *Proceedings of the American Philosophical Society* 102:25–52.

Kuznets, S. 1975. Immigration of Russian Jews to the United States: Background and Structure. *Perspectives in American History* 9:35–124.

Kuznets, S., and E. Rubin. 1954. *Immigration and the Foreign-Born.* New York: National of Bureau of Economic Research.

Lai, W. L. 2002. Asian Contract and Free Migrations to the Americas. In *Coerced and Free Migration: Global Perspectives*, ed. D. Eltis, 229–258. Stanford: Stanford University Press.

Lalonde, R. J., and R. H. Topel. 1991. Labor Market Adjustments to Increased Immigration. In *Immigration, Trade and the Labor Market*, ed. J. M. Abowd and R. B. Freeman, 167–199. Chicago: University of Chicago Press.

Lalonde, R. J., and R. H. Topel. 1992. The Assimilation of Immigrants in the U.S. Labor Market. In *Immigration and the Workforce: Economic Consequences for the United States and Source Areas*, ed. G. J. Borjas and R. B. Freeman, 67–92. Chicago: University of Chicago Press.

Landes, D. S. 1998. *The Wealth and Poverty of Nations: Why Some Are So Rich and Some Are So Poor.* New York: Norton.

Latham, A. J. H. 1978. *The International Economy and the Undeveloped World, 1865–1914.* London: Croom Helm.

Latham, A. J. H. 1981. *The Depression and the Developing World, 1914–1939.* London: Croom Helm.

Latham, A. J. H., and L. Neal. 1983. The International Market in Rice and Wheat, 1868–1914. *Economic History Review* 36:260–275.

Lebergott, S. 1964. *Manpower in Economic Growth: The American Record since 1800.* New York: McGraw-Hill.

Lee, K. K. 1998. *Huddled Masses, Muddled Laws: Why Contemporary Immigration Policy Fails to Reflect Public Opinion.* Westport, CT: Praeger.

Lee, R. D., and T. W. Miller. 1997. The Future Fiscal Impact of Current Immigrants. In *The New Americans*, ed. J. P. Smith and B. Edmonston, 297–362. Washington, DC: National Academy Press.

Leff, N. H. 1972. Economic Development and Regional Inequality: Origins of the Brazilian Case. *Quarterly Journal of Economics* 86:243–262.

Leff, N. H. 1992. Economic Development in Brazil, 1822–1913. First Boston Working Paper FB-92–02, Columbia University, New York.

Lewis, W. A. 1954. Economic Development with Unlimited Supplies of Labour. *Manchester School of Economic and Social Studies* 22:139–191.

Lewis, W. A. 1978a. *Growth and Fluctuations, 1870–1913.* London: Allen and Unwin.

Lewis, W. A. 1978b. *The Evolution of the International Economic Order.* Princeton: Princeton University Press.

Liebfritz, W., P. O'Brien, and J.-P. Dumont. 2003. Effects of Immigration on Labour Markets and Government Budgets: An Overview. Working Paper 874, Center for Economic Studies–Ifo Institute for Economic Research (CESifo), University of Munich.

Liebig, T., and A. Sousa-Poza. 2004. Migration, Self-selection and Income Inequality: An International Analysis. *Kyklos* 57:125–146.

Lindert, P. H. 1978. *Fertility and Scarcity in America*. Princeton: Princeton University Press.

Lindert, P. H. 2003. *Growing Public: Social Spending and Economic Growth since the Eighteenth Century*. Cambridge: Cambridge University Press.

Lindert, P. H., and J. G. Williamson. 1983. English Workers' Living Standards during the Industrial Revolution: A New Look. *Economic History Review* 36:1–25.

Lindert, P. H., and J. G. Williamson. 2003. Does Globalization Make the World More Unequal? In *Globalization in Historical Perspective*, ed. M. Bordo, A. M. Taylor, and J. G. Williamson, 227–275. Chicago: University of Chicago Press.

Lindley, J. K. 2002. Economic Assimilation and the Labour Market Performance of British Refugees and Economic Migrants. Globalisation and Labour Markets Research Paper 2002/06, University of Nottingham, Nottingham, UK.

Lovejoy, P. E. 1983. The Volume of the Atlantic Slave Trade: A Synthesis. *Journal of African History* 23:473–501.

Lucas, R. E. 1988. On the Mechanics of Economic Development. *Journal of Monetary Economics* 22:3–42.

Lucas, R. E. B. 1985. Migration among the Batswana. *Economic Journal* 95:358–382.

Lucas, R. E. B. 1987. Emigration to South Africa's Mines. *American Economic Review* 77:313–330.

Maddison, A. 1991. *Dynamic Forces in Capitalist Development: A Long-run Comparative View*. New York: Oxford University Press.

Maddison, A. 1994. Explaining the Economic Performance of Nations. In *Convergence of Productivity: Cross-national Studies and Historical Evidence*, ed. W. Baumol, R. Nelson, and E. Wolff, 20–61. New York: Oxford University Press.

Maddison, A. 1995. *Monitoring the World Economy, 1820–1992*. Paris: Organization for Economic Development Development Centre Studies.

Madgwick, R. B. 1937. *Immigration into Eastern Australia, 1788–1851*. Sydney: Sydney University Press.

Magee, S. P., W. A. Brock, and L. Young. 1989. *Black Hole Tariffs and Endogenous Policy Theory*. New York: Cambridge University Press.

Makanya, S. T. 1994. The Desire to Return. In *When Refugees Go Home*, ed. T. Allen and H. Morsink, 105–125. London: Africa World Press.

Mankiw, N. G., D. Romer, and D. N. Weil. 1992. A Contribution to the Empirics of Economic Growth. *Quarterly Journal of Economics* 107:407–437.

Manning, C., and P. Bhatnager. 2003. The Movement of Natural Persons in ASEAN: How Natural? Unpublished paper, Australian National University, Canberra.

Margo, R. D. 1992. Wages and Prices during the Ante Bellum Period: A Survey and New Evidence. In *American Economic Growth and Standards of Living before the Civil War*, ed. R. E. Gallman and J. J. Wallis, 173–210. Chicago: University of Chicago Press.

Marshall, M. G. 1999. *Third World War: System, Process and Conflict Dynamics*. Boulder, CO: Rowman and Littlefield.

Marshall, M. G. 2002. Measuring the Societal Impact of War. In *From Reaction to Conflict Prevention: Opportunities for the UN System*, ed. F. O. Hampson and D. M. Malone, 63–104. Boulder, CO: Rienner.

Martin, P. L. 1998. *Germany: Reluctant Land of Immigration*. Washington, DC: American Institute for Contemporary German Studies.

Marvel, H. P., and E. J. Ray. 1983. The Kennedy Round: Evidence on the Regulation of International Trade in the United States. *American Economic Review* 73:190–197.

Massey, D. S. 1988. Economic Development and International Migration in Comparative Perspective. *Population and Development Review* 14:383–413.

Mayda, A. M. 2003. Who Is against Immigration? A Cross-country Investigation of Individual Attitudes toward Immigrants. Unpublished paper, Harvard University, Cambridge, MA.

Mayda, A. M., and D. Rodrik. 2001. Why Are Some People (and Countries) More Protectionist than Others? Working Paper 8461, National Bureau of Economic Research, Cambridge, MA.

McClean, R. R. 1990. Scottish Emigration to New Zealand, 1840–1880: Motives, Means and Background. Ph.D. diss., University of Edinburgh.

McDonald, J., and R. Shlomowitz. 1990. Mortality on Immigrant Voyages to Australia. *Explorations in Economic History* 27:84–113.

McDonald, J., and R. Shlomowitz. 1993. Contract Prices for Bulk Shipping of Passengers in Sailing Vessels, 1816–1904: An Overview. *International Journal of Maritime History* 5:65–93.

McDonald, J. T., and C. Worswick. 1998. The Earnings of Immigrant Men in Canada: Job Tenure, Cohort and Macroeconomic Conditions. *Industrial and Labor Relations Review* 51:465–482.

McInnis, M. 1994. Immigration and Emigration: Canada in the Late Nineteenth Century. In *Migration and the International Labor Market, 1850–1939*, ed. T. J. Hatton and J. G. Williamson, 139–155. London: Routledge.

McKeown, A. 2004. Global Migration, 1846–1940. *Journal of World History* 15:155–189.

Meredith, D. 1988. Full Circle? Contemporary Views on Transportation. In *Convict Workers: Reinterpreting Australia's Past*, ed. S. Nicholas, 14–27. Cambridge: Cambridge University Press.

Miller, P. W., and L. M. Neo. 2003. Labour Market Flexibility and Immigrant Adjustment. *Economic Record* 79:336–356.

Milazi, D. 1998. Migration within the Context of Poverty and Landlessness in Southern Africa. In *Emigration Dynamics in Developing Countries*. Vol. 1, *Sub-Saharan Africa*, ed. R. Appleyard, 145–164. Aldershot, UK: Ashgate.

Minns, C. 2000. Income, Cohort Effects, and Occupational Mobility: A New Look at Immigration to the United States at the Turn of the 20th Century. *Explorations in Economic History* 37:326–350.

Mitchell, B. R. 1983. *International Historical Statistics: Europe.* New York: Stockton.

Mokyr, J. 1980. The Deadly Fungus: An Econometric Investigation into the Short-Term Demographic Impact of the Irish Famine, 1846–1851. *Research in Population Economics* 2:237–277.

Mokyr, J. 1985. *Why Ireland Starved: A Quantitative and Analytical History of the Irish Economy, 1800–1845,* rev. ed. London: Allen and Unwin.

Molinas, C., and L. Prados. 1989. Was Spain Different? Spanish Historical Backwardness Revisited. *Explorations in Economic History* 26:385–402.

Money, J. 1997. No Vacancy: The Political Geography of Immigration Control in Advanced Industrial Countries. *International Organization* 51:685–720.

Money, J. 1999. *Fences and Neighbors: The Political Geography of Immigration Control.* Ithaca: Cornell University Press.

Moon, D. 2002. Peasant Migration, the Abolition of Serfdom, and the Internal Passport System in the Russian Empire. In *Coerced and Free Migration: Global Perspectives,* ed. D. Eltis, 324–357. Stanford: Stanford University Press.

Moreda, V. P. 1987. Spain's Demographic Modernization, 1800–1930. In *The Economic Modernization of Spain, 1830–1930,* ed. N. Sanchez-Albornoz, 13–41. New York: New York University Press.

Morrison, J., and B. Crosland. 2001. The Trafficking and Smuggling of Refugees: The End Game in European Asylum Policy? Working Paper 39, United Nations High Commissioner for Refugees, Geneva.

Moses, J. W., and B. Letnes. 2003. If People Were Money: Estimating the Potential Gains from Increased International Migration. Discussion Paper 2003/42, World Institute for Development Economics Research, Helsinki.

Mountford, A. 1997. Can a Brain Drain Be Good for Growth in the Source Economy? *Journal of Development Economics* 53:287–303.

Mundell, R. A. 1957. International Trade and Factor Mobility. *American Economic Review* 47:321–355.

Nelli, H. S. 1983. *From Immigrants to Ethnics: The Italian Americans.* New York: Oxford University Press.

New Zealand Bureau of Statistics. Various years. *New Zealand Official Yearbook.* Wellington: Government Printer.

Nicholas, S., and S. P. Shergold. 1988. Convicts as Migrants. In *Convict Workers: Reinterpreting Australia's Past,* ed. S. Nicholas, 43–61. Cambridge: Cambridge University Press.

Nickell, S. J. 1997. Unemployment and Labor Market Rigidities: Europe versus North America. *Journal of Economic Perspectives* 11:55–74.

Noll, G. 2000. *Negotiating Asylum: The EU Acquis, Extraterritorial Protection and the Common Market of Deflection.* The Hague: Nijhoff.

North, D. C. 1958. Ocean Freight Rates and Economic Development, 1750–1913. *Journal of Economic History* 18:538–555.

Northrup, D. 1995. *Indentured Labor in the Age of Imperialism, 1834–1922.* Cambridge: Cambridge University Press.

Northrup, D. 2002. Freedom and Indentured Labor in the French Caribbean, 1848–1900. In *Coerced and Free Migration: Global Perspectives*, ed. D. Eltis, 205–228. Stanford: Stanford University Press.

Nugent, J. B., and V. Saddi. 2003. When and How Do Land Rights Become Effective? Historical Evidence from Brazil. Unpublished paper, Department of Economics, University of Southern California.

Nugent, W. 1995. Migration from the German and Austro-Hungarian Empires to North America. In *The Cambridge Survey of World Migration*, ed. R. Cohen, 103–108. Cambridge: Cambridge University Press.

Obstfeld, M., and A. M. Taylor. 2003. Globalization and Capital Markets. In *Globalization in Historical Perspective*, ed. M. Bordo, A. M. Taylor, and J. G. Williamson, 121–187. Chicago: National Bureau of Economic Research.

OECD. *See* Organization for Economic Cooperation and Development.

ÓGráda, C. 1984. Malthus and the Pre-famine Economy. In *Economists and the Irish Economy*, ed. A. E. Murphy, 75–95. Dublin: Irish Academic Press.

ÓGráda, C. 1988. *Ireland before and after the Famine: Explorations in Economic History, 1800–1925.* Manchester, UK: Manchester University Press.

ÓGráda, C. 1994. *Ireland, 1780–1939: A New Economic History.* Oxford: Oxford University Press.

ÓGráda, C., and K. H. O'Rourke. 1997. Migration as Disaster Relief: Lessons from the Great Irish Famine. *European Review of Economic History* 1:3–25.

Ohlin, B. 1933. *Interregional and International Trade.* Cambridge, MA: Harvard University Press.

Olson, M. 1965. *The Logic of Collective Action.* Cambridge, MA: Harvard University Press.

Organization for Economic Cooperation and Development. 1993. *Main Economic Indicators: Historical Statistics.* Paris: Organization for Economic Cooperation and Development.

Organization for Economic Cooperation and Development. 1997. *Trends in International Migration, 1996.* Paris: Organization for Economic Cooperation and Development.

Organization for Economic Cooperation and Development. 2000a. *Combating the Illegal Employment of Foreign Workers.* Paris: Organization for Economic Cooperation and Development.

Organization for Economic Cooperation and Development. 2000b. *Trends in International Migration.* Paris: Organization for Economic Cooperation and Development.

Organization for Economic Cooperation and Development. 2001a. *Economic Outlook.* Paris: Organization for Economic Cooperation and Development.

Organization for Economic Cooperation and Development. 2001b. *Trends in International Migration, 2000.* Paris: Organization for Economic Cooperation and Development.

Organization for Economic Cooperation and Development. 2003. *Trends in International Migration, 2002*. Paris: OECD.

O'Rourke, K. H. 1991. Did the Great Irish Famine Matter? *Journal of Economic History* 51:1–21.

O'Rourke, K. H. 1995. Emigration and Living Standards in Ireland since the Famine. *Journal of Population Economics* 8:407–421.

O'Rourke, K. H. 2003. Heckscher-Ohlin Theory and Individual Attitudes towards Globalization. Paper presented at the Eli Heckscher Celebratory Symposium, Stockholm, May 22–24.

O'Rourke, K. H., and R. Sinnott. 2001. What Determines Attitudes towards Protection? Some Cross-Country Evidence. In *Brookings Trade Forum 2001*, ed. S. M. Collins and D. Rodrik, 157–206. Washington, DC: Brookings Institution Press.

O'Rourke, K. H., and R. Sinnott. 2004. The Determinants of Individual Attitudes towards Immigration. Unpublished paper, Trinity College, Dublin.

O'Rourke, K. H., A. M. Taylor, and J. G. Williamson. 1996. Factor Price Convergence in the Late Nineteenth Century. *International Economic Review* 37:499–530.

O'Rourke, K. H., and J. G. Williamson. 1997. Around the European Periphery, 1870–1913: Globalization, Schooling and Growth. *European Review of Economic History* 1:153–191.

O'Rourke, K. H., and J. G. Williamson. 1999. *Globalization and History: The Evolution of a Nineteenth-century Atlantic Economy*. Cambridge, MA: MIT Press.

O'Rourke, K. H., J. G. Williamson, and T. J. Hatton. 1994. Mass Migration, Commodity Market Integration and Real Wage Convergence. In *Migration and the International Labor Market, 1850–1939*, ed. T. J. Hatton and J. G. Williamson, 203–220. London: Routledge.

Oucho, J. 1996. *Urban Migrants and Rural Development in Kenya*. Nairobi: University of Nairobi Press.

Piketty, T., and E. Saez. 2003. Income Inequality in the United States, 1913–1998. *Quarterly Journal of Economics* 118:1–39.

Pincus, J. J. 1977. *Pressure Groups and Politics in Antebellum Tariffs*. New York: Columbia University Press.

Piore, M. 1979. *Birds of Passage: Migrant Labor in Industrial Societies*. London: Cambridge University Press.

Pischke, J.-S., and J. Velling. 1997. Employment Effects of Immigration to Germany: An Analysis Based on Local Labor Markets. *Review of Economics and Statistics* 79:594–604.

Pollard, S. 1978. Labour in Great Britain. In *The Cambridge Economic History of Europe: Volume VII: The Industrial Economies: Capital, Labour, and Enterprise, Part I*, ed. P. Mathias and M. M. Postan, 97–179. Cambridge: Cambridge University Press.

Pope, D., and G. Withers. 1994. Wage Effects of Immigration in Late-Nineteenth Century Australia. In *Migration and the International Labor Market, 1850–1939*, ed. T. J. Hatton and J. G. Williamson, 240–262. London: Routledge.

Prebisch, R. 1950. *The Economic Development of Latin American and Its Principal Problems*. New York: United Nations Economic Commission for Latin America.

Price, C. 1987. Immigration and Ethnic Origin. In *Australians: Historical Statistics*, ed. W. Vamplew, 2–22. Sydney: Fairfax, Syme and Weldon.

Pritchett, L. 1997. Divergence, Big Time. *Journal of Economic Perspectives* 11:3–17.

Pritchett, L. 2001. Where Has All the Education Gone? *World Bank Economic Review* 15:367–391.

Puri, S., and T. Ritzema. 1994. Migrant Worker Remittances, Micro-finance and the Informal Economy: Prospects and Issues. Working Paper 21, International Labour Organization, Geneva.

Ramcharan, R. 2001. Globalization and Human Capital Formation: Theory and Evidence from the U.S. High School Movement. IMF Working Paper 02/123, International Monetary Fund, Washington, DC.

Ramcharan, R. 2003. Migration and Human Capital Formation: Evidence from the U.S. States, 1900–1930. Unpublished paper, International Monetary Fund, Washington, DC.

Ramos, F. A. 1992. Out-Migration and Return Migration of Puerto Ricans. In *Immigration and the Workforce: Economic Consequences for the United States and Source Areas*, ed. G. J. Borjas and R. B. Freeman, 49–66. Chicago: University of Chicago Press.

Rasmussen, H. K. 1997. *No Entry: Immigration Policy in Europe*. Copenhagen: Copenhagen Business School Press.

Ratha, D. 2003. Worker's Remittances: An Important and Stable Source of External Development Finance. In *Global Development Finance*, 157–175. Washington, DC: World Bank.

Richards, E. 1993. How Did Poor People Emigrate from the British Isles to Australia in the Nineteenth Century? *Journal of British Studies* 32:250–279.

Robinson, V. 1994. Marching into the Middle Classes? The Long Term Resettlement of East African Asians in the UK. *Journal of Refugee Studies* 6:230–227.

Rodrik, D. 2002. Feasible Globalizations. Working Paper 9129, National Bureau of Economic Research, Cambridge, MA.

Rodríguez, F., and D. Rodrik. 2001. Trade Policy and Economic Growth: A Skeptic's Guide to the Cross-national Evidence. In *Macroeconomics Annual 2000*, ed. B. Bernanke and K. S. Rogoff, 261–325. Cambridge, MA: MIT Press.

Rogge, J. R. 1994. Repatriation of Refugees. In *When Refugees Go Home*, ed. T. Allen and H. Morsink. London: Africa World Press.

Rogowski, R. 1989. *Commerce and Coalitions: How Trade Effects Domestic Political Arrangements*. Princeton: Princeton University Press.

Rosenberg, N. 1967. Anglo-American Wage Differences in the 1820s. *Journal of Economic History* 27:221–229.

Rotte, R., M. Vogler, and K. Zimmermann. 1997. South-North Refugee Migration: Lessons for Development Co-operation. *Review of Development Economics* 1:99–115.

Roy, A. D. 1951. Some Thoughts on the Distribution of Earnings. *Oxford Economic Papers* 3:135–146.

Roy, T. 2000. *The Economic History of India, 1857–1947*. Oxford: Oxford University Press.

Rybczynski, T. M. 1955. Factor Endowments and Relative Commodity Prices. *Economica* 22:336–341.

Sachs, J. D., and A. Warner. 1995. Economic Reform and the Process of Global Integration. *Brookings Papers on Economic Activity* 1:1–118.

SAMP. *See* South African Migration Project.

Samuelson, P. A. 1964. *Economics*, 6th ed. New York: McGraw-Hill.

Sánchez-Albornoz, N. 1994. The First Transatlantic Transfer: Spanish Migration to the New World, 1493–1810. In *Europeans on the Move: Studies on European Migration, 1500–1800*, ed. N. Canny, 26–36. Oxford: Clarendon.

Sanchez-Alonso, B. 1995. *Las causas de la emigracion Espanola, 1880–1930*. Madrid: Alianza Editorial.

Sanchez-Alonso, B. 1998. What Slowed Down the Mass Migration from Spain in the Late Nineteenth Century? Paper presented at the Conference on Long-run Economic Change in the Mediterranean Basin, Istanbul, June 4–7.

Sarkar, N. K. 1957. *The Demography of Ceylon*. Colombo: Ceylon Government Press.

Scheve, K. F., and M. J. Slaughter. 2001a. Labor Market Competition and Individual Preferences over Immigration Policy. *Review of Economics and Statistics* 83:133–145.

Scheve, K. F., and M. J. Slaughter. 2001b. *Globalization and the Perceptions of American Workers*. Washington, DC: Institute for International Economics.

Schmeidl, S. 1997. Exploring the Causes of Force Migration: A Pooled Time-Series Analysis, 1971–1990. *Social Science Quarterly* 78:284–308.

Schmidt, C. 2000. Aggregate-Level Migration Studies as a Tool for Forecasting Future Migration Streams. Discussion Paper 183, Institute for the Study of Labor (IZA), Bonn.

Schultz-Nielsen, M. L., and A. Constant. 2004. Employment Trends for Immigrants and Natives. In *Migrants, Work, and the Welfare State*, ed. T. Tranæs and K. F. Zimmermann, 119–146. Odense: University Press of Southern Denmark.

Self, R., and B. K. Zutshi. 2002. Temporary Entry of Natural Persons as Service Providers: Issues and Challenges in Further Liberalization under the Current GATS Negotiations. Paper presented at the Joint World Trade Organization–World Bank Symposium on the Movement of Natural Persons (Mode 4) under the GATS, Geneva.

Sen, A. K. 1981. *Poverty and Famines: An Essay on Entitlement and Deprivation*. Oxford: Oxford University Press.

Shah Mohammed, S., and J. G. Williamson. 2004. Freight Rates and Productivity Gains in British Tramp Shipping, 1869–1950. *Explorations in Economic History* 41:172–203.

Shaw, A. G. L. 1966. *Convicts and the Colonies*. Melbourne: Melbourne University Press.

Shughart, W., R. Tollison, and M. Kimenyi. 1986. The Political Economy of Immigration Restrictions. *Yale Journal on Regulation* 4:79–97.

Singer, H. W. 1950. The Distribution of Gains between Investing and Borrowing Countries. *American Economic Review* 40:473–485.

Sinn, H.-W., and M. Werding. 2001. Immigration Following EU Eastern Enlargement. *CESIfo [Center for Economic Studies–Ifo Institute for Economic Research] Forum* 2:40–47.

Siok-Hwa, C. 1968. *The Rice Industry of Burma, 1852–1940.* Singapore: University of Malaya Press.

Sjastaad, L. 1962. The Costs and Returns of Human Migration. *Journal of Political Economy* 70:80–93.

Skeldon, R. 2000. Myths and Realities of Chinese Irregular Migration. Migration Research Series 1/2000, International Office for Migration, Geneva.

Slaughter, M. J. 1995. The Antebellum Transportation Revolution and Factor-Price Convergence. Working Paper 5303, National Bureau of Economic Research, Cambridge, MA.

Smith, A. E. 1947. *Colonialists in Bondage: White Servitude and Convict Labor in America.* Chapel Hill, NC: University of North Carolina Press.

Smith, J. P., and B. Edmonston, eds. 1997. *The New Americans: Economic, Demographic and Fiscal Effects of Immigration.* Washington, DC: National Academy Press.

Snodgrass, D. R. 1966. *Ceylon: An Export Economy in Transition.* Homewood, IL.: R. D. Irwin.

Sokoloff, K. L., and S. L. Engerman. 2000. Institutions, Factor Endowments, and Paths of Development in the New World. *Journal of Economic Perspectives* 14:217–232.

Solberg, C. 1978. Mass Migrations in Argentina, 1870–1970. In *Human Migration: Patterns and Policies,* ed. W. H. McNeill and R. S. Adams, 146–170. Bloomington: Indiana University Press.

Souden, D. 1984. English Indentured Servants and the Transatlantic Colonial Economy. In *International Migration: Historical Perspectives,* ed. S. Marks and P. Richardson, 19–33. London: Institute for Commonwealth Studies.

South African Migration Project. 2001. The Point of No Return: Evaluating the Amnesty for Mozambican Refugees in South Africa. Migration Policy Brief 6, South African Migration Project, Queen's University, Kingston, Ontario, Canada.

Stalker, P. 1994. *The Work of Strangers: A Survey of International Labor Migration.* Geneva: International Labour Organization.

Stark, O. 1991. *The Migration of Labor.* Oxford: Blackwell.

Storesletten, K. 2000. Sustaining Fiscal Policy through Immigration. *Journal of Political Economy* 108:300–323.

Storesletten, K. 2003. Fiscal Implications of Immigration: A Net Present Value Calculation. Unpublished paper, University of Stockholm.

Swierenga, R. P. 1976. Dutch International Migration and Occupational Change: A Structural Analysis of Multinational Linked Files. In *Migration Across Time and Distance, Population Mobility in Historical Context,* ed. I. A. Glazier and L. de Rosa, 95–124. New York: Holmes and Meier.

Taylor, A. M. 1994. Mass Migration to Distant Southern Shores. In *Migration and the International Labor Market, 1850–1939,* ed. T. J. Hatton and J. G. Williamson, 91–115. London: Routledge.

Taylor, A. M., and J. G. Williamson. 1997. Convergence in the Age of Mass Migration. *European Review of Economic History* 1:27–63.

Thernstrom, S. 1973. *The Other Bostonians: Poverty and Progress in the American Metropolis.* Cambridge, MA: Harvard University Press.

Thiara, R. K. 1995. Indian Indentured Workers in Mauritius, Natal and Fiji. In *The Cambridge Survey of World Migration*, ed. R. Cohen, 63–68. Cambridge: Cambridge University Press.

Thielemann, E. R. 2003. Why EU Policy Harmonisation Undermines Burden Sharing. National Europe Centre Paper 101, Australian National University, Canberra.

Thomas, B. 1954. *Migration and Economic Growth.* Cambridge: Cambridge University Press.

Thomas, B. 1972. *Migration and Urban Development.* London: Methuen.

Thomas, D. S. 1941. *Social and Economic Aspects of Swedish Population Movements.* New York: Macmillan.

Timmer, A., and J. G. Williamson. 1996. Racism, Xenophobia or Markets? The Political Economy of Immigration Policy Prior to the Thirties. Working Paper 5867, National Bureau of Economic Research, Cambridge, MA.

Timmer, A., and J. G. Williamson. 1998. Immigration Policy Prior to the Thirties: Labor Markets, Policy Interaction, and Globalization Backlash. *Population and Development Review* 24:739–771.

Tinker, H. 1974. *A New System of Slavery: The Export of Indian Labour Overseas, 1830–1920.* London: Oxford University Press.

Todaro, M. P. 1969. A Model of Labor Migration and Urban Unemployment in Less Developed Countries. *American Economic Review* 59:138–148.

Tortella, G. 1994. Patterns of Retardation and Recovery in South-Western Europe in the Nineteenth and Twentieth Centuries. *Economic History Review* 47:1–21.

Tyrrell, I. 1991. American Exceptionalism in an Age of International History. *American Historical Review* 96:1031–1055.

UNHCR. *See* United Nations High Commissioner for Refugees.

United Kingdom Home Affairs Committee. 2003. *Asylum Removals.* Vol. 1, *Report and Proceedings of the Committee.* London: House of Commons.

United Nations. 1979. *Trends and Characteristics of International Migration since 1950.* New York: United Nations.

United Nations. 1997. *Demographic Yearbook 1997.* New York: United Nations.

United Nations. 1999. *World Population Prospects: The 1998 Revision.* New York: United Nations.

United Nations. 2000a. *World Migration Report.* New York: United Nations.

United Nations. 2000b. *Replacement Migration: Is It a Solution to Declining and Ageing Populations?* New York: United Nations.

United Nations. 2002a. *International Migration Report, 2002*. New York: United Nations.

United Nations. 2002b. *International Migration from Countries with Economies in Transition: 1980–1999*. New York: United Nations. http://www.un.org/esa/population/publications/ittmig2002/ittmigrep2002.htm.

United Nations. 2003. *World Population Prospects: The 2002 Revision*. New York: United Nations.

United Nations. Various issues. *World Population Monitoring*. New York: United Nations.

United Nations High Commissioner for Refugees. 2001. *The State of the World's Refugees: Fifty Years of Humanitarian Action*. Geneva: United Nations High Commissioner for Refugees.

United Nations High Commissioner for Refugees. 2002. *Statistical Yearbook, 2001*. Geneva: United Nations High Commissioner for Refugees.

United States Bureau of the Census. 1926. *Statistical Abstract of the United States, 1925*. Washington, DC: U.S. Government Printing Office.

United States Citizenship and Immigration Services. 2003. *2002 Yearbook of Immigration Statistics*. Washington, DC: U.S. Citizenship and Immigration Services.

United States Committee for Refugees. Various years. *World Refugee Survey*. Washington, DC: U.S. Committee for Refugees.

United States Immigration Commission. 1911. *Reports*, 61st Congress, 3rd Session. Washington, DC: U.S. Government Printing Office.

Venturini, A. 2004. *Postwar Migration in Southern Europe, 1950–2000: An Economic Analysis*. Cambridge: Cambridge University Press.

Vertovec, S. 1995. Indian Indentured Migration to the Caribbean. In *The Cambridge Survey of World Migration*, ed. R. Cohen, 57–62. Cambridge: Cambridge University Press.

Walmsley, T. L., and L. A. Winters. 2004. Relaxing the Restrictions on the Temporary Movement of Natural Persons: A Simulation Analysis. Unpublished paper, University of Sheffield, Sheffield, UK.

Wegge, S. A. 2002. Occupational Self-Selection of European Emigrants: Evidence from Nineteenth Century Hesse-Cassel. *European Review of Economic History* 6:365–394.

Weiner, M. 1997. Bad Neighbours, Bad Neighbourhoods: An Enquiry into the Causes of Refugee Flows, 1969–1992. In *Migrants, Refugees and Foreign Policy: U.S. and German Policies towards Countries of Origin*, ed. R. Münz and M. Weiner, 183–229. Oxford: Berghahn.

Weiner, M., and T. Hanami, eds. 1998. *Temporary Workers or Future Citizens? Japanese and U.S. Migration Policies*. New York: New York University Press.

Wellisch, D., and U. Walz. 1998. Why Do Rich Countries Prefer Free Trade over Free Migration? The Role of the Modern Welfare State. *European Economic Review* 42:1595–1612.

Williamson, J. G. 1974. *Late Nineteenth Century American Development: A General Equilibrium History*. Cambridge: Cambridge University Press.

Williamson, J. G. 1979. Inequality, Accumulation, and Technological Imbalance: A Growth-Equity Conflict in American History? *Economic Development and Cultural Change* 27:231–253.

Williamson, J. G. 1982. Immigrant-Inequality Trade-Offs in the Promised Land: American Growth, Distribution and Immigration Prior to the Quotas. In *The Gateway: U.S. Immigration Issues and Policies*, ed. B. Chiswick, 251–288. Washington, DC: American Enterprise Institute.

Williamson, J. G. 1986. The Impact of the Irish on British Labor Markets during the Industrial Revolution. *Journal of Economic History* 56:693–720.

Williamson, J. G. 1990. *Coping with City Growth during the British Industrial Revolution.* Cambridge: Cambridge University Press.

Williamson, J. G. 1995. The Evolution of Global Labor Markets since 1830: Background Evidence and Hypotheses. *Explorations in Economic History* 32:141–196.

Williamson, J. G. 1996. Globalization, Convergence and History. *Journal of Economic History* 56:1–30.

Williamson, J. G. 1997. Globalization and Inequality, Past and Present. *World Bank Research Observer* 12:117–135.

Williamson, J. G. 2000a. Real Wages and Factor Prices around the Mediterranean, 1500–1940. In *The Mediterranean Response to Globalization before 1950*, ed. S. Pamuk and J. G. Williamson, 45–75. London: Routledge.

Williamson, J. G. 2000b. Globalization, Factor Prices and Living Standards in Asia before 1940. In *Asia Pacific Dynamism, 1550–2000*, ed. A. J. H. Latham and H. Kawakatsu, 13–45. London: Routledge.

Williamson, J. G. 2002. Land, Labor and Globalization in the Third World, 1870–1940. *Journal of Economic History* 62:55–85.

Williamson, J. G. 2004. Globalization and the Poor Periphery before the Modern Era. The Ohlin Lectures, Stockholm School of Economics, Stockholm, October.

Williamson, J. G. 2005. Explaining World Tariffs, 1870–1938: Stolper-Samuelson, Strategic Tariffs and State Revenues. Forthcoming in *Eli F. Heckscher, 1879–1952: A Celebratory Symposium*, ed. R. Findlay, R. Henriksson, H. Lindgren, and M. Lundahl. Cambridge, MA: MIT Press.

Williamson, J. G., and P. H. Lindert. 1980. *American Inequality: A Macroeconomic History.* New York: Academic Press.

Wilson, J. Q. 1980. *The Politics of Regulation.* New York: Basic Books.

Winklemann, R. 2001. Immigration Policies and Their Impact: The Case of Australia and New Zealand. In *International Migration: Trends, Policies and Economic Impact*, ed. S. Djajic, 1–20. London: Routledge.

Winters, L. A., T. L. Walmsley, Z. K. Wang, and R. Grynberg. 2003. Liberalising Temporary Movement of Natural Persons: An Agenda for the Development Round. *World Economy* 26:1137–1161.

Wokeck, M. S. 1999. *Trade in Strangers: The Beginnings of Mass Migration to North America.* University Park: Pennsylvania State University Press.

Wolff, E. N. 1991. Capital Formation and Productivity Convergence over the Long Term. *American Economic Review* 81:565–579.

Wooden, M., R. Holton, G. Hugo, and J. Sloan. 1994. *Australian Immigration: A Survey of the Issues*. Canberra: Australian Government Printing Service.

World Bank. 2000. *World Development Report 2000/1: Attacking Poverty*. Washington, DC: World Bank.

Wright, G. 1986. *Old South, New South*. New York: Basic Books.

Wright, G. 1990. The Origins of American Industrial Success, 1879–1940. *American Economic Review* 80:651–668.

Wrigley, E. A., and R. S. Schofield. 1981. *The Population History of England, 1541–1871*. Cambridge, MA: Harvard University Press.

Yang, D. 2004a. Why Do Migrants Return to Poor Countries? Evidence from Philippine Migrants' Responses to Exchange Rate Shocks. Photocopy, Department of Economics, University of Michigan, Ann Arbor.

Yang, D. 2004b. International Migration, Human Capital, and Entrepreneurship: Evidence from Philippine Migrants' Exchange Rate Shocks. Photocopy, Department of Economics, University of Michigan, Ann Arbor.

Yang, P. Q. 1995. *Post-1965 Immigration to the United States*. Westport, CT: Praeger.

Yasuba, Y. 1978. Freight Rates and Productivity in Ocean Transportation for Japan, 1875–1943. *Explorations in Economic History* 15:11–39.

Yuengert, A. 1994. Immigrant Earnings Relative to What? The Importance of Earnings Function Specification and Comparison Points. *Journal of Applied Econometrics* 9:71–90.

Zetter, R., D. Griffiths, S. Ferretti, and M. Pearl. 2003. An Assessment of the Impact of Asylum Policies in Europe, 1990–2000. Online Report 17/03, UK Home Office, London. http://www.homeoffice.gov.uk/rds/horspubs1.html.

Zlotnick, H. 1998. International Migration, 1965–1996: An Overview. *Population and Development Review* 24:429–468.

Zunz, O. 1982. *The Changing Face of Inequality: Industrial Development and Immigrants in Detroit, 1880–1920*. Chicago: University of Chicago Press.

Index